THE Admiralty Regrets

BRITISH WARSHIP
LOSSES OF THE
20TH CENTURY

This book is dedicated to my friend Gus Britton (1922–97) of the Royal Navy's submarine museum, who taught me more about naval history than I care to remember. His comments – both constructive and profound – on my various books were always perceptive and enlightening.
He is greatly missed.

THE Admiralty Regrets

BRITISH WARSHIP LOSSES OF THE 20TH CENTURY

PAUL KEMP

SUTTON PUBLISHING

First published in the United Kingdom in 1999 by
Sutton Publishing Limited · Phoenix Mill
Thrupp · Stroud · Gloucestershire · GL5 2BU

British Library Cataloguing in Publication Data
A catalogue record for this book is available from the British Library.

ISBN 0-7509-1567-6

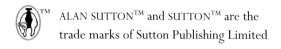

ALAN SUTTON™ and SUTTON™ are the
trade marks of Sutton Publishing Limited

Typeset in 11/14 pt Perpetua.
Typesetting and origination by
Sutton Publishing Limited.
Printed in Great Britain by
Butler & Tanner, Frome, Somerset.

CONTENTS

Acknowledgements   vii

Note to Text   viii

Abbreviations   ix

Introduction   xi

Losses 1904–1914   1

Losses 1915   14

Losses 1916   28

Losses 1917   46

Losses 1918   62

Losses November 1918–August 1939   84

Losses September–December 1939   101

Losses 1940   105

Losses 1941   137

Losses 1942   165

Losses 1943   206

Losses 1944   227

Losses January–July 1945   248

Losses October 1945–to date   255

Select Bibliography   265

Alphabetical List of Ships   269

ACKNOWLEDGEMENTS

I would like to express my thanks to those who have helped with the writing of this book: the Commonwealth War Graves Commission, Debbie Corner of the Royal Navy Submarine Museum, Brian Head, David Hill, Peter Jung of the Kriegsarchiv in Vienna; Kent County Council Central Reference Library at Springfield; Public Record Office; Service Historique de la Marine in Paris, Dott. Achille Rastelli, Bob Todd of the National Maritime Museum and David Webb. Special thanks are due to to my editor, Jonathan Falconer at Sutton Publishing, a true prince among publishers, and to production and editorial staff for producing the layout.

Paul Kemp
April 1999

NOTE TO TEXT

As many details as possible are given for each warship, although in some cases, perhaps because of reporting restrictions and/or the nature of the loss, little information is available or traceable today. The following data is listed wherever it has been possible to do so:

Name of Warship	**Location when lost**
Class	**Cause of Loss**
Date when built	**Number of Casualties**
Commanding Officer	**Number of Survivors**

Should readers know of other details, the author and publisher would be delighted to learn of these for future reference.

ABBREVIATIONS

A-Arcs	The limits to which a gun turret can be trained. To 'open A-Arcs' is to alter course in relation to the bearing of the target in order that all guns can be brought to bear
ABS	Armed Boarding Steamer
AMC	Armed Merchant Cruiser
Asdic	British underwater sound location device. Now better known as *Sonar*
BDV	Boom Defence Vessel
CAM	Catapult Armed Merchant (Ship)
Casing	Free-flooding boat-shaped structure built on to the pressure hull of a submarine
CC	*Capitano di Corvetta:* Italian Navy Lieutenant-Commander
CinC	Commander in Chief
CVE	Standard USN notation for an Escort Carrier
DSEA	Davis Submarine Escape Apparatus
ECG	*Ecogoniometro*: Italian Navy's version of British Asdic
EMB	Explosive Motor Boat
ERA	Engine Room Artificer
FAT	*Federapparat*: a German torpedo that could run in a zig-zag pattern after firing
GNAT	British acronym: German Naval Acoustic Torpedo
HMAS	His (Her) Majesty's Australian Ship
HMCS	His (Her) Majesty's Canadian Ship
HMNZS	His (Her) Majesty's New Zealand Ship
IJN	Imperial Japanese Navy
JAAF	Japanese Army Air Force
JNAF	Japanese Navy Air Force
Mas	*Motoscafi Anti Sommergibile*: Italian Navy anti-submarine motor boat
OOW	Officer of the Watch
PDM	Passive Delay Mechanism: a device used to delay the explosion of a mine (usually an acoustic, magnetic or pressure mine) until a certain number of ships had passed over it
RAN	Royal Australian Navy
RCN	Royal Canadian Navy
RN	Royal Navy
RNR	Royal Naval Reserve. The addition of the appropriate letter, A, C or NZ, would indicate an officer of the Australian, Canadian or New Zealand Naval Reserves
RNVR	Royal Naval Volunteer Reserve. The addition of the appropriate letter, A, C or NZ, would indicate an officer of the Australian, Canadian or New Zealand Naval Volunteer Reserves
RNZN	Royal New Zealand Navy

SANF	South African Naval Forces
S/M	Submarine
SSV	Special Service Vessel – Q-Ship
STV	*Sotto Tenente di Vascello*: Italian Navy Sub Lieutenant
TB	Torpedo Boat
TV	*Tenente di Vascello*: Italian Navy Lieutenant

INTRODUCTION

This book is a list. It is a list of ships which have flown the White Ensign and which have been sunk either by accident in peacetime or in wartime this century. But it is not a complete list and therefore I must offer an apology. The book concentrates on capital ships, aircraft carriers, monitors, depot ships, cruisers, destroyers, sloops, submarines, minesweepers, frigates and corvettes. For reasons of space the legion of auxiliary craft have been omitted. I offer an apology to those who served in such craft who may be disappointed at finding their ship not included here.

However, this book is more than just a list. It is also, in a way, a chronicle of the tremendous technological change which has transformed naval warfare in the twentieth century. No preceding century has seen such rapid change and development in construction techniques, propulsion and weapons. Wooden ships gave way to iron and then steel. Sail made way for steam, diesel and other forms of mechanical propulsion. The gun became larger and longer ranged while its accuracy was transformed with the development of sophisticated fire control techniques and with the development of radar. New naval weapons such as the torpedo, the mine and the guided missile were introduced while the development of new weapons carriers such as the aircraft carrier, the aeroplane and the submarine transformed naval warfare into a three-dimensional battlefield. At Trafalgar in 1805 Nelson was concerned with events on the water around him. One hundred and forty years later Admiral Sir Bertram Ramsay, commanding the naval forces for the Normandy landings, was concerned with events on, under and above the water. Developments in naval technology were supplemented by a political climate in which the size of a country's navy was directly related to its great power status.

Losses of British warships reflect these developments, but they also show what has remained substantially the same in naval warfare. Despite the tremendous technological advances, the human element has remained unchanged. Writing after the 1918 raid on Zeebrugge Captain Alfred Carpenter, who commanded the *Vindictive*, wrote, 'It is the men that matter. You who have placed your faith in technology have followed a false God.' Carpenter is quite correct – in an age where tradition seems to be regarded as irrelevant. The sailors who remained at their posts in the smoke-filled computer room in HMS *Sheffield* in May 1982 are of the same stamp as those who fought in HMS *Exeter* until she sank beneath them in 1942 and those who took the blockships into Zeebrugge in 1918. These virtues are not solely reserved for war. The Royal Navy has had its share of peacetime accidents which have particularly affected the Submarine Service. The courage shown by Lieutenant Samuel Anderson in crawling into the tiny 17 in torpedo tube in *C.16* to try to escape in 1917 and Surgeon Sub Lieutenant C.E. Rhodes in returning again and again to *Sidon*'s burning interior in 1955 are the equal of any wartime exploit. Technology may change but human courage and *esprit de corps* are eternal. This book is therefore also a record of courage and sacrifice in the face of adversity.

None of the sinkings can be viewed as an isolated technical act without considering the human dimension. The Royal Navy has always been a close family even with its massive wartime expansion in two world wars. When the words 'The Admiralty Regrets . . .' announced that yet another ship was missing, officers and men who had never served in that ship or even seen her, felt genuine grief. As Nicholas Monsarrat expresses it in

Families greet sailors from a British submarine (in this case HMS *Ursula*) on their return from patrol. For the families of the crews of seventy-five British submarines there would be no such reunion – only the dreaded telegram from the Admiralty.

the marvellous novel, *The Cruel Sea*, when the commanding officer tells his engineer about the loss of his previous ship, '. . . He knows all about it, like everyone else in the Navy whether they're in destroyers in the Mediterranean or attached to the base at Scapa Flow: it's part of a linked feeling, part of a family bereavement'.

LOSSES 1904–1914

18 March 1904

Name	*A.1*	**Location**	Off Spithead, near the Nab
Class	*A* class submarine		Tower
Built	9 July 1902	**Cause**	Collision
CO	Lt L.C.O. Mansergh RN	**Casualties**	11
		Survivors	None

Notes   *A.1* was engaged in a practice attack on the cruiser HMS *Juno* and was not aware of the approach of the liner *Berwick Castle* until too late. The Master of the *Berwick Castle* believed he had struck a floating torpedo and reported this to Captain Roger Bacon RN, the head of the Royal Navy's submarine service, who was observing the exercise from the gunboat HMS *Hazard*. When *A.1* failed to surface, the significance of the *Berwick Castle*'s signal was appreciated. The two officers and nine men who made up *A.1*'s ship's company were the first of over 5,000 submariners of the Royal Navy to die in action and through accidents during the twentieth century. *A.1* was raised on 18 April 1904, but did not return to service and was sunk as a target in August 1911. The crew are buried at the Royal Navy cemetery at Haslar near Portsmouth.

13 August 1904

Name	*Decoy*	**Cause**	Collision
Class	Torpedo boat	**Casualties**	1
Built	2 August 1894	**Survivors**	40
Location	English Channel, between the Scilly		
	Isles and Wolf Rock		

Notes   As a sign of increased training for war, night exercises were held in 1904 in which for the first time ships did not burn the usual running lights. *Decoy* was part of the 'Red' fleet and was steaming ahead of her capital ships. In the bad weather and darkness she was rammed by HMS *Arun*, one of Blue Fleet's destroyers. *Arun*'s bow sliced into *Decoy*'s engine room, into which the sea began to pour, enveloping *Decoy* in clouds of steam. The latter immediately began to settle in the water and buckled in the middle. The order was given to abandon ship and all her crew save one were rescued by *Arun* and *Sturgeon*.

   Arun's commanding officer, Lieutenant Reginald Tyrwhitt, was subsequently found guilty of hazarding both his ship and *Decoy*, and was reprimanded. There was much sympathy for the young officer in the press. 'This sentence cannot fail to act as a most unfortunate check on the dash and enterprise of the officers of our destroyer flotillas' was the verdict of the *Globe*. It evidently did Tyrwhitt's career no harm for during the First World War he won fame as commander of the Harwich Force.

8 June 1905

Name	*A.8*	**Location**	South coast of England, Plymouth
Class	*A* class submarine		Sound
Built	23 January 1905	**Cause**	Foundered
CO	Lt H.C. Candy RN	**Casualties**	15
		Survivors	4

Notes   The submarine *A.8* was conducting exercises when she was shaken by an internal explosion of considerable violence and then sank. The wreck was further destroyed by two more explosions. A court of enquiry subsequently found that a rivet was missing from the forward petrol tank, which meant that water would be admitted into the boat at a rate of 1 ton every 10 minutes. This was undoubtedly the cause of the foundering; the cause of the three internal explosions that subsequently wrecked the submarine is unclear but was probably water shorting the electrical circuits and igniting petrol vapour or a battery explosion. *A.8* was salvaged on 12 June 1905, and eventually sold for breaking up at Dartmouth on 8 October 1920.

16 October 1905

Name	*A.4*	**Location**	English Channel, Stokes Bay, 2 miles
Class	*A* class submarine		west of Portsmouth
Built	9 June 1903	**Cause**	Accident
CO	Lt Martin Dunbar-Nasmith RN	**Casualties**	None
		Survivors	11

Notes   *A.4* sank as a result of flooding through a ventilation shaft while engaged in exercises with *TB.26*. Dunbar-Nasmith managed to bring the boat to the surface and he and his crew clambered out on the casing. On checking the number of men present Dunbar-Nasmith realised two were missing and so re-entered the submarine to find them still at their posts because they had not heard the order to abandon ship. *A.4* was taken in tow by HMS *Hazard* and returned to Portsmouth. However, as she was about to enter the dry dock the submarine suffered three internal explosions, probably the result of petrol vapour igniting, and foundered in Portsmouth Harbour. *A.4* was subsequently raised and returned to service. She was finally sold to J. Lee of Bembridge for breaking up in January 1920.

Lieutenant Dunbar-Nasmith was reprimanded for 'hazarding His Majesty's Submarine A.4' but the judgement did not affect his career for after winning the Victoria Cross in command of *E.11* in the Dardanelles, he retired as Admiral Sir Martin Dunbar-Nasmith VC. Sub-Lieutenant Godfrey Herbert, *A.4*'s first lieutenant, was involved in the sinking of four of HM submarines, of which *A.4* was the first. (See the entries for *D.5*, *E.22* and *K.13*.) This is a record and he can thus be regarded as the 'Jonah' of the Royal Navy's Submarine Service.

17 April 1906

Name	*TB.84*	**Cause**	Collision
Class	Torpedo boat	**Casualties**	1
Location	Mediterranean, off Malta	**Survivors**	18

Notes   *TB.84* sank following a collision with the destroyer HMS *Ardent* during night exercises off Malta.

17 May 1906

Name	*TB.56*	Cause	Foundered
Class	Torpedo boat	Casualties	7
Location	Mediterranean, off Damietta	Survivors	8

Notes *TB.56* had been engaged in patrol duties off the northern entrance to the Suez Canal during the 1906 Turkish Crisis. She was being returned to Malta in the tow of the cruiser HMS *Arrogant*. During the tow the weather worsened and, when off Damietta, *TB.56* suddenly capsized.

30 May 1906

Name	*Montague*	Location	British Channel, Lundy Island
Class	*Duncan* class battleship	Cause	Grounded
Built	5 March 1901	Casualties	None
CO	Capt T.B. Adair RN	Survivors	720

Notes HMS *Montague* was heading up the Bristol Channel for a rendezvous with the Channel Fleet. The weather was extremely foggy but Captain Adair pressed on, determined to be at the rendezvous on time, rather than anchoring to wait for the fog to clear. However, in those pre-radar and satellite navigation days, *Montague*'s track was well to the south of where her navigating officer thought it was. She was lucky to round Hartland Point but went hard aground on the Shutters, a rocky ledge on the south-west point of Lundy Island. It proved impossible to float her off so the decision was taken to remove every item of equipment that could be salved and leave the hulk to be broken up *in situ*. Access to the wreck was by a precarious ropeway strung from the clifftop and she became quite an item of local interest. A number of articles from the wreck are still displayed on Lundy.

18 September 1906

Name	*Phoenix*	Location	Port of Hong Kong
Class	*Phoenix* class sloop	Cause	Accident
Built	25 April 1895	Casualties	None
CO	None appointed	Survivors	Not applicable

Notes *Phoenix* was in dry dock and out of commission in Hong Kong when the colony was struck by a typhoon. The shoring could not support the sloop against the force of the wind and she fell over in the dock. After survey it was considered that she was beyond economical repair. Her wreck was sold on 7 January 1907.

19 April 1907

Name	*Ariel*	Location	Mediterranean, entrance to Grand Harbour, Valetta
Class	*D* class destroyer		
Built	5 March 1897	Cause	Grounded
		Casualties	None

Notes *Ariel* grounded and was wrecked on Ricasoli Breakwater while trying to enter Grand Harbour during a night exercise to test harbour defences.

2 April 1908

Name	*Tiger*	**Location**	English Channel, off Isle of Wight,	
Class	*C* class destroyer		18 miles S of St Catherine's Point	
Built	19 May 1900	**Cause**	Collision	
CO	Lt Cdr W.E. Middleton RN	**Casualties**	36	
		Survivors	22	

Notes   *Tiger* was one of a number of destroyers engaged in night manoeuvres off the Isle of Wight in which all participating ships had extinguished their navigation lights. While attempting to cross the bows of the cruiser *Berwick*, her commanding officer misjudged the distance with the result that the cruiser hit *Tiger* amidships on the starboard side and cut the frail destroyer in half.

25 April 1908

Name	*Gladiator*	**Location**	English Channel, the Solent
Class	*Arrogant* class light cruiser	**Cause**	Collision
Built	18 December 1896	**Casualties**	27
CO	Capt W. Lumsden RN	**Survivors**	372

Notes   HMS *Gladiator* collided with the US liner *St Paul* in bad weather in the Solent. The liner suddenly emerged from the fog and rammed the *Gladiator* on her starboard side. *Gladiator* headed for the coast and eventually ran aground near the Black Rock Buoy where she capsized. *St Paul's* boats showed great seamanship in rescuing her crew who were gathered on the upturned port side of her hull. Raised in October 1908 she was found to be beyond economical repair and was sold for breaking up.

27 April 1908

Name	*Gala*	**Cause**	Collision
Class	*River* class destroyer	**Casualties**	None
Built	7 Janaury 1905	**Survivors**	58
Location	North Sea, near Outer Gabbard Light Vessel		

Notes   HMS *Gala* was rammed and sunk by the cruiser HMS *Attentive* during night exercises off Harwich.

6 April 1909

Name	*Blackwater*	**Cause**	Collision
Class	*River* class destroyer	**Casualties**	3
Built	25 July 1903	**Survivors**	55
Location	English Channel, off Dungeness		

Notes   HMS *Blackwater* was sunk in collision with the SS *Hero* in the English Channel.

14 July 1909

Name	*C.11*	**Location**	North Sea, off Cromer, 4.5 miles
Class	*C* class submarine		NW of the Haisborough Light
Built	27 May 1907	**Cause**	Collision
CO	Lt C.G. Brodie RN	**Casualties**	13
		Survivors	3

Notes *C.11* was sunk in collision with the merchant ship *Eddystone*. The accident happened at night despite the fact that *C.11*, in company with eight other submarines, eight torpedo boats and the depot ship *Bonaventure*, were all brightly illuminated. *Eddystone* ploughed straight into the formation and sliced the submarine's stern off and *C.11* sank in 40 seconds. It was suggested that the *Eddystone*'s Master, Captain T.B. Pritchard, was not on the bridge at the time, despite his ship being in a crowded shipping lane, but was enjoying the company of his wife in the privacy of his cabin. The three survivors – Lieutenant C.G. Brodie, commanding officer, Lieutenant G. Watkins, first lieutenant, and Able Seaman J. Stripes – were in the conning tower at the time of the collision and were able to scramble out before the submarine sank.

5 October 1909

Name	*Lee*	**Cause**	Grounding
Class	Torpedo boat	**Casualties**	None
Built	27 January 1899	**Survivors**	56
Location	Ireland, Blacksod Bay		

Notes HMS *Lee* ran aground in Blacksod Bay and was a total loss. Her wreck was sold for breaking up in December 1909.

21 August 1910

Name	*Bedford*	**Location**	East China Sea, Samarang Rocks near
Class	*Monmouth* class cruiser		Quelpart Island
Built	31 August 1901	**Cause**	Grounded
CO	Capt E.S. Fitzherbert RN	**Casualties**	18

Notes HMS *Bedford* was conducting a full power trial in the Straits of Korea when she drove hard aground on the Samarang Rocks. She hit the rocks at a speed of 19 knots, the impact immediately flooding her machinery spaces so that no more power was available. Although only a small portion of the bow was aground, further damage was done to the hull by the heavy seas working the ship to and fro. The Japanese Navy offered assistance but, as with *Montague*, it proved impossible to refloat her. After all the equipment had been removed, her hull was sold to local breakers on 10 October 1910.

6 February 1912

Name	*A.3*	**Location**	English Channel, off Bembridge on
Class	*A* class submarine		the W coast of the Isle of Wight
Built	9 March 1903	**Cause**	Collision
CO	Lt F.T. Ormand RN	**Casualties**	14
		Survivors	None

Notes   A.3 was sunk in collision with HMS *Hazard* during exercises. The small submarine surfaced directly under the bows of the gunboat. It was too late for *Hazard* to take avoiding action and she tore a huge hole in *A.3*'s side. The submarine sank so quickly that none of the fourteen crew could escape to safety. *A.3* was subsequently raised and eventually sunk by gunfire of the battleship HMS *St Vincent* on 7 May 1912. The crew are buried at the Royal Navy cemetery at Haslar near Portsmouth.

4 October 1912

Name	*B.2*	**Location**	English Channel, 4 miles NE of
Class	*B* class submarine		Dover
Built	31 October 1905	**Cause**	Collision
CO	Lt P.B. O'Brien RN	**Casualties**	15
		Survivors	1

Notes   B.2 was sunk following a collision with the Hamburg–America liner *Amerika*. The 23,000 ton liner, which was outward bound for Southampton and then New York, was intent on making a fast passage and her Master, evidently one of the 'Ram You – Damn You' liner captains so often criticised in the contemporary press, believed that all other craft would get out of his way. The submarine's look-outs apparently thought that the liner would pass clear of her for no avoiding action was taken until it was too late. The sole survivor, Lieutenant Richard Pulleyne, had been swept off the conning tower but had to spend some hours in the water before being rescued by the submarine *C.16*. Lieutenant Pulleyne was later killed while commanding the submarine *E.34* (see p. 76).

A subsequent investigation found that *Amerika* had sighted *B.2*'s conning tower about 60 ft ahead of her. *Amerika* was steaming at 17 knots and although the order for full astern was given the liner had too much way on her to stop.

10 December 1913

Name	*C.14*	**Location**	English Channel, Plymouth Sound
Class	*C* class submarine	**Cause**	Collision
Built	7 December 1907	**Casualties**	None
CO	Lt W.E. Naper RN	**Survivors**	20

Notes   C.14 collided with *Admiralty Hopper* No. 27. The collision occurred in fog as the submarine was passing between Drakes Island and Devil's Point. The pressure hull was holed but the boat sank very slowly, allowing the crew to jump clear and swim to safety.

16 January 1914

Name	*A.7*	**Location**	English Channel, Whitesand Bay
Class	*A* class submarine	**Cause**	Accident
Built	23 January 1905	**Casualties**	11
CO	Lt G.M. Welman RN	**Survivors**	None

Notes   A.7 is presumed to have sunk as a result of a dive in which control of the submarine was lost and she became stuck in the mud and unable to free herself. Divers found the wreck on the 23rd. *A.7* was lying on the bottom with a bow up angle of between 30° to 40° and with nearly 22 ft of her stern buried in the mud. It proved impossible to raise the submarine and salvage was abandoned on 27 February.

LOSSES 1914

6 August 1914

Name	*Amphion*	**Location**	North Sea, off Harwich
Class	*Active* class cruiser	**Cause**	Mine
Built	4 December 1911	**Casualties**	151
CO	Capt C.H. Fox RN	**Survivors**	174

Notes The first British casualty of the First World War, *Amphion* had just scored the Royal Navy's first success of the war by sinking the German auxiliary minelayer *Köningen Luise* on the 5th. Returning from that operation she altered course so as to avoid the minefield just laid by the *Köningen Luise*. However, as was so often the case, her dead reckoning position was wrong and she just clipped a corner of the German minefield. At 0630 hrs on the 6th there was a shattering explosion, shortly followed by another as *Amphion* struck a second mine. She was then abandoned. In addition to the 151 of *Amphion*'s ship's company who were killed, eighteen of the twenty survivors from the *Köningen Luise* were also drowned.

September 1914 *gave a striking demonstration of the capability of a new weapon of war – the submarine. The sinking of* Pathfinder *swiftly followed by that of* Aboukir, Hogue *and* Cressy *came as a terrible shock to the Royal Navy.*

3 September 1914

Name	*Speedy*	**Cause**	Mine
Class	*Alarm* class torpedo gunboat	**Casualties**	None
Built	18 May 1893	**Survivors**	124
Location	North Sea, off the Humber		

Notes The Germans had laid extensive minefields off the Tyne and the Humber and it was while sweeping off the Humber that *Speedy* was mined and sunk. As a result of her loss the Admiralty took the decision not to attempt clearance of entire minefields but merely to clear swept channels through them.

5 September 1914

Name	*Pathfinder*	**Location**	Scotland, Firth of Forth
Class	*Pathfinder* class cruiser	**Cause**	Submarine attack
Built	16 July 1904	**Casualties**	256
CO	Capt M. Leake RN	**Survivors**	12

Notes HMS *Pathfinder* was on patrol off the Firth of Forth when she was attacked by *U21* (*Kapitanleutnant* Otto Hersing). Standing Orders emphasised a minimum speed of 15 knots in waters where U-boats might be expected to operate, but *Pathfinder* was doing only 6 knots on account of the requirements of her task (she was patrolling in the Firth of Forth) and her small coal bunkers. Consequently she was almost a 'sitting duck' for Hersing. The torpedo was seen approaching the starboard side and the helm was put over but it was too late.

The torpedo hit the starboard side under the bridge and set off the forward magazine – the explosion blew Captain Leake aft and into the upper deck meat-safe. The bows were literally blown off and then she started to sink as water poured into her hull. Four minutes later she had disappeared.

8 September 1914

Name	*Oceanic*	**Cause**	Grounded
Class	AMC	**Casualties**	None
Location	Shetland Islands	**Survivors**	400

Notes   HMS *Oceanic* was operating as part of the Northern Patrol, enforcing the naval blockade of Germany. On 8 September she went aground on Foula Island in the Shetlands and could not be refloated.

19 September 1914

Name	*AE.1*	**Location**	Pacific, off New Britain, exact
Class	*E* class submarine		position unknown
CO	Lt Cdr T.E. Besant RN	**Casualties**	30
		Survivors	None

Notes   *AE.1* was covering the occupation by Australian forces of New Britain and other German possessions in the Bismarck Archipelago. She was spotted by the destroyer *Parramata* at 1530/19 but was never seen again. When she failed to reappear by 2000 hrs that evening the alarm was raised. Although a major search was carried out nothing, not even an oil slick, was found. It is presumed that in approaching Blanche Island while submerged, *AE.1* grounded on a coral reef.

20 September 1914

Name	*Pegasus*	**Location**	Indian Ocean, off Zanzibar
Class	*Pelorus* class cruiser	**Cause**	Gunfire
Built	4 March 1897	**Casualties**	31
CO	Cdr J.A. Ingles RN		

Notes   HMS *Pegasus* was undergoing routine maintenance at the harbour of Zanzibar when it was reported that the German cruiser *Konigsberg* was in the area. Consequently all other British warships had gone to cover a troop convoy taking British troops to France from India, leaving *Pegasus* alone. Commander Ingles had taken such precautions as he could: a tug was stationed at the harbour entrance to give warning, his men slept at their posts and steam was kept raised. However, at 0525 hrs on 20 September, when the *Konigsberg* appeared, she merely brushed past the tug, which failed to pass on any warning, and opened fire on *Pegasus* from a range of 9,000 yards. At this range *Pegasus'* guns could not reply and within eight minutes all her broadside guns were disabled. At 0555 hrs *Konigsberg* discontinued the action, leaving *Pegasus* in a sinking condition. The crew tried to beach her but *Pegasus* capsized.

22 September 1914

Name	*Aboukir*	**Location**	North Sea, off the Dutch coast,
Class	*Cressy* class cruiser		52 18'N, 03 41'E
Built	16 May 1900	**Cause**	Submarine attack
CO	Capt Drummond		

Notes The cruisers *Aboukir*, *Cressy* and *Hogue* were on patrol off the Dutch coast to prevent German forces from moving south to attack Channel troop convoys. Owing to bad weather the three cruisers were without their destroyer screen. At 0630 hrs on 20 September there was a violent explosion on *Aboukir*'s starboard side. She quickly assumed a 20° list to starboard while efforts were made to right the ship by counterflooding. However, the list kept on increasing until it was clear that she was going to capsize. Abandon Ship was ordered and the *Hogue* prepared to rescue her crew. As 0655 hrs hrs *Aboukir* capsized and floated bottom up for a while before sinking. Captain Drummond thought that his ship had been mined but in fact she had been torpedoed by *U9* (*Kapitanleutnant* Otto Weddigen).

Name	*Hogue*	**Location**	North Sea, off the Dutch coast,
Class	*Cressy* class cruiser		52 18'N, 03 41'E
Built	13 August 1900	**Cause**	Submarine attack
CO	Capt W. Nicholson RN		

Notes As *Aboukir* was sinking, Captain Nicholson took *Hogue* up to rescue her crew. *Hogue*'s crew threw anything that would float over the side to their comrades in the water. Almost immediately *Hogue* was struck on her port side by two torpedoes fired by *U9* and she began to sink by the stern. At the same time the submarine broached on the cruiser's port quarter and was immediately fired on by every gun that would bear. Ten minutes after being hit *Hogue* rolled over on to her beam ends and sank.

Name	*Cressy*	**Location**	North Sea, off the Dutch coast,
Class	*Cressy* class cruiser		52 18'N, 03 41'E
Built	4 December 1899	**Cause**	Submarine attack
CO	Capt R.W. Johnson RN		

Notes It was now abundantly clear to Captain Johnson what had been responsible for sinking his two consorts. Nevertheless, *Cressy* remained stopped picking up *Hogue*'s and *Aboukir*'s survivors. She thus became Weddigen's third victim in little less than an hour, struck by two torpedoes and sinking equally quickly.

In total, 60 officers and 777 men were saved from the three ships which means that the death toll from the three ships was 1,459 – greater than the total British casualties at the Battle of Trafalgar. Among the dead were many boy seamen from HMS *Ganges* and officer cadets from the Britannia Royal Naval College at Dartmouth.

15 October 1914

Name	*Hawke*	**Location**	North Sea, between Peterhead and
Class	*Edgar* class cruiser		the Naze
Built	11 March 1891	**Cause**	Submarine attack
CO	Capt H.P.E. Williams RN	**Casualties**	500
		Survivors	70

Notes HMS *Hawke* was on patrol with the other units of the 12th Cruiser Squadron. On the morning of the 15th she had stopped to collect mail from *Endymion*. She was just getting under way again when at 1030 hrs she was hit by a torpedo fired by Weddigen's *U9* and sank very quickly. Even so, 3 officers and 46 men got away in a boat, were collected by a Norwegian steamer and taken in to Aberdeen the next day. A further 21 survivors were rescued by HMS *Swift* after a search.

18 October 1914

Name	*E.3*	**Location**	North Sea, off the Ems estuary
Class	*E* class submarine	**Cause**	Submarine attack
Built	29 October 1912	**Survivors**	None
CO	Lt Cdr G.F. Cholmley RN		

Notes   *E.3* was the first British submarine to be sunk in action and the first to be sunk by another submarine. Cholmley was patrolling off the Ems estuary when *E.3* was sighted by *U27* (*Kapitanleutnant* Bernhard Wegener). Wegener took his time making his approach, noting that the six men on *E.3*'s bridge were concentrating on looking toward land and that no all round lookout was being maintained. He therefore manoeuvred until he was attacking from the direction of the sun, to give him a clearer target – all he could see was *E.3*'s conning tower – and hopefully hide his periscope in the glare of the sun off the sea. He fired one torpedo from a range of 300 yards and watched *E.3* break in half and sink. Wegener saw four men in the water but made no attempt to surface for fear of another British submarine in the area. When he eventually surfaced 30 minutes later the men had gone and all that was left of *E.3* was wreckage.

27 October 1914

Name	*Audacious*	**Location**	Atlantic, off Lough Swilly, 55 34'N,
Class	*King George V* class battleship		08 12'W
Built	14 September 1912	**Cause**	Mine
CO	Capt C.F. Dampier RN	**Casualties**	None
		Survivors	860

Notes   In the confusion following various submarine alarms, the Grand Fleet was dispersed to various anchorages in Scotland and Ireland. As she was leaving Lough Swilly for gunnery practice, *Audacious* struck a mine. At 0845 hrs the OOW recorded a dull thump and thought that one of the aft 13.5 in guns had been 'accidentally' fired. The ship then took a list to port and by 0900 hrs it was clear that *Audacious* was in trouble. An examination of the ship found massive flooding on the port side around the port wing engine room and the dynamo room. Counterflooding failed to correct the list and it was reported that water was leaking through the longitudinal bulkhead into the centre and starboard compartments. By 1000 hrs all engine rooms had to be abandoned and the ship lay dead in the water; by 1100 hrs all steam power had failed. Non-essential personnel were disembarked leaving a towing party of around 250 who prepared a tow line. Three attempts were made to tow the ship, the first by the liner *Olympic*, the second by HMS *Liverpool* and the third by the collier *Thornhill*. All failed because *Audacious* was virtually unmanageable.

By 1700 hrs *Audacious'* quarterdeck was awash and water was entering the ship through the smashed mushroom vents aft. At 1815 hrs she was abandoned and lay dead in the water rolling heavily, but at 2045 hrs she suddenly turned turtle and floated upside down. Then at 2100 hrs there was a terrific explosion, caused by fused shells (*Audacious* carried 1,120 13.5 in shells and 2,400 4 in shells) breaking out of their racks and hitting the 'floor', exploding and igniting the cordite charges. Immediately after this explosion *Audacious* was seen to sink. The subsequent enquiry found that the longitudinal bulkhead was inadequate to prevent water reaching the central part of the ship. The shock of the explosion buckled bulkheads and distorted doors and valves, all of which made it extremely difficult to stop the ship filling up with water.

The minefield in which *Audacious* was sunk had been laid on the night of 23 October by the German auxiliary minelayer *Berlin* whose commander, *Kapitan zur See* Hans Pfundheller, had been unable to lay the mines in the Clyde as ordered and thought he might as well lay them outside Lough Swilly as anywhere else. The Admiralty was desperate to keep the loss of *Audacious* a secret but it was a futile effort. There had been a number of Americans on board *Olympic* and the Germans knew of the loss of *Audacious* within a week. Nevertheless, to preserve the fiction, her name continued to be included in the Navy List until the end of the war.

31 October 1914

Name	*Hermes*	**Location**	English Channel, 8 miles WNW of
Class	Seaplane carrier		Calais
Built	7 April 1898	**Cause**	Submarine attack
CO	Capt Charles Lambe RN	**Casualties**	44
		Survivors	400

Notes In 1912 the cruiser HMS *Hermes* had been converted to a seaplane carrier. On the morning of 31 October she left Dunkirk, where she had arrived the previous evening from Portsmouth with a number of seaplanes. At 0930 hrs a signal was made for her to return on account of a submarine alarm but at 0940 hrs the destroyer *Liberty* reported that *Hermes* had been torpedoed and sunk. Her assailant had been Wegener's *U27*.

November 1914 *saw Britain's first significant defeat in the First World War when Admiral Craddock's squadron was virtually annihilated by the German East Asia Squadron off the coast of Chile. Though the sinking of the* Good Hope *and the* Monmouth *were speedily avenged, it was nevertheless a bitter blow to British prestige.*

1 November 1914

Name	*Good Hope*	**Location**	E Pacific, off Coronel on the Chilean
Class	*Drake* class cruiser		coast
CO	Capt P. Franklin RN, flagship of Rear	**Cause**	Gunfire
	Adm Christopher Craddock	**Casualties**	900
		Survivors	None

Notes HM Ships *Good Hope*, *Monmouth*, *Glasgow* and *Ortanto* were operating in the E Pacific, searching for the German East Asia Squadron under the command of Admiral Maximilian Graf von Spee, which was attempting to return to Germany via Cape Horn. On the evening of 1 December the two squadrons met. Initially the British had the advantage for the Germans were silhouetted against the setting sun, but von Spee used his superior speed to avoid action. After the sun set the British ships were illuminated by the afterglow while the German ships were hidden in the dusk and it was at this juncture that von Spee initiated the action. The British ships were further hampered by bad weather which meant that their lower casemate guns could not be worked. Another factor was that, while von Spee's ships were manned by well-trained regulars who had worked and trained together, the British ships had only recently recommissioned with crews made up of reservists. Under the circumstances it was very one-sided engagement. Firing began just after 1900 hrs and by 1952 hrs *Good Hope* had been battered into a wreck by the German cruisers *Scharnhorst* and *Gneisenau*. In the dark and driving rain it was difficult to see how or when she sank but observers did see a large explosion after which the stern portion was seen floating.

Name	*Monmouth*	Location	Pacific Ocean, off Coronel on the
Class	*Monmouth* class cruiser		Chilean coast
Built	13 November 1901	Cause	Gunfire
CO	Capt F. Brandt	Casualties	900
		Survivors	4

Notes *Monmouth* had endured a similar battering from the German cruisers but after the sinking of the flagship she had broken away to try to escape to the north. At 2100 hrs she was found by the German cruiser *Nurnberg*, listing to port and with steam escaping amidships. The list was so steep that none of the guns on *Monmouth*'s port side could be worked, so by remaining on her port side *Nurnberg* could maintain an uninterrupted fire with no risk of damage to herself. After firing a few rounds *Nurnberg* paused to see if *Monmouth* would strike her colours but to no avail. *Nurnberg* opened fire again and then *Monmouth* capsized. The rough weather prevented *Nurnberg* from lowering any boats.

The four survivors were Mate Robert Roe and three ratings who had been landed on the Albrohos Rocks to establish a lookout/signal station. They therefore escaped the fate of their crewmates.

Mate Robert Roe (centre) who survived the sinking of HMS *Monmouth* by default when he and four ratings were put ashore on Albrohos Rocks to set up a signal station. Roe later became a successful submarine commander. (Author)

3 November 1914

Name	*D.5*	**Location**	North Sea, off Yarmouth
Class	*D* class submarine	**Cause**	Mine
CO	Lt Cdr Godfrey Herbert RN	**Survivors**	5

Notes *D.5* was off Yarmouth when she was mined. She sank very quickly and only those on the bridge survived and were picked up by the drifter *Faithful*.

12 November 1914

Name	*Niger*	**Location**	English Channel, off the port of Deal
Class	*Alarm* class torpedo gunboat	**Cause**	Submarine attack
CO	Lt Cdr A.P. Moore RN	**Casualties**	None

Notes HMS *Niger* was torpedoed while at anchor off Deal. The ship was abandoned and her crew taken off by the Deal and Kingsdown lifeboats, watched by hundreds of people on the shore. She then exploded.

25(?) November 1914

Name	*D.2*	**Location**	North Sea, exact location unknown
Class	*D* class submarine	**Survivors**	None
CO	Lt Cdr C. Head RN		

Notes *D.2* sailed for patrol on 24 November 1915 and thereafter nothing more was heard from her. She may have been mined or lost as a result of an accident arising from materiel or drill failure.

26 November 1914

Name	*Bulwark*	**Location**	Thames estuary, off Sheerness
Class	*London* class battleship	**Cause**	Accident
Built	18 October 1899	**Survivors**	12
CO	Capt G.L. Sclater RN		

Notes HMS *Bulwark* was taking on ammunition at a buoy off Sheerness when she suddenly blew up. An enquiry concluded that the most likely cause of the explosion was careless handling of black powder charges on her upper deck.

27 December 1914

Name	*Success*	**Cause**	Wrecked
Class	Destroyer	**Survivors**	60
Location	N coast of Scotland, off Fifeness		

Notes HMS *Success* went aground off Fifeness in bad weather and was wrecked. She was not refloated and the wreck was left *in situ*.

LOSSES 1915

1 January 1915

Name	*Formidable*	**Location**	English Channel, 25 miles off
Class	*Formidable* class battleship		Portland
Built	17 November 1898	**Cause**	Submarine attack
CO	Capt A.N. Loxley RN, flagship of	**Casualties**	547
	Vice Admiral Sir Lewis Bayly	**Survivors**	233

Notes   HMS *Formidable* was leading the eight battleships of the 5th Battle Squadron down the English Channel screened by two light cruisers. The destroyers had been sent back to Harwich when the ships passed Folkestone. The squadron had been spotted by *U24* (*Kapitanleutnant* Rudolph Schneider) but he had been unable to manoeuvre into an attacking position and had to watch as the ships sailed by. Shortly after 1900 hrs the British ships made a 16-point turn in accordance with orders that course should be altered after dark in areas where submarines were known to be operating. Again at 0200 hrs a second 16-point turn was made so that *Formidable* and her consorts were steaming back along their course and towards *U24*. This time Schneider was in a perfect position and at 0225 hrs fired a torpedo against *Formidable*, the last ship in the line. It hit her on the starboard side by the fore funnel. Her machinery spaces began to flood and she assumed a list to starboard. At 0315 hrs Schneider fired a second torpedo which hit *Formidable* on the port side. On board *Formidable* the dynamos failed although the crew maintained perfect discipline in the listing and darkened ship. At 0445 hrs she capsized and then sank.

Bayly was ordered to haul down his flag as a result of this loss. His request for a court martial was refused despite prominent and vocal support for him in the House of Lords. In the end Bayly became the highly successful commander of Anglo-American forces operating from Queenstown in southern Ireland.

4(?) January 1915

Name	*C.31*	**Location**	Unknown, possibly off Zeebrugge
Class	*C* class submarine	**Survivors**	None
CO	Lt George Pilkington RN		

Notes   *C.31* sailed from Harwich on 4 January for a patrol off Zeebrugge and was never seen or heard from again. When she failed to return the Royal Naval Air Service was asked to observe the waters off Zeebrugge carefully for signs of any German activity indicating a salvage operation. However, nothing was seen. It is presumed that *C.31* struck a mine though her loss as the result of an accident cannot be ruled out.

13 January 1915

Name	*Viknor*	**Cause**	Unknown
Class	AMC	**Casualties**	295
CO	Cdr E.O. Ballantyne	**Survivors**	None
Location	North Sea, off Tory Island		

Notes HMS *Viknor* is presumed to have been mined while on blockade duty. Nothing by way of wreckage or bodies was ever found.

18(?) January 1915

Name	*E.10*	**Location**	North Sea, off Heligoland
Class	E class submarine	**Cause**	Mine
Built	29 November 1913	**Survivors**	None
CO	Lt Cdr W. St J. Fraser RN		

Notes *E.10* left Harwich on 18 January in company with *E.15* (Lieutenant-Commander T.S. Brodie) for a patrol off Heligoland. *E.10*'s patrol area was NNW of the island. Nothing more was heard from her and it is presumed that she was sunk in a German minefield laid on 22 December 1914, and the existence of which was then unknown to the British.

3 February 1915

Name	*Clan MacNaughton*	**Cause**	Presumed mined
Class	AMC	**Casualties**	261
CO	Cdr Robert Jeffreys RN	**Survivors**	None

Notes HMS *Clan MacNaughton* was employed on blockade duty when she disappeared. Wreckage – but no survivors – was subsequently found and it is presumed that she was mined.

6 February 1915

Name	*Erne*	**Location**	North Sea, E coast of Scotland
Class	*River* class destroyer	**Cause**	Grounded
Built	14 January 1903	**Casualties**	None

Notes HMS *Erne* went aground off Rattray Head, Aberdeenshire, in bad weather. The wreck was subsequently sold for breaking up *in situ*.

18/19 February 1915

Name	*Goldfinch*	**Location**	Orkney Islands, Start Point
Class	*Acorn* class destroyer	**Cause**	Grounded
Built	12 July 1910	**Casualties**	None

Notes HMS *Goldfinch* went aground in fog on Start Point on Sunday Island in the Orkneys. Her wreck was sold for breaking up in 1919.

March 1915 *saw the beginning of the Dardanelles Campaign, which would cost the Royal Navy 5 battleships, 1 destroyer, 4 submarines and a number of other vessels.*

11 March 1915

Name	*Bayano*	**Cause**	Submarine attack
Class	AMC	**Casualties**	195
CO	Cdr H.C. Carr RN	**Survivors**	26
Location	10 miles WNW of Corsewall Point		

Notes *Bayano* was torpedoed at 0505 hrs on 11 March by *U27*, commanded by *Kapitanleutnant* Bernhard Wegener.

18 March 1915

Name	*Irresistible*	**Location**	E Mediterranean, the Dardanelles
Class	*Formidable* class battleship	**Cause**	Mined after shore battery fire
Built	15 December 1898	**Casualties**	200
CO	Capt D.L. Dent RN	**Survivors**	610

Notes HMS *Irresistible* was engaged in operations off the Cape Helles Peninsula to silence the Turkish forts and force a passage through the Dardanelles into the Sea of Marmora and thence to Constantinople. It was a task that seemed comparatively easy but the forts proved hard to hit and mobile batteries of field artillery kept up harassing fire on the battleships and the trawlers which were attempting to clear mines. *Irresistible* was first hit by gunfire from the fort Hamedieh 1. She stopped and then drifted into a row of mines which had been laid parallel to the shore at Eren Kuel Bay by the Turkish minelayer *Nousret*. This field had already damaged the battle cruiser *Inflexible*. Efforts to save the ship failed and she was abandoned.

Name	*Ocean*	**Location**	E Mediterranean, the Dardanelles
Class	*Canopus* class battleship	**Cause**	Mine
Built	5 July 1898	**Casualties**	None
CO	Capt A. Hayes-Saddlet RN	**Survivors**	683

Notes HMS *Ocean* was the third British victim of *Nousret*'s minefield. After the loss of *Irresistible* the British battleships were ordered to withdraw. As *Ocean* turned around her course took her past Eren Kuel Bay and on to *Nousret*'s mines at 1805 hrs on 18 March. She foundered during the night.

21 March 1915

Name	*TB.064*	**Location**	Aegean
Class	Torpedo boat	**Cause**	Grounded
Built	1886	**Casualties**	None

Notes *TB.064* went aground in bad weather.

17 April 1915

Name	*E.15*	**Location**	Mediterranean, the Dardanelles, on
Class	*E* class submarine		Kephez Point
CO	Lt C.S. Brodie RN	**Cause**	Grounded
		Casualties	1

Notes   A number of British submariners had considered the possibility of sailing up the Dardanelles and into the Sea of Marmara where they could harass Turkish shipping taking supplies to their troops on Cape Helles. *E.15* (under the command of Lieutenant-Commander T.S. Brodie who had commanded *C.11* when she was sunk in 1909) was the first British submarine selected for the attempt. The passage of the Dardanelles is a tricky one and to help with navigation Lieutenant C.S. Palmer RNVR, who before the war had been British Vice Consul at Chanak, was appointed to submarine in the hope that his local knowledge would prove useful.

E.15 sailed on the night of 16 April but early the next morning she was caught in a fierce eddy and grounded on Kephez Point on the Asiatic shore. She was fired on by the guns of Fort Dardanos and abandoned by her crew. Brodie was killed as he climbed out of the conning tower but the rest of his crew were taken prisoner.

The Royal Navy now regarded the destruction of *E.15*'s wreck as a matter of urgency to prevent the Turks from salvaging her. Bombing from the air, bombardment by battleships, an attack by the submarine *B.6* and torpedo attacks by destroyers all failed. In the end two 56 ft picket boats specially converted to carry torpedoes did the job. *E.15* would never fly the Turkish ensign.

Turkish and German personnel (the naval officer on the foreground is undoubtedly German despite the *fez*) examine the wreck of the British submarine *E.15* aground near Kephez Point in the Dardanelles. (Author)

30 April 1915

Name	*AE.2*	**Location**	Sea of Marmara
Class	*E* class submarine	**Cause**	Scuttled
Built	18 June 1913	**Casualties**	None
CO	Lt Cdr H.G. Stoker RN	**Survivors**	30

Notes   *AE.2* was the first 'British' submarine (although she was officially part of the Royal Australian Navy) to make the passage of the Dardanelles into the Marmara. On 20 April Stoker was proceeding to Ataki Bay for a meeting with *E.14*, which had followed *AE.2* into Marmara, when he sighted the Turkish gunboat *Sultan Hissar*. Stoker dived but *AE.2* suddenly assumed a large bow up angle and broached in full view of the gunboat, about 100 yards off her bow. *Sultan Hissar*'s crew were very much on the *qui vive* for they opened fire immediately, scoring a number of hits on the submarine. Stoker brought *AE.2* to the surface long enough for her crew to abandon her. In his book *Straws in the Wind*, Stoker described the last moments of his submarine: '. . . slowly and gracefully, like the lady she was, without sound or sigh, without causing an eddy or a ripple on the water, *AE.2* just slid away on her last and longest dive.'

1 May 1915

Name	*Recruit*	**Cause**	Submarine attack
Class	Torpedo boat	**Casualties**	43
Location	North Sea, near the Galloper Bank	**Survivors**	26

Notes   HMS *Recruit* was torpedoed by *U6*. The explosion blew the little torpedo boat in half and she sank very quickly.

7 May 1915

Name	*Maori*	**Cause**	Mine
Class	*Tribal* class destroyer	**Casualties**	None
Built	24 May 1909	**Survivors**	95 plus *Crusader*'s boat crew
CO	Cdr B.W. Barron RN		

Notes   HMS *Maori* and HMS *Crusader* had been ordered to carry out certain observations off Ostende in preparation for a bombardment. Experience would later teach the Royal Navy that the Belgian coast should not be approached at low water, when German moored mines were nearer the surface. It was low water as *Maori* approached to take her observations and was sunk by a mine. *Crusader* lowered a boat but was forced to withdraw when fired on by German shore batteries. Thus *Maori*'s entire ship's company plus *Crusader*'s boat crew went ashore to become prisoners of war.

13 May 1915

Name	*Goliath*	**Location**	E Mediterranean, Morto Bay
Class	*Canopus* class battleship	**Cause**	Torpedo
Built	25 March 1898	**Casualties**	570
CO	Capt T.L. Shelford RN	**Survivors**	180

Notes HMS *Goliath* had been doing excellent work bombarding Turkish positions on Cape Helles. She anchored for the night of 12 May in Morto Bay, an exposed anchorage. The effectiveness of her fire had disturbed the German/Turkish command so the Turkish destroyer *Muavenet*, under the command of the German *Kapitanleutnant* Rudolph Firle, sortied from the Dardanelles and torpedoed the elderly battleship.

25 May 1915

Name	*Triumph*	**Location**	E Mediterranean, W shore of Cape Helles
Class	*Swiftsure* class battleship		
Built	15 January 1903	**Cause**	Submarine attack
CO	Capt M.S. Fitzmaurice RN	**Casualties**	73
		Survivors	500

Notes The concentration of significant numbers of British forces in the eastern Mediterranean to support the Gallipoli landings proved an irresistible lure for German U-boats. *U21* (*Kapitanleutnant* Otto Hersing) arrived off Cape Helles on the 24th but made no attacks that day. The next day he fired at *Vengeance* but missed, and later on sighted *Triumph*. The battleship was lying at anchor with torpedo nets out and a destroyer circling round her. *Triumph* was supporting Australian troops on ANZAC beach when Hersing fired one torpedo from a range of 300 yards. The torpedo struck and the great battleship slowly heeled over and then sank. The spectacle brought the land fighting to a halt as Australian and Turkish troops crowded out of their trenches to watch.

The battleship HMS *Triumph* which was torpedoed off Cape Helles by the German *U21* on 25 May 1915. (US National Archives)

HMS *Majestic* listing to port before sinking on 27 May 1915 after being torpedoed by *U21*. (M. Piovano)

27 May 1915

Name	*Majestic*	**Location**	E Mediterranean, W shore of Cape
Class	*Majestic* class battleship		Helles
Built	31 January 1895	**Cause**	Submarine attack
CO	Capt H.F. Talbot RN	**Casualties**	40
		Survivors	737

Notes Two days later, after sinking *Triumph*, Hersing's *U21* was back off Cape Helles. There he found the *Majestic* lying at anchor, but with her torpedo nets out and circled by destroyers, bombarding Turkish positions on W beach at the southern end of Cape Helles. Again one torpedo sufficed to send the battleship to the bottom.

The strategic consequences of Hersing's actions were enormous. The loss of *Goliath*, *Triumph* and *Majestic* caused the CinC, Admiral de Roebeck, to order that capital ships would no longer be exposed off Cape Helles. As a result the army lost their heavy artillery support. The soldiers felt abandoned – whatever the effectiveness of their fire, the battleships had been impressive to watch – and there was a general lowering of morale.

Name	*Princess Irene*	**Location**	Thames estuary, port of Sheerness
Class	Minelayer	**Cause**	Accident
Built	Commissioned in January 1915	**Casualties**	51, plus 77 civilian workers
CO	Capt M.H. Cole RN	**Survivors**	2 crew plus 1 civilian

Notes The minelayer *Princess Irene*, a ferry taken up from trade for minelaying duties, was lying at Sheerness when she was destroyed by an internal explosion on 27 May.

30 June 1915

Name	*Lightning*	**Location**	English Channel, off Kentish Knock
Class	Torpedo boat	**Cause**	Mine
CO	Lt D. Cavendish RN		

Notes   HMS *Lightning* was mined in the Channel.

4(?) August 1915

Name	*C.33*	**Location**	North Sea
Class	C class submarine	**Survivors**	None
CO	Lt G.E.B. Carter RN		

Notes   *C.33* had been working with the trawler *Weelsby* as part of a plan to lure U-boats to destruction. The plan was for the submarine to remain submerged but connected to the trawler by telephone cable. When a U-boat surfaced to sink the trawler it would in turn be torpedoed by the submarine; the combination worked and *U40* and *U23* were sunk. On the 4th Carter parted company with *Weelsby* to proceed independently and was last heard from in a signal timed 2150 hrs. Searches failed to find any wreckage or survivors so it is presumed that she was sunk by a mine. However, the possibility that she was lost as the result of an accident cannot be ruled out.

8 August 1915

Name	*India*	**Cause**	Mine
Class	AMC	**Casualties**	160
CO	Cdr W.G.A. Kennedy RN	**Survivors**	141
Location	Norwegian Sea, off Hellevoer		

Notes   The armed merchant cruiser *India* was mined while on the Northern Patrol.

Name	*The Ramsay*	**Class**	ABS

Notes   No details are known.

9 August 1915

Name	*Lynx*	**Location**	North Sea, off the Moray Firth
Class	*Acasta* class destroyer	**Cause**	Mine
Built	20 March 1913	**Casualties**	70
CO	Cdr J.F. Cole RN	**Survivors**	26

Notes   HMS *Lynx* was mined in a field laid off the Moray Firth by the German raider *Meteor*.

18 August 1915

Name	*E.13*	**Location**	Danish coast, off the island of
Class	E class submarine		Saltholme
Built	22 September 1914	**Cause**	Grounding
CO	Lt Cdr G. Layton RN	**Casualties**	15
		Survivors	23

E.13 aground off the island of Saltholme in August 1915 after she had been abandoned by her crew. (Royal Danish Navy)

A detail of the port side of *E.13* after the submarine had been taken into Copenhagen. Shell holes are clearly visible on the casing and conning tower. (Royal Danish Navy)

Notes   *E.13* was on her way to the Baltic when at 2300 hrs on 18 August she grounded on the island of Salthome – in Danish territorial waters – owing to a defective gyro compass. The Danish authorities, in the shape of the torpedo boat *Narhwalen*, were firm but correct: Layton had 24 hours from 0500 hrs on the 19th to repair his boat and leave or he would be interned. A German torpedo boat, *G132*, appeared but made no attempt to intervene. However, just after 0928 hrs two more German destroyers appeared, one of which fired two torpedoes at *E.13* after which both destroyers raked the submarine with gunfire. *E.13* could offer no resistance and her crew began to jump over the side – only to be fired on again by the Germans. However, the Danish torpedo boat *Soulven* placed herself between the swimmers and the German destroyers while her commanding officer made a very forthright protest. The survivors were picked up and landed in Copenhagen the following evening.

   E.13's crew were interned in very comfortable surroundings. If they gave their parole they were free to do as they liked. However, these conditions soon irked Layton and his first lieutenant, Paul Eddis. Both men withdrew their parole and successfully escaped back to the UK, although it does seem that the Danes did very little to hamper their departure! As for *E.13*, she was sold to the Danish government and scrapped. Some of her machinery was still in use in various Danish businesses as late as 1952!

29 August 1915

Name	*C.29*	**Location**	North Sea, off the Humber, 33 59'N,
Class	*C* class submarine		01 25'E
Built	16 June 1909	**Cause**	Mine
CO	Lt W.R. Schofield RN	**Survivors**	None

Notes   *C.29* was participating in the trawler-submarine 'trap'. On 29 August she was proceeding submerged in tow of the trawler *Ariadne*. Suddenly there was a massive explosion and the towrope went slack. *C.29* had inadvertently been towed into a minefield.

4 September 1915

Name	*E.7*	**Location**	Dardanelles, off Nagara Point
Class	*E* class submarine	**Cause**	Scuttled
Built	2 October 1913	**Casualties**	None
CO	Lt Cdr A.D. Cochrane RN	**Survivors**	38

Notes   *E.7* was on her way up the Dardanelles into the Marmara when she became entangled with the submarine net off Nagara Point. Cochrane tried various combinations of blowing and flooding tanks together with using his motors to free the submarine but to no avail. However, all this manoeuvring made a good deal of disturbance on the surface. Watching with interest was *Leutnant zur See* Heino von Heimburg, the commanding officer of *U14*. Heimburg had himself rowed out to the spot in a small boat; according to Heimburg the seaman doing the rowing was his cook, and they took a small mine with them. Using a grapple to locate *E.7*'s position they then lowered the mine down and fired it near the submarine's estimated position. Cochrane realised that it was only a matter of time before a larger charge did even more damage to his submarine. In the circumstances he had no choice but to surface and allow his crew to surrender. Von Heimburg dined out on the story for years.

E.7 leaves Mudros for her second and final patrol in the Sea of Marmara. She was subsequently scuttled after becoming entangled in nets by Nagara Point. (Gus Britton)

25 October 1915

Name	*Velox*	**Location**	North Sea
Class	Torpedo boat	**Cause**	Mine

Notes No further details are known.

28 October 1915

Name	*Argyll*	**Location**	E coast of Scotland, near the port of
Class	*Devonshire* class cruiser		Dundee
Built	3 April 1904	**Cause**	Grounded
CO	Capt J.C. Tancred RN	**Casualties**	None
		Survivors	655

Notes HMS *Argyll* was returning to Scapa Flow, having just completed a refit at Devonport, when she grounded in very bad weather on the Bell Rock near Dundee. Damage done by the grounding was worsened by the action of the storm working the ship to and fro on the rocks. She was considered to be beyond repair.

30 October 1915

Name	*Louis*	**Location**	E Mediterranean, Suvla Bay
Class	*Laforey* class destroyer	**Cause**	Grounded
Built	30 December 1913	**Casualties**	None
CO	Lt Cdr A.D.A. Hall RN	**Survivors**	102

Notes   During 30/31 December the Gallipoli Peninsula was struck by a storm of fierce proportions. HMS *Louis* was anchored off Suvla Bay but her anchors began to drag and she was driven ashore and abandoned. Her hull was too tempting a target for the Turkish artillery which pounded her into a wreck over the next weeks.

1 November 1915

Name	*TB.96*	**Location**	Mediterranean, off Gibraltar
Class	Torpedo boat	**Cause**	Collision
Built	1893	**Casualties**	None

Notes   *TB.96* was sunk following a collision with the troopship *Tringa*.

5 November 1915

Name	*Tara*	**Cause**	Submarine attack
Class	ABS	**Casualties**	10
CO	Capt G.S. Gwatkin-Williams RN	**Survivors**	95
Location	Mediterranean, off Sollum		

Notes   The steamer *Tara* was sunk by *U35* (*Kapitanleutnant* Wilhelm Kophamel). Kophamel towed the survivors in their lifeboats to the port of Bardia where they were handed over to the Turks.

For the survivors their troubles were just beginning. The Turks handed them over to the Senussi tribesmen who were fighting the Italians. The Senussi were defeated in November 1915 and Bardia was reoccupied in March 1916. It was then learned that *Tara*'s survivors were being held at a camp in the desert 120 miles W of Bir Hakim. A column of motor ambulances and armoured cars of the Duke of Westminster's Armoured Car Squadron made a 14-hour dash across the unmapped desert to rescue them and take them to Sollum. Four had died during their captivity.

6 November 1915

Name	*E.20*	**Location**	Sea of Marmara
Class	*E* class submarine	**Cause**	Submarine attack
Built	22 September 1914	**Casualties**	27
CO	Lt Cdr C.H. Warren RN	**Survivors**	9

Notes   *E.20* had just arrived in the Mediterranean, fresh from the builders. Uniquely she was armed with a 6 in howitzer which she was to use against railway lines and bridges to disrupt Turkish communications. On 6 November she was due to rendezvous with the French submarine *Turquoise* (*Lieutenant de Vaisseau* Henri Ravenel). However, *Turquoise* had been abandoned on 30 October and her crew had made no effort to destroy charts, documents or secret instructions. As a result the Germans and Turks knew the details of *E.20*'s rendezvous. It would now be the German *UB14* (*Leutnant* Heino von Heimburg) that was waiting for her. Heimburg remained submerged in the area until he sighted *E.20* lying stopped on the surface at 1600 hrs on the 6th. At 1710 hrs *E.20* was still lying stopped and on the surface when Heimburg fired one torpedo from a range of 550 yards. After seeing his torpedo explode Heimburg surfaced and rescued the survivors.

After the war *LV* Ravenel was court martialled for the loss of his submarine and the consequent loss of *E.20*. The court found him not guilty on all charges.

A fine view of *E.20* on commissioning. The 6 in howitzer which was fitted for shore bombardment purposes can be seen forward of the conning tower. (Vickers Shipbuilding & Engineering)

Lieutenant de Vaisseau Henri Ravenel, commanding officer of the French submarine *Turquoise*, whose negligence led to the sinking of the British submarine *E.20* in November 1915. (Service Historique de la Marine, Paris)

26 December 1915

Name	*E.6*	**Location**	North Sea, off Harwich
Class	*E* class submarine	**Cause**	Mine
Built	12 November 1912	**Casualties**	38
CO	Lt Cdr W.J. Foster RN	**Survivors**	None

Notes   *E.6* had left Harwich on 26 December with orders to patrol off the Horns Reef and intercept any U-boats. She had barely cleared the harbour when she struck a mine near the Sunk Light Vessel and sank with all hands. The sinking is quite bizarre because the existence of that minefield had been known for some time; the trawler *Resono* had only recently been mined there. Moreover as she headed out a torpedo boat signalled her that she was heading into danger. *E.6* acknowledged the signal but continued on her course and blew up in full view of the TB's horrified crew.

27 December 1915

Name	*TB.046*	**Class**	Torpedo boat

Notes   No details are known.

31 December 1915

Name	*Natal*	**Location**	W coast of Scotland, Cromarty Firth
Class	*Warrior* class cruiser	**Cause**	Accident
Built	30 September 1905	**Casualties**	404
CO	Capt E.P.C. Back RN	**Survivors**	299

Notes   HMS *Natal* was at anchor at Cromarty when she was destroyed by an internal explosion. A subsequent enquiry attributed the explosion to faulty cordite charges. For many years her wreck was visible at low tide, fitted with markers bow and stern.

LOSSES 1916

6 January 1916

Name	*E.17*	**Location**	North Sea, off Texel
Class	*E* class submarine	**Cause**	Grounded
Built	16 January 1915	**Casualties**	None
CO	Lt Cdr J.R.G. Moncreiffe RN	**Survivors**	33

Notes   *E.17* was on patrol north of Texel when she struck an uncharted sandbank. Moncreiffe surfaced and after inspecting such parts of the hull that he could see, decided that *E.17* just might make England. Just then a cruiser was sighted approaching and, unsure of whether the ship was German or Dutch (the ship was approaching bows on) Moncreiffe decided to dive. *E.17* was taking on water as a result of the grounding and Moncreiffe realised that he had to surface. The warship was the Dutch cruiser *Noord Brabant* which closed *E.17* on sighting the latter's distress flares. The crew were taken off and Moncreiffe watched *E.17* sink at 1140 hrs. The survivors were taken to Den Helder and then to an internment camp at Groningen, known facetiously as HMS *Timber*, to await the end of the war.

E.17's conning tower has been salvaged and is now on display at the Royal Navy Submarine Museum, Gosport.

Name	*King Edward VII*	**Location**	N of Scotland, off Cape Wrath
Class	*King Edward VII* class battleship	**Cause**	Mine
Built	27 March 1903	**Casualties**	None
CO	Capt C. MacLachlan RN	**Survivors**	777

Notes   HMS *King Edward VII* was mined off Cape Wrath in a field laid by the German raider *Moewe* in November 1915. The explosion flooded her machinery spaces and she lay dead in the water. She was towed for 9 hours but as the flooding gained, she became unmanageable and eventually capsized.

19 January 1916

Name	*H.6*	**Location**	North Sea, on Ameland Island,
Class	*H* class submarine		2 miles W of Schiermonnikoog
Built	10 June 1915		Lighthouse
CO	Lt R.N. Stopford RN	**Cause**	Grounded
		Casualties	None
		Survivors	22

Notes   *H.6* was at sea covering an attack by seaplanes from HMS *Vindex* on Zeppelin sheds at Nordeich and Hoyer. She was to attack any German warships which emerged to look for the carrier and also to be on hand to rescue any downed aircrew. In the event she did neither of these things for in bad visibility she went aground on the Dutch island of Ameland at 0355 hrs on 19 January. On hearing of the grounding, Commodore Tyrwhitt cancelled the operation and ordered destroyers to search for *H.6*. She was found at 1145 hrs by HMS *Firedrake*. By this time *H.6* was hard aground with both propellers out of the water. She had already been visited by the two Dutch lighthouse-keepers who informed Stopford that a Dutch warship was on her way.

Since *H.6* could evidently not be hauled off, the question was now one of evacuating as many of her key personnel as possible and saving her confidential books. Accordingly a boat was sent over to her from the destroyer *Medea* and returned with four officers (not including Stopford), the coxswain, chief ERA and several ratings. With the falling tide, worsening weather and a report of an increase in German wireless traffic – possibly indicating a German interest in proceedings – it was not possible to send the boat back for a second trip. Stopford and the remainder of his crew became internees of the Dutch and joined *E.17*'s crew at HMS *Timber*.

H.6 had a varied life. Salved and purchased by the Dutch she became Her Netherlands Majesty's Submarine *O.8*. In May 1940 she was scuttled by the Dutch at Willemsoord. She was subsequently raised by the Germans and commissioned as *UD1*. On 3 May 1945 she was scuttled at Wilhelmshaven and eventually broken up there.

20 January 1916

Name	*TB.13*	**Class**	Torpedo boat

Notes No details are known.

10 February 1916

Name	*Arabis*	**Location**	North Sea
Class	Minesweeping sloop	**Cause**	Gunfire
Built	6 November 1915	**Casualties**	76
CO	Lt Cdr Hallowell-Carew RN	**Survivors**	14

Notes HMS *Arabis* was part of the newly formed 10th Minesweeping Flotilla and was engaged in keeping their swept channels in the minefields east of Dogger Bank clear for the Grand Fleet. On the night of 10 February warning of a sortie by the German High Seas Fleet for a sweep east of Dogger Bank was given by Room 40, the Admiralty's code-breaking organisation. Accordingly the Grand Fleet and Harwich Force were ordered to sea to cut off the Germans. In the event the German light cruisers and destroyers sailed. In order to preserve wireless silence and thereby not alert the Germans about British moves, the decision was taken not to warn the 10th Minesweeping Flotilla that the Germans were heading in their direction. Armed with just two 4 in guns, the little *Arabis* stood no chance when she was engaged by German destroyers. Her wireless was quickly knocked out and her main steam pipe cut, so that she could neither summon help nor try to escape. The first three German destroyers then disappeared but later six German destroyers returned to finish her off. The survivors were picked up by the Germans and treated with considerable courtesy.

In 1919 Lieutenant-Commander Hallowell-Carew was awarded the DSO for this action.

11 February 1916

Name	*Arethusa*	**Location**	North Sea, approaches to Harwich,
Class	*Arethusa* class light cruiser		off the North Cutler Buoy
Built	25 October 1913	**Cause**	Mine
CO	Cdre Reginald Tyrwhitt	**Casualties**	8 plus a cat
		Survivors	272

Notes   It was while returning from the abortive sweep to look for the German High Seas Fleet that the famous light cruiser *Arethusa* was lost. She was steaming at 20 knots and had just entered the Sledway Channel when she struck a mine which had been laid by *UC7* the previous evening. The explosion occurred under the machinery spaces and she lost power and began to settle. The destroyers *Lightfoot* and *Loyal* tried to take her in tow but on each occasion the tow rope parted. Eventually *Arethusa* drifted on to the Cutler Shoal and broke in half. Six men were killed in the explosion and another two drowned when their Carley float overturned. Tyrwhitt was the last to leave the ship, having remained to look for his cat. After Tyrwhitt's boat had pushed off a bearded figure was seen to rush on to the quarterdeck. This was a stoker who had not only slept through the explosion but slept on through all the subsequent activity! Trapped below, he had clambered up the inside of the after funnel and then out on to the quarterdeck.

The next day salvage of papers and portable items of equipment could be carried out since the cruiser's upperworks were still above the water. However, wind and tide slowly buried the ship in the sandbank where she lies to this day.

29 February 1916

Name	*Alcantara*	**Location**	North Sea, 60 miles NE of the
Class	AMC		Shetlands
CO	Capt T.E. Wardle RN	**Cause**	Gunfire
		Casualties	69

Notes   HMS *Alcantara* was sunk in a mutually fatal engagement with the German raider *Greif*. *Alcantara* was on blockade duty when she sighted a 'Norwegian' ship coming up from the south. *Alcantara* closed to establish the stranger's identity, only to find the 'Norwegian' ship – which was the raider *Greif* – hoisting German colours and opening fire. In a very short but intense duel the two ships inflicted such damage on each other that they both sank. (See HMS *Sydney*, p. 157, for a similar engagement.) *Alcantara* had a heavy list to port, having received numerous shell hits and been struck by a torpedo. After she sank her survivors were rescued by HMS *Munster*, leaving the *Greif* to be finished off by HMS *Andes* and HMS *Comet*.

1 March 1916

Name	*Primula*	**Cause**	Torpedo
Class	Minesweeping sloop	**Casualties**	3
Built	6 December 1916	**Survivors**	107
Location	Mediterranean, near Cerigo Island		

Notes   HMS *Primula* was attacked by the German *U35* (*Kapitanleutnant* Lothar von Arnauld de la Perriere). The torpedo blew off the sloop's bows yet she turned and went astern in an attempt to ram the submarine. A second and a third torpedo both missed and it was *U35*'s fourth torpedo that eventually sent the sloop to the bottom. 'Four torpedoes for that tiny wasp' was de la Perriere's outraged comment.

7(?) March 1916

Name	*E.5*	**Location**	North Sea, exact position unknown
Class	*E* class submarine	**Casualties**	33
Built	17 May 1912	**Survivors**	None
CO	Lt Cdr H. Edwards RN		

Notes *E.5* had departed for a patrol off the Ems estuary on 4 March. She was possibly sighted by *E.26* on the afternoon of 6 March north of Juist Island. At 0810 hrs on the 7th German destroyers escorting the battle cruiser *Seydlitz* attacked a submarine in this area. A few hours later another submarine was sighted by the cruiser *Regensburg*. The position of that sighting lies not far from a minefield. It is likely that *E.5* was mined but the possibility that she was lost by accident cannot be ruled out.

7 March 1916

Name	*TB.11*	**Location**	North Sea
Class	Torpedo boat	**Cause**	Mine
Built	1907	**Casualties**	23
CO	Lt J. Legh RN	**Survivors**	12

Notes HMS *TB.11* was mined in the North Sea and sank very quickly.

Name	*Coquette*	**Cause**	Mine
Class	Torpedo boat	**Casualties**	22
CO	Lt V. Seymour RN	**Survivors**	11
Location	North Sea		

Notes HMS *Coquette* struck a mine not long after *TB.11* and sank equally quickly.

9 March 1916

Name	*Fauvette*	**Location**	English Channel, off the North Foreland
Class	ABS		
CO	Cdr H.W. Wilson RNR	**Cause**	Mine
		Casualties	14

Notes The armed boarding steamer was on Examination Service duty in the Downs when she struck a mine. As she drifted helpless, she struck a second mine which completed her destruction and she sank.

24 March 1916

Name	*E.24*	**Location**	North Sea
Class	*E* class submarine	**Casualties**	34
Built	9 December 1915	**Survivors**	None
CO	Lt Cdr George Naper RN		

Notes *E.24* left Harwich on 21 March for a minelaying operation in the Heligoland Bight and was not heard from again. She was going to lay her mines in an area 3 miles from the field laid on her previous patrol. In view of the nature of submarine navigation at the time the possibility exists that she might have gone into her own field and been mined. This is but one possibility: the whole of the Heligoland Bight was covered in minefields – both British and German – and *E.24* might have been lost in any one of them. It must also be considered that *E.24* might have been sunk by accident.

25 March 1916

Name	*Medusa*	**CO**	Lt Cdr Hemans RN
Class	*M* class destroyer	**Location**	North Sea, Heligoland Bight
Built	27 March 1915	**Cause**	Foundered following ramming

Notes   On 24 March the Harwich Force screened the seaplane carrier *Vindex* in an air attack on the Zeppelin sheds at Hoyer. The attack took place the next morning and while the destroyers were searching for three aircraft which were missing, two German armed trawlers were sighted, chased and sunk between the islands of Rom and Sylt. As the destroyers were reforming they were attacked by German aircraft and in the confusion *Medusa* was rammed by *Laverock* and sustained such damage that she could steam at only 6 knots. She was then taken in tow by *Lightfoot* and the force began a slow withdrawal. However, the weather worsened during the night of the 25th and she was abandoned at 2100 hrs.

The affair had a curious sequel. On 3 April *Medusa*'s waterlogged hull was found by a Dutch ship which took the derelict in tow and headed for Terschelling. However, *Medusa* hit a sandbank at the entrance to the harbour and was a total loss.

25 April 1916

Name	*E.22*	**Location**	North Sea, off Yarmouth
Class	*E* class submarine	**Cause**	Submarine attack
Built	27 August 1915	**Survivors**	2
CO	Lt Cdr R.T. Dimsdale RN		

Notes   *E.22* was proceeding to sea in company with three other submarines when she was attacked by *UB18* (*Kapitanleutnant* Otto Steinbrinck). Steinbrinck's first torpedo missed and *E.22* turned towards her assailant as if to ram. *UB18* went under *E.22*, catching her net cutter on *E.22*'s hull as she did so. Steinbrinck was not deterred and fired again: his second torpedo hit the submarine which sank very quickly leaving two men, ERA F. Buckingham and Signalman Harrod, in the water. By coincidence *E.22* had been fitted with a wooden platform on her casing for carrying aircraft. The splintered remains of this wooden planking kept Buckingham and Harrod afloat until *UB18* surfaced to rescue them.

27 April 1916

Name	*Nasturtium*	**Location**	Mediterranean, off Malta
Class	Minesweeping sloop	**Cause**	Mine
Built	21 December 1915	**Casualties**	7
CO	Lt R.W. Lloyd RN		

Notes   On 25 April *U73* (*Kapitanleutnant* Gustav Siess) laid a field of twenty-two mines off Malta. This was to prove an especially profitable venture. The sloop HMS *Nasturtium* was the first victim.

Name	*Russell*	**Location**	Mediterranean, off Malta
Class	*Duncan* class battleship	**Cause**	Mine
Built	19 February 1901	**Casualties**	124
CO	Capt W. Bowden-Smith RN	**Survivors**	625

The after casing of *E.22* showing her seaplane platform. After the submarine had been torpedoed on 25 April 1916 it was the shattered remnants of the seaplane platform that kept the survivors afloat until they were resuced. (Author)

Notes HMS *Russell* was the second victim of *U73*'s minelaying activities. While approaching Malta she was mined and sank very quickly. As with *Nasturtium*, the nearness of land and the presence of many small craft for rescue purposes prevented a greater loss of life. The third victim of *U73*'s minefield was the yacht *Aegusa*.

14 May 1916

Name	*M.30*	**Location**	Mediterranean, Gulf of Smyrna, off
Class	*M* class monitor		Cape Aspro
Built	23 June 1915	**Cause**	Shore battery fire
CO	Lt Cdr E. Lockyer RN	**Casualties**	2

Notes Following the evacuation of Gallipoli, an airfield was built on Long Island in the Gulf of Smyrna so that a watch could be maintained over the Dardanelles in case the *Goeben* should sortie. The Turks did not remain passive in the face of this development and brought up artillery which they used to shell the island and British patrol vessels. On the night of 14 May at about 2200 hrs *M.30* was on her way to Long Island with a cargo of stores when she was fired upon. While she was trying to locate the battery, a 5.9 in shell burst inside her machinery space, damaging a boiler and blowing a hole in her bottom. She lay dead in the water while a massive fire took hold amidships. Ships gathered round but there was little they could do but take off the survivors. Eventually *M.30* grounded 200 yards from the shore. Over the next couple of weeks as much equipment as possible was salvaged from the wreck, including her two 6 in guns, after which she was destroyed by a 100 lb guncotton charge.

24 May 1916

Name	*E.18*	**Location**	Baltic, exact position unknown
Class	*E* class submarine	**Casualties**	38
Built	4 March 1915	**Survivors**	None
CO	Lt Cdr R.C. Halahan RN		

Notes The cause of *E.18*'s loss is unknown. She had been active until 23 May because on that day she had blown the bows off the German destroyer *V100*. Thereafter nothing was heard from her. There are claims that she was sunk by a German decoy vessel but there is no hard evidence to support this. Other possibilities include being sunk by a mine and being the victim of an accident.

31 MAY/1 JUNE 1916: THE BATTLE OF JUTLAND

31 May 1916 *was 'Der Tag', the long-awaited clash between the Grand Fleet and the German High Seas Fleet. The actions at Heligoland Bight and Dogger Bank had been mere curtain-raisers – this was to be the main event. The Royal Navy won an impressive strategic victory but the significance of that success was blunted by the fact that the Grand Fleet lost more ships than the German High Seas Fleet: 3 battle cruisers, 3 armoured cruisers and 8 destroyers, compared with German losses of 1 pre-dreadnought battleship, 1 battle cruiser, 4 light cruisers and 5 destroyers. The situation was not helped by inept handling of the news by the British authorities which stressed the* materiel *losses but overlooked the fact that after the battle the Royal Navy was still at sea while the German ships had scuttled back to port. The public mood changed from 3 June onwards and is caught by this poem:*

> *The Germans cry aloud, 'We've won!'*
> *But surely 'tis a curious view*
> *That those are conquerors who run*
> *And those the vanquished who pursue.*

Nevertheless the damage was done. The Battle of Jutland and, more to the point, who was to blame for the losses at Jutland, remained the source of much debate in the Royal Navy during the interwar period. The battle still occupies an ambivalent place in British naval history.

31 May 1916

Name	*Indefatigable*	**Location**	North Sea, off the Jutland Peninsula,
Class	*Indefatigable* class battlecruiser		56 50'N, 05 36'E
Built	28 October 1909	**Cause**	Gunfire
CO	Capt C.F. Sowerby RN	**Casualties**	1,022
		Survivors	2

Notes *Indefatigable* was at the rear of the battle cruiser line and was engaged in a private duel with her opposite number in the German line, the *Von der Tann*. At 1602 hrs two shells fell on her upper deck causing 'X' magazine to explode. She hauled out of line sinking by the stern. She was then hit again on the forecastle and there followed a much larger explosion in which the ship was totally destroyed. Two survivors were rescued by a German destroyer.

Name	*Queen Mary*	Location	North Sea, off the Jutland Peninsula,
Class	Battle cruiser		56 42'N, 05 40'E
Built	20 March 1912	**Cause**	Gunfire
CO	Capt C.I. Prowse RN	**Casualties**	1,266
		Survivors	20

Notes *Queen Mary* was the crack gunnery ship of the Battle Cruiser Fleet. She was fitted with the Argo fire control director, an instrument which many believed was superior to the Dreyer instrument fitted throughout the rest of the fleet. *Queen Mary* was firing at her opposite number in the German line, the *Seydlitz*, and just after 1615 hrs she went into rapid-fire mode. However, *Queen Mary* was also being engaged by the *Derfflinger* which, owing to an error by *Princess Royal*, ahead of *Queen Mary* in the British line, was not being fired on. *Derfflinger*, like *Queen Mary* a crack gunnery ship, settled down to some undisturbed target practice. Just after 1626 hrs she hit *Queen Mary*'s 'Q' turret: the right-hand gun was disabled but the left-hand gun carried on firing. Then she was struck by two 12 in shells on the forecastle and 'A' and 'B' magazines exploded. The forward part of the ship was totally destroyed as far back as the foremast. As she listed to port she was destroyed by a further massive explosion. The last sight of the *Queen Mary* was of her stern sinking, the propellers revolving slowly. It was after the sinking of the *Queen Mary* that Beatty is said to have commented, 'There is something wrong with our bloody ships today.'

Name	*Nestor*	Location	North Sea, off the Jutland Peninsula,
Class	*M* class destroyer		56 43'N, 05 58'E
Built	9 October 1915	**Cause**	Gunfire
CO	Cdr the Hon. Edward Bingham RN	**Casualties**	6
		Survivors	80

Notes At 1609 hrs Beatty ordered an attack on the German line by his destroyers which were led out with extraordinary *élan* by *Nestor*. As they approached the German line, they were engaged by fifteen German destroyers led by the cruiser *Regensburg*. A fierce duel developed between the two destroyer forces, with gun ranges down to as little as 600 yards. *Nestor* got to within 3,000 yards of the German line to fire three torpedoes but was badly damaged by gunfire. Both her boilers were disabled and she lay dead in the water. *Nicator* offered assistance but Bingham ordered her away on the grounds that she would endanger herself by remaining. *Nestor* remained dead in the water as the German battle fleet approached her. She was sinking by the stern but still fired her fourth and last torpedo at the head of the German line. She was abandoned while under heavy fire and sank.

Name	*Nomad*	Location	North Sea, off the Jutland Peninsula,
Class	*M* class destroyer		54 42'N, 06 00'E
Built	7 February 1916	**Cause**	Gunfire
CO	Lt Cdr Paul Whitfield RN	**Casualties**	7
		Survivors	72

Notes   *Nomad* followed *Nestor* into the attack on the German battle cruisers but was hit in her engine room and brought to a stop. Two torpedoes fired by German destroyers passed under her but her luck ran out when she was fired on by leading battleships in the German fleet approaching from the south. The damage was such that she had to be abandoned: while her crew were going over the side, she was hit once more on the forecastle. The magazine exploded and she sank very quickly.

Name	*Shark*	Location	North Sea, off the Jutland Peninsula,
Class	*Acasta* class destroyer		57 00'N, 06 04'E
Built	30 July 1912	Cause	Gunfire
CO	Cdr Loftus Jones RN	Casualties	86
		Survivors	2

Notes   In between the engagement between the two battle cruiser fleets and the main engagement between the battle fleets, there was a short but vicious battle between the British 3rd Battle Cruiser Squadron and the German 2nd, 6th and 9th Destroyer Flotillas. After the German ships had delivered their torpedo attack, which the British ships easily avoided, the four British destroyers *Shark*, *Acasta*, *Ophelia* and *Christopher* began their own torpedo attack. As they did so the head of the German battle cruiser fleet came out of the fog and what had started as a destroyer duel now assumed a very different character. *Shark* was brought to a standstill by a barrage of gunfire and began to sink by the bow. Jones had lost a leg but continued to fight his ship and ensured that her colours were flying until the little destroyer sank beneath him.

Jones was posthumously awarded the Victoria Cross. A few weeks later his body was washed ashore on the coast of Sweden and buried in the village of Kviberg.

Name	*Defence*	Location	North Sea, off the Jutland Peninsula,
Class	*Minotaur* class cruiser		57 02'N, 05 53'E
Built	24 April 1907	Cause	Gunfire
CO	Capt S.V. Ellis RN, flagship of Rear	Casualties	907
	Adm Robert Arbuthnot MVO	Survivors	None

Notes   *Defence* was the flagship of Rear Admiral Robert Arbuthnot, a noted disciplinarian and physical fitness enthusiast. As the Grand Fleet deployed for action Arbuthnot had to move to his position at the rear of the British line – armoured cruisers like *Defence* were considered too vulnerable to remain in the line of battle. Arbuthnot could either pass down the disengaged side of the British fleet or the engaged side. So keen was he to get at the enemy that he did the latter and steamed straight for the head of the German line. At 1816 hrs *Defence* was fired on by *Derfflinger* and four dreadnoughts and at 1820 hrs blew up in a massive explosion.

Name	*Invincible*	Location	North Sea, off the Jutland Peninsula,
Class	Battle cruiser		57 03'N, 06 07'E
Built	13 April 1907	Cause	Gunfire
CO	Capt Arthur Cay RN, flagship of	Casualties	1,026
	Rear Adm the Hon. Horace Hood	Survivors	6
	CB MVO DSO		

Notes As the two main fleets went into action, so a brief duel developed between the two battle cruiser fleets. The four surviving British battle cruisers were reinforced by *Invincible* and her two consorts of the 3rd BCS. The British shooting was superb but at 1829 hrs the mist cleared slightly and *Invincible* was silhouetted sharply against the sky. *Derfflinger*'s gunners needed no urging and opened fire on this target. At 1833 hrs one of *Derfflinger*'s shells landed on *Invincible*'s 'Q' turret. Shortly afterwards the magazines for 'Q' and 'P' turrets exploded. *Invincible* was torn in two and sank in only 180 ft of water. Since the ship was 587 ft long, her middle rested on the bottom while her bow and stern rose above the surface. Survivors were clinging to both portions and they cheered as the rest of the British battle cruisers raced by.

Horace Hood was killed. He was an outstanding commander who would undoubtedly have attained the highest ranks of the Service. Writing after his death Beatty said, 'You should have seen him bring his squadron up into action, it would have done your heart good. No one could have died a more glorious death.'

The night action that followed the main battle was one of the most savage in naval history. The German High Seas Fleet heading east crossed the stern of the Grand Fleet steaming south. There was a succession of sudden, fierce engagements as isolated units ran into one another. Better night-fighting training gave the Germans the advantage.

1 June 1916

Name	*Tipperary*	**Location**	North Sea, off the Jutland Peninsula,
Class	*Faulknor* class flotilla leader		56 12'N, 06 06'E
Built	5 March 1915	**Cause**	Gunfire
CO	Capt C.J. Wintour RN	**Casualties**	185
		Survivors	15

Notes At 2315 hrs on 31 May *Tipperary*, leading the 4th Destroyer Flotilla, sighted the silhouettes of three cruisers. The destroyer made her challenge and in reply the German cruisers *Elbing*, *Pillau* and *Frankfort* switched on a blaze of searchlights and opened fire. *Tipperary* was hit forward, set on fire and brought to a standstill. She sank at 0145 hrs on 1 June. The survivors were rescued by HMS *Sparrowhawk*.

Name	*Sparrowhawk*	**Location**	North Sea, off the Jutland Peninsula,
Class	*Acasta* class destroyer		56 16'N, 06 06'E
Built	12 October 1912	**Cause**	Scuttled after a double ramming
CO	Lt Cdr S. Hopkins RN	**Casualties**	6
		Survivors	plus 15 from *Tipperary*

Notes After *Tipperary* was disabled *Sparrowhawk* sighted a large ship on her starboard bow. This was the German battleship *Westfalen* which challenged and then opened fire. The leading British destroyer HMS *Broke* turned away but as she did so she was hit on the bridge and continued turning, making a 360° turn until she rammed *Sparrowhawk*. In the confusion the destroyer *Contest* failed to avoid the two destroyers locked together and sliced through *Sparrowhawk*'s stern. *Sparrowhawk* could not be brought home and had to be sunk by gunfire by HMS *Marksman*.

Name	*Black Prince*	Location	North Sea, off the Jutland Peninsula,
Class	*Duke of Edinburgh* class armoured		56 02'N, 06 06'E
	cruiser	Cause	Gunfire
Built	14 June 1904	Casualties	862
CO	Capt T.P. Bonham RN	Survivors	None

Notes   Since the loss of the *Defence* and the crippling of *Warrior*, the *Black Prince* had proceeded independently, loosely following the track of the Grand Fleet. At 10 minutes past midnight on 1 June she came across the German battleship *Thuringen*, which opened fire first, sinking the cruiser outright.

Name	*Fortune*	Location	North Sea, off the Jutland Peninsula,
Class	*Acasta* class destroyer		56 01'N, 06 07'E
Built	17 March 1913	Cause	Gunfire
CO	Lt Cdr F.G. Terry RN	Casualties	67
		Survivors	None

Notes   Just after midnight the 4th Destroyer Flotilla's clash with the German High Seas Fleet continued when the six remaining destroyers sighted the capital ships at the head of the German line. *Fortune* was simply overwhelmed by gunfire and sank quickly.

Name	*Ardent*	Location	North Sea, off the Jutland Peninsula,
Class	*Acasta* class destroyer		55 59'N, 06 13'E
Built	8 September 1913	Cause	Gunfire
CO	Lt Cdr Arthur Marsden RN	Casualties	78
		Survivors	2

Notes   At 0019 hrs on 1 June *Ardent*, which had just observed *Fortune*'s end, headed away to the east but was fired on by a squadron of German battleships. She attacked immediately but was left in a sinking condition; she then took another pounding by the following German squadron as it went by. The survivors abandoned ship and *Ardent* sank with colours flying. The survivors were five hours in the water before being rescued by HMS *Obdurate* and HMS *Marksman*.

Name	*Turbulent*	Location	North Sea, off the Jutland Peninsula,
Class	*Talisman* class destroyer		55 57'N, 06 17'E
Built	5 January 1916	Cause	Rammed
CO	Lt Cdr D. Stuart	Casualties	100
		Survivors	13

Notes   At 0025 hrs on 1 June *Turbulent*, in company with the 13th Flotilla, encountered the German 1st Battle Squadron. In the mêlée that followed *Turbulent* was rammed by the *Westfalen* and sank. *Turbulent* had only been in commission for three weeks at the time of her loss.

Name	*Warrior*	Location	North Sea, off the Jutland Peninsula,
Class	*Warrior* class cruiser		57 39'N, 02 57'E
Built	25 November 1905	**Cause**	Scuttled after damage by gunfire
CO	Capt V.B. Molteno RN	**Casualties**	71

Notes   After *Defence* had blown up *Warrior* was fired on by the German fleet but was saved by the battleship *Warspite*, which was making two complete 360° turns after her steering had jammed. *Warrior* went to the rear of the British line but was in a sorry state. The engine rooms flooded and just after 2000 hrs on 31 May she was taken in tow by the *Engadine*. There was every hope that she would make port but during the night the weather worsened and seas began washing over her upper deck. By 0745 hrs on 1 June she had no reserves of buoyancy left and so Molteno ordered *Engadine* to come alongside and take off the crew. This task was done in rising seas and were it not for the fact that *Engadine* was a former cross-Channel ferry fitted with a large rubbing-strake, it is doubtful whether she could have withstood the grinding against *Warrior*'s side.

5 June 1916

Name	*Hampshire*	Cause	Mine
Class	*Devonshire* class cruiser	**Casualties**	650
Built	4 September 1903	**Survivors**	12
CO	Capt H.J. Savill RN		

Notes   On 5 June 1916 *Hampshire* left Scapa Flow carrying Lord Kitchener and a military mission to Russia for talks. The weather was dreadful and her escorting destroyers were sent back, the seas being too rough. Three hours after clearing the Hoxa Gate, the cruiser ran on to a mine laid by *U75* a week earlier. *U75*'s commander had observed British warships passing close inshore off the Orkneys on a previous patrol and these observations determined where he would lay his mines. Only twelve men survived the sinking – Kitchener and all his staff perished.

Kitchener's death sparked off many rumours that there was more to the affair than met the eye but the circumstances of his death and *Hampshire*'s loss were purely accidental.

18 June 1916

Name	*Eden*	Location	North Sea
Class	*River* class destroyer	**Cause**	Collision
CO	Lt A.C. Farguhar RN		

Notes   Lost in collision. No further details are known.

6 July 1916

Name	*E.26*	Location	North Sea, off the Ems estuary
Class	*E* class submarine	**Casualties**	31
Built	11 November 1915	**Survivors**	None
CO	Lit E.W. Ryan RN		

Notes *E.26* was on patrol off the Ems estuary. On 3 July *E.55*, about 20 miles to the north of *E.26*'s area, heard the sound of depth-charging which may have marked the end for *E.26*. However, there are no German claims to have sunk a submarine on this day. Alternative explanations for her loss include mining and accident.

15 July 1916		**Location**	Adriatic, off the port of Cattaro
Name	*H.3*	**Cause**	Mine
Class	*H* class submarine	**Casualties**	22
Built	3 June 1915	**Survivors**	None
CO	Lt George Jenkinson RN		

Notes *H.3* was on a routine patrol in the Adriatic to attack Austrian and German U-boats entering or leaving the port of Cattaro. During the day it was the practice to move close inshore while dived and then withdraw at night to charge batteries on the surface. The Austrian coastwatching service was extremely efficient and *H.3* was sighted on the morning of the 15th. That afternoon watchers on Punta d'Ostro outside Cattaro noticed a massive explosion in the middle of a minefield. Small boats were sent out and recovered wreckage including parts of a clock made in Glasgow, parts of a British torpedo and other debris, all of which clearly indicated that a British submarine had been sunk.

26 July 1916			
Name	*TB.9*	**Class**	Torpedo boat

Notes No details are known.

A very rare photograph of the submarine *H.3* taken on 15 June 1915 at St Johns, Newfoundland, before her voyage to the UK. *H.3* was mined just over one year later in the Adriatic. (Public Archives of Canada)

9 August 1916

Name	*B.10*	**Cause**	Air attack
Class	*B* class submarine	**Casualties**	None
CO	Lt K. Michell RN	**Survivors**	15
Location	N. Adriatic, port of Venice		

Notes *B.10* has the distinction of being the first submarine to be sunk by air attack, albeit indirectly. The Austrian aircraft that attacked Venice on the evening of 9 August merely dropped their bombs and left. *B.10* was lying alongside the depot ship *Marco Polo* at the time; she was hit on the port bow at 2230 hrs and sank. She was subsequently raised on 23 August and taken into dock where the bomb damage was compounded by a fire. An Italian workman had started drilling next to a petrol tank which had not been emptied – despite warnings from the British to the Italian dockyard authorities. The sparks from the drill caused the petrol to ignite. The resulting conflagration was such that the dock had to be flooded. *B.10* was considered beyond repair and she was sold locally, for 45,000 lire, for breaking up.

13 August 1916

Name	*Lassoo*	**Location**	North Sea, off the Maas Light Vessel
Class	*Laforey* class destroyer	**Cause**	Mine
Built	24 August 1915		

Notes HMS *Lassoo* was mined off the Maas Light Vessel. No further details are known.

B.10 in dry dock at Venice in August 1916 after being sunk in an Austrian air raid. The hole made by the bomb in *B.10*'s port bow is clearly visible. (Museo Storico Navale, Venice)

15 August 1916

Name	*E.4*	**Location**	North Sea, off Harwich, E of the
Class	*E* class submarine		Cork Light Vessel
Built	5 February 1912	**Cause**	Collision
CO	Lt Cdr J. Tenison RN	**Casualties**	33
		Survivors	None

Notes   During routine exercises *E.4* was making a submerged attack on *E.41* which was on the surface. During the exercise *E.4*, which was dived, rammed *E.41* just forward of the conning tower and sank. She was subsequently raised and recommissioned.

Name	*E.41*	**Location**	North Sea, off Harwich, E of the
Class	*E* class submarine		Cork Light Vessel
Built	28 July 1915	**Cause**	Collision
CO	Lt M. Winser RN	**Casualties**	18
		Survivors	15

Notes   The impact of *E.4*'s ramming was barely felt inside *E.41*. However, water soon began rushing into the submarine from forward. As many men as possible got out through the conning tower but First Lieutenant T.F. Voysey RN and Lieutenant Money were trapped in the control room when water poured down the conning tower hatch. The build-up of air pressure in the boat eventually blew the hatch open and carried Voysey and Money to the surface. *E.41* sank in less than 90 seconds, leaving only fourteen men struggling in the water. Astonishingly, 90 minutes later when the watchers on the surface had given up all hope of saving any more men from the submarine, Stoker Petty Officer William Brown came to the surface. Trapped alone in the engine room in complete darkness, he had carried out a textbook escape. Like *E.4*, *E.41* was repaired and returned to service.

19 August 1916

Name	*Nottingham*	**Location**	North Sea
Class	*Birmingham* class cruiser	**Cause**	Submarine attack
Built	18 April 1913	**Casualties**	38
CO	Capt C.D. Miller RN	**Survivors**	442

Notes   In August 1916 the German High Seas Fleet made its first sortie into the North Sea since the Battle of Jutland. As usual the Grand Fleet was forewarned and put to sea with every expectation of bringing the Germans to battle. As part of the German plan a line of U-boats had been deployed across the Germans' line of advance. Just before 0700 hrs the cruiser screen of the Battle Cruiser Fleet passed through the U-boat line and *Kapitanleutnant* Walther Hans in *U52* selected the cruiser *Nottingham* as his target. Just after 0700 hrs he fired three torpedoes and scored two hits in the machinery spaces which destroyed the generators and doused the boiler fires leaving the ship dead in the water without power. A third torpedo fired at 0710 hrs completed the destruction.

Name	*Falmouth*	**Location**	North Sea, off Flamborough Head
Class	*Weymouth* class cruiser	**Cause**	Submarine attack
Built	20 September 1910	**Casualties**	1
CO	Capt J.D. Edwards RN	**Survivors**	375

Falmouth was the second British cruiser to be struck on the 19th. When it became clear that the High Seas Fleet was not at sea, Jellicoe ordered the Grand Fleet to retire – an order which inadvertently took the Grand Fleet back across the U-boat line. At 1652 hrs *U66* (*Kapitanleutnant* von Botha) hit *Falmouth* with two torpedoes on her starboard side. A determined depth-charge attack drove off *U66* and prevented *U49* from finishing the cruiser off. *Falmouth* remained afloat and proceeded towards the Humber under her own steam throughout the night until early on the 20th when she was taken in tow by tugs sent out from Immingham. Alas, her route took her across a third U-boat patrol line and early on the morning of the 20th she was hit by two more torpedoes fired by *U52* (*Kapitanleutnant* Otto Schulze). *Falmouth* remained afloat for another 8 hours before rolling over and sinking when only 7½ miles from Flamborough Head. All her crew were taken off by destroyers. Her sole casualty was a stoker who died of his injuries some days later.

22 August 1916

Name	*E.16*	**Location**	North Sea
Class	E class submarine	**Casualties**	31
Built	22 September 1914	**Survivors**	None
CO	Lt Cdr Kenneth Duff-Dunbar DSO RN		

Notes   *E.16* had put to sea on 18 August in anticipation of the German fleet operation in which *Nottingham* and *Falmouth* were sunk. Nothing further was heard from her. No German claim was made for her sinking, other than a vague report of an attack on a periscope on the 22nd, so loss by mine or accident are the likely explanations.

25 August 1916

Name	*Duke of Albany*	**Cause**	Submarine attack
Class	ABS	**Casualties**	24
CO	Cdr George Ramage RNR	**Survivors**	86
Location	20 miles E of the Skerries		

Notes   No further details are known.

23 October 1916

Name	*Genista*	**Location**	W coast of Ireland
Class	Minesweeping sloop	**Cause**	Mine
Built	22 February 1916	**Casualties**	78
CO	Lt Cdr J. White RN	**Survivors**	12

Notes   No further details are known.

25 October 1916

Name	*Flirt*	**Cause**	Gunfire
Class	Torpedo boat	**Casualties**	80
CO	Lt R. Kellett	**Survivors**	4
Location	English Channel		

Notes   On the night of 25 October HMS *Flirt* was the duty destroyer in the Dover Patrol tasked with supporting the drifters in the centre of the Channel should they encounter a submarine. That night the Germans despatched two groups of destroyers into the Channel to disrupt the A/S forces. *Flirt* sighted one group of these destroyers heading for Dover but did not report them as Kellett thought they were British destroyers returning from Dunkirk. Later that night *Flirt* heard gunfire and while proceeding toward the sound found the drifter *Waveney* in a sinking condition. There were men in the water and *Flirt* used her searchlight to pinpoint them. These were survivors from drifters sunk by the Germans. *Flirt*'s gunner thought he saw destroyers in the glare of the searchlight but did not report his suspicions because he thought the destroyers were French. *Flirt*'s boat, manned by her Gunner and a rating, was sent away to rescue the men in the water while her first lieutenant and a rating jumped over the side to offer immediate assistance. Almost immediately, *Flirt* was illuminated by searchlights and raked with gunfire. *Flirt* disappeared in a cloud of steam, leaving not so much as a scrap of wreckage on the surface. The German ships had watched *Flirt* as she went about the rescue and then opened fire. The only survivors from *Flirt* were the gunner and rating in the boat and the first lieutenant and the other rating who had jumped over the side.

27 October 1916

Name	*Nubian*	**CO**	Cdr M.R. Bernard RN
Class	*Tribal* class destroyer	**Location**	English Channel
Built	21 April 1909	**Cause**	Torpedo

Notes   The 6th Destroyer Flotilla had been called out from Dover following a report that the Germans were raiding the Channel and was tearing after the German ships, trying to cut them off. At 0040 hrs *Nubian* sighted five destroyers ahead and made the challenge. The reply was a burst of gunfire as the German ships passed down *Nubian*'s port side at close range. Commander Bernard ordered the helm to be put over and tried to ram the last destroyer in the German line but instead *Nubian* was struck under the bridge by a torpedo. As she lay disabled the forward fuel tanks ignited and for a while the forward part of the ship was blazing furiously. At 0147 hrs she was taken in tow by *Lark* but at 0548 hrs the tow parted and *Nubian* drifted ashore under the South Foreland, west of St Margaret's Bay.

8 November 1916

Name	*Zulu*	**Location**	English Channel
Class	*Tribal* class destroyer	**Cause**	Mine
Built	16 September 1909	**Casualties**	None
CO	Lt John Brooke RN		

Notes   While on passage from Dover to Dunkirk *Zulu* was mined. The mine exploded under the engine room, throwing parts of the turbines on to the forecastle. The ship was held together only by the upper deck and eventually the motion of the sea caused the stern to break off and sink. The forward part was towed into Calais by the French destroyer *Capitaine Mehl*.

Admiral Bacon, commanding the Dover Patrol, now had the stern part of one *Tribal* class destroyer (*Nubian*) and the forward part of another (*Zulu*). The solution seemed to be to join the two together. The task was performed at Chatham dockyard and was not easy, not least because *Zulu* and *Nubian* had different builders and their hulls were not identical. However, the job was done and on 17 June 1917 the hybrid HMS *Zubian* was commissioned.

15(?) October 1916

Name	*E.30*	**CO**	Lt Cdr G.N. Biggs RN
Class	*E* class submarine	**Location**	North Sea
Built	29 June 1915	**Casualties**	33
		Survivors	None

Notes   *E.30* left for patrol on 15 November and was not heard from again. She might have been mined in her patrol area in the Heligoland Bight or perhaps in a new field off Orford Ness, which lay across her route home. The existence of this field was only discovered on 25 November.

1 December 1916

Name	*E.37*	**Location**	North Sea, off Harwich
Class	*E* class submarine	**Cause**	Mine
Built	2 September 1915	**Casualties**	38
CO	Lt Cdr R.F. Chisholm RN	**Survivors**	None

Notes   The same minefield may have accounted for *E.37*. Early on the morning of 1 December the officers in *E.54* heard a significant explosion. Knowing that *E.37* was outward bound at the time, they attributed the explosion to her striking a mine.

21 December 1916

Name	*Negro*	**Cause**	Collision
Class	*M* class destroyer	**Casualties**	None
Built	8 March 1916	**Survivors**	80
Location	Norwegian Sea, off the Orkney Islands		

Notes   See the entry on HMS *Hoste* below.

Name	*Hoste*	**Cause**	Collision
Class	*Parker* class destroyer	**Casualties**	None
Built	16 August 1916	**Survivors**	116
Location	Norwegian Sea, off the Orkney Islands		

Notes   *Hoste* was commissioned on 13 November 1916 and her operational career lasted just thirty-eight days. On 19 December, while at sea screening the Grand Fleet, her steering engine broke down and she returned to Scapa Flow with *Negro* as an escort. While on passage on 21 December the two ships collided. The shock of the collision rolled two depth-charges off *Hoste*'s stern into the sea where they detonated. The explosion blew off *Hoste*'s stern and blew in *Negro*'s bottom plating. *Negro* foundered shortly afterwards with great loss of life. *Marmion* and *Marwel* tried to take *Hoste* in tow but she was eventually abandoned after her crew had been taken off.

LOSSES 1917

11 January 1917

Name	*Ben-my-Chree*	**Location**	Mediterranean, off Castellorizo
Class	Seaplane carrier	**Cause**	Shore battery fire
Built	23 March 1908	**Casualties**	None
CO	Wg Cdr C.R. Samson DSO RNAS	**Survivors**	250

Notes HMS *Ben-my-Chree* was owned by the Isle of Man Steam Packet Company and had been requisitioned for war service in 1915 as a seaplane carrier. After service in the Red Sea she returned to the Mediterranean. While anchored off Castellorizo, she was engaged by a Turkish field artillery battery. She received a number of hits but one shell hit her magazine and caused her to blow up.

Name	*Cornwallis*	**Location**	Mediterranean, E of Malta
Class	*Duncan* class battleship	**Cause**	Submarine attack
Built	13 July 1901	**Casualties**	15
CO	Capt A.P. Davidson DSO RN	**Survivors**	655

Notes HMS *Cornwallis* was torpedoed by *U32* (*Kapitanleutnant* Kurt Hartwig) just a few miles off Malta. Hartwig put two torpedoes into the old battleship's starboard side and then, despite random depth-charge attacks from escorting destroyers, he remained to observe the results of his handiwork. *Cornwallis* assumed a list to starboard which was corrected by flooding the engine and boiler rooms. However, after a while it became clear that she was sinking so the destroyer *Beagle* came alongside to take off the survivors. Just as *Beagle* sheered off *Cornwallis* was struck by a third torpedo on the port side: Hartwig had fired again to make sure she had sunk but had waited until *Beagle* had moved away. 'A battleship is enough for one day' he told his control room crew.

19 January 1917

Name	*E.36*	**Location**	North Sea, off Harwich
Class	*E* class submarine	**Cause**	Collision
Built	16 September 1916	**Survivors**	None
CO	Lt T.B. MacGregor-Robertson RN		

Notes The submarines *E.36* and *E.43* were proceeding to sea together. *E.43* was ahead but had stopped to sink a drifting mine and then repair her canvas bridge screen. In the meantime *E.36* had caught up but had altered course to the east in order to avoid a group of trawlers. This took her directly across the track of *E.43* which was now coming up fast. *E.43* rammed *E.36* about 10 ft from her stern on her starboard side. In the dark less than 15 seconds elapsed between *E.43* sighting *E.36* and the collision – there was no time for avoiding action. Although *E.43* searched the area she found no survivors.

23 January 1917

Name	*Laurentic*	**Cause**	Mine
Class	AMC	**Casualties**	None
CO	Capt R.A. Norton RN	**Survivors**	368
Location	N coast of Ireland, off Lough Swilly		

Notes *Laurentic* ran over two mines laid outside the entrance to Lough Swilly. The ship was holed under the bridge and under the funnels on the port side. Within minutes she lost all power, rolled over and sank.

Name	*Simoom*	**Location**	North Sea, between the Maas and
Class	*R* class destroyer		North Hinder Light Vessels
Built	30 October 1916	**Cause**	Torpedo
CO	Cdr Inman RN	**Casualties**	47
		Survivors	43

Notes On the night of 22 January the Harwich Force put to sea to intercept the German 6th Destroyer Flotilla en route from the Heligoland Bight to Zeebrugge. On paper the British possessed significant superiority: 6 cruisers and 18 destroyers against 11 destroyers. However, in the confusion of the night the Germans got through and the destroyer *S.50* torpedoed HMS *Simoom*. She was hit in the magazine but remained afloat but she had to be sunk at 1040 hrs on the 23rd by HMS *Nimrod*.

28 January 1917

Name	*TB.24*	**CO**	Lt H.B. Wrey RN
Class	Torpedo boat	**Location**	Dover harbour
Built	19 March 1908	**Cause**	Wrecked

Notes *TB.24* collided with a breakwater while trying to enter the harbour in bad weather.

29 January 1917

Name	*K.13*	**Cause**	Accident
Class	*K* class submarine	**Casualties**	24 ship's company and associated
Built	11 November 1916		naval personnel together with 7
CO	Lt Cdr Godfrey Herbert RN		representatives of the builders,
Location	W coast of Scotland, off Shandon in		Fairfield & Co.
	the Gareloch, Firth of Clyde	**Survivors**	48

Notes This was the first accident to befall one of the Royal Navy's steam-driven K class fleet submarines. In time the class would acquire a horrific reputation for accidents: of the 18 boats in the class, 8 suffered disasters, 16 had major accidents and there were innumerable minor incidents. *K.13* was on her acceptance trials in the Gareloch. All had gone well during the morning trials and a further dive was scheduled for the afternoon. As *K.13* submerged one of the indicator lights on the control room panel showing the status of the engine room ventilators (which had to be closed before diving) was seen to be flickering. The Engineer Officer, Lieutenant Arthur Lane, said it was a faulty connection, but an ERA who had been sent to the boiler room to check came

Commander Francis Goodhart who was killed while escaping from *K.13* to summon assistance. (Author)

back with the grim news that the boiler room was flooding rapidly. The submarine could not be brought back to the surface and settled on the bottom.

After the submarine sank, Commander Francis Goodhart RN, the commanding officer of *K.14* who was observing the trials, volunteered to make an escape from the conning tower to try to alert the authorities as to the submarine's plight. Goodhart was killed during the escape but Lieutenant-Commander Herbert, who was assisting him, was carried to the surface. Herbert was able to work with the rescue authorities who had been alerted to *K.13*'s disappearance by the submarine *E.51*, which had seen her dive, and a high pressure air hose was connected to the submarine. The ballast tanks were then blown and *K.13*'s bows were hauled to the surface and a hole cut with oxy-acetylene equipment. Fifty-four hours after she had sunk, the first survivor crawled out to a huge cheer of welcome. *K.13* was raised on 15 March 1917 and recommissioned as *K.22*; she was sold for breaking up on 16 December 1926.

When the submarine was salvaged the body of Commander Goodhart was found wedged in the wheelhouse. He had hit his head on leaving the submarine, been rendered unconscious and drowned. Goodhart had previously commanded the submarine *E.8* in the Baltic with considerable success. This was the fourth submarine accident in which Herbert had been involved. He never served in submarines again.

8 February 1917

Name	*Gurkha*	**Location**	English Channel, 4 miles SE of
Class	*Tribal* class destroyer		Dungeness
Built	29 April 1907	**Cause**	Mine
CO	Lt H.C. Woolcombe-Boyce RN		

Notes   HMS *Gurkha* was a member of the 6th Destroyer Flotilla serving the Dover Patrol. She was mined while proceeding south-east of Dungeness.

1 March 1917

Name	*Pheasant*	**Location**	Pentland Firth
Class	*M* class destroyer	**Cause**	Mine
Built	23 October 1916	**Casualties**	100

Notes   HMS *Pheasant* was mined in rough weather while on routine despatch duties between the Grand Fleet base at Scapa Flow and the mainland. *Pheasant*'s hull was located and explored by Army divers in 1996. As befits her status as a war grave, her wreck was left undisturbed.

12 March 1917

Name	*E.49*	**Location**	Shetland Islands, off Huney Island
Class	*E* class submarine	**Cause**	Mine
Built	18 September 1916	**Survivors**	None
CO	Lt B.A. Beal		

Notes   At 1255 hrs on 12 March *E.49* was observed by the coastal patrol leaving Balta Sound in the Shetlands. As she passed behind Huney Island there was a sharp explosion, followed by the appearance of a cloud of smoke. *E.49* was not seen again. A search of the area revealed a wooden grating and some sailors' caps. Subsequently the area was dragged, and the wreck was found and examined. Divers discovered that *E.49*'s bows had been completely blown off, indicating that she had been mined. An inspection of German records after the war revealed that the field in question had been laid by *UC70*.

15 March 1917

Name	*Foyle*	**Location**	English Channel, Straits of Dover
Class	*River* class destroyer	**Cause**	Mine
Built	1903		

Notes   No further details are known.

17 March 1917

Name	*Mignonette*	**Location**	Atlantic, SW coast of Ireland
Class	*Arabis* class sloop	**Cause**	Mine
Built	26 January 1916		

Notes   No further details are known.

18 March 1917

Name	*Paragon*	**Location**	English Channel, Straits of Dover
Class	*Acasta* class destroyer	**Cause**	Gunfire
Built	21 February 1913	**Survivors**	10
CO	Lt J. Bowyer RN		

Notes   On the night of 17 March twelve German destroyers made a sustained attack on the Dover Barrage. Despite the British having some advance warning of the attack the Germans were able to slip through the patrols and shell Ramsgate and Broadstairs. *Paragon* was patrolling to the south-west of 11A buoy of the barrage when she sighted three or four destroyers approaching from the east and steaming across her bow. Lieutenant Bowyer thought they were friendly and made the challenge then in force. Almost immediately *Paragon* was hit by a torpedo in her engine room and received a number of hits from shells fired at close range. Within 8 minutes *Paragon* broke in half and sank. As she did so the depth-charges on her stern, which had not been set to 'safe', rolled into the sea and exploded, killing many of her survivors in the water.

Name	*Alyssum*	**Location**	Atlantic, SW coast of Ireland
Class	*Arabis* class sloop	**Cause**	Mine
Built	5 November 1915		

Notes   No further details are known.

23 March 1917

Name	*Laforey*	**Location**	English Channel
Class	*Laforey* class destroyer	**Cause**	Mine
Built	28 March 1911		

Notes   No further details are known.

26 March 1917

| **Name** | *Myrmidon* | **Location** | English Channel |
| **Class** | B class destroyer | **Cause** | Collision |

Notes   HMS *Myrmidon* was sunk in collision with the SS *Hamborn*.

7 April 1917

| **Name** | *Jason* | **Location** | W coast of Scotland |
| **Class** | Torpedo gunboat | **Cause** | Mine |

Notes   HMS *Jason* was serving as a minesweeper when she was lost off the west coast of Scotland.

16 April 1917

Name	*C.16*	**Location**	North Sea, 7 miles E of Harwich,
Class	C class submarine		near Rough Wreck Light Vessel
Built	19 March 1908	**Cause**	Collision
CO	Lt H. Boase RN	**Casualties**	16
		Survivors	None

Notes   On the morning of 16 April *C.16* and *C.25* were exercising off Harwich with the destroyer *Melampus*. During the exercises *C.16*'s periscope was sighted crossing *Melampus*' track. There was no time to avoid a collision and although *Melampus* went full astern and the helm was put over, *C.16* struck the destroyer's starboard bow and then bumped along her bottom before sinking. *Melampus* immediately buoyed the position and radioed for assistance. Later that afternoon *C.16*'s hull was found by a minesweeper and subsequently raised.

An examination of the boat provided some clues as to what had happened. The position of the hydroplanes and instruments showed that Boase had been trying to dive when *C.16* struck. The collision had forced the upper conning tower hatch off its seating, allowing water to flood into the boat through the lower hatch which, though shut, had been distorted by the collision. This ingress of water had to some extent been contained by stuffing the leaking hatch with clothing, wedges and tallow. The survivors had then tried to blow the main

The battered conning tower of *C.16*. The photograph was taken after the submarine had been raised following her collision with HMS *Melampus*. (Author)

ballast tanks but because the stop cock to the whistle valve had been left open, the air simply vented out through the whistle pipe which had been broken in the collision. A combination of the water entering the boat flowing aft and the blowing of main ballast caused the bow to rise until it was just 16 ft below the surface. Boase decided to let First Lieutenant Samuel Anderson RN try to escape through the port bow torpedo tubes. However, this attempt failed and Anderson's body was subsequently found wedged inside the tube. He had most likely drowned while the tube had been flooded up. Boase and the rest of the survivors now tried to escape from the *C16* through the conning tower hatch. The starboard torpedo tube was opened to the sea allowing the boat to flood. When Boase judged that the pressure inside equalled the sea pressure outside, he tried to lift the lid. However, he could not raise the hatch sufficiently. When he tried to close it, the hatch jammed open on a pig of lead that had swung under the joint and the hatch was held open by 2 inches. The precious air lock was lost and all inside drowned.

30 April 1917

Name	*Tulip*	**Location**	Atlantic, SW of Ireland
Class	SSV or *Aubretia* class sloop	**Cause**	Submarine attack
Built	15 July 1916	**Casualties**	None
CO	Cdr Lewis RN		

Notes *Aubretia* class sloops were built to resemble merchant ships in the hope that a U-boat would be careless and approach within range. (They were known as Q-ships.) In *Tulip*'s case the disguise proved singularly unsuccessful for she was torpedoed by *U62* (*Kapitanleutnant* Ernst Hashagen). The torpedo struck between the engine room and the stokehold. The boilers then exploded and *Tulip* was almost blown in half, being held together solely by the keel. She was abandoned. *U62* then surfaced and took *Tulip*'s captain prisoner before sinking *Tulip* by gunfire. As he climbed on to *U62*'s casing, Commander Lewis asked when and where he was going to be shot, only to be told by an amused Hashagen, 'Not yet! Come below and have a drink!' Hashagen's suspicions had been aroused by the brand-new Red Ensign flying at *Tulip*'s stern – this was unusual at a time when British merchant ships hardly wore any distinguishing colours.

2 May 1917

Name	*Derwent*	**Location**	Atlantic, off Le Havre
Class	*River* class destroyer	**Cause**	Mine

Notes   HMS *Derwent* was mined off the approaches to Le Havre.

5 May 1917

Name	*Lavender*	**Location**	English Channel
Class	*Acacia* class sloop	**Cause**	Submarine attack
Built	12 June 1915		

Notes   HMS *Lavender* was torpedoed and sunk by *UC75*.

17 May 1917

Name	*Setter*	**Cause**	Collision
Class	*R* class destroyer	**Casualties**	None
Built	18 August 1916	**Survivors**	82
Location	North Sea, off Harwich		

Notes   HMS *Setter* was sunk as a result of a collision in thick fog with HMS *Sylph*.

25 May 1917

Name	*Hilary*	**Cause**	Submarine attack
Class	AMC		

Notes   HMS *Hilary* was torpedoed and sunk by *U88* (*Kapitanleutnant* Walter Schwieger).

10 June 1917

Name	*TB.117*	**Cause**	Collision
Class	Torpedo boat	**Casualties**	5
Built	18 February 1904	**Survivors**	45
Location	English Channel		

Notes   *TB.117* sank following a collision with SS *Kamouraska*.

14 June 1917

Name	Avenger	**Cause**	Submarine attack
Class	AMC	**Casualties**	1
Location	North Atlantic		

Notes   HMS *Avenger* was sunk by torpedo.

19 June 1917

Name	CMB.1	**Cause**	Mine?
Class	CMB	**Casualties**	None
Built	1917	**Survivors**	4
Location	English Channel, off Ostend		

Notes   No further details are known.

20 June 1917

Name	Salvia	**CO**	Lt Cdr W. Olphert DSO DSC RN
Class	SSV	**Location**	Atlantic, W coast of Ireland
Built	16 June 1916	**Cause**	Submarine attack

Notes   HMS *Salvia* was another Q-ship whose disguise failed to impress a German commander for she was torpedoed and sunk by a U-boat. *Salvia* was struck on the starboard quarter by a torpedo that not only disabled her machinery spaces, but blew her 4 in gun over the side. The crew abandoned ship. Like the unfortunate Commander Lewis, Lieutenant-Commander Olphert was also taken prisoner.

30 June 1917

Name	Cheerful	**Cause**	Mine
Class	B class destroyer	**Casualties**	None
Built	14 July 1897	**Survivors**	60
Location	Shetland Islands		

Notes   HMS *Cheerful* was mined off the Shetland Islands.

4 July 1917

Name	Aster	**Location**	Mediterranean, off Malta
Class	Acacia class sloop	**Cause**	Mine
Built	1 May 1915	**Casualties**	10
CO	Lt Cdr Hodson RN	**Survivors**	83

Notes   *Aster* and *Azalea* were escorting the steamer *Abbasieh* to Mudros from Malta. The sloops were too small to carry paravanes and thus had no protection when they strayed into a minefield. *Aster* hit a mine and sank very quickly to the shock of those on *Azalea*'s bridge, who now began to see the mines all around them in the clear water. As *Azalea* tried to back out of the field, the current carried her on to a mine. She was lucky: the damage was slight and she managed to return to Malta.

6 July 1917

Name	*Itchen*	**Location**	North Sea
Class	*River* class destroyer	**Cause**	Submarine attack
Built	17 March 1903		

Notes   HMS *Itchen* was torpedoed by *U99*.

17 July 1917

Name	*C.34*	**Location**	North Sea, between the Orkneys and
Class	C class submarine		the Shetlands, 59 30'N, 00 05'E
CO	Lt I.S. Jefferson RN	**Cause**	Submarine attack
		Casualties	15
		Survivors	1

Notes   It was the practice to deploy two C class submarines on patrol between the Orkneys and the Shetlands to prevent German U-boats using this route on their way to the Atlantic. On 16 July *C.34* sailed for such a patrol from Scapa Flow for the area around Fair Isle. The next day at 1335 hrs she was lying stopped and trimmed down on the surface when she was attacked by *U52* (*Kapitanleutnant* Walther Hans, who had previously sunk HMS *Nottingham*). When Hans surfaced and ran over the spot he found one survivor, Stoker Frank Scoble, and a mass of wreckage. A very fine memorial to Lieutenant Jefferson was subsequently erected in Ripon Cathedral.

9 July 1917

Name	*Vanguard*	**Location**	Scapa Flow
Class	*St Vincent* class battleship	**Cause**	Accident
Built	22 April 1909	**Casualties**	804
CO	Capt J.D. Dick RN	**Survivors**	2

Notes   On the afternoon of the 9th *Vanguard* had been exercising Abandon Ship and had then dropped anchor near the north shore of Scapa Flow at 1830 hrs. At 2320 hrs she blew up and sank. From the many varying accounts of her loss it seems that smoke was seen to issue from the area just below the foremast. Then there was an explosion, followed a sheet of flame after which the ship was enveloped in a dense pall of smoke. No one actually saw *Vanguard* sink. Ships nearby were showered with wreckage and when these pieces were examined they were found to come from compartments round *Vanguard*'s 'P' and 'Q' turrets. The enquiry set up to investigate what had happened to the ship spent some time considering all the evidence and ruled out a number of theories including sabotage. They eventually concluded that coal sacks had been stowed around 'P' and 'Q' handling rooms which cut off the natural ventilation in the area. The temperature in the magazine then rose until the cordite ignited spontaneously, blowing the ship apart.

23 July 1917

Name	*Otway*	**Location**	W coast of Scotland, off Loch Ewe
Class	AMC	**Cause**	Submarine attack
CO	Capt P.H. Columb RN		

Notes HMS *Otway* had just left the safety of Loch Ewe and was heading to take up her position in the patrol line off the Norwegian coast when she was torpedoed and sunk.

26 July 1917

Name	*Ariadne*	**Location**	English Channel, off Beachy Head
Class	*Diadem* class cruiser	**Cause**	Submarine attack
Built	22 April 1898	**Casualties**	38

Notes The cruiser *Ariadne* had been converted to a minelayer with a capacity of over 400 mines. She laid over 700 mines off Heligoland and in the Dover Straits. However, on the night of 26 July 1917 she was torpedoed off Beachy Head by *UC65*.

9 August 1917

Name	*Recruit*	**Location**	North Sea
Class	*R* class destroyer	**Cause**	Submarine attack
Built	9 December 1916		

Notes HMS *Recruit* was torpedoed and sunk by *U16*.

13 August 1917

Name	*Bergamot*	**Location**	Atlantic
Class	*Anchusa* class sloop	**Cause**	Submarine attack
Built	5 May 1917	**Casualties**	None
CO	Lt P.T. Perkins RNR	**Survivors**	98

Notes Like the *Aubretia* class the *Anchusa* class sloops were built to resemble merchant ships and, generally, their armament was concealed as much as possible. HMS *Bergamot* had been in service barely two months when she was torpedoed by a U-boat in the Atlantic. Following the attack *Bergamot*'s crew tried to lure the U-boat to the surface where she could be attacked but the U-boat failed to take the challenge. *Bergamot* subsequently foundered in rough weather.

20(?) August 1917

Name	*E.47*	**CO**	Lt E.C. Carre RN
Class	*E* class submarine	**Location**	North Sea
Built	29 May 1916	**Survivors**	None

Notes *E.47* failed to return from patrol on 20 August 1917. There is no clear explanation for her loss, which can only be ascribed to either a mine or an accident.

September 1917 *The accidental sinking of* G.9 *by the destroyer* Pasley *was an indication of how difficult the art of recognition was becoming at sea with the introduction of the submarine. It also showed the need for thorough and rigorous staffwork to ensure that friendly forces were kept aware of each other's location. Sadly, this was not the last incident of this type.*

Stoker William Drake (right), the sole survivor from HM Submarine *G.9*, rammed in error by the destroyer HMS *Pasley*. (Author)

16 September 1917

Name	*G.9*	**Location**	North Sea
Class	G class submarine	**Cause**	Rammed
Built	15 June 1916	**Survivors**	1
CO	Lt Cdr Byron Cary RN		

Notes   *G.9* was on patrol in the North Sea and had been warned about a U-boat operating in her area. It appeared that *G.9* mistook the destroyer HMS *Pasley*, which was escorting a convoy to Lerwick, for the U-boat and fired two torpedoes at her just after midnight on 16 September. One torpedo missed astern while the other struck the destroyer abreast her engine room but did not explode. Just how this mistake occurred is not clear for *Pasley* was displaying a white light halfway up her foremast as a guide for the merchantmen in her charge. No U-boat would burn a white light at night in enemy waters. Moreover *G.9* had been warned about *Pasley*'s convoy passing through her area.

Just after the torpedoes had been fired *G.9* must have realised her mistake for she made the correct challenge using the brightest light on board which lit up the entire submarine. But it was too late. The submarine was only 100 yards from the *Pasley* and steaming across her bows from starboard to port while the destroyer was swinging to starboard and increasing speed to ram. *Pasley* struck *G.9* abreast the conning tower and she sank very quickly leaving only one survivor, Stoker William Drake.

27 September 1917

Name	*CMB.8*	**Location**	English Channel
Class	Coastal motor boat	**Cause**	Scuttled

Notes   No further details are known.

October 1917 *saw a daring German cruiser raid on a Scandinavian convoy that resulted in two destroyers and nine merchant ships being sunk, despite the presence of numerous covering forces.*

2 October 1917

Name	*Drake*	**Location**	N coast of Ireland
Class	*Drake* class cruiser	**Cause**	Submarine attack
Built	5 March 1901	**Casualties**	None
CO	Capt S.H. Radcliffe RN		

Notes HMS *Drake* was torpedoed by *U79*. She managed to reach Church Bay in Rathlin Sound under her own power and then anchored. However, the flooding could not be contained and she began to list and eventually capsized. The wreck became popular with divers and demolition of *Drake*'s hull did not start until 1970.

9 October 1917

Name	*Champagne*	**Location**	Irish Sea
Class	AMC	**Cause**	Submarine attack
CO	Capt Percy Brown RN	**Casualties**	56

Notes No further details are known.

12 October 1917

Name	*Begonia*	**Location**	Mediterranean, off Casablanca
Class	SSV	**Cause**	Collision
Built	26 August 1915	**Casualties**	100
CO	Lt Cdr Basil Noake RN	**Survivors**	None

Notes HMS *Begonia* was an *Azalea* class sloop that was converted in 1916–17 at Haulbowline to resemble a small coaster. She then served as a Q-ship under the names *Dolcis*, *Jessop* and *Q.10*. On the morning of the 12th *Begonia* was sighted by *U151* (KK Walter Kophamel) which dived to avoid detection. Kophamel brought *U151* up to periscope depth when he thought it was safe but as he did so *Begonia* ran over the U-boat's after casing, tearing away the decking and leaving parts of her propeller blades embedded in the casing structure. A few moments later *Begonia* was seen to stop, heel over and then explode. Evidently the damage done to her hull by the collision had caused massive flooding followed by explosion of her boilers.

17 October 1917

Name	*Strongbow*	**Location**	North Sea, 75 miles E of Lerwick
Class	R class destroyer	**Cause**	Gunfire
Built	30 September 1916	**Casualties**	47
CO	Lt Cdr E. Brooke RN	**Survivors**	39

Notes With HMS *Mary Rose* and two trawlers HMS *Strongbow* was escorting a convoy of twelve merchantmen to Lerwick in the Shetlands from Norway. At 0600 hrs on the 17th *Strongbow* was surprised by the appearance of the German minelaying cruisers *Brummer* and *Bremse* which had broken through the patrols and were now 'on the loose'. The two German ships were armed with 5.9 in guns and had a top speed of 34 knots. *Strongbow* was no match for them but Brooke took his ship into action none the less. However, before *Strongbow* could even come within range of the Germans, she was disabled by a shell that burst in her engine room, severing the main steam pipe. She was then abandoned and sank at about 0730 hrs.

Name	*Mary Rose*	**Location**	North Sea, 75 miles E of Lerwick
Class	*M* class destroyer	**Cause**	Gunfire
Built	8 October 1915	**Casualties**	83
CO	Lt Cdr C.L. Fox RN	**Survivors**	5

Notes   On hearing the gunfire which marked the end of *Strongbow*, *Mary Rose* turned back. She too was outgunned by her opponents and soon brought to a standstill. Nevertheless Lieutenant-Commander Fox continued to encourage his men to fight the ship until she sank under them with her colours flying. *Brummer* and *Bremse* then sank nine of the twelve merchant ships before returning, unchallenged, to port.

19 October 1917

Name	*Orama*	**Location**	Atlantic
Class	AMC	**Cause**	Submarine attack

Notes   HMS *Orama* was torpedoed by *U62* (*Kapitanleutnant* Ernst Hashagen). The submarine had the satisfaction of intercepting *Orama*'s distress call and thus was certain of her victim's identity.

21 October 1917

Name	*Marmion*	**Location**	North Sea, off the Shetland Islands
Class	*M* class destroyer	**Cause**	Collision
Built	28 May 1915		

Notes   HMS *Marmion* was sunk off the port of Lerwick following a collision in bad weather with the destroyer *Tirade*.

22 October 1917

Name	*C.32*	**Location**	Baltic, Vaist Bay
Class	*C* class submarine	**Cause**	Scuttled after grounding
Built	29 September 1909	**Casualties**	None
CO	Lt C.P. Satow RN		

Notes   *C.32* grounded in Vaist Bay on the Estonian coast as a result of a faulty compass and Satow's reluctance to approach the land to look for marks since he did not know if the coast was held by the Germans. Although a tug arrived *C.32* could not be pulled clear and was destroyed by scuttling charges. Destruction was completed when Satow re-entered the submarine and opened the torpedo tubes.

2 November 1917

Name	*CMB.11*	**Cause**	Fire
Class	CMB	**Casualties**	None
Location	English Channel	**Survivors**	4

Notes   *CMB.11* burned out following a collision.

11 November 1917

		Location	Eastern Mediterranean, off Deir el Belah
Name	*M.15*		
Class	*M* class monitor	**Cause**	Submarine attack
Built	28 April 1915	**Casualties**	26

Notes   *M.15* was one of a number of ships supporting Allenby's army in Palestine. When the rapid advance of the army had placed them beyond the range of naval gunfire support the monitors were withdrawn. When reports of a U-boat were received the monitors and other warships withdrew behind a line of nets secured 2 miles offshore. However, *Oberleutnant* Hans Wendlandt in *UC38* was not deterred. Slipping past the patrols and around the end of the net he torpedoed *M.15* at 1735 hrs. The torpedo hit on the port bow causing a serious cordite fire in the forward magazine. *M.15* sank in less than 3 minutes.

Name	*Staunch*	**Location**	Eastern Mediterranean, off Deir el Belah
Class	*Acorn* class destroyer		
Built	29 October 1910	**Cause**	Submarine attack

Notes   HMS *Staunch* was the second of *UC38*'s victims. Wendlandt escaped unscathed after both sinkings.

18 November 1917

Name	*K.1*	**Location**	North Sea, off the Danish coast
Class	*K* class submarine	**Cause**	Scuttled following collision
Built	14 November 1916	**Casualties**	None
CO	Lt Cdr C.S. Benning RN	**Survivors**	56

Notes   *K.1* was engaged in a Grand Fleet sweep off the Danish coast with *K.3*, *K.4* and *K.7* and the light cruiser *Blanche*. The cruiser was leading followed by *K.1*, *K.3*, *K.4* and *K.17*. *Blanche* had to make a sudden alteration of course in order to avoid ships of the 5th Light Cruiser Squadron. As she did so *K.1* lost power owing to salt water entering her fuel lines. In the confusion caused by *Blanche*'s alteration of course and *K.1* slowing down, *K.3* passed *K.1* on her port side but *K.4* collided with *K.1*, hitting her on the port side just aft of the conning tower. The submarine quickly began to flood and the crew were forced out on to the casing as the battery began to give off chlorine gas. After a quick consultation it was decided that she was beyond saving. It was impossible for anyone to try to re-enter the submarine because of the gas. A more important consideration was that the whole force had been lying stopped in enemy waters for more than an hour with all navigation lights and searchlights burning on a very clear night. They could not expect to remain unmolested for long. After the crew was taken off *K.1* was sunk by four 4 in shells from *Blanche*.

The subsequent enquiry found that Benning was at fault for not using the way on *K.1* when her engine failed to haul out of line and so pre-empt the possibility of a collision.

24 November 1917

Name	*Candytuft*	**Location**	Mediterranean, near Bougie
Class	SSV	**Cause**	Submarine attack
CO	Cdr W.O. Cochrane RN		

Notes   HMS *Candytuft*, another *Aubretia* class sloop, was escorting the merchant ship *Tremayne* from Gibraltar to Malta when she was attacked by a U-boat. The first torpedo hit the starboard quarter and blew off her stern. A second torpedo then hit under the bridge and broke the remainder of her hull in two: the bow sank almost immediately but the bridge grounded.

December 1917 *saw a second successful German attack on a Scandinavian convoy. The Royal Navy had increased the strength of the covering forces for the Scandinavian convoys since the sinking of the* Mary Rose *but the Germans seemed to be able to act with impunity. Worse was to follow for German minelaying off the Hook of Holland accounted for the loss of three brand-new destroyers and over 250 men in one night.*

12 December 1917

Name	*Partridge*	**Location**	Norwegian Sea, SW of Bjorne Fjord
CO	Lt Cdr R.H. Ranson RN	**Cause**	Gunfire and torpedo

Notes   On 11 December 1917 HMS *Partridge*, accompanied by HMS *Pellew* and four trawlers, left Lerwick for Bergen with a six ship convoy. At 1145 hrs on the 12th the convoy was attacked by four German destroyers, *G.101*, *G.103*, *G.104* and *V.100*. *Partridge* was hit almost immediately by a shell that severed her main steam pipe and left her lying dead in the water. She did fire a torpedo, which hit *V.100*, but unfortunately this failed to explode before she was struck by a torpedo herself. Ranson gave the order to abandon ship and *Partridge* was then hit by a further two torpedoes. The German destroyers sank all six merchant ships and the trawler escorts and escaped under cover of bad weather, leaving the damaged *Pellew* as the only survivor.

Name	*Wolverine*	**Location**	NW coast of Ireland
Class	*Beagle* class destroyer	**Cause**	Collision
Built	5 January 1910		

Notes   *Wolverine* was sunk following a collision with the sloop HMS *Rosemary*.

16 December 1917

Name	*Arbutus*	**Location**	St George's Channel
Class	*Anchusa* class sloop	**Cause**	Submarine attack
Built	8 September 1917	**Casualties**	9
CO	Cdr Charles Oxlade RNR	**Survivors**	84

Notes   HMS *Arbutus* was torpedoed by a U-boat. The ship remained seaworthy but bad weather subsequently caused her to founder.

23 December 1917

Name	*Torrent*	**Location**	North Sea, near the Maas Buoy
Class	*R* class destroyer	**Cause**	Mine
Built	26 November 1916		

Name	*Surprise*	**Location**	North Sea, near the Maas Buoy
Class	*R* class destroyer	**Cause**	Mine
Built	23 November 1916		

Name	*Tornado*	**Location**	North Sea, near the Maas Buoy
Class	*R* class destroyer	**Cause**	Mine
Built	4 August 1917		

Notes   It was one of the many responsibilities of the Harwich Force to escort the Dutch convoy traffic and it was their usual practice, since they could not enter Dutch waters, to meet the convoy off the Maas Light Buoy. The Germans were aware of this and had laid fields of mines near the Maas Buoy in which the mines were all linked together by wires. The effect of a ship fouling the wire would be to draw one or more mines on to the ship concerned. The idea worked perfectly. On the night of 23 December the destroyers *Radiant*, *Surprise*, *Torrent* and *Tornado* had gone to meet a convoy and ran into the field. In an incident oddly reminiscent of the sinking the *Cressy*, *Hogue* and *Aboukir* three years earlier (see pp. 8–9), *Torrent* was the first to be mined and while going to her assistance *Surprise* was also mined. *Tornado* tried to get clear by going astern but in the process she struck two more mines and sank quickly. Undeterred by the carnage Commander G.F.S. Nash of *Radiant* remained to rescue the survivors before getting clear – remarkably unscathed. A total of 12 officers and 240 men were killed in the three destroyers.

30 December 1917

Name	*Attack*	**Location**	Mediterranean, off Alexandria
Class	*Acheron* class destroyer	**Cause**	Mine
Built	12 December 1911		

Notes   No further details are known.

LOSSES 1918

January 1918 saw the last sinking of a British warship by a German capital ship when the battle cruiser Goeben *made a brief foray into the Aegean. Poor deployment of available British warships allowed the Germans to sink two monitors at no cost to themselves, though honours were evened later in the day when* Goeben *ran into a minefield and then grounded while her consort* Breslau *sank after striking no fewer than five mines. However, the affair was a potent demonstration that even in the last year of the war the German Navy was still a force to be reckoned with.*

9 January 1918

Name	*Racoon*	**Location**	N coast of Ireland
Class	*Beagle* class destroyer	**Cause**	Grounded
Built	15 February 1910	**Casualties**	91
CO	Lt George Napier RN	**Survivors**	9

Notes HMS *Racoon* ran aground in bad weather. Her hull was subsequently broken up by the action of the storm.

14(?) January 1918

Name	*G.8*	**Location**	North Sea
Class	*G* class submarine	**Casualties**	30
Built	1 May 1916	**Survivors**	None
CO	Lt J.F. Tryon RN		

Notes *G.8* failed to return to harbour from patrol on 14 January. There are no firm causes for her loss so it must be assumed that she was the victim of either a mine or an accident.

12 January 1918

Name	*Narborough*	**Location**	Scapa Flow
Class	*M* class destroyer	**Cause**	Collision
Built	2 March 1916		

Name	*Opal*	**Location**	Scapa Flow
Class	*M* class destroyer	**Cause**	Collision
Built	11 September 1915		

Notes HMS *Opal* and *Narborough* collided in rough weather while entering Scapa Flow with the Grand Fleet. Both ships suffered such damage in the encounter that they subsequently foundered.

19(?) January 1918

Name	*H.10*	**CO**	Lt C. Collier RN
Class	*H* class submarine	**Location**	North Sea
Built	27 June 1915	**Casualties**	22

Notes   *H.10* failed to return to harbour from patrol on 19 January. There are no firm causes for her loss so it must be assumed that she was the victim of either a mine or an accident.

20 January 1918

Name	*Raglan*	**Location**	E Mediterranean, Kusu Bay, on the
Class	*Abercrombie* class monitor		NE corner of the island of Imbros
Built	29 April 1915	**Cause**	Gunfire
CO	Capt the Viscount Broome RN	**Casualties**	127
		Survivors	93

Notes   On the morning of 20 January the battle cruiser *Goeben* and the cruiser *Breslau* slipped out of the Dardanelles, passing Cape Helles at 0540 hrs, for a brief raiding cruise in the Aegean. Lookouts on Mavro Island to the south of the Dardanelles failed to spot the two ships and it was not until 0720 hrs that they were first sighted by the destroyer *Lizard* which raised the alarm despite heavy radio jamming by the two German ships. Almost at the same time *Raglan*, anchored in Kusu Bay, sighted the two ships and closed up for action while trying to raise steam.

At first *Raglan* held fire since Broome felt the German ships might not have seen the monitor under the shore. He was mistaken. After driving off the *Lizard*, *Breslau* opened fire on *Raglan* and with her fourth salvo destroyed the monitor's spotting top, killing the gunnery officer and wounding Broome. *Raglan*'s twin 14 in turret now had to be operated in local control. Once *Breslau* had the range she began firing rapid salvoes which did a considerable amount of damage and she was soon joined by the *Goeben*. One 11 in shell from *Goeben* penetrated the barbette armour on the port side, starting a cordite fire and causing the evacuation of the turret. *Raglan*'s position was hopeless: she was lying at anchor close to the shore with her armament out of action and with no hope of escape. The first lieutenant, realising the ship's position, and thinking Broome was killed, gave the order to abandon ship. The two German ships kept up their rapid fire, coming as close as 4,000 yards. One German shell set off the 12 pdr magazine, after which *Raglan* sank by the bow at 0815 hrs. She settled on an even keel in 40 ft of water with her mast, funnel and part of her bridge protruding above the water.

The subsequent court martial found that the conduct of Broome (a nephew of Lord Kitchener) and his ship's company was 'in accordance with the traditions of the Service and that no blame was attributable to any of them'. However, the local CinC, Rear Admiral A. Hayes-Saddler, was criticised for having used the battleship *Lord Nelson* to take him on a routine visit to Salonika, thus removing her from the theatre, when he could have used another vessel.

Name	*M.28*	**Location**	E Mediterranean, Kusu Bay, on the
Class	*M* class monitor		NE corner of the island of Imbros
Built	28 June 1915	**Cause**	Gunfire
CO	Lt Cdr D.P. MacGregor RN	**Casualties**	8
		Survivors	58

Notes *M.28* shared the same fate as *Raglan*. *Breslau* hit her amidships with her second salvo, igniting the cordite and oil fuel tanks in one fierce explosion. The single 9.2 in gun then had to be abandoned as flames from the magazine below were coming up around the gun through the hatch in the deck. A shell from *Breslau* then burst on the 9.2 in gun, killing MacGregor and many around him. At 0827 hrs the cordite fire reached the shell room and *M.28* blew up in a massive explosion that showered debris and human remains over a wide area.

28 January 1918

Name	*E.14*		**Location**	E Mediterranean, Dardanelles
Class	*E* class submarine		**Cause**	Gunfire
Built	7 July 1914		**Casualties**	21
CO	Lt Cdr G.S. White RN		**Survivors**	9

Notes After her foray into the Aegean *Goeben* had reached the safety of the Dardanelles but had gone aground near Nagara Point. The Royal Navy was determined to destroy this ship and after attempts to bomb her from the air had failed, the submarine *E.14* was summoned from Corfu to use more reliable methods of destruction. Air reconnaissance on the 27th showed *Goeben* at anchor, so *E.14* sailed from Mudros that evening. Alas, no one on the British side was aware that as *E.14* was slipping out of Mudros, tugs were towing *Goeben* off and beginning the passage to Constantinople.

E.14 successfully broke through the anti-submarine net at Chanak but White was disappointed to find that *Goeben* had gone. He turned about and headed back down the Straits and at 0845 hrs on the 28th fired a torpedo at a Turkish transport. Just 11 seconds after the torpedo had been fired, there was a massive explosion. Either the torpedo had dived and exploded on hitting the bottom or the warhead had armed prematurely and exploded – either way *E.14* began to take on water through the torpedo loading hatch which had been sprung open by the blast. White brought the boat to the surface to find that the Turkish gunners were very much awake. For nearly 30 minutes *E.14* ran down the Straits under continuous gunfire but the combination of flooding and shell damage meant that her position was hopeless. White ordered her to be run ashore before he was killed. Shortly afterwards *E.14* sank, the survivors being rescued by the Turks.

Lieutenant-Commander White was posthumously awarded the Victoria Cross. *E.14* only ever had two commanding officers: Lieutenant Courtney Boyle and Lieutenant-Commander White. Both these officers were awarded the Victoria Cross.

Name	*Hazard*		**Location**	English Channel, off Portland
Class	Torpedo gunboat		**Cause**	Collision
Built	1894			

Notes HMS *Hazard* was sunk in a collision with a merchant ship off Portland.

31 January 1918

Name	*K.4*		**Cause**	Collision
Class	*K* class submarine		**Casualties**	59
CO	Lt Cdr D. de B. Stocks RN		**Survivors**	None
Location	Firth of Forth, off May Island			

Notes See the section on *K.17* below.

Name	*K.17*	**Cause**	Collision
Class	*K* class submarine	**Casualties**	50
CO	Lt Cdr H.J. Hearn RN	**Survivors**	9
Location	Firth of Forth, off May Island		

Notes   *K.4* and *K.17* were both sunk in what has since become known as the 'Battle of May Island'. On the night of 31 January elements of the Grand Fleet were putting to sea for an exercise. The force included two flotillas of *K*-boats: the 13th Flotilla consisting of *K.22*, *K.14*, *K.11*, *K.12* and *K.17* led by Commander E. Leir in the light cruiser *Ithuriel*, and the 12th Flotilla consisting of *K.4*, *K.6*, *K.7* and *K.3* led by Commander Charles Little in the light cruiser *Fearless*. The night was pitch black with occasional patches of mist. The ships were running without lights except for a very dim, blue stern light and wireless silence was enforced.

In the darkness *K.14* sighted a number of armed minesweeping trawlers ahead of her which had not been told of the fleet's movements. As she altered course to avoid the minesweepers her helm jammed and she was then rammed by *K.22* (ex-*K.13*, *q.v.*). As the two submarines lay locked together they were overtaken by the heavier units of the Grand Fleet coming up astern of them. *K.22* was rammed by the battle cruiser *Inflexible*. Both *K.14* and *K.22* survived the evening.

The real chaos was just beginning. Hearing the garbled interchange of signals between *K.22* and *K.14* Commander Leir in HMS *Ithuriel* made the humanitarian but unwise decision to turn around, taking *K.11*, *K.12* and *K.17* with him, to see what help he could offer. This meant that he was running on a reciprocal course to the main body of the Grand Fleet which was now coming up fast, unaware either that the light cruiser and three submarines were heading back or that there had been a collision. Although he turned on navigation lights to make his ships more visible, Leir had to make a rapid alteration of course to avoid the battle cruiser *Australia*, dead ahead on an opposite course. This turn took him straight across the track of HMS *Fearless* leading the second flotilla of *K* boats (*K.4*, *K.6*, *K.7* and *K.3*). At 2032 hrs *Fearless* collided with *K.17* which sank 8 minutes later. Around eighteen men made an escape from the engine room but only nine of them were rescued. Destroyers passed through the area of her sinking at high speed, unaware of what had happened, and running down the survivors. Astern of *Fearless K.4* swung out of line to port to avoid the mêlée and stopped. *K.6* tried to do the same and ploughed into *K.4*, cutting her in half. As *K.4* settled in the water she was run down by *K.7* which bumped over her sinking hull.

A total of 103 submariners were killed in this series of collisions which unleashed a storm of controversy in the Navy about the wisdom of operating submarines with the surface fleet and about the competence of submarine officers in navigation and station-keeping. No less a personage than Sir Eric Geddes, the First Lord of the Admiralty, commented, 'this chapter of accidents looks as if there was something wrong with the standard of efficiency of the officers'. One of the participants blamed the poor construction of the *K*s, saying they had: 'the speed of a destroyer, the turning circle of a battleship and the bridge control facilities of a picket boat'.

31(?) January 1918

Name	*E.50*	**Location**	North Sea
Class	*E* class submarine	**Casualties**	30
CO	Lt R.E. Snook RN	**Survivors**	None

Notes   *E.50* failed to return to harbour from patrol on 31 January. There are no firm causes for her loss so it must be assumed that she was the victim of either a mine or an accident.

8 February 1918

Name	*Boxer*	**Location**	English Channel
Class	*A* class destroyer	**Cause**	Collision
Built	1894		

Notes   HMS *Boxer* sank following a collision with SS *Patrick* in bad weather.

1 March 1918

Name	*Calgarian*	**Location**	N of Ireland
Class	AMC	**Cause**	Submarine attack
CO	Capt R.A. Newton RN	**Casualties**	49

Notes   The armed merchant cruiser *Calgarian* was torpedoed by *U19* (*Kapitanleutnant* Johann Spiess). However, her crew quickly contained the flooding and she remained afloat while signalling for help. Thinking he was about to be cheated of a major prize, Spiess watched appalled as *Calgarian* was soon surrounded by seven destroyers, three sloops and a number of trawlers. Undeterred, he penetrated the screen and fired two more torpedoes which were sufficient to send the AMC to the bottom.

6 March 1918

Name	*H.5*	**Cause**	Rammed
Class	*H* class submarine	**Casualties**	25
CO	Lt A.W. Forbes RN	**Survivors**	None
Location	Irish Sea, 53 04'N, 4 40'W		

Notes   At the end of February 1918 *H.5* departed from Bantry Bay for a patrol in the southern Irish Sea. At 2030 hrs on 2 March the steamer *Rutherglen* sighted a submarine crossing her bows at considerable speed. *Rutherglen*'s Master identified the submarine as a U-boat and rammed her. Cries were heard and men were seen swimming in the water but none was picked up. Since no U-boats were operating in the area at the time, *Rutherglen*'s victim was almost certainly *H.5*. One of those killed was Ensign E.F. Childs of the United States Navy, an American submariner who was on board *H.5* for some war 'experience'. He was one of the first American casualties of the First World War. It is interesting to note that *H.5* had an exceptionally experienced crew – no fewer than five ratings had been awarded the DSM for previous war service. It is not clear whether *Rutherglen* had been warned that a British submarine was operational along her route. Certainly neither party made any attempt to identify themselves. The Admiralty was not desperately concerned about the incident, for *Rutherglen*'s crew were told that they had sunk a U-boat and they received the usual reward. The deception went so far as to sanction the award of the Distinguished Service Cross to *Rutherglen*'s Master . . . *pour encourager les autres*. The reason for this was that the Admiralty constantly exhorted merchant ship masters to attack U-boats at every opportunity: the news that a British submarine had been rammed might well make others cautious.

12 March 1918

Name	*D.3*	**Cause**	Air attack
Class	*D* class submarine	**Casualties**	25
CO	Lt W. Maitland-Dougall RN	**Survivors**	None
Location	English Channel, off Dieppe		

Notes   HM Submarine *D.3* was on anti-submarine patrol in the English Channel off Dieppe when she was sighted by the French airship AT-0. *D.3* attempted to identify herself using rocket signals but the crew of the airship thought the rockets were being fired at their vulnerable hydrogen-filled balloon. Moreover the rockets were not the recognised inter-Allied recognition signal. Accordingly they returned fire with a machine-gun and the submarine dived. The airship crew immediately (and reasonably) assumed that the submarine was German and dropped six 52 kg depth-bombs. Amid the explosions *D.3* came to the surface briefly before sinking back into the depths. Four survivors were left swimming in the water, one of whom apparently yelled to the airship crew as they hovered overhead, 'You got us!' (the true response was probably a good deal stronger) whereupon Lieutenant Saint Remy, AT-0's commander, realised that they might be British. He could not pick them up and while he was searching for a ship to rescue them, the men sadly drowned.

22 March 1918

Name	*Gaillardia*	**Cause**	Mine
Class	Sloop	**Casualties**	85
Location	North Sea	**Survivors**	8

Notes   HMS *Gaillardia* was engaged in the laying of the northern barrage, a massive deep minefield covering the gap between the Orkneys and Norway to stop U-boats using this route into the Atlantic. While recovering Danbuoys marking the location of one of the minefields, she inadvertently fouled a mine, blew up and sank. There was some concern at her loss since the little sloop drew just 12 ft and the mines were supposed to be moored at a depth of 65 ft – there should have been 53 ft clearance!

23 March 1918

Name	*Arno*	**Cause**	Collision
Class	*Arno* class destroyer	**Casualties**	None
Built	22 December 1914	**Survivors**	70+
Location	E Mediterranean, the Dardanelles		

Notes   HMS *Arno* was sunk in a collision with the destroyer HMS *Hope* off the Dardanelles.

27 March 1918

Name	*Kale*	**Location**	North Sea
Class	*River* class destroyer	**Cause**	Mine
Built	8 November 1904		

Notes   *Kale* was mined while returning to Harwich.

April 1918 *was a fairly momentous month. The operations of the E and C class submarines in the Baltic were brought to a conclusion when the remaining boats were scuttled in the face of a deteriorating political and military situation. April also saw the St George's Day raid on Zeebrugge and Ostende. Though the operation failed in its primary objective of blocking the exit from these ports for German destroyers and submarines, the heroism and gallantry of those who took part was a massive morale-booster for the country at large, at a time when the war on land seemed no nearer a conclusion. Vice-Admiral Roger*

Keyes, Commander of the Dover Patrol, voiced his hopes for the venture, which remain the most accurate verdict: '. . . even if we don't actually achieve all we are setting to do – we will accomplish a good deal for the credit of the Service and give the enemy a bad night'.

1 April 1918

Name	*Falcon*	**Location**	North Sea
Class	*C* class destroyer	**Cause**	Collision

Notes   HMS *Falcon* was sunk in collision with the drifter *John Fitzgerald*. In August 1914 *Falcon* had survived a direct hit from a German 8.2 in shell on her bridge, which had killed her commanding officer and 23 others out of her ship's company of 60.

3 April 1918

Name	*E.1*	**Location**	Baltic, 10 miles S of Helsingfors,
Class	*E* class submarine		near Grohara Lighthouse
Built	9 November 1912	**Cause**	Scuttled
CO	Out of commission	**Casualties**	None

Notes   In April 1918 the decision was taken to scuttle the submarines of the British squadron which had done such good work in the Baltic since 1915. After the Bolshevik Revolution, the flotilla had moved to Helsingfors in Finland. However, in 1918 they were trapped: they could be captured by the advancing Germans or by the Bolshevik government which under the terms of the Treaty of Brest Litovsk (17 November 1917) would have had to surrender the British submarines to the Germans. Thus on 3 April *E.1*, *E.8*, *E.9* and *E.19* were towed out by the tug *Zavtra*, and scuttling charges were set and fired. *E.1* sank immediately. While in commission, under the command of Lieutenant-Commander Noel Laurence RN, she had torpedoed and damaged the German battle cruiser *Moltke*.

Name	*E.9*	**Location**	Baltic, 10 miles S of Helsingfors,
Class	*E* class submarine		near Grohara Lighthouse
Built	29 November 1913	**Cause**	Scuttled
CO	None appointed	**Casualties**	None

Notes   Scuttled with *E.1*. *E.9* had formerly been commanded by Commander Max Horton and her operations had been so effective that the Germans had named the Baltic '*Hortonsee*'.

Name	*E.19*	**Location**	Baltic, 10 miles S of Helsingfors,
Class	*E* class submarine		near Grohara Lighthouse
Built	13 May 1915	**Cause**	Scuttled
CO	None appointed	**Casualties**	None

Notes   Scuttled with *E.1*.

4 April 1918

Name	*E.8*	**Location**	Baltic, 10 miles S of Helsingfors,
Class	E class submarine		near Grohara Lighthouse
Built	30 October 1913	**Cause**	Scuttled
CO	None appointed	**Casualties**	None

Notes   Scuttled with *E.1*. *E.8* had formerly been commanded by Commander Francis Goodhart who was killed in *K.13* (*q.v.*). On 23 October 1915 she had sunk the German cruiser *Prinz Adalbert*. The scuttling charges set on the 3rd failed to fire so she was left overnight and sunk the next day with the C class boats.

Name	*C.26*	**Location**	Baltic, 10 miles S of Helsingfors,
Class	C class submarine		near Grohara Lighthouse
Built	20 March 1909	**Cause**	Scuttled
CO	None appointed	**Casualties**	None

Notes   On 4 April the three C class submarines were towed out to the same location. *C.26* was secured alongside *E.8* and both were destroyed in the same explosion.

5 April 1918

Name	*C.35*	**Location**	Baltic, 10 miles S of Helsingfors,
Class	C class submarine		near Grohara Lighthouse
Built	2 November 1909	**Cause**	Scuttled
CO	None appointed	**Casualties**	None

Notes   *C.35* had been towed out with *C.26*, but as with *E.8* the charges failed to explode and she was left until the 5th and sunk with *C.27*.

Name	*C.27*	**Location**	Baltic, 10 miles S of Helsingfors,
Class	C class submarine		near Grohara Lighthouse
Built	22 April 1909	**Cause**	Scuttled
CO	None appointed	**Casualties**	None

Notes   The failure of the explosive charges in *E.8* and *C.35* caused the British to adopt a different procedure for the last two boats. Each was trimmed down by the bow, the fore hatch was opened and then the bow caps and rear doors of the two bow torpedo tubes were opened. As water rushed into the submarines, the scuttling parties fled up the conning tower ladders to safety.

8 April 1918

Name	*Bittern*	**Cause**	Collision
Class	C class destroyer	**Survivors**	None
Location	English Channel, off Portland		

Notes   In thick fog the SS *Kenilworth* collided with *Bittern* off Portland.

12 April 1918

Name	*CMB.18A*	**Cause**	Collision
Class	CMB	**Casualties**	None
Location	English Channel	**Survivors**	5

Notes   The first attack on Zeebrugge and Ostende took place on the night of 11 April. However, the operation was aborted when the wind dropped and shifted, as this would have deprived the British ships of the benefits of a smokescreen. In the manoeuvring associated with a 16-point turn carried out in pitch darkness, the low-lying *CMB.18* was run down by another vessel and was sunk.

Name	*CMB.33A*	**Cause**	Grounded
Class	CMB	**Casualties**	None
Location	English Channel, off Ostende	**Survivors**	5

Notes   *CMB.33* had run aground on shoals near the entrance to the harbour at Ostende. Her commanding officer had disobeyed instructions that confidential documents were not to be taken to sea. He then neglected to destroy either the documents or his boat with the result that the Germans were able to learn that an attack was planned on Ostende and much else besides. However, other than issuing an order for increased vigilance along the coast, the German command did not profit much from this unexpected intelligence windfall.

23/24 APRIL 1918: THE ATTACK ON ZEEBRUGGE

The plan called for the sinking of blockships in the harbour entrances of the ports of Zeebrugge in order to deny the Germans the use of these ports as a base for destroyers and submarines. The old cruisers Thetis, Intrepid *and* Iphigenia *were selected for Zeebrugge. Here the harbour entrance was protected by a long curving mole which the Germans had extensively fortified. In order to capture the mole the cruiser* Vindictive *and the Mersey ferries* Iris *and* Daffodil *were fitted out as assault ships carrying 700 Royal Marines and 200 armed sailors. They were to come alongside the seaward side of the mole and disembark their troops from specially hinged ramps. The last element in the plan was to blow up the viaduct linking the mole to the shore, using two old C class submarines packed with explosive, and thereby prevent the Germans from reinforcing the mole.*

23 April 1918

Name	*C.3*	**Location**	Belgian coast, port of Zeebrugge
Class	*C* class submarine	**Cause**	Expended
Built	3 October 1906	**Casualties**	None
CO	Lt R. Sandford RN	**Survivors**	6

Notes   Although the submarines *C.1* and *C.3* were selected for destruction in the operation, *C.1* dropped out leaving *C.3* to proceed alone. While the German guards' attention was diverted by the severe fighting at the other end of the mole, where *Vindictive* and her two consorts were putting the troops ashore in the face of severe opposition, *C.3*, packed with 5 tons of explosive, crashed into the viaduct and became wedged firm in its supports. Sandford and his crew of five now set the fuses and abandoned the submarine using a small motor boat that had been lashed to the conning tower. Unfortunately, as the boat was being dropped into the sea, the propeller was dashed against the submarine's side and the shaft snapped. The boat had to be rowed to safety as

The mole at Zeebrugge, showing the gap made in it by the explosion of HM Submarine *C.3*, 23 April 1918. (US Navy).

the German guards fired on it, wounding three of the crew. All five men were subsequently picked up by a motor launch. *C.3* exploded on time, just as a company of German infantry, mounted on bicycles, were crossing the viaduct. A seaman in HMS *Iphigenia* remembered seeing a German soldier, still sitting astride his machine, frantically pedalling as he sailed through the air before turning a complete somersault and hitting the water!

Sandford was awarded the Victoria Cross for the operation. On 23 November 1918, just seven months later, he died of typhoid in a Yorkshire hospital.

Name	*Thetis*	**CO**	Cdr F. Sneyd RN
Class	*Apollo* class cruiser	**Location**	Belgian coast, port of Zeebrugge
Built	13 December 1890	**Cause**	Expended as blockship

Notes The Germans were so occupied with *Vindictive* and the fighting on the mole that *Thetis* and her two consorts were able to come level with the mole before they were sighted. All three ships were fired on but the Germans seemed to concentrate on *Thetis*, the lead ship. She was repeatedly holed on her starboard side, swept to port by the tide and then became entangled with anti-submarine nets. Commander Sneyd fought to keep her on course but the ship was losing power – her interiors were shot to pieces by German gunfire and she grounded on the port side of the channel before she reached the harbour entrance. Once aground her gunners continued to man the three surviving 6 in guns and cheered *Intrepid* and *Iphigenia* on as they swept by. However, Engineer Lieutenant-Commander Ronald Boddie succeeded in restoring power on the starboard engine and slowly *Thetis* was manoeuvred into the middle of the channel where Sneyd fired the scuttling charges.

Name	*Intrepid*	**Location**	Belgian coast, port of Zeebrugge
Class	*Apollo* class cruiser	**Cause**	Expended as blockship
Built	20 June 1891	**Survivors**	87
CO	Lt S.S. Bonham-Carter RN		

Notes   *Intrepid* steamed into the harbour almost unnoticed as the Germans concentrated on the unfortunate *Thetis*. Bonham-Carter brought his ship successfully into the canal but when he tried to swing across the canal mouth, he found that the sides had been inefficiently dredged and that *Intrepid* was grounding fore and aft as he worked her engines furiously to get the vessel across the canal before he scuttled her. He was partially successful but was then rammed by *Iphigenia* coming up astern, which had the effect of pushing *Intrepid* back into the middle of the canal. Bonham-Carter then blew the scuttling charges and *Intrepid* sank.

Name	*Iphigenia*	**CO**	Lt E.W. Billyard-Leake RN
Class	*Apollo* class cruiser	**Location**	Belgian coast, port of Zeebrugge
Built	19 November 1891	**Cause**	Expended as blockship

Notes   *Iphigenia* was the last of the blockships. Following her collision with *Intrepid*, Billyard-Leake also had to work her engines furiously to get the *Iphigenia* across the canal. He too was frustrated by the accumulated silt on the sides of the canal but when satisfied, he blew the charges and abandoned the ship. His crew, and that of *Intrepid*, were taken off by motor launches.

Sub-Lieutenant M. Lloyd of *Iphigenia* had been mortally wounded in the attack and was hastily evacuated back to the UK. Lloyd had proudly borne *Iphigenia*'s ensign away so that it would not be taken by the Germans but strips from the flag had to be used to bind his wounds. Neither Lloyd nor another officer, Lieutenant Keith Wright, from one of the motor launches, was expected to live long. Acting on urgent representations from Keyes, King George V granted the immediate award of the Distinguished Service Cross to both officers without waiting for formal recommendations to arrive in the usual way. Lloyd died of his wounds but Wright survived to collect his medal.

24 April 1918

Name	*North Star*	**Location**	Belgian coast, port of Zeebrugge
Class	*M* class destroyer	**Cause**	Scuttled after damage from shore
Built	9 November 1916		battery gunfire
CO	Lt Cdr K.C. Helyar RN		

Notes   During the attack on Zeebrugge, HMS *North Star* had lost touch with her consorts, *Warwick* and *Phoebe*, and while running south-west down the Belgian coast found herself inside the sweep of the mole at Zeebrugge. She tore out of the harbour at full speed, firing all four torpedoes at German destroyers anchored on the inside of the mole but as she passed the end of the mole at 0125 hrs on the 24th, she was hit in the engine room and boiler room by two salvoes fired at incredibly close range. She lay stopped in the water less than 400 yards from the mole and was fired on by the Germans.

The destroyer *Phoebe* laid a smokescreen which effectively concealed both ships and tried to take *North Star* under tow; however, the tow parted and the smoke cleared, leaving both ships cruelly exposed. Further attempts at salvage were hopeless, so after taking off *North Star*'s survivors, *Phoebe* scuttled her with a torpedo.

Although German destroyers and U-boats continued to use the port of Zeebrugge, the operation had been worth it. The casualty list was enormous: 170 dead, 400 wounded and 45 missing, together with a destroyer and two motor launches sunk as well as the three blockships. Nevertheless for once the Navy was seen to be acting on the offensive, instead of reacting to German initiatives. Keyes was created KCB and eleven Victoria Crosses were awarded. It was a thrilling success which came at just the right time, soon after the German spring offensive on the western front. As Keyes had rightly said, 'we will accomplish a good deal for the credit of the Service and give the enemy a bad night'.

23/24 APRIL 1918: THE ATTACK ON OSTENDE

Ostende was selected for blocking for the same reasons as Zeebrugge. In this operation, because the approach to the harbour mouth was comparatively simple, only two cruisers, Sirius *and* Brilliant, *were used as blockships and there were no covering forces.*

23 April 1918

Name	*Brilliant*	CO	Cdr A.E. Godsal RN
Class	*Apollo* class cruiser	Location	Belgian coast, port of Ostende
Built	24 June 1891	Cause	Expended as blockship

Notes   See the entry for HMS *Sirius* below.

Name	*Sirius*	CO	Lt Cdr H.N. Hardy RN
Class	*Apollo* class cruiser	Location	Belgian coast, port of Ostende
Built	27 October 1890	Cause	Expended as blockship

Notes   The attack on Ostende was a complete disaster. The wind shifted suddenly, sweeping away the smokescreens and revealing the calcium flare buoys laid by the British to mark the route to the harbour entrance. The flare buoys were shot out by German gunfire making the approach route very indistinct. To add to the confusion the Germans (possibly as a result of the intelligence gleaned from *CMB.33*) had shifted the light buoy that marked the harbour entrance a mile to the east. Both blockships were fired on by the German batteries and both were badly damaged. In the confusion *Brilliant* slowed to a stop and *Sirius* ran into her, driving her aground. There was nothing either Godsal or Hardy could do but evacuate the crews by motor launch and scuttle their ships.

25 April 1918

Name	*Cowslip*	Location	Mediterranean, off Cape Spartel
Class	*Anchusa* class sloop	Cause	Submarine attack
Built	19 October 1917		

Notes   No further details are known.

Name	*TB.90*	**Built**	1892
Class	140 ft torpedo boat	**Location**	Atlantic, W of Gibraltar
		Cause	Foundered in heavy weather

Notes   No further details are known.

28 April 1918

Name	*CMB.39B*	**Built**	1918
Class	CMB	**Location**	English Channel
		Cause	Accident

Notes   *CMB.39B* burned out following a petrol fire.

5 May 1918

Name	*Rhododendron*	**Built**	5 October 1917
Class	*Anchusa* class sloop	**Location**	North Sea
		Cause	Submarine attack

Notes   No further details are known.

7 May 1918

Name	*CMB.10*	**Built**	1918
Class	CMB	**Location**	English Channel
		Cause	Accident

Notes   *CMB.10* burned out following a petrol fire.

10 May 1918

Name	*Vindictive*	**CO**	Cdr A.E. Godsal RN
Class	*Arrogant* class cruiser	**Location**	Belgian coast, port of Ostende
Built	9 December 1897	**Cause**	Expended as blockship

Notes   The battered *Vindictive* which had survived the ordeal alongside the mole at Zeebrugge was selected for use as a blockship in the second attack on Ostende. *Vindictive* had difficulty in finding the harbour entrance and when she did so she came under heavy fire. At this critical moment Godsal and his navigator were killed. Owing to the fact that her port propeller had been damaged at Zeebrugge (and not repaired) she would not answer the helm and crashed up against the pier on the eastern side of the harbour entrance and remained there, leaving the channel completely clear. There the scuttling charges were blown and her crew taken off by motor launch.

Her battered remains were still visible along the eastern pier at the end of the war. Her wreck was raised on 16 August 1920 and subsequently broken up.

14 May 1918

Name	*Phoenix*	**Location**	Mediterranean, Straits of Otranto
Class	*Acheron* class destroyer	**Cause**	Submarine attack
Built	9 October 1911		

Notes   HMS *Phoenix* has the unlucky distinction of being the only warship to be sunk while supporting the Otranto Barrage, and the only British warship to be sunk by the Austrian Navy. At 1135 hrs she was torpedoed by the Austrian *U27* (*Linienschiffsleutnant* Josef Holub), which was homeward bound to Cattaro following a Mediterranean patrol.

23 May 1918

Name	*Moldavia*	**Cause**	Submarine attack
Class	AMC	**Casualties**	Crew + 56 US soldiers
Location	English Channel, off Beachy Head		

Notes   HMS *Moldavia* was operating in the dual role of commissioned warship and troop transport, carrying US troops to Europe. She was torpedoed by *U57* while escorting convoy *HC.1*.

31 May 1918

Name	*Fairy*	**Location**	North Sea, 53 57'N, 00 09'E
Class	B class destroyer	**Cause**	Ramming
Built	1897	**Casualties**	None

Notes   *Fairy* was escorting an east coast convoy that was attacked by *UC75*. The U-boat was located by the steamer *Blaydonian*, which tried to ram but instead scraped over the submarine's casing. Badly damaged in the encounter *UC75* came to the surface and found herself in the middle of the convoy. The CO of the destroyer HMS *Fairy* could not believe that a U-boat had appeared in the middle of his convoy; he assumed that the boat was British and offered the challenge then in force. When no reply was received he rammed the U-boat's stern on the basis that if she was a British boat, all the crew would be able to get out. There was evidently a certain amount of confusion in the submarine for one man in the conning tower indicated that the U-boat was surrendering while others manned the deck gun. *Fairy* then came around for a second deliberate ramming, striking *UC75* between the deck gun and the conning tower. Two of *UC75*'s crew simply jumped from the casing on to *Fairy*'s forecastle where they stood with their hands raised in surrender. Another twelve were picked up from the water.

   Fairy's bows were badly damaged in the two rammings. Launched in 1897, she had just sunk an opponent one and a half times her size and considerably more stoutly built. Damage control could not stem the water pouring into her shattered bows and she eventually sank.

13 June 1918

Name	*Patia*	**Location**	Bristol Channel
Class	AMC	**Cause**	Submarine attack
CO	Capt W.G. Howard	**Casualties**	16

Notes   No further details are known.

28 June 1918

Name	*D.6*	**Location**	Atlantic, off W coast of Ireland
Class	D class submarine	**Cause**	Submarine attack
Built	23 October 1911	**Casualties**	25
CO	Lt S.A. Brooks RN	**Survivors**	None

Notes   *D.6* was attacked and sunk by *U73*.

9 July 1918

Name	*CMB.2*	**Built**	1918
Class	CMB	**Location**	English Channel
		Cause	Accident

Notes *CMB.2* burned out following a petrol fire.

10 July 1918

Name	*Anchusa*	**Built**	21 April 1917
Class	*Anchusa* class sloop	**Location**	N coast of Ireland
		Cause	Submarine attack

Notes No further details are known.

19 July 1918

Name	*CMB.50*	**Built**	1918
Class	CMB	**Location**	English Channel
		Cause	Scuttled

Notes The circumstances of *CMB.50*'s loss are unclear.

20(?) July 1918

Name	*E.34*	**Location**	North Sea, exact position unknown
Class	*E* class submarine	**Casualties**	30
Built	27 January 1917	**Survivors**	None
CO	Lt R.I. Pulleyne RN		

Notes The most likely cause of *E.34*'s loss was that she was mined in a British minefield off the Dutch coast. *E.34* was probably out of position, submarine navigation at the time being a very 'rough and ready' business. The submarine was evidently mined while on the surface because the bodies of Lieutenant Pulleyne and the submarine's coxswain, both wearing outdoor clothing and seaboots, were later washed up on the West Friesian islands. Both men were buried locally. Lieutenant Pulleyne was the only survivor from *B.2*'s collision with *Amerika* in 1912 (see p. 6). Other bodies from *E.34* were also washed ashore and are now buried in the British military cemetery in Hamburg.

23 July 1918

Name	*Marmora*	**Location**	Atlantic, W coast of Ireland
Class	AMC	**Cause**	Submarine attack
CO	Capt W.E. Woodward DSO RN	**Casualties**	10

Notes No further details are known.

24 July 1918

Name	*Pincher*	**Location**	Seven Stones
Class	*Beagle* class destroyer	**Cause**	Wrecked
Built	15 March 1910		

Notes HMS *Pincher* was wrecked on the Seven Stones rocks in bad weather.

The crew of HM Submarine *E.34*, photographed at Harwich shortly before the submarine was sunk in July 1918. Lieutenant Pulleyne, her commanding officer (shown on the right on the conning tower) had been the only survivor from *B.2*, rammed and sunk in 1912. (US Navy)

August 1918 *On 11 August striking demonstrations took place of the capabilities of naval air power. On the same day that a Sopwith Camel took off from a lighter towed by the destroyer* Redoubt *of the Harwich Force and shot down the Zeppelin L.53 over Terschelling, the German Naval Air Force delivered a more telling display of the effectiveness of air power, sinking three out of a force of six British CMBs and damaging two others so severely that they had to be towed into Dutch harbours. Pearl Harbor was twenty-three years away but naval air power had arrived. There were lessons here for those who chose to see them.*

2 August 1918

Name	*Vehement*	**Location**	North Sea
Class	*V* class destroyer	**Cause**	Mine
Built	6 July 1917		

Notes On 1 August 1918 the 20th Destroyer Fleet sailed from the Humber to lay a minefield at the seaward end of one of the German-swept channels through their minefield in the Heligoland Bight. All was going to plan and the force was within 20 miles of its objective when, at 2347 hrs, *Vehement* struck a mine which exploded her forward magazine and blew off the whole forward section of the ship forward of the forward funnel. *Vehement* was taken in tow by *Abdiel* and after an hour or so, and when all fires had been extinguished, there seemed every hope of saving the ship. However, at 0400 hrs on the 2nd *Vehement*'s stern suddenly rose into the air and it was clear that the tow could not be continued. After all hull valves had been opened and the survivors taken off, *Vehement* was sunk by gunfire from *Telemachus* and *Vanquisher*.

Name	*Ariel*	**Built**	26 September 1911
Class	*Acheron* class destroyer	**Location**	North Sea
		Cause	Mine

Notes *Ariel* was the second victim of the 20th Destroyer Flotilla's sortie into the Bight. While trying to manoeuvre clear of the minefield she also struck a mine. Her bows were blown clean away and she sank in less than 50 minutes. Her survivors were rescued by HMS *Vanoc*.

6 August 1918

Name	*Comet*	**Built**	23 June 1910
Class	*Acorn* class destroyer	**Location**	Mediterranean
		Cause	Submarine attack

Notes No further details are known.

11 August 1918

Name	*CMB.40*	**Location**	North Sea
Class	CMB	**Cause**	Air attack

Name	*CMB.42*	**Name**	*CMB.47*
Class	CMB	**Class**	CMB
Location	North Sea	**Location**	North Sea
Cause	Air attack	**Cause**	Air attack

Notes These three vessels were part of a force of six CMBs escorted across the North Sea by cruisers of the Harwich Force. When the British force reached a point 25 miles north of the island of Vlieland the CMBs were detached. They had orders to cross the minefields, their shallow draft giving them immunity, and torpedo any German ships found at the mouth of the River Ems. The CMBs should have had air cover but there was no wind that morning and the seaplanes due to escort them could not take off.

The CMBs stayed outside Dutch waters and had just passed Terschelling when they were attacked by six, later eight, German flying boats, Brandenburg W.12 and W.28 types and Friedrichshafen FF.49C types, from the Borkum Naval Air Station. The six CMBs closed up to concentrate the defensive fire of their .303 Lewis guns but when they turned to the west to rejoin the Harwich Force the German seaplanes suddenly had the sun behind them. The original eight seaplanes were now joined by five more from Nordeney to complete the rout. The CMBs *40, 42* and *47* sank, riddled with bullets. Two more drifted into Dutch waters and were taken in tow by the Dutch Navy who had observed the entire operation. Only *CMB.41* survived.

15 August 1918

Name	*Ulleswater*	**Location**	North Sea, off the coast of Holland
Class	R class destroyer	**Cause**	Submarine attack
Built	4 August 1917		

Notes *Ulleswater* was torpedoed by *UC17*.

Name	*Scott*	**Location**	North Sea
Class	*Scott* class destroyer flotilla leader	**Cause**	Submarine attack
Built	18 October 1917		

Notes *Scott* probably sank as the result of a torpedo attack by the German *UC17*.

8 September 1918

Name	*Nessus*	**Location**	North Sea
Class	M class destroyer	**Cause**	Collision
Built	24 August 1915		

Notes HMS *Nessus* was lost following a collision with HMS *Ampithrite* in thick fog.

16 September 1918

Name	*Glatton*	**CO**	Cdr N.W. Diggle RN
Class	Monitor	**Location**	English Channel, port of Dover
Built	8 August 1914	**Cause**	Accident

Notes HMS *Glatton* was a coast defence battleship built for the Royal Norwegian Navy in Britain under the name *Bjorgvin* but which was purchased, along with her sister ship *Nidaros*, in January 1915. On the evening of the 16th Diggle had gone for a walk with Keyes on the cliffs above the harbour to discuss the part his ship was to play in the Army's forthcoming offensive. At 1815 hrs they were appalled to see *Glatton* blow up.

By the time the two men reached the harbour, tugs had already arrived on the scene and it was clear that the situation was serious. Huge yellow flames from *Glatton*'s midships 6 in magazine continued to shoot out of 'Q' turret, reaching as high as the mast head. Moored only 150 yards ahead at the next berth was the loaded ammunition ship *Gransha*. Even though tugs were beginning to pull her clear there was still a very real danger of her blowing up – and destroying most of the town. Keyes and Diggle boarded *Glatton* and ordered the forward magazine flooded but could not flood the after magazines and attempts to sink the ship by opening the seacocks also failed. Since it was only a matter of time before the fire reached the after magazine, Keyes ordered the destroyer *Cossack* to sink *Glatton* with a torpedo. However, two torpedoes from *Cossack* were not sufficient to defeat *Glatton*'s extensive anti-torpedo protection so the destroyer *Myngs* was ordered to fire another two torpedoes at 2015 hrs. This attack was successful for *Glatton* rolled over to starboard until her port anti-torpedo bulge was above the water. The fires were extinguished and Dover was saved from destruction.

What had caused the explosion? Any number of theories were examined but the most likely reason was the stokers' habit of heaping red hot ashes from nos 2 and 3 boilers against the after bulkhead of the boiler room, unaware that the 6 in cordite magazine lay on the other side of the bulkhead. The magazine was insulated with 5 inches of cork and ¾ inches of wood panelling. However, the insulation was compromised by rivets having been omitted from the bulkhead, allowing hot air into the magazine by virtue of the forced draught pressure in the boiler room, and by the possible presence of newspapers stuffed behind the insulation by shipyard workers – newspapers had been found in the same place in *Glatton*'s sister ship *Gorgon*, and there was no reason why *Glatton* should have been any different. Red hot ashes piled against the bulkhead could well have ignited such newspapers with hot air being supplied from the boiler room through the open rivet holes. Under these conditions the cork panelling in the magazine would have started to give off flammable gases and eventually ignited the cordite charges.

Glatton was raised in March 1926. Her hull was abandoned at the north-east end of the harbour and now lies buried under the Eastern Docks car ferry terminal.

30 September 1918

Name	*Seagull*	**Built**	1889
Class	Torpedo gunboat		

Notes No further details are known.

? October 1918

Name	*C.12*	**Location**	E coast of England, port of
Class	C class submarine		Immingham
Built	9 September 1907	**Cause**	Collision
CO	Lt N. Manley RN	**Casualties**	None
		Survivors	16

Notes *C.12* had just arrived at Immingham when her motors failed. Before they could be restarted or the submarine anchored, the tide swept her against a destroyer secured to the eastern jetty. *C.12* was holed and began to sink. Manley and First Lieutenant G.H. Sullivan RN remained in the boat after sending the other fourteen men up on to the casing. Then they sealed themselves in the conning tower, drawing the lower lid after them. They then flooded up the conning tower and escaped. *C.12* was later raised and returned to service.

3 October 1918

Name	*L.10*	**Location**	North Sea, off Terschelling
Class	L class submarine	**Cause**	Gunfire
Built	24 April 1918	**Survivors**	None
CO	Lt Cdr A.E. Whitehouse RN		

Notes *L.10* was the only member of her class to be sunk during the First World War. On 3 October she observed a force of four German destroyers, *S.33*, *S.34*, *V.28* and *V.29*. *S.34* struck a mine and sank, and the other three stopped to rescue survivors. Whitehouse promptly torpedoed *S.33* but after firing *L.10* lost her trim and broached in full view of the German destroyers. *V.28* and *V.29* lost no time in opening fire. *L.10* was hit several times and sank, leaving a large oil slick on the surface.

6 October 1918

Name	*Otranto*	**Cause**	Collision
Class	AMC	**Casualties**	351
Location	W coast of Scotland, off the Isle of Islay	**Survivors**	367

Notes HMS *Otranto* collided with the P&O liner *Kashmir* in thick fog. She then drifted ashore on Islay and was wrecked.

15 October 1918

Name	*CMB.71 A*	**Location**	English Channel, off the Belgian coast, exact position unknown
Class	CMB	**Cause**	Foundered

Notes No further details are known.

Name	*J.6*	**Location**	North Sea, between the Firth of Forth and Blyth
Class	*J* class submarine		
Built	9 September 1915	**Cause**	Gunfire
CO	Lt Cdr G. Warburton RN	**Casualties**	29
		Survivors	15

Notes On 15 October 1918 the Q-ship *Cymric* was on patrol in the North Sea between the Firth of Forth and Blyth where a U-boat had been reported. It was a busy day for *Cymric*'s crew, for two submarines had already been sighted but identified as friendly. Just after 1600 hrs a third submarine was sighted which was identified as an enemy boat. One of the factors in the decision was that the submarine appeared to have a large white 'U' painted on her conning tower. The ensign flown by the submarine could not be made out, but it would not have made any difference to *Cymric*'s commanding officer as he had once been deceived by a U-boat masquerading under the white ensign. In any case the white ensign and the war ensign of the Imperial German Navy looked remarkably similar when viewed from a distance.

    Cymric's 4 in guns had been tracking the submarine and when the order to open fire was given, the submarine was engaged at point-blank range. The very first shell was on target. Meanwhile men on the submarine were trying to make a recognition signal. An officer trying to fire a rifle grenade was killed while another emerged from the fore hatch waving a white tablecloth. *Cymric* ceased fire but when the submarine altered course and headed for a fog bank, *Cymric*'s captain believed he was being fooled again, so headed after her, continuing to fire until the submarine was lost to sight in the fog.

    Cymric went after her into the fog and was rewarded when the fog lifted and the submarine was seen ahead in a sinking condition. Only a small part of the conning tower was visible, while the bows were well out of the water. Some of the crew had boarded a small collapsible boat while others floundered in the water. When the collapsible drew alongside the Q-ship, it was noticed that all the men wore cap tallies inscribed HM Submarines. Rescue work now began with a will, with many of *Cymric*'s crew diving into the icy water to support the survivors until they could be rescued.

    The submarine that had identified the *Cymric* as a German vessel was the *J.6* – her error hardly surprising given that *Cymric* was disguised to allay the suspicions of the most hard-bitten U-boat commander. The 'U' on *J.6*'s conning tower was made up by something hanging down from the conning tower and completing the loop of the 'J'. This was a tragic case of mutual misidentification, but it was asking for trouble to have a Q-ship and a submarine operational in the same area.

20 October 1918

Name	*M.21*	**Cause**	Mine
Class	*M* class monitor	**Casualties**	5
Built	27 May 1915	**Survivors**	64
Location	English Channel, off Ostende		

Notes   *M.21* was operating off Ostende when she ran into a minefield laid by the Germans shortly before they evacuated the port. It may have been a minefield of the type that ensnared *Tornado*, *Torrent* and *Surprise* in 1917 for at 1735 hrs *M.21* was shaken by two massive explosions which destroyed the forward part of the ship. She could still steam so she was brought back to Dover but sank a mile from the West Pier.

28 October 1918

Name	*Ulysses*	**Location**	W coast of Scotland, Firth of Clyde
Class	*R* class destroyer	**Cause**	Collision
Built	24 March 1917		

Notes   HMS *Ulysses* was sunk in collision with SS *Ellerie* in thick fog in the Clyde.

1(?) November 1918

Name	*G.7*	**Location**	North Sea
Class	*G* class submarine	**Casualties**	30
Built	4 March 1916	**Survivors**	None
CO	Lt C.A.C. Russell RN		

HMS *Britannia*, the last British battleship to be sunk in the First World War. On 9 November 1918 she was torpedoed by off Cape Trafalgar by *UB50* (*Leutnant zur See* Heinrich Kukat). (US Navy)

Notes   There is no explanation for the loss of *G.7* and it must be presumed that she was either mined or the victim of an accident. She was the last of fifty-nine British submarines to be lost during the First World War.

5 November 1918

Name	*Campania*	**Location**	E coast of Scotland, Firth of Forth
Class	Seaplane carrier	**Cause**	Collision
Built	8 September 1893	**Casualties**	None

Notes   HMS *Campania* was a former Cunard liner which had been taken up from trade and converted as a seaplane/kite balloon carrier. On 5 November she was at anchor in the Firth of Forth when in heavy weather she dragged her anchor, drifted across the bows of the battleship HMS *Revenge* and subsequently foundered.

9 November 1918

Name	*Britannia*	**Location**	Atlantic, W of Gibraltar
Class	*King Edward VII* class battleship	**Cause**	Submarine attack
Built	10 December 1904		

Notes   At 0715 hrs on 9 November *Britannia* was approaching Gibraltar from the west when she was attacked by *UB50* (*Leutnant zur See* Heinrich Kukat) which was homeward bound to Germany from the Mediterranean. One of Kukat's three torpedoes missed but the other two struck amidships and set off a large quantity of cordite. *Britannia* stayed afloat for 3½ hours and her secondary armament repeatedly fired on Kukat's periscope as he observed the results of his handiwork.

At 1100 hrs on 11 November 1918 hostilities with Germany came to an end and the Armistice came into effect. Hostilities with Turkey had ended on 30 October and an armistice with Austria-Hungary had been signed on 4 November. The First World War was over.

LOSSES NOVEMBER 1918– AUGUST 1939

NOVEMBER 1918 – LOSSES AFTER THE ARMISTICE

22 November 1918

Name	*G.11*	**Location**	North Sea, near the village of
Class	*G* class submarine		Howick
Built	22 February 1916	**Cause**	Grounded
CO	Lt Cdr G.F. Bradshaw RN	**Casualties**	2
		Survivors	29

Notes *G.11* grounded south of Craster coastguard station while returning to harbour from patrol in foggy weather. Bradshaw estimated that he was still some 16 miles from land but just after 1830 hrs *G.11* ran aground on rocks at a speed of 9 knots, forcing her bow clear of the water. Tremendous damage was done to her hull by the impact: most of the keel was torn away from the pressure hull.

Bradshaw saw that the submarine was in danger of capsizing and ordered the crew up on to the casing. First Lieutenant C.A. Smith RN then went over the bow with a rope and made his way ashore, using the rope to establish a handhold for the rest of the crew. While Bradshaw remained on the conning tower, the rest of *G.11*'s crew went over the bow and clambered ashore using the rope Smith had laid out. Two of the crew, Telegraphist G.P. Back and Stoker P. Foster, were drowned but the rest of the crew got ashore safely and were put up in local houses. Bradshaw was the last to leave the submarine at 1930 hrs.

December 1918 *No sooner had the First World War finished than the Royal Navy found itself involved in operations in the Baltic, supporting the White Russian forces against the Bolsheviks and dealing with the many different 'private armies' that had grown up in the Baltic States following the collapse of German and Imperial Russian authority. Although no formal state of hostilities existed, it was nevertheless a 'hot' war and would eventually cost the Navy a brand-new light cruiser, a destroyer, a submarine, two monitors and a number of smaller craft.*

5 December 1918

Name	*Cassandra*	**Location**	Baltic, Gulf of Finland
Class	*Caledon* class cruiser	**Cause**	Mine
Built	25 November 1916	**Casualties**	11
CO	Capt E.C. Kennedy RN	**Survivors**	333

Notes *Cassandra*, named after the unlucky daughter of King Priam of Troy, had the shortest career of the four ships in her class. Commissioned in June 1917, her service life lasted just under 1½ years. On 5 December she was operating in the Gulf of Finland when she struck a mine and sank.

4 June 1919

Name	*L.55*	**Location**	Baltic, Gulf of Finland
Class	*L* class submarine	**Casualties**	42
Built	21 September 1918	**Survivors**	None
CO	Lt C.M. Chapman DSC RN		

Notes   *L.55* was operating far up the Gulf of Finland between Caporski Bay and Bjorka Bay when she was sunk. It is still not clear as to whether she was mined or sunk by the Soviet destroyers *Gavril* and *Azard*. In August 1928 her hull was raised and the submarine repaired and subsequently commissioned into the Soviet Navy. The bodies of the forty-two officers and ratings were returned to Britain and now lie together in one grave at the Royal Navy cemetery at Haslar.

24 June 1919

Name	*Sword Dance*	**Location**	Russia, Dvina River
Class	*Dance* class minesweeper	**Cause**	Mine
Built	1917		

Notes   *Sword Dance* was mined during clearance operations on the Dvina River.

3 July 1919

Name	*Fandango*	**Location**	Russia, Dvina River
Class	*Dance* class minesweeper	**Cause**	Mine
Built	1917		

Notes   *Fandango* was mined during clearance operations on the Dvina River.

16 July 1919

Name	*Myrtle*	**Location**	Baltic, Gulf of Finland
Class	*Azalea* class sloop	**Cause**	Mine
Built	11 October 1915		

Notes   *Myrtle* was mined during clearance operations on the Dvina River.

Name	*Gentian*	**Location**	Baltic, Gulf of Finland
Class	*Arabis* class sloop	**Cause**	Mine
Built	23 December 1915		

Notes   *Gentian* was mined during clearance operations in the Gulf of Finland.

September 1919 *saw the British trying to extricate themselves from Russia. The White Russian forces were unreliable and following a mutiny by White Russian troops in July, the decision was taken to withdraw. However, the ships in the Dvina had to wait until September for the level of the river to rise sufficiently to allow them to clear the sandbars and reach Archangel. However, it proved impossible to get two monitors away and they had to be abandoned.*

1 September 1919

Name	*Vittoria*	**Location**	Baltic
Class	*V* class destroyer	**Cause**	Submarine attack
Built	1 September 1919		

Notes HMS *Vittoria* was attacked and sunk by the Soviet submarine *Pantera*.

16 September 1919

Name	*M.25*	**Location**	Russia, Dvina River
Class	*M* class monitor	**Cause**	Scuttled
Built	24 July 1915	**Casualties**	None

Notes See the entry for *M.27* below.

Name	*M.27*	**Location**	Russia, Dvina River
Class	*M* class monitor	**Cause**	Scuttled
Built	8 September 1915	**Casualties**	None

Notes It proved impossible to lighten *M.25* and *M.27* sufficiently to enable them to clear the sandbars. Efforts were made to blast a channel through the sandbars for them but when this was unsuccessful, both ships were stripped of all useful equipment and then scuttled on 16 September.

18 October 1919

Name	*H.41*	**Cause**	Collision
Class	*H* class submarine	**Casualties**	None
CO	Lt Cdr N.R. Peploe RN	**Survivors**	22
Location	NE England, Port of Blyth		

Notes *H.41* was secured alongside the depot ship HMS *Vulcan* when the latter's commanding officer gave approval for a slow speed engine trial in the basin, 'forgetting' that a submarine was secured alongside. As *Vulcan* slowly went astern the suction from her propellers drew *H.41* towards her and despite the efforts of both ships' crews to keep the two apart, *Vulcan*'s propeller sliced into the submarine's starboard quarter causing massive flooding. She sank alongside. The fact that the majority of the submarine's crew were up on the casing undoubtedly prevented loss of life.

20 January 1921

Name	*K.5*	**Location**	Atlantic, WSW of the Scilly Isles,
Class	*K* class submarine		48 53'N, 08 52'W
Built	16 December 1916	**Cause**	Accident
CO	Lt Cdr J.A. Gaimes RN	**Casualties**	57
		Survivors	None

Notes On 20 January five *K* class submarines including *K.5* were participating in Atlantic fleet exercises. *K.5* was last seen at 1144 hrs diving normally; she was not seen again. That afternoon when *K.5* failed to surface a

HM Submarine *H.41* after her 'ramming' by the depot ship HMS *Vulcan*. (Author)

search was established around her last known position. A large oil slick was found together with wooden wreckage identified as coming from a *K* boat. The following morning the lid of a ditty box belonging to one of *K.5*'s crew was found.

The *K* class submarines were very difficult to handle when dived. If a large bow-down or bow-up angle developed it was difficult to rectify since the broad casing acted as an enormous hydroplane causing the boat to see-saw. With a diving depth of only 183 ft and a hull length of over 300 ft, the bow could be below crush depth in seconds if the dive was a steep one. Such was probably the fate of *K.5*.

25 June 1921

Name	*K.15*	**Location**	Port of Portsmouth, inside the tidal
Class	*K* class submarine		basin
Built	30 October 1917	**Cause**	Accident
CO	Lt Cdr G.F. Bradshaw RN	**Casualties**	None

Notes   *K.15* was undergoing a routine refit at the Royal Dockyard in Portsmouth. It was a hot day and the oil in the hydraulic system which closed the vents on the external ballast tanks had expanded. In the coolness of the evening the oil contracted, causing a loss of pressure and allowing the main vents to open slightly. The ballast tanks slowly began to fill and the submarine sank slowly by the stern. The few men on board were able to jump to the cruiser HMS *Canterbury*, secured alongside. (Most of the crew were on leave at the time of the accident.) Bradshaw was an unlucky commanding officer. Two years earlier he had lost *G.11* (see p. 84). *K.15* was subsequently raised and broken up.

23 March 1922

Name	*H.42*	**Location**	E Atlantic, off Gibraltar
Class	*H* class submarine	**Cause**	Collision
Built	5 November 1918	**Survivors**	None
CO	Lt D.C. Sealy RN		

Notes   The destroyer HMS *Versatile* (Commander V. Campbell RN) was steaming off Europa Point when *H.42* surfaced dead ahead and only 120 yards away. The submarine's number was clearly visible on the conning tower. There was no time to take avoiding action before *Versatile* cut the submarine in two, just aft of the conning tower. *H.42* sank very quickly and gave up no survivors.

8 August 1922

Name	*Raleigh*	**Cause**	Grounding
Class	*Cavendish* class cruiser	**Casualties**	None
Built	28 August 1919	**Survivors**	712
Location	Belleisle Strait, off the coast of Labrador		

Notes   In bad weather *Raleigh* grounded on Point Armour in the Belleisle Strait. Salvage operations succeeded in recovering a large amount of equipment but it proved impossible to refloat the wreck. *Raleigh*'s remains were blown up in 1927 by a party from HMS *Calcutta*.

29 August 1922

Name	*ML.196*	**Cause**	Accident
Class	Motor launch	**Casualties**	None
Built	1916	**Survivors**	8
Location	River Danube, city of Poszony (now Bratislava)		

Notes   *ML.196* was the last survivor of the nine MLs that had been sent to the Danube in 1918. On the evening of the 29th she and the gunboat *Glowworm* had anchored at Poszony and most of the crews of both vessels had gone ashore. At 2300 hrs the alarm was raised when smoke was seen rising from the ML's engine room. It proved impossible to control the fire so the ML was veered astern and allowed to drift into mid-river where she later capsized and sank. The Austrian and Hungarian press ascribed the fire to unsafe ammunition stowage and used the incident as a pretext for demanding the withdrawal of British forces from the river. However, the Royal Navy enquiry concluded that a petrol fire which had got out of control was responsible for the ML's loss. *ML.196*'s loss is notable because it must have taken place further from the sea than any other loss in this volume.

18 August 1923

Name	*L.9*	**Location**	Hong Kong harbour
Class	*L* class submarine	**Cause**	Typhoon
Built	29 January 1918	**Casualties**	None
CO	None appointed	**Survivors**	4

Notes   *L.9* was part of the Reserve Submarine Flotilla in Hong Kong and was thus not in full commission when the colony received a typhoon warning in August 1923. The safest practice was to secure the submarines to buoys in the harbour with a maintenance party of four ratings on board and let them ride out the storm. *L.9* was secured to no. 13 buoy with four ratings under the command of PO Willi Gordon.

The typhoon struck Hong Kong at 0940 hrs on the 18th and within minutes the line securing *L.9* to the buoy had parted and she was blown against the dockyard wall. Believing that the repeated pounding of the submarine against the dock wall had caused serious damage, Gordon ordered his men to abandon the submarine. *L.9* was now completely at the mercy of the elements. The wind drove her against the bows of the Japanese ship *Ginyo Maru*, despite the efforts of Lieutenant T.H. Dickson who had single-handedly boarded the submarine and tried to secure her. However, *L.9* had now suffered such damage from bumping against the wall and the *Ginyo Maru* that she was taking in massive amounts of water. Dickson felt the engine room bulkhead collapse and then had to abandon the submarine as she sank stern first.

L.9 was subsequently raised and was recommissioned, being sold locally for breaking up in 1927.

10 January 1924

Name	*L.24*	**Location**	English Channel, off Portland
Class	*L* class submarine	**Cause**	Collision
Built	19 February 1919	**Survivors**	None
CO	Lt Cdr P.L. Eddis RN		

Notes   *L.24* was accidentally rammed and sunk by the battleship HMS *Resolution* during exercises off Portland (**see** photograph overleaf).

12 November 1925

Name	*M.1*	**Location**	English Channel, 50 00'N, 03 36'W
Class	*M* class submarine	**Cause**	Collision
Built	9 July 1917	**Casualties**	69
CO	Lt Cdr A. Carrie RN	**Survivors**	None

Notes   On 12 November *M.1* was participating with four other submarines, two submarine depot ships and four minesweepers in a simulated convoy action in the English Channel. The exercises went ahead despite the presence of numerous merchant ships in the area but that evening *M.1* failed to surface or report her position, and she was presumed to have sunk.

Four days later the Swedish merchant ship *Vidar*, which had witnessed the exercises, arrived at the Kiel Canal. On hearing of *M.1*'s loss her Master reported that at 0745 hrs on the 12th he and his officers had felt a severe double shock and that *Vidar* momentarily failed to answer her helm. When she subsequently docked in Sweden, *Vidar*'s bow plates were found to be buckled and scarred with grey-green paint of the same colour and composition as the paint used on *M.1*. It was clear that as *M.1* was surfacing *Vidar*'s bow had pitched down in the

A memorial postcard produced to mark the loss of the submarine *L.24* in January 1924. Photographers in the main naval ports could produce such commemorative items within 24 hours of the event. (Author)

trough of a wave, slicing into the submarine's pressure hull. The next wave lifted *Vidar* clear but *M.1* was already on her way to the bottom. Divers found her wreck in 1967 but out of respect for those who lost their lives on board, they did not divulge the position.

The loss of *M.1* highlighted the need for accurate casualty reporting. At the time *M.1* was manned from a common pool of seamen as an economy measure. When it came to issuing the casualty notices, no one had an accurate idea of who was on board. The result was the laying down of clear guidelines about notification of who was present on a submarine and the establishment of special teams of clerks and typists who could be called upon to issue accurate reports of casualties in the event of major disasters in the future.

9 August 1926

Name	*H.29*	**Location**	Devonport dockyard
Class	*H* class submarine	**Cause**	Accident
Built	8 June 1918	**Casualties**	5 civilian workers and 1 sailor
CO	Lt F.H. Skyrme RN		

Notes   *H.29* lay secured fore and aft along the South Wall in No. 2 Basin in Devonport Dockyard for a routine refit. It was the intention to test the firing mechanism on the bow tubes and for this the submarine had to be brought down to normal trim – she was riding high in the water owing to the auxiliary tanks having been blown. First Lieutenant M.E. Wevell announced his intention to put some water into nos 2 and 3 main ballast tanks.

This 'intention' was interpreted as an order by Petty Officer George Aske who flooded both tanks, bringing the submarine down to normal trim. However, what Wevell did not notice was that every hatch on the upper deck was open and that the stern was now very low in the water. Water began to pour into the submarine through the after hatch which could not be shut owing to the presence of a 4 in ventilation pipe which had been left in the hatchway. As the civilian workmen began to abandon the submarine, Lieutenant Skyrme vainly tried to shut the after hatch and all watertight doors. The submarine sank alongside the wall.

The subsequent enquiry found that *H.29* had sunk when the flooding of no. 3 ballast tank had brought the after hatch under water. This accident is unique in that more civilian than naval personnel were killed. It has ominous similarities with the loss of HMS *Artemis* in July 1971 (see p. 258).

22 October 1926

Name	*Valerian*	**Location**	Caribbean, S of Bermuda
Class	*Arabis* class sloop	**Cause**	Foundered
Built	21 February 1916	**Casualties**	86
CO	Cdr W.J. Usher RN	**Survivors**	29

Notes   The sloop *Valerian* was on passage to Bermuda when a hurricane struck the area. At 0800 hrs she reported that she was 5 miles from the harbour but could make out neither the entrance nor any navigational marks because of wind and spray. Accordingly she turned around and sought more sea room to ride out the storm. Commander Usher subsequently reported that *Valerian*'s engines lacked sufficient power to hold the ship against wind and sea, the force of which laid the ship over on her beam ends so that water had poured down the funnels and into the boilers. She later capsized. An alternative explanation was that she grounded on a reef and was then capsized by the force of the wind and sea. The survivors were later found on a Carley float by the cruiser *Curlew*.

9 July 1929

Name	*H.47*	**Location**	Irish Sea, off the coast of
Class	*H* class submarine		Pembrokeshire
Built	19 November 1918	**Cause**	Collision
CO	Lt R.J. Gardner RN	**Casualties**	19
		Survivors	3

Notes   *H.47* was rammed by *L.12* as both boats were leaving Lamlash. *L.12* was just ahead of *H.47*'s beam and had made an alteration of course which resulted in her ramming *H.47* on the port side just forward of the conning tower. So deeply were *L.12*'s bows embedded in *H.47*'s side that she was dragged down with *H.47* until she tore herself free. One of *H.47*'s crew leapt for *L.12*'s jumping wire just before the collision and hung on for dear life. When *L.12* finally surfaced he informed them in no uncertain terms that they had just sunk *H.47*.

One of the three survivors, telegraphist Sydney Cleburne, was a lucky man. He had earlier sailed in *M.1* and had been drafted from her just 48 hours before she sailed her last voyage (see p. 89).

9 June 1931

Name	*Poseidon*	**Location**	Yellow Sea, N of Wei Hai Wei
Class	*P* class submarine	**Cause**	Collision
Built	21 June 1929	**Casualties**	21
CO	Lt Cdr B.W. Galpin RN	**Survivors**	34

Notes *Poseidon* was rammed by the Japanese merchant ship *Yuta*. *Poseidon* had surfaced at 1145 hrs and remained stationary on a course of 235°. At 1205 hrs the *Yuta* was 1,500 yards away on the port beam and steering north-west. *Poseidon* went ahead and then hard to starboard so that the *Yuta* was now on her port beam. At 1209 hrs *Yuta* suddenly altered course to starboard and rammed into the submarine, cutting a V-shaped hole in the pressure hull. The submarine sank in 130 ft of water in less than 2 minutes but twenty-nine men managed to scramble out of the conning tower and into the water where they were picked up. Eighteen men were trapped in the after ends and were unable to escape. Eight men were trapped in the fore ends under the command of Petty Officer P.W. Willis. Willis took charge and distributed the new DSEA sets and then began flooding up the compartment – a task that took over 2½ hours to achieve. When the water was up to the necks of the survivors Willis tried to force the torpedo loading hatch open; it moved and two men, Able Seamen Arthur Lovock and Edmund Holt, shot to the surface. Both were picked up although Lovock died almost immediately. It took another 45 minutes to repressurise the compartment before Willis tried the hatch again. This time all six escaped although only four reached the surface.

Lieutenant-Commander Galpin was tried by court martial for the loss of his ship and was found guilty of 'negligently or by default hazarding HMS *Poseidon*'. He was sentenced to be severely reprimanded.

11 November 1931

Name	*Petersfield*	**Location**	South China Sea, Tung Yung Island
Class	*Aberdare* class minesweeper	**Cause**	Grounding
CO	Lt D. Allen RN	**Casualties**	None

Notes HMS *Petersfield* was employed on the China Station as the CinC's despatch vessel. In November 1931 *Petersfield* was to take the CinC, Vice Admiral Sir Howard Kelly, Lady Kelly and staff, from Shanghai to Foochow. Kelly was one of the most forceful characters in the Royal Navy, a tremendously competent officer but one whose heavy sarcasm alienated those around him.

During the passage, in rough weather, *Petersfield* had collided with a buoy with sufficient force to throw Lady Kelly from her bunk and had then sighted a disabled junk, loaded with coffins, which was taken in tow but subsequently had to be abandoned in rising seas. Lieutenant Allen was extremely seasick and Kelly, a navigation specialist, helped him lay off the course he should steer. If carried to its natural conclusion the course led directly to the rocks of Tung Yung Island and Kelly assumed that *Petersfield*'s captain would take the appropriate action. A light should have been sighted at 0200 hrs, which would have indicated that a change in course was necessary. However, on this morning the light was obscured and Lieutenant Allen held to the course given him the previous evening. The result was that at 0300 hrs on 11 November *Petersfield* took the ground on Tung Yung Island as predicted. Fortunately all were got ashore, including the admiral's dog and Lady Kelly's canaries. The admiral's steward proved very resourceful and brought an enormous hamper of food ashore. All were subsequently rescued by the cruiser *Suffolk*. *Petersfield* was a total wreck and was abandoned *in situ*.

As is the custom of the Service, Lieutenant Allen had to stand trial by court martial for the loss of his ship. The case became something of a *cause célèbre* on the China Station since Admiral Kelly was, at one and the same time, the convening officer for the court martial, the chief witness for the prosecution and the officer who would review the verdict. Allen's defence was that Kelly, by helping him lay off a course, had taken *de facto* command of *Petersfield* and that therefore responsibility for the grounding was Kelly's. This defence was rejected and Allen was found guilty on two out of three counts. However, the case had aroused such passions on the Station that the Navy paid for Allen to be sent home in a P&O liner (despite an economy drive forbidding such practices) rather than have him wait around for the next UK-bound warship.

An interesting sequel to this tale concerns Kelly's turbulent relationship with his brother, Admiral Sir John Kelly. When John Kelly heard of his brother's misfortunes he cabled 'Glad you're safe' and received the reply 'Glad you're glad!'

26 January 1932

Name	*M.2*	**Location**	English Channel, off Portland,
Class	*M* class submarine		50 34'N, 02 33'W
Built	19 October 1918	**Cause**	Accident
CO	Lt Cdr J.D. de M. Leathes RN	**Casualties**	60
		Survivors	None

Notes   *M.2* was the second of the four submarines of the *M* class. Originally built to carry one 12 in gun, she had been converted between 1925 and 1927 to carry a Parnell Peto seaplane in a hangar built forward of the conning tower.

On 26 January *M.2* was exercising off Portland. She had dived just after 1000 hrs and when she had not sent a surfacing signal by 1615 hrs a search was put in hand for her. Searching for the submarine was difficult because West Bay, the area where *M.2* had been working, is littered with wrecks. Just as the Navy was beginning to become concerned about *M.2* it was reported that she had been observed diving stern first at 1130 hrs by Captain A. Howard, Master of the coaster *Tynesider*. He had thought nothing of it but had carried on with his voyage to Gravelines in France after coaling at Portland, where he had mentioned his sighting of the boat that morning. When these facts were known the destroyer *Scimitar* was sent racing across to Gravelines to obtain precise details from Captain Howard. Even with Howard's evidence it was not until 3 February that *M.2* was found lying on an even keel in 102 ft of water.

Salvage work was begun at once under the direction of Ernest Cox who had made his name by raising the ships of the German High Seas Fleet scuttled at Scapa Flow. Divers found that *M.2*'s hangar door was open, as was the access hatch from the pressure hull up to the hangar and the conning tower hatch. This discovery seemed to suggest how *M.2* had met her end. The submarine was surfacing to launch her aircraft and the order to open the hangar door had been given as soon as the conning tower was clear of the water but before the hangar door was clear. Water sloshed into the hangar, down into the pressure hull through the access hatch and into the boat, causing her to sink. However, some doubted this theory saying that if this had been the case then the submarine would not have sunk stern first, and damage to the submarine's stern and grooves on the seabed confirmed that she *had* sunk stern first.

An alternative explanation was that the vent valves to the after tanks had inadvertently been left open allowing ther tanks to start filling again once *M.2* was on the surface. When Leathes, who had gone up to the bridge, realised this, he went below to order the tanks to be blown but not before the submarine sank by the stern, allowing water to flood into the open hangar and down into the submarine. A third explanation for her loss put forward by officers who had formerly served in *M.2* was that a motor or hydroplane failure occurring while the submarine was being driven upwards in order to get the hangar clear of the water could well have turned a routine manoeuvre into a disaster. The submarine would have lost power, begun to sink back in the water and flooding would have occurred through the hangar. In both the second and third explanations, the bow-up angle of *M.2* during the surfacing would have meant that flood water would have run aft, thus accounting for the submarine sinking stern first.

The decision was taken to salvage the submarine and to this end the hangar access and conning tower hatches were sealed with quick drying cement. As the divers worked they uncovered two bodies which indicated that *M.2* had been about to launch her aircraft when she sank. On 18 March the body of Leading Seaman Albert Jacob was found in the hangar and brought to the surface. On 1 July the body of Leading Aircraftman Leslie Gregory was discovered, wearing flying overalls. Sadly, the weather and tides conspired against the salvagemen and on 7 December, after a number of lifts had failed, the operation was abandoned.

M.2 remains on the bottom off Portland. While the Navy retained a presence at Portland she was used as a bottom target for sonar operators. Her wreck has also been visited and filmed by amateur divers. However, visiting the wreck is not easy – tides and the salvage cables that still festoon her make it a dangerous experience. In 1970 a diver was killed while trying to reach *M.2*.

June 1939 *saw the loss of HMS Thetis. It was one of the most horrifying peacetime accidents to befall a British submarine. As one observer recalled, 'Never will I forget the films and photographs of the stern of* Thetis *swinging in the tide of Liverpool Bay with men doomed to die so soon and so near to apparent help.' What made the disaster almost inexplicable was that it took place within easy reach of one of the country's biggest ports and shipbuilding centres. Moreover* Thetis *herself represented the*

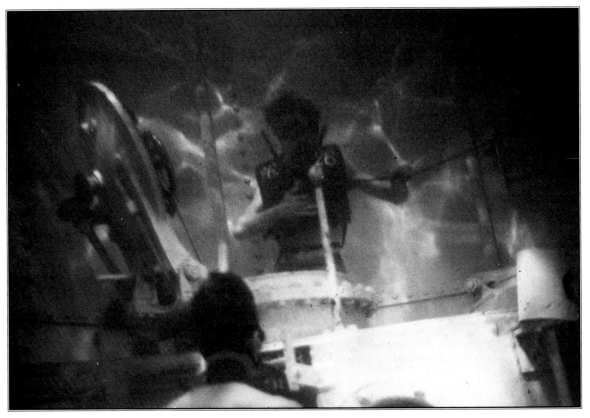

Submarine escape training using the Davis Submarine Escape Apparatus taking place in the 10 ft escape tank at HMS *Dolphin*.
The artificiality of such training is apparent. (US Navy)

latest in submarine escape technology, the lessons learned following the loss of Poseidon. *She boasted two four-man escape chambers situated at either end of the submarine which in theory would allow the crew to escape without the need to flood up whole compartments.*

1 June 1939

Name	*Thetis*	**CO**	Lt Cdr Guy Bolus RN
Class	*T* class submarine	**Location**	W coast of England, Liverpool Bay
Built	29 June 1938	**Cause**	Accident

Casualties 99. These were: 4 officers and 47 ratings of the ship's company; 4 officers from other submarines building at Cammell Laird; 4 naval officers associated with *Thetis'* construction; 7 Admiralty officials; 25 employees of Cammell Laird & Co. Ltd; 4 employees of Vickers Armstrong Ltd; 2 employees of City Caterers (Liverpool) Ltd; 1 employee of Brown Bros & Co; 1 Mersey River pilot.

Survivors 4. These were: Captain H.P. Oram RN, Captain 5th Submarine Flotilla; Lieutenant Frederick Woods RN, *Thetis'* torpedo officer; Leading Stoker Walter Arnold, HMS *Thetis*; Frank Shaw, a Cammell Laird fitter.

Notes   In essence *Thetis* was sunk because the rear door to no. 5 torpedo tube was opened while the bow cap was also open to the sea. However, the story is a good deal more complicated than that. There were four factors involved in this tragic loss. Firstly, owing to a series of errors in the construction process it was possible to open

A very rare photograph of HMS *Thetis* taken during her trials in the Gareloch, May 1939. (Author)

the rear door to no. 5 torpedo tube while the bow cap was open to the sea. Secondly, those in *Thetis* failed to shut the watertight door and expel the water from the submarine once the flooding had started. Thirdly, those inside the submarine failed to escape using DSEA sets and fourthly, those outside the submarine failed to render effective assistance.

Thetis was the first of the *T* class submarines to be built by Cammell Laird at Birkenhead and by March 1939 she was ready for her trials. Her first diving trials in the Gareloch were abandoned owing to equipment problems, so her first dive was planned to take place in Liverpool Bay on 1 June 1939. At 1400 hrs on the 1st Bolus gave the order to dive but *Thetis* was reluctant to submerge, even with all ballast and auxiliary tanks flooded and with the hydroplanes at 10° to dive. Bolus ordered a check to be made that *Thetis* was carrying all the water indicated on the trim statement. This involved checking whether nos 5 and 6 torpedo tubes were full. Since each tube held 1,600 lb of water, the weight would make the difference between *Thetis* being able to dive or not.

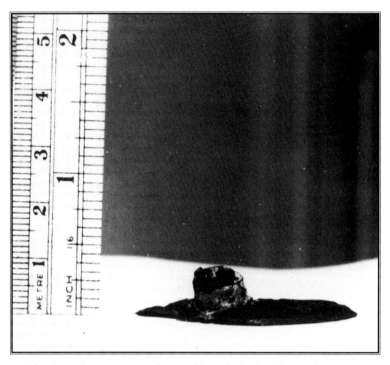

The piece of bitumastic enamel removed from the inside of the rear door to no. 5 tube which blocked the test cock, rendering it useless. (Author)

Lieutenant Frederick Woods, the torpedo officer, went forward into the tube space and used the test cock on each tube to check whether it was full or not. All proved empty except for no. 6 tube which was at least half full. However, Woods was not to know that the test cock for no. 5 tube was inoperable: when the inside of the tube door had been given a coat of enamel, the painter had omitted to plug the 'hole' of the test cock, but had simply painted over it. Woods then decided to inspect the inside of all six tubes. He inspected the bow cap indicators located between the two banks of tubes, to ensure that the bow doors were shut. Yet his inspection of the bow cap indicators was not as thorough as it should have been. When the submarine was salved the indicator for no. 5 tube was found set in the 'open' position. Yet the fault does not lie entirely with Woods. Unbelievably, the six indicators were arranged in a single vertical line in the order 1, 2, 3, 4, 6 and 5, so that the bottom indicator was for no. 5 tube. Moreover the indicator for no. 5 tube was partially obscured by a metal bar. Worse still, the relative positions for 'shut' and 'open' were different on each indicator. On that for no. 5 tube, 'shut' was at five o'clock but on the other five indicators 'shut' was at eleven o'clock. Woods probably looked down the row of indicators, saw that all six pointers lined up and assumed that all was well. In fact the bow cap indicator for no. 5 tube pointed at 'open' – all that stood between *Thetis* and the sea was the rear door of no. 5 tube **(Factor Number 1)**.

Woods then proceeded to inspect the inside of the first four torpedo tubes and found nothing amiss.

However, when Leading Seaman Hambrook tried to open the rear door to no. 5 tube he found that the lever was stiff. Flinging his full weight against the lever, Hambrook was knocked aside as the door sprang open and a 21-in thick column of water poured into the submarine.

Immediately Bolus ordered main ballast blown to bring *Thetis* to the surface. Had the flooding been confined to the tube space *Thetis* might have been saved. However, it proved impossible to shut the watertight door connecting the tube space to the fore-ends: there were four doors in this bulkhead and on this occasion three of them were already clipped shut. It proved impossible to pull this single door 'up hill' against *Thetis*' increasing bow-down angle. Moreover the door was secured by eighteen single turnbuckles, one of which was jammed. Water was now flowing into the fore-ends: if it spilled further aft there was chance it would flow into the battery and create chlorine gas. Bolus ordered this second compartment evacuated as *Thetis* bottomed in 150 ft of water. Her situation was dire: two of her six compartments were flooded and she had twice the normal number of men on board.

Bolus now tried to drain down the flooded fore-ends since with only one compartment flooded *Thetis* could surface. The plan was for one man, wearing a DSEA set, to enter the fore-ends, via the forward escape chamber. He would then go forward and close the door in the bulkhead between the tube space and the fore-ends. He would then open the two main line suction valves and ballast pumps would expel the water. Four members of *Thetis*' ship's company showed the utmost gallantry in attempting this hazardous operation but on each occasion had to give up on account of the pain caused by the pressure on their ears as the escape chamber was flooded up. **(Factor Number 2)** Bolus' next plan was to raise his submarine's stern to bring the after escape chamber nearer the surface and by morning some 18 ft of *Thetis*' stern was above the surface.

What was happening on the surface? *Thetis*' escort, the tug *Grebecock*, carried naval personnel for liaison purposes. Lieutenant R.E. Coltart, the liaison officer, had been alarmed by the sudden way in which *Thetis* had dived and by her subsequent failure to carry out any of the prearranged manoeuvres. But it was not until 1615 hrs that he sent a signal asking about the duration of *Thetis*' dive. Due to series of misfortunes Coltart's signal was not received at Fort Blockhouse until 1815 hrs. Fortunately the naval authorities were already concerned, not having received *Thetis*' surfacing signal, and Coltart's signal prompted the ordering of a major search.

At dawn on 2 June the destroyer HMS *Brazen* (Lieutenant-Commander R.H. Mills), which was *en route* for Devonport, was diverted to Liverpool Bay and found *Thetis*' stern sticking above the water. *Brazen* had in fact been searching all night but her task had been complicated by a series of false reports. No sooner had *Brazen* dropped explosive charges in the water alongside *Thetis* to indicate her arrival than two heads appeared in the water. The first two men had escaped and it looked as if all would be well.

Bolus had delayed ordering escapes until he knew that help was at hand. However, the deteriorating conditions in the submarine, in particular the growing concentration of CO_2 in the air, forced him to proceed. **(Factor Number 3)** The first two out were Captain H.P. Oram, Captain of 5th Submarine Flotilla, and Lieutenant Woods. Oram had been selected because Bolus considered that a senior submarine officer's presence on the surface would provide some specialist knowledge to the rescuers. Oram brought notes written by *Thetis*' engineer officer on how to salve the submarine. The notes included an injunction to *Brazen* 'to keep constant watch for men escaping from the after chamber'. This injunction was to have a powerful effect on the rescuers.

At 1000 hrs two more men escaped, Leading Stoker Walter Arnold and Frank Shaw, a Cammell Laird fitter. Arnold reported that conditions in the boat were now dire and that help was needed desperately. There would be no more escapes from *Thetis*. After Arnold and Shaw had left, the chamber was drained down and prepared for another escape. Unfortunately the rating working the chamber, exhausted and starved of oxygen, did not release the gearing on the upper hatch so it could not be opened from within: in effect the chamber was locked. Four men tried to use the chamber but were dragged out dead or dying, having failed to open the hatch.

The salvage vessel *Vigilant* closes *Thetis'* stern in a last desperate attempt to free those trapped inside the submarine. Moments later *Thetis* slipped beneath the waves for the last time. (Author)

Thetis' battered conning tower immediately after salvage. (Author)

Thetis' fore-ends after salvage, looking forward, showing the two doors leading forward into the tube space. At the time of the accident the starboard door was closed but it proved impossible to close the port door and secure the eighteen turnbuckles, and so stem the flow of water against *Thetis'* increasing bow down angle. The single clip at the top right was secured by *Thetis'* TGM, Petty Officer E. Mitchell, who gallantly remained in the compartment until ordered to leave. (Author)

The remains of *Thetis* beached at Moelfre Bay in Anglesey, awaiting the attentions of the Board of Enquiry. (US Navy)

Another memorial postcard, this one produced for the loss of HMS *Thetis*. Stoker Arnold's name appears, erroneously, in the second column, fourth from the top. (Author)

Sometime during the afternoon of 2 June two more desperate men entered the escape chamber. They too failed to move the hatch. But as they opened the door to return to the motor room they failed to turn off the flooding valve so that for the second time in 24 hours, *Thetis* was once more open to the sea. The inrush of water pushed up the dangerously high CO_2 level so that the ninety-nine men still in the submarine were mercifully killed by the gas before the water had risen sufficiently to drown them.

On the surface *Brazen* had since been joined by a small flotilla of craft including the salvage vessel *Vigilant*. Throughout the morning of 2 June they waited and did nothing, mindful of Bolus' injunction to keep clear of the stern. **(Factor Number 4)** By the afternoon of the 2nd, desperation drove them into action. Wreckmaster Brock clambered on to *Thetis*' stern. He hoped to be able to open a manhole to Z tank and then pass through the tank and into the steering machinery compartment. It was a bold plan but as Brock worked on the cover plate for Z tank, *Thetis* began to twist violently in the tide and he was forced to come down. Just after 1500 hrs *Vigilant* came alongside *Thetis* with the intention of cutting a hole in her stern. However, the force of the tide now proved too strong for the wires holding the two vessels and at 1510 hrs the cable parted and *Thetis* sank from sight. It was now all over and the operation became one of salvage rather than rescue.

On 23 October 1939 she was raised and returned to Birkenhead. Her salvage had cost the life of a diver, Petty Officer Harry Perdue, making the death toll one hundred. Had it been peacetime she would probably have been broken up. However, the country was now at war and *Thetis*' hull represented a £300,000 investment at a time when every boat was desperately needed. She was recommissioned under the name *Thunderbolt* (see p. 209).

LOSSES
SEPTEMBER–DECEMBER
1939

10 September 1939

Name	*Oxley*	**Location**	Norwegian Sea, off Obrestad
Class	*Oxley* class submarine	**Cause**	Submarine attack
Built	29 June 1926	**Survivors**	2
CO	Lt Cdr H.G. Bowerman RN		

Notes   The first British warship loss of the Second World War was due to friendly fire. *Oxley* was on patrol off Norway but owing to navigational error had moved into the area occupied by HMS *Triton* (Lieutenant-Commander H.P. de C. Steel RN). Shortly before 2100 hrs *Triton*, which was proceeding on the surface, sighted

Commander H.P. de C. Steel RN, commanding officer of HMS *Triton*
when she attacked and sank HMS *Oxley* on 10 September 1939.
(Author)

another submarine. Steel was cautious and ordered the challenge then in force to be given using a signal lamp. When no reply was received the challenge was repeated. Again when no reply was received Steel ordered the challenge to be repeated, using a rifle grenade. When no reply was received to this third challenge Steel ordered two torpedoes to be fired. Just after the torpedoes had been fired what was described as 'indeterminable flashing' was observed from the other submarine. It could not be read and in any case was obliterated by the explosion of *Triton*'s torpedoes. Any elation felt by *Triton*'s crew at this their first sinking quickly evaporated when the two survivors plucked from the water turned out to be Lieutenant-Commander Bowerman and Able Seaman Gluckes.

The subsequent enquiry absolved Steel of any blame in the affair – indeed Steel was congratulated for his tactical proficiency. *Oxley* had drifted to the east owing to the strong tidal sets in the area and thus out of her patrol area and into *Triton*'s. Navigational error was (and is) an ever-present hazard but in this case it was compounded by a lack of vigilance on the part of *Oxley*'s lookouts and OOW. Bowerman was only called to the bridge when *Triton*'s rifle grenade burst – by which time *Triton* had had *Oxley* under observation for some time – and then it was too late for him to influence events. Bowerman never served in submarines again, but had a distinguished war career in escort vessels.

17 September 1939

Name	*Courageous*	**Location**	Atlantic, SW of Ireland, 50 10'N, 14 45'W
Type	Aircraft carrier		
Built	5 February 1916	**Cause**	Submarine attack
CO	Capt W.T. Makeig-Jones RN	**Casualties**	518
		Survivors	742

Notes After covering the passage of the BEF to France, *Courageous* was employed in anti-submarine operations in the Western Approaches. At 2000 hrs the ship was just turning into the wind to recover aircraft when she was struck on the port side by two torpedoes fired by *U29* (*Kapitanleutnant* Otto Schuhart). Damage control parties were unable to stem the flooding and 5 minutes after the torpedo struck the order was given to abandon ship. *Courageous* sank ten minutes later. Captain Makeig-Jones was lost with his ship. Experience was to show that anti-submarine warfare was a highly specialised task and that patrolling without up-to-date intelligence in an area where U-boats were known to be operating was as unproductive as it was dangerous.

14 October 1939

Name	*Royal Oak*	**Location**	Orkney Islands, Scapa Flow
Class	*Royal Sovereign* class battleship	**Cause**	Submarine attack
		Casualties	786

Notes On the night of 13 October *U47* (*Kapitanleutnant* Gunther Prien) entered the great anchorage of Scapa Flow, German air reconnaissance having revealed the inadequacy of the booms and fixed defences of the British main base in Home Waters. Prien entered the anchorage without difficulty and at 2358 hrs fired four torpedoes at the *Royal Oak*. One torpedo struck the ship forward but the explosion was put down to an air attack or an internal explosion. At 0016 hrs Prien carried out his second attack with three torpedoes: all hit and the *Royal Oak* sank in less than 15 minutes. Prien and *U47* then withdrew to sea and a hero's welcome at Wilhelmshaven. The loss of the *Royal Oak* made little appreciable difference to the balance of naval forces in Home Waters but the attack, carried out in the heart of Scapa Flow, was an important psychological and propaganda victory for the Germans.

The wreck was subsequently covered with a net to prevent debris rising to the surface. Even so, a persistent trickle of fuel oil continues to rise to the surface, marking the last resting place of the *Royal Oak*.

November 1939 *The Luftwaffe began a minelaying campaign off the east coast of the UK in November 1939 using the newly developed magnetic mine. Lying on the sea bed in shallow water, these mines were actuated by the magnetic field present in every ship's hull. Although counter-measures were swiftly devised, the magnetic mine was to inflict a significant number of casualties throughout the war.*

13 November 1939

Name	Blanche	**Built**	29 May 1930
Class	B class destroyer	**Location**	Thames estuary, 51 29'N, 01 30'E
		Cause	Mine

Notes *Blanche* was the first vessel to be sunk by a magnetic mine during the Second World War. At the time of her loss she was escorting the minelayer *Adventure*, which had been damaged by a mine several hours earlier.

21 November 1939

Name	Gypsy	**Location**	North Sea, off Harwich, 51 57'N, 01 19'E
Class	G class destroyer		
Built	7 November 1935	**Cause**	Mine

Notes *Gypsy* was leaving Harwich when she ran over a magnetic mine laid by a German aircraft the night before. Although her crew managed to beach the ship, a survey found that her back had been broken by the explosion and that she was beyond repair.

23 November 1939

Name	Rawalpindi	**Location**	Atlantic, E of Iceland, 63 40'N, 12 31'W
Class	AMC		
Built	1925	**Cause**	Gunfire
CO	Capt E.C. Kennedy RN	**Casualties**	270
		Survivors	37

Notes *Rawalpindi* was on blockade duty when she was sighted and engaged by the German battle cruiser *Scharnhorst*. Armed with only four 6 in guns against the *Scharnhorst*'s nine 11 in guns, *Rawalpindi* conducted a heroic defence until every gun was out of action and the ship was ablaze from stem to stern before she sank. Her last message was received at 1605 hrs but the cruiser *Newcastle*, hastening to her aid, saw the flashes of her final engagement at 1746 hrs. Three boats got away from the ship: one with eleven survivors was found by the armed merchant cruiser *Chitral*; the other two were picked up by the Germans.

12 December 1939

Name	*Duchess*	**Location**	North Channel, 9 miles off the Mull of Kintyre, 55 19'N, 06 06'W
Class	D class destroyer		
Built	19 July 1932	**Cause**	Collision

Notes   *Duchess* sank following a collision with the battleship HMS *Barham*.

LOSSES 1940

7 January 1940

Name	*Undine*	**Location**	North Sea, SW of Heligoland
Class	*U* class submarine	**Cause**	Scuttled after depth-charge attack
Built	5 October 1937	**Casualties**	None
CO	Lt Cdrr A.S. Jackson RN		

Notes   *Undine* had carried out an unsuccessful attack on two German minesweeping trawlers, *M1207* and *M1201* of the 12th Minesweeper Flotilla, and was then subjected to a severe depth-charging. She sustained considerable damage: the fore ends were flooded, there were two leaks in the pressure hull and the forward hydroplanes were jammed at 'hard to rise'. Despite flooding the 'Q' quick diving tank, *Undine* continued to rise until she broke surface in full view of the trawlers. Jackson ordered all CBs and charts to be burnt. The crew was ordered to abandon the submarine after which First Lieutenant Michael Harvey opened the main vents and the submarine began to sink. The survivors were picked up by the Germans. In captivity Lieutenant Harvey made a thorough nuisance of himself and was sent to the *Straflager* at Colditz. There he became a 'ghost', remaining in hiding within the castle for 352 days in order to cover the escapes of fellow prisoners. Eventually he made his own escape but was caught within the castle walls. Since he could not be charged with escaping, he received a 28-day sentence for being absent from '1,326 roll calls including three Gestapo Appells'.

Name	*Seahorse*	**Location**	North Sea, Heligoland Bight,
Class	*S* class submarine		54 19'N, 07 30'E
Built	15 November 1932	**Cause**	Depth-charge?
CO	Lt D.S. Massey-Dawson RN	**Survivors**	None

Notes   *Seahorse* was thought to have been mined but an examination of German records reveals an attack by vessels of the 1st Minesweeper Flotilla, which may well account for her loss. A total of eighteen depth-charges were dropped after which all engine noises from the target disappeared. Heavy seas prevented any sighting of wreckage or oil on the surface.

9 January 1940

Name	*Starfish*	**CO**	Lt T.A. Turner RN
Class	*S* class submarine	**Location**	North Sea, SW of Heligoland
Built	14 March 1933	**Cause**	Scuttled after depth-charge attack

Notes   *Starfish* had attempted an attack at 0950 hrs on the German minesweeper *M7* (which had been identified as a destroyer) but owing to an error in drill no torpedoes had been fired. Instead *Starfish*'s periscope had been spotted and the submarine was subjected to a series of depth-charge attacks in which the single minesweeper was joined by a number of other vessels. By 1800 hrs the situation inside the submarine was serious and Turner decided that his best course of action was to surface and hope to be able to slip away under cover of darkness. However, on surfacing Turner found an enemy vessel on either bow which opened fire on *Starfish* with machine-guns. Turner gave the order to flood main ballast and abandon ship. *Starfish* was the third British submarine to have been lost in as many days. Unlike the *Seahorse*'s commander, Lieutenant Turner survived.

19 January 1940

Name	*Grenville*	**Location**	North Sea, 23 miles E of the Kentish
Class	G class destroyer leader		Knock Light Vessel, 51 39'N, 02 17'E
Built	15 August 1935	**Cause**	Mine

Notes   *Grenville* had been engaged in the third of a series of four anti-shipping sweeps off the Dutch coast and was returning to the UK when she was mined.

21 January 1940

Name	*Exmouth*	**Location**	North Sea, off Tarbet Ness, Moray
Class	E class destroyer leader		Firth, 58 18'N, 02 25'W(?)
Built	7 February 1934	**Cause**	Torpedo
		Survivors	None

Notes   *Exmouth* had been ordered to sea in search of a U-boat (*U55*) which had just torpedoed a Danish merchant vessel, the *Tekla*. Nothing further was heard from her. At 0444 and 0448 hrs the motor vessel *Cyprian Prince*, which had been following *Exmouth*, heard two explosions. It was not until after the war that it was learned that the destroyer had been torpedoed and sunk by *U22* (*Kapitanleutnant* Karl-Heinrich Jenisch). It had been noted by the superstitious that *Exmouth*'s cat had deserted the ship just before she had sailed.

3 February 1940

Name	*Sphinx*	**Cause**	Air attack
CO	Cdr J.R.N. Taylor RN	**Casualties**	41
Location	North Sea, 15 miles N of Moray Firth, 57 57'N, 02 00'W		

Notes   *Sphinx* was one of a number of ships – naval and mercantile – sunk or damaged during intense air attacks that developed along the length of the east coast throughout 3 February. The CO and forty of the crew were killed in the attack but under the command of the first lieutenant efforts were made to save the ship. However, the damage proved too great and she foundered the next day.

18 February 1940

Name	*Daring*	**Location**	North Sea, 40 miles E of Duncansby
Class	D class destroyer		Head, 58 38'N, 01 40'W
Built	7 April 1932	**Cause**	Submarine attack
		Survivors	15

Notes *Daring* was torpedoed and sunk by *U23* (*Leutnant zur See* Otto Kretschmer) while she was escorting the homeward bound convoy HN.12. Kretschmer was shadowing the convoy and sighted *Daring* as she carried out a zigzag. Instead of diving Kretschmer carried out a snap attack, aided by inadequate black-out precautions in his target – lights were showing through poorly covered doorways on the upper deck. Two torpedoes were fired and Kretschmer and those on duty on *U23*'s bridge were able to watch as the destroyer sank. In the darkness only fifteen of her crew were rescued by HM Submarine *Thistle*.

April 1940 *saw the German invasion of Denmark and Norway marked the first major turning point in the war at sea. The first British loss of the campaign was a destroyer that sank as the result of an unexpected encounter with a German heavy cruiser and her destroyer escort.*

8 April 1940

Name	*Glowworm*	**Location**	Norwegian Sea, W of Trondheim,
Class	G class destroyer		64 27'N, 06 28'E
Built	22 July 1935	**Cause**	Gunfire
CO	Lt Cdr G.B. Roope RN	**Casualties**	40

Notes *Glowworm* was screening the battle cruiser HMS *Renown* during operation Wilfrid (minelaying in Norwegian waters) when she detached to look for a seaman lost overboard. At 0855 hrs on the 8th she reported that she was in contact with another vessel and this was followed at 0904 hrs by another signal, which faded out. Nothing further was heard from her. It was not until after the war, when her survivors were repatriated, that the Admiralty learned that she had encountered the German destroyer *Bernd von Arnim* and the cruiser *Hipper*. Initially the *Hipper* held her fire since she was unable to distinguish which ship was *Glowworm* and which was *Bernd von Arnim* and it was not until 0857 hrs that the German cruiser opened fire. Despite being hit several times *Glowworm* fired a salvo of torpedoes, which *Hipper* avoided, before retiring behind a smokescreen. The *Hipper* followed *Glowworm* into the smoke and, failing to answer the helm owing to the heavy seas, found the *Glowworm* heading straight for her. *Glowworm* rammed *Hipper* just aft of the starboard anchor, wrecking her own bows, then crashed down *Hipper*'s starboard side, tearing away some 130 ft of the armour belt, before she drifted astern, listing heavily and with her torpedo tubes under water. She then blew up and sank. *Hipper* made every effort to pick up survivors (**see** photograph overleaf). Lieutenant-Commander Roope was being hauled onboard and had just reached the level of the deck when, exhausted, he let go of the rope and was drowned.

As a result of the evidence offered by *Glowworm*'s survivors, Lieutenant-Commander Roope was posthumously awarded the Victoria Cross. Although Roope's VC was the first to be won, owing to circumstances it was one of the last to be formally gazetted, in September 1945.

9 April 1940

Name	*Gurkha*	**Location**	Norwegian Sea, off Bergen, 59 13'N,
Class	*Tribal* class destroyer		04 00'E
Built	7 June 1937	**Cause**	Air attack
CO	Cdr A.W. Buzzard RN	**Survivors**	190

Notes *Gurkha* was screening the Home Fleet when the ships were attacked by a mixed force of Ju.87 and He.111 dive-bombers. Commander Buzzard altered course to open the A-Arcs of his AA guns but in doing so left the mutual protection afforded by being part of the screen. The German aircraft concentrated on the lone

Oil-soaked survivors from HMS *Glowworm* waiting their turn to go up a ladder to the deck of the *Admiral Hipper*. (US Navy)

destroyer. The first bomb blew a huge hole in the stern which started flooding. Soon the stern was awash and the ship had a 45° list to starboard. All lights were extinguished, and the wounded were brought up on to the forecastle. Many had been blinded by fuel oil. Most were put into boats or on Carley floats although one man with a broken leg was lashed to a table and floated off to be picked up later. Just as *Gurkha* rolled over on to her starboard side, the cruiser *Aurora* appeared to rescue survivors. At 1900 hrs HMS *Gurkha* rolled over and sank: she was the first of the magnificent *Tribal* class to be sunk and the first British destroyer to be sunk by air attack. When they heard of her loss every officer and man in the Gurkha Brigade contributed a day's pay to provide for another ship of the same name (see p. 165).

10 April 1940

Name	*Hardy*	**CO**	Capt B.A.W. Warburton-Lee RN
Class	*H* class destroyer	**Location**	Narvik, Otofjord, 68 23'N, 17 06'E
Built	7 April 1936	**Cause**	Gunfire

Notes   The five destroyers of the 2nd Destroyer Flotilla had entered the network of fjords leading to the port of Narvik and found the enemy there in superior numbers: ten German destroyers. Warburton-Lee nevertheless decided to attack and in the mêlée that followed the German destroyers *Anton Schmidt* and *Wilhelm*

Heidkamp were sunk. However, while withdrawing the British ships were engaged by five more German destroyers. *Hardy* was hit on the bridge by a 5.9 in shell and in the vacuum caused by Warburton-Lee's death, she was beached on the south side of Otofjord. The wreck floated off at the next high tide and drifted east for some 2½ miles before grounding near Skjomnes where she remained.

On 7 June 1940 HM King George VI approved the posthumous award of the Victoria Cross to Captain Warburton-Lee; it was the second VC to be won but the first to be awarded (see p. 107).

Name	*Hunter*	CO	Lt Cdr L. de Villiers RN
Class	*H* class destroyer	Location	Narvik, Otofjord, 68 20'N, 17 04'E
Built	25 February 1936	Cause	Gunfire and collision

Notes HMS *Hunter* was the second British casualty of the First Battle of Narvik. After *Hardy* was hit *Hunter* was the Germans' next victim. She was brought to a standstill by repeated hits from 5.9 in shells before she collided with the damaged *Hotspur*. The two ships remained locked together for some time before *Hotspur* was able to get clear.

Name	*Thistle*	Location	Norwegian Sea, off Skudesnes
Class	*T* class submarine	Cause	Submarine attack
Built	25 October 1938	Survivors	None
CO	Lt Cdr W.F. Haselfoot RN		

Notes *Thistle* had been on patrol off Skudesnes and had unsuccessfully attacked the German *U4*. Haselfoot remained in the area in the hope of sighting the U-boat again. Unfortunately it was *Kapitanleutnant* Hans-Peter Hinsch's *U4* which made the first sighting. *U4* attacked at 0113 hrs on the 10th and although Hinsch surfaced to look for survivors, he found nothing but oil. *U4* was one of the very few German U-boats to remain in continuous commission throughout the Second World War.

Name	*Tarpon*	Location	Norwegian Sea, 57 43'N, 06 33'E
Class	*T* class submarine	Cause	Depth-charge
Built	17 October 1939	Survivors	None
CO	Lt Cdr H.J. Caldwell RN		

Notes *Tarpon* had the briefest career of any British submarine. After completion and commissioning in Glasgow she proceeded south to the sound range at Portland and then to Portsmouth for orders. She was then ordered to proceed to Rosyth in company with convoy FN.39 but en route was diverted to patrol on account of the invasion of Norway. On the 10th a submarine (which must have been *Tarpon* since the attack took place very near to *Tarpon*'s patrol position of 57N 06E) attacked the German Q-ship *Schiff 40*. The German vessel immediately sought and obtained Asdic contact but was forced to suspend operations while an RAF Hudson aircraft circled overhead. When the aircraft moved off the attack commenced at 0905 hrs and continued until 1252 hrs when a pattern blew a large amount of wreckage, including publications, personal effects and human remains, to the surface. *Schiff 40* remained in the area until 0500 hrs on the 11th. *Tarpon* remains the only British submarine to have been sunk by a decoy vessel.

Lieutenant-Commander Caldwell was an officer of exceptional promise, who, unusually, had been promoted from the lower deck. Sadly, he was lost with his submarine.

17(?) April 1940

Name	*Sterlet*	**Location**	Skagerrak
Class	S class submarine	**Casualties**	30
Built	22 September 1937	**Survivors**	None
CO	Lt Cdr G.H. Haward RN		

Notes   There is no clear explanation for the loss of *Sterlet*. On 15 April she sank the German gunnery training ship *Brummer*, but made no report of this action which might suggest that she was sunk in the counter-attack. Alternatively she might have been sunk by the minesweeper *M.75* on 17 April. The minesweeper sighted a submarine, which almost certainly was *Sterlet*, on the surface in position 58 57'N, 10 12'E and attacked with depth-charges. If *Sterlet* survived this attack then she could well have been mined in a field laid by the Germans on 8 April, and which lay directly astride her route home on the night of 22 April. The file on HMS *Sterlet* remains open.

29 April 1940

Name	*Unity*	**Location**	North Sea, off the port of Blyth
Class	U class submarine	**Cause**	Collision
Built	16 February 1938	**Casualties**	4
CO	Lt J.F. Brooks RN		

Notes   *Unity* had put to sea at 1730 hrs on the 29th and had entered the swept channel off Blyth when the fog descended and visibility was reduced to 100 yards. Brooks did not know that coming toward him down the channel was a six ship convoy from Methil to the Tyne. At 1907 hrs *Unity*'s OOW heard a long siren blast. Ordering a long blast in reply the wheel was put over to starboard at the same time as another blast was heard fine on the starboard bow. The wheel was put amidships and full astern ordered but it was too late. The Norwegian freighter *Atle Jarl* came out of the fog and rammed *Unity* on the port bow. The crew clambered out on to the casing as *Unity* sank beneath them. Boats from the *Atle Jarl* rescued the survivors but Able Seaman Hare and Stoker Shelton drowned before they could be rescued. First Lieutenant John Low and Able Seaman Henry Miller were subsequently awarded the Empire Gallantry Medal (later exchanged for the George Cross) for remaining in the submarine to ensure that the crew got out. They remained inside the boat too long and went with *Unity* on her final dive.

   The subsequent court martial found that Brooks had been unaware of the convoy's presence since he had not received signal 1428 hrs on the 29th which warned him of the convoy's passage through the swept channel. The signal office staff at the depot at Blyth were unsure as to whether or not Leading Seaman Percy Moon from *Unity* had collected the signal – Moon declared that he had not. Moon testified that he had collected *Unity*'s 'mail' from the signal office on the afternoon of the 29th and had given all signals to the first lieutenant. Since Low was dead and *Unity*'s signal logs at the bottom of the North Sea, the court could not pursue the matter further. However, the court did consider that, at 8 knots, *Unity* had been proceeding too fast down the channel, given the poor visibility, and that Brooks should have made more use of his siren.

   Lieutenant Brooks subsequently commanded HMS *Upright* but was relieved of command in December 1940. On 3 June 1943 he was observing air operations from a Beaufighter of 236 Squadron when the aircraft was engaged by eight Ju.88s. Brooks took over the rear gun but was mortally wounded and did not survive the Beaufighter's forced landing at Predannack in Cornwall.

30 April 1940

Name	*Bittern*	**Location**	Norwegian Sea, off Namsos,
Class	*Sloop*		64 28'N, 11 30'E
Built	14 July 1937	**Cause**	Scuttled after air attack
CO	Lt T. Johnston RN		

Notes   Disabled in an air attack, *Bittern* had to be sunk by HMS *Carlisle* during the evacuation of Namsos.

Name	*Dunoon*	**Location**	North Sea, off Great Yarmouth,
Class	*Minesweeper*		52 45'N, 02 23'E
		Cause	Mine

Notes   *Dunoon* sank during routine mine clearance operations off Great Yarmouth.

May 1940   *The order to evacuate the British Expeditionary Force through the port of Dunkirk was given on the evening of 26 May and operations continued until they formally ceased on the morning of 4 June. During this period more than 335,000 British, French and Belgian servicemen and refugees were brought to England. Though a resounding defeat in military terms, the evacuation, which was carried in the face of sustained air attacks by the Luftwaffe, inspired the nation. The cost to the Royal Navy was high: of the 721 vessels (of all shapes and sizes) involved, 71 were lost. The most serious losses were 6 of the Royal Navy's 38 destroyers; many others were so badly damaged that they would be in dockyard hands for months to come.*

3 May 1940

Name	*Afridi*	**Cause**	Air attack
Class	*Tribal* class destroyer	**Casualties**	49 crew plus 13 soldiers from the
Built	8 June 1937		York & Lancaster Regiment and
CO	Capt P.L. Vian RN		more than 30 survivors from the
Location	Norwegian Sea, off Namsos,		*Bison*
	66 14'N, 05 45'E		

Notes   During the evacuation of Namsos, *Afridi* had just rescued a large number of survivors from the French destroyer *Bison* when she was attacked by aircraft. Two Ju.87 aircraft attacked her from each side and *Afridi* was caught between them. One bomb exploded in no. 1 boiler room starting a severe fire in the after area of the messdecks. A second bomb hit the port side forward of the bridge. At 1445 hrs *Afridi* sank by the bow. It was only the second anniversary of her commissioning.

5 May 1940

Name	*Seal*	**Location**	Kattegat
Class	*Porpoise* class submarine minelayer	**Cause**	Captured after mine damage
Built	27 September 1938	**Casualties**	None
CO	Lt Cdr Rupert Lonsdale RN		

Golf enthusiasts in *Seals*' ship's company heading ashore before the submarine's last patrol in May 1940. (Author)

Seal alongside a German armed trawler at Frederikshavn in Denmark on the evening of 5 May 1940 after being captured. (Royal Danish Navy)

A crowd of curious German soldiers admiring *Seal* alongside the jetty at Frederikshavn. (Royal Danish Navy)

Some of *Seal*'s ship's company share a hot meal in a school yard (their temporary PoW camp) at Frederikshavn. On the right is Chief ERA 'Tubby' Lister who later achieved singular distinction as one of only two non commissioned officers (the other was also a submariner) to be sent to the *Straflager* at Colditz for 'bad behaviour'. True to form both men subsequently escaped and reached Switzerland. (Royal Danish Navy)

Seal's ship's company begin the long march into captivity. (Royal Danish Navy)

May 1945: all that can be seen of *Seal* (or *UB* as she was known in German service) is her conning tower sticking forlornly above the water. (Author)

A fine pre-war view of the submarine minelayer HMS *Seal*. (Wright & Logan)

Notes   *Seal* had completed a minesweeping operation in the Kattegat on 4 May and was attempting to clear the area while being harried by a number of A/S trawlers. As Lonsdale manoeuvred away, he inadvertently strayed into a minefield and detonated a mine with *Seal*'s stern. The submarine settled on the bottom while the crew began a series of exhausting efforts to bring her to the surface. All these efforts failed and by evening officers and men were badly affected by CO_2 poisoning. Lonsdale, a deeply religious man, suggested that all in the control room should say a prayer before making one final attempt to raise the submarine. The last of the compressed air was then blown into the ballast tanks and as if by miracle *Seal* broke free of the bottom and came to the surface at 0130 hrs on the 5th – 23 hours after she had dived. Her predicament, though, was serious. She was unable to dive since the drop keel had been jettisoned as part of the efforts to surface. Lonsdale signalled to the Admiralty his intention to head for neutral Sweden and internment before ordering the wireless, Asdic and CBs to be destroyed. *Seal* was then sighted by two Arado aircraft that commenced a series of strafing runs, inflicting some damage on the submarine. Lonsdale realised that the position was hopeless and gave the order to his crew to cease all efforts at resistance. One Arado, flown by *Leutnant zur See* Karl Schmidt, landed alongside *Seal* and ordered Lonsdale to swim over. Lonsdale complied and was taken off into captivity. Subsequently a virtual armada of surface craft arrived, took off the rest of *Seal*'s officers and men, and began the slow process of taking *Seal* back to Germany. One of *Seal*'s crew, Chief ERA 'Tubby' Lister, was not destined to remain a PoW for long. Even Colditz camp failed to contain him and together with another submariner, ERA F. Hammond of *Starfish*, he successfully made a 'home run'.

Seal was repaired and recommissioned by the *Kriegsmarine* as a U-boat although she was never much more than a propaganda showpiece. In 1945 she was scuttled.

Lonsdale spent the rest of the war as a prisoner, acting as an inspiration to all around him in difficult conditions. He constantly pondered the correctness of his decision to surrender. He was not to know that following his signal indicating his intention to head for Sweden, the Admiralty had replied, concurring with his decision and adding that the safety of his crew was his prime concern. At his court martial in April 1946 Lonsdale was fully and honourably acquitted of any charges in respect of the loss of his command. Lonsdale subsequently left the Navy and took Holy Orders.

15 May 1940

Name	*Valentine*	**Location**	North Sea, off Terneuzen on the
Class	*V* class destroyer leader		Schelde estuary, 51 20'N, 03 49'E
Built	24 March 1917	**Cause**	Beached following air attack

Notes   *Valentine* was one of four British destroyers engaged in operation 'FA' – the provision of naval gunfire support to the left flank of the Belgian Army. On the 15th she was badly damaged in an attack by Ju.87 dive-bombers and beached.

18 May 1940

Name	*Effingham*	**Location**	Norwegian Sea, off Narvik, 67 17'N,
Class	*Hawkins* class cruiser		13 58'E
Built	8 June 1921	**Cause**	Grounding
CO	Capt J.M. Howson RN	**Casualties**	None

Notes   *Effingham* went aground on a submerged rock pinnacle. The subsequent court martial showed that the thick pencil used on the cruiser's chart had obscured the chart symbol marking the rock's position. The cruiser was exactly on track and struck the rock. After salvage of usable equipment *Effingham*'s hull was destroyed by gunfire on 21 May.

19 May 1940

Name	*Whitley*	**Location**	English Channel, 2 miles off
Class	*W* class destroyer		Nieuport, 51 11'N, 02 40'E
Built	13 April 1918	**Cause**	Beached after air attack

Notes   *Whitley* was attacked by German aircraft and sustained severe damage after being struck by two bombs. She was beached off Nieuport but the damage was such that she was destroyed by gunfire on the same day by HMS *Keith*.

24 May 1940

Name	*Wessex*	**Location**	English Channel, off Calais, 51 00'N,
Class	*W* class destroyer		01 46'E
Built	12 March 1918	**Cause**	Air attack

Notes   The destroyers *Wessex*, *Wolfhound*, *Vimiera* and the Polish *Burza* were deployed off Calais to give what assistance they could to the Guards Brigade and the Rifle Brigade who were holding the town in a last-ditch effort to cover the retreat of the BEF to Dunkirk. The four ships were subjected to repeated air attacks on the 24th and *Vimiera* and *Burza* were damaged. *Wessex* was less fortunate and was sunk.

26 May 1940

Name	*Curlew*	**Location**	Norway, Skudenes, Lavang Fjord,
Class	C class cruiser		67 32'N, 16 37'E
Built	5 July 1917	**Cause**	Air attack
CO	Capt B.C. Brooke RN		

Notes   In a series of severe air attacks on British and French ships in the Narvik area, *Curlew* was overwhelmed and sunk.

29 May 1940

Name	*Wakeful*	**Location**	English Channel, 13 miles N of
Class	*V & W* class destroyer		Nieuport, 51 22'N, 02 43'E
Built	6 October 1917	**Cause**	Scuttled following torpedo attack
CO	Cdr R.L. Fisher RN	**Casualties**	*c.* 650 crew and embarked soldiers
		Survivors	25, plus 1 embarked soldier.

Notes   *Wakeful* was returning to Dover from Bray Beach off Dunkirk carrying 600 troops when she was attacked by the German *Schnellboot S-30* at 0045 hrs. Although *Wakeful* avoided the first torpedo, the second struck her in the forward boiler room. The ship broke in half and sank, leaving the bow and stern sections remaining above the water. The soldiers were all below decks and only one survived. Together with the minesweeper HMS *Gossamer*, the *Lydd* tried to rescue as many of the *Wakeful*'s company as possible. *Lydd* had picked up around ten men from the water when the destroyer HMS *Grafton* arrived on the scene, also returning from La Panne with 800 men on board. *Gossamer* returned to Dover leaving *Grafton* and *Lydd* to carry on with the rescue work. Also on the scene was the drifter *Comfort* which had been en route to La Panne with the drifter *Nautilus*. *Comfort* picked up sixteen of *Wakeful*'s crew, including her CO, Commander R.L. Fisher RN. She then went alongside *Wakeful*'s stern portion to rescue more men but found that it had capsized.

Name	*Grafton*	**Location**	English Channel, 13 miles N of
Class	G class destroyer		Nieuport
Built	18 September 1935	**Cause**	Torpedo
CO	Cdr G.E.C. Robinson RN		

Notes   See the entry for HMS *Comfort* below.

Name	*Comfort*	**Location**	English Channel, 13 miles N of
Class	Trawler		Nieuport
		Cause	Ramming

Notes   The loss of HMS *Wakeful* was but the first element in a disastrous night for the Royal Navy. After *Comfort* had found *Wakeful*'s stern section capsized, she went alongside *Grafton*'s starboard side to warn her of the danger of *Schnellboote* in the area. It was at this juncture that the *U62* (*Kapitanleutnant* Hans Michalowski) appeared on the scene and fired one torpedo that struck *Grafton*'s port side and blew away her stern. A second explosion (cause unknown, for *U62* fired only one torpedo) wrecked *Grafton*'s bridge, killing her CO Commander Robinson, and three others. The torpedo explosion swamped the *Comfort* (some of her crew and *Wakeful*'s survivors, including

Commander Fisher, were washed overboard) so she cast off, and circled round until within 50 yards of the *Grafton*. In the darkness and confusion, *Lydd* and *Grafton* mistook *Comfort* for a *Schnellboot* and opened a heavy and accurate fire upon her with 4 in and Lewis guns. *Lydd* then turned in and rammed the drifter squarely amidships, cutting her in half. Some of *Comfort*'s crew attempted to jump on to the *Lydd* but were repelled with rifle fire, the minesweeper's crew thinking that they were hostile boarders. Two determined men did manage to gain the minesweeper's deck and it was then discovered that the rammed vessel was the *Comfort*. Only five men were saved from the *Comfort*, of whom four were survivors from *Wakeful*. After this tragic incident *Lydd* set course for Ramsgate since *Grafton* was floating on an even keel and seemed able to look after herself. (She was sunk later that day by HMS *Ivanhoe* after her troops and ship's company had been taken off.) Commander Fisher was left swimming until 0515 hrs when he was picked up by the SS *Hird*. Following the loss of *Grafton* orders were issued to all British destroyers involved in the evacuation that they were not to stop to aid other ships in distress.

Name	*Waverley*	**Location**	English Channel, near Kwint Bank
Class	Paddle minesweeper		Buoy
CO	T/y Lt S.F. Harmer Elliott RNVR	**Cause**	Air attack

Notes *Waverley* was returning to Dover with 600 men on board when she was attacked by German aircraft. A bomb hit her on her port quarter and passed straight through the ship. Four of the 600 troops she had embarked at La Panne were killed and a number wounded. Another 150 soldiers drowned after *Waverley* sank.

Name	*Grenade*	**CO**	Cdr R.C. Boyle RN
Class	G class destroyer	**Location**	Port of Dunkirk, alongside the east mole
Built	12 November 1935	**Cause**	Air attack

Notes *Grenade* was secured alongside the east mole at Dunkirk awaiting the embarkation of troops when she was first damaged and then sunk in a series of four air attacks that developed from 1530 hrs. In the first attack *Grenade* received some splinter damage and took some casualties. At about 1750 hrs a near miss blew a hole in her port side. Almost immediately after this *Grenade* received two direct hits. Her machinery was disabled and a serious fire started on the upper deck. At 1815 hrs she was abandoned. Commander Boyle arranged with the piermaster for her burning hull to be towed clear of the main channel. She burned fiercely for some hours and then blew up.

June 1940 *The collapse of France and the Low Countries meant the abandonment of the Norwegian campaign even though allied troops were firmly established in Narvik. Over 27,000 men were brought away from Norway without loss in the first week of June. However, a dubious decision to use one of the Navy's precious fleet carriers to evacuate fighter aircraft and her captain's poor tactical awareness led to the Germans scoring a significant success.*

1 June 1940

Name	*Keith*	**Location**	English Channel, off Bray, 51 06'N,
Class	B class destroyer leader		02 32'E
Built	10 July 1930	**Cause**	Air attack
CO	Capt E.L. Berthon DSC RN, flagship of Rear Adm Wake-Walker	**Casualties**	136: 36 lost in original attack, 100 more lost in the tug *St Abbs* (sunk with *Keith* survivors on board)

Notes *Keith* had just cleared the deserted eastern beaches when she was attacked by a large number of Ju.87 aircraft. Although the ship's freedom to manoeuvre was restricted by shoals, magnetic mines and wrecks, she was not hit. However, a bomb that exploded astern of her jammed the steering. Just after 0800 hrs a large hole was blown in the starboard side of the ship at the forward end of the after engine room. Two further hits on the port side caused the ship to list to port. Rear Admiral Wake-Walker transferred his flag to *MTB.102* and *Keith*'s battered hull was then sunk in a further series of bombing attacks.

Name	*Basilisk*	**Location**	English Channel, off La Panne,
Class	B class destroyer		51 08'N, 02 35'E
Built	6 August 1930	**Cause**	Scuttled following air attack
CO	Cdr M. Richmond OBE RN	**Survivors**	131

Notes *Basilisk* was overwhelmed in a series of air attacks which took place from 0800 hrs while *Keith* was being attacked further up the coast and while no RAF cover was operating overhead. *Basilisk* was hit first in no. 3 boiler room, losing main steam pressure and putting all her machinery out of action. Six other bombs exploded alongside or underneath the ship, causing her side to buckle. At noon the Luftwaffe returned and finished off her battered hull. *Basilisk* sank in shallow water and her hull was destroyed by depth-charges dropped by HMS *Whitehall*.

Name	*Havant*	**Location**	English Channel, off Dunkirk,
Class	Ex-Brazilian *Javary*		51 04'N, 02 35'E
Built	17 July 1939	**Cause**	Air attack
CO	Lt Cdr A. Burnell Nugent DSC RN	**Casualties**	8

Notes *Havant* had just departed from Dunkirk with 500 troops embarked from the damaged *Ivanhoe*. At 0906 hrs she was attacked and hit by two bombs that entered the engine room. A third bomb exploded as the ship passed over it. Despite the loss of all power the ship was anchored and the soldiers transferred to the *Saltash* and *Grive* under continual air attack. Concussion from a number of near misses caused the ship to list to port so the majority of her ship's company were evacuated. By 1000 hrs her decks were awash and she was abandoned, and at 1015 hrs she rolled over and sank.

Name	*Skipjack*	**Location**	English Channel, off Malo les Bains,
Class	Minesweeper		51 03'N, 02 24'E
CO	Lt Cdr F.B. Proudfoot RN	**Cause**	Air attack
		Casualties	Crew and 270 soldiers

Notes *Skipjack* had been busy evacuating British and French troops from Malo les Bains. She had been fighting off continuous air attacks since 0530 hrs and by 0845 hrs her ammunition supply had been reduced to less than a dozen rounds per gun. In a fierce attack at about 0850 hrs the little minesweeper was overwhelmed in an attack in which she was hit five times. She capsized and floated bottom up before sinking. Most of her 270+ soldier passengers were below and were drowned. The few survivors were machine-gunned in the water.

Name	*Mosquito*	**Location**	English Channel, off Dunkirk
Class	River gunboat		harbour
CO	Lt D.H.P. Gardiner RN	**Cause**	Air attack

Notes *Mosquito* was one of a number of river gunboats which had been built for service on the Yangtse River in China. The evacuation of the BEF required her presence in waters nearer home where her shallow draught and manoeuvrability were considerable assets. However, she was neither built nor designed to operate unsupported against aircraft. At 1330 hrs she was attacked by more than twenty Ju.87s and sustained damage to her boiler and engine room. Her steering gear was damaged and she assumed a heavy list to port. Leading Seaman Ronald Thirlwall kept the pom-pom in action despite being severely wounded, while Able Seaman C.A. Hirschfield kept the 0.5 in machine-gun in action single-handed after all its crew were killed. Eventually *Mosquito* rolled over to port and her survivors were picked up by two drifters.

7 June 1940

Name	*Carinthia*	**Location**	Atlantic, NW of Ireland, 53 13'N, 10 40'W
Class	AMC		
		Cause	Submarine attack

Notes *Carinthia* was torpedoed by *U46* (*Kapitanleutnant* Engelbert Endrass) while engaged in the Northern Patrol blockade duty.

8 June 1940

Name	*Juniper*	**Cause**	Gunfire
Class	Trawler	**Survivors**	4
Location	Norwegian Sea, 67 26'N, 04 23'E		

Notes *Juniper* had been given the task of escorting the tanker *Oil Pioneer* which was bound for the UK from Tromso. At 0531 hrs the two ships were sighted by the German battle cruisers *Scharnhorst* and *Gneisenau*, accompanied by the cruiser *Hipper* and four destroyers. The little trawler stood no chance and was swiftly despatched by gunfire along with the tanker. It was an auspicious beginning to what would be an outstandingly successful day for the Germans.

Name	*Glorious*	**Casualties**	76 officers and 1,086 ratings plus 41 RAF personnel
Class	Aircraft carrier		
Built	20 April 1916	**Survivors**	43: 3 officers and 35 ratings picked up by the Norwegian vessel *Borgund* on 11 June and landed in the Faroes; 5 picked up by the Norwegian trawler *Svalbard II* – they became PoWs
CO	Capt Guy D'Oyly-Hughes RN		
Location	Norwegian Sea, SW of Narvik, 68 45'N, 04 30'E		
Cause	Gunfire		

Notes *Glorious* was heading back to the UK, escorted by the destroyers *Ardent* and *Acasta*, having embarked seventeen RAF fighters from Narvik. She was steaming at 17 knots but had no aircraft on patrol around the ship. At 1600 hrs the two German battle cruisers were sighted to the north-west. Orders were given to ready the Swordfish aircraft for a strike, but none was flown off. In almost perfect weather conditions *Scharnhorst* opened fire at 1631 hrs, followed by her consort. Despite both destroyers laying a smokescreen *Glorious* was hit in the forward upper hangar. This hit left a massive hole in the flight deck and started a severe fire. The bridge was hit at around 1700 hrs and an 11 in shell hit aft at around 1715 hrs. Armed only with sixteen 4.7 in guns *Glorious* was hopelessly outranged. The order to abandon ship was given at 1720 hrs and at 1740 hrs she rolled over to starboard and sank.

The loss of the *Glorious* has been the focus of much attention in recent years with various conspiracy theories being given an airing. Most do not bear serious consideration. The facts of the matter are that it was a questionable decision to use such a valuable ship to evacuate only seventeen fighters (ten of which were biplanes of dubious value). Secondly *Glorious*' CO lacked tactical awareness in not having any aircraft up and patrolling around the ship. Lastly, when an aircraft carrier armed with no more than sixteen 4.7 in guns and escorted by two destroyers armed with four 4.7 in guns and eight torpedoes apiece runs into two battle cruisers armed with eighteen 11 in guns between them, the outcome is almost inevitable.

Name	*Ardent*	**Cause**	Gunfire
Class	A class destroyer	**Casualties**	10 officers and 142 ratings
Built	26 June 1929	**Survivors**	2: picked up by a German seaplane
CO	Lt Cdr J.F. Barker RN		on 11 June
Location	Norwegian Sea, SW of Narvik, 68 45'N, 04 30'E		

Notes   When *Glorious* came under fire from the two German ships *Ardent* moved out towards the enemy at high speed, making smoke. She fired one salvo of eight torpedoes but was then hit several times and sank at 1728 hrs.

Name	*Acasta*	**Location**	Norwegian Sea, SW of Narvik, 68 45'N, 04 30'E
Class	A class destroyer		
Built	8 August 1929	**Cause**	Gunfire
CO	Cdr C.E. Glasfurd RN	**Casualties**	8 officers and 152 ratings
		Survivors	1: Able Seaman C. Carter

Notes   After *Ardent* sank, *Acasta* continued to engage the German ships though hopelessly outgunned and outranged. Even though Glasfurd could have escaped behind a smokescreen he chose to make one final torpedo attack. One torpedo hit *Scharnhorst* just aft of her after 11 in turret. During this attack *Acasta* was hit hard and she sank just after 1810 hrs. Commander Glasfurd was last seen on the bridge of his ship calmly lighting a cigarette while he exhorted his men to save themselves.

12 June 1940

Name	*Calypso*	**Location**	Mediterranean, S of Crete, 33 45'N, 23 32'E
Class	C class cruiser		
Built	24 January 1917	**Cause**	Submarine attack
		Casualties	39

Notes   The Italian government announced to the British and French governments that from midnight on 10 June 1940 a state of war would exist between their countries. Determined not to be caught on the hop, the combined British and French fleets put to sea from Alexandria to catch any Italian forces found off Benghazi or Tobruk. At 0200 hrs the cruiser *Calypso* reported that she had been torpedoed and was sinking. She eventually sank at 0330 hrs. The British doubted that a submarine was responsible and considered her loss to be due to a mine. However it was the Italian submarine *Bagnolini* (*CC* Franco Tosoni-Pittoni) which was responsible for the *Regia Marina*'s first major success of the war.

13 June 1940

Name	*Scotstoun*	**Location**	Atlantic, N of Ireland, 57 00'N, 09
Class	AMC		57'W
Built	1925	**Cause**	Submarine attack

Notes   *Scotstoun* was torpedoed and sunk by *U25* (*Kapitanleutnant* Heinz Beduhn) at 0715 hrs while en route from the Clyde to her allocated area with the Northern Patrol.

14 June 1940

Name	*Odin*	**Location**	Mediterranean, Gulf of Taranto
Class	*O* class submarine	**Cause**	Depth-charge
Built	5 May 1928	**Casualties**	53
CO	Lt Cdr K.M. Woods RN	**Survivors**	None

Notes   Taranto was the principal base for the Italian Navy and the approaches to the harbour were always well guarded. *Odin* was a large submarine, recently arrived in the Mediterranean from the Far East, and she left Malta on 11 June for a patrol right in the *Regia Marina*'s back yard. At 2321 hrs on the 13th the escort *Strale*, on anti-submarine patrol in the Gulf of Taranto, sighted a large submarine – HMS *Odin* – that she attacked with a torpedo (which was seen to strike), gunfire and depth-charges. At 0157 hrs on the 14th the escort *Baleno* sighted a submarine in the same area – 9 miles from the position of *Strale*'s attack – that she attacked with depth-charges. Aerial surveys of the scene on the 14th and 15th revealed an oil slick that eventually covered 10 square miles.

16 June 1940

Name	*Grampus*	**Location**	Mediterranean, between Augusta and
Class	*Grampus* class submarine minelayer		Syracuse
Built	25 February 1936	**Cause**	Depth-charge
CO	Lt Cdr C.A. Rowe RN	**Casualties**	59
		Survivors	None

Notes   *Grampus* had also left Malta on 10 June and on the 13th she reported having successfully laid mines in the swept channel between Augusta and Syracuse. That was the last ever heard from the submarine. At 1902 hrs on the 16th she was sighted by the Italian escort *Circe*, which had left Syracuse at 1830 hrs that same day in company with *Clio*, *Calliope* and *Polluce* for a routine anti-submarine patrol. *Grampus* was not going to give up, for Rowe fired one torpedo at *Circe* and two at *Polluce* but to no avail. The three Italian ships manoeuvred with considerable skill, dropping sixty-one depth-charges over the spot in 15 minutes. At 1907 hrs there was a massive underwater explosion and a considerable amount of wreckage came to the surface.

Name	*Andania*	**Location**	Atlantic, SE of Iceland, 62 36'N,
Class	AMC		15 09'W
		Cause	Submarine attack

Notes   The perils of service for AMCs on the Northern Patrol had already been made clear by the sinkings of the *Carinthia* and *Scotstoun*. Now the *UA* (the ex-Turkish submarine *Batiray*, commanded by *Korvettenkapitan* Hans Cohausz) sank the *Andania*, the third such vessel to be sunk within a month.

19(?) June 1940

Name	*Orpheus*	**Location**	Mediterranean, off Benghazi
Class	*Odin* class submarine	**Casualties**	53
Built	26 February 1929	**Survivors**	None
CO	Lt Cdr J.A. Wise RN		

Notes   *Orpheus* had left Malta on 10 June and on the 19th had been ordered to patrol off Benghazi. She acknowledged receipt of a signal at 2115 hrs on the 19th. At that time she was 100 miles north-west of Benghazi. Nothing further was heard from her and it is presumed that she was either mined or the victim of an accident. *Orpheus* was the third British submarine to be sunk in a week in the Mediterranean: over 170 submariners had been killed and there had been nothing to show for the sacrifice.

22 June 1940

Name	*Khartoum*	**Location**	Red Sea, off Perim Island, 12 38'N,
Class	*K* class destroyer		43 24'E
Built	6 February 1939	**Cause**	Accident

Notes   The destroyers *Khartoum*, *Kandahar* and *Kingston*, with the sloops *Shoreham* and *Indus*, found the Italian submarine *Torricelli* (CC Salvatore Pelosi) north of Perim Island. Pelosi chose to fight it out on the surface and there followed a 40 minute gun and torpedo duel. During the engagement *Khartoum* sustained one hit from a 10 cm shell which burst near the after bank of 21 in torpedo tubes. A splinter caused the air vessel of a torpedo to explode. It proved impossible to contain the resulting fire and the ship was beached on Perim Island.

23 June 1940

Name	*Pathan*	**Cause**	Submarine attack
Class	Sloop	**Casualties**	5
Location	Indian Ocean, off Bombay, 18 56'N,		
	72 45'E		

Notes   *Pathan* was on patrol off Bombay when she was shaken by a large explosion at 0100 hrs. She eventually sank early on the morning of the 24th. In addition to the five killed, twenty-two of her complement were wounded. Her loss was originally ascribed to a contact mine since it was thought that no Axis submarines were operating that far to the east. However, it was the Italian submarine *Galvani* (CC Spano) that was responsible. Twenty-four hours later *Galvani* was herself rammed and sunk by HMS *Falmouth*.

25 June 1940

Name	*Fraser*	**Location**	Atlantic, off the Gironde estuary,
Class	*C* class destroyer		45 44'N, 01 31'W
Built	29 September 1931	**Cause**	Collision
		Survivors	130

Notes *Fraser* was sunk in collision with the cruiser HMS *Calcutta* during operations to evacuate the last British and Allied personnel from France.

4 July 1940

Name	*Foylebank*	**Location**	English Channel, Portland harbour
Class	Auxiliary AA vessel	**Cause**	Air attack

Notes *Foylebank* was sunk in a German air attack on Portland Harbour.

5 July 1940

Name	*Whirlwind*	**Location**	Atlantic, 120 miles W of Lands End,
Class	*W* class destroyer		50 17'N, 08 48'W
Built	15 December 1917	**Cause**	Submarine attack
		Casualties	57

Notes *Whirlwind* was torpedoed at 1825 hrs by *U34* (*Kapitanleutnant* Wilhelm Rollmann). Though she did not sink as a result of the attack, she was considered beyond repair and was scuttled 4 hours later by HMS *Westcott*. *U34* was the first German U-boat to enter the newly acquired bases on the French Atlantic coast. Her arrival was made much of by the German propaganda service and mention was made of the attack on *Whirlwind*.

6 July 1940

Name	*Shark*	**Location**	Norwegian Sea, 30 miles SW of
Class	*S* class submarine		Stavanger
Built	31 May 1934	**Cause**	Scuttled
CO	Lt Cdr P. Buckley RN	**Casualties**	3

Notes At 2200 hrs on the 5th July *Shark* came to the surface off Stavanger to charge her battery. Even at that late hour it was still light and therefore *Shark* was easy prey for an aircraft which attacked her at 2250 hrs and caused severe damage to her rudder, port propeller and pressure hull, so that she could not dive. *Shark* was then subjected to more than five hours of air attacks by a series of He.111, Do.17 and Me.110 aircraft, and had to fight it out on the surface, shooting down a Do.17 bomber in the process. However, in the end the sheer weight of numbers told against the submarine. When all the ammunition had been expended, and with three of her crew killed and eighteen wounded, Buckley reluctantly decided to surrender. An Arado seaplane landed astern of them and promptly sank! The aircrew came aboard the submarine claiming that one of the Arado's float had been damaged by gunfire. However, Buckley felt that they had damaged the float in a bad landing and weren't going to admit it. It was a strange situation – who were the prisoners? The Germans remained on the bridge as *Shark*'s wounded were brought up and laid on the casing while inside the submarine the first lieutenant led an orgy of destruction. (**See** photograph overleaf.)

At 0500 hrs on the 6th a twin-engined Dornier seaplane landed alongside and Buckley was taken on board together with Sub Lieutenant Barnes, who was badly wounded. As they flew off they saw *Shark* lying stern down with at least ten aircraft circling overhead. At 0730 hrs four trawlers arrived from Stavanger and took off the wounded. The Germans were very considerate and had sent medical staff with the trawlers. However, as soon as the Germans tried to tow *Shark* away, she reared up her bows and sank stern first.

The White Ensign is draped unceremoniously over the port side of the conning tower as the Germans prepare to take the submarine in tow on 6 July 1940. *Shark* subsequently sank and thus was spared the fate that had befallen *Seal*. (US Navy)

9 July 1940

Name	*Salmon*	**Location**	Norwegian Sea, 57 22'N, 05 00'E
Class	*S* class submarine	**Cause**	Mine
Built	30 April 1934	**Casualties**	30
CO	Cdr E.O. Bickford RN	**Survivors**	None

Notes *Salmon* sailed for patrol on 4 July and nothing more was heard from her. After the war, when the positions of German minefields became known, it was found that *Salmon* had been routed across a German minefield that had only just been laid.

Name	*Foxglove*	**Location**	English Channel, 8 miles south of
Class	*Acacia* class sloop		the Nab Tower
Built	30 March 1915	**Cause**	Air attack

Notes   *Foxglove* was attacked by German aircraft off the Isle of Wight. She was badly damaged but was towed back to Portsmouth. However, it was considered that she was not worth restoring to a fully seagoing condition. Instead she was patched up and despatched to the River Royle in Northern Ireland where she served as a base ship until 1945.

11 July 1940

Name	*Escort*	**Location**	Mediterranean, N of Algiers, 36
Class	*E* class destroyer		11'N, 03 36'E
Built	29 March 1934	**Cause**	Submarine attack
		Casualties	None

Notes   *Escort* was screening Force H, which was returning from an attack on the island of Cagliari, when she was attacked by the Italian submarine *Marconi* at 0215 hrs. None of her complement was killed and she was sunk at 1115 hrs after her crew had been transferred to HMS *Forester*.

16 July 1940

Name	*Phoenix*	**Location**	Mediterranean, off Augusta
Class	*Parthian* class submarine	**Cause**	Depth-charge
Built	3 October 1929	**Casualties**	53
CO	Lt Cdr G.H. Nowell RN	**Survivors**	None

Notes   *Phoenix* had left Alexandria on 3 July but the last heard from her was at 2350 hrs on the 14th. At 1252 hrs on the 16th *Phoenix* attacked the tanker *Dora C* which was protected by the escort *Albatros*. *Capitano di Fregata* Alessandro Mazzetti, commanding officer of the *Albatros*, lost no time and raced down the torpedo tracks to deliver a ten-charge pattern directly over the submarine. The speed of the attack was such that *Phoenix* could have moved no more than a hundred yards and she was undoubtedly sunk by *Albatros*.

Name	*Imogen*	**Location**	English Channel, off Duncansby
Class	*I* class destroyer		Head, 58 34'N, 02 54'W
Built	30 October 1936	**Cause**	Collision

Notes   While returning to Scapa Flow in thick fog, *Imogen* collided with the cruiser HMS *Glasgow*. *Imogen* subsequently caught fire and had to be abandoned.

20 July 1940

Name	*Brazen*	**Location**	English Channel, Straits of Dover,
Class	*B* class destroyer		51 01'N, 01 17'E
Built	25 July 1930	**Cause**	Air attack

Notes   *Brazen* was escorting Channel convoy CW7 when she was attacked by a force of around thirty bombers with fighter escort off Dover. She was taken in tow but sank later.

23 July 1940

Name	*Narwhal*	**Location**	Norwegian Sea, 55 30'N, 01 10'E
Class	*Grampus* class submarine minelayer	**Cause**	Air attack
Built	29 August 1935	**Casualties**	59
CO	Lt Cdr R.J. Burch RN	**Survivors**	None

Notes   *Narwhal* had left Blyth at 1500 hrs on the 22nd with orders to lay a minefield in position 63 16'N, 07 13'E. Her orders were to proceed on the surface until within 30 miles of 59 29'N, 02 34'E. Twenty-four hours later, almost to the minute, she was sunk by a Dornier flying boat at 1455 hrs on the 23rd. *Narwhal's* estimated position at this time tallied exactly with the position given by the Dornier.

27 July 1940

Name	*Codrington*	**Location**	English Channel, port of Dover
Class	*A* class destroyer leader	**Cause**	Air attack
Built	7 August 1929		

HMS *Narwhal* sunk off Norway in July 1940. (Wright & Logan)

Notes *Codrington* was sunk in an air raid on Dover carried out by around 120 German aircraft. The destroyer *Walpole* and sloop *Sandhurst* were damaged. The ferocity of this attack caused the Admiralty to abandon Dover as an advanced base for destroyers.

27 July 1940

Name	*Wren*	**Location**	North Sea, off Aldeburgh, 52 10'N,
Class	W class destroyer		02 06'E
Built	11 November 1919	**Cause**	Air attack

Notes *Wren* was providing AA cover for minesweepers engaged in routine sweeping operations when the force was attacked by German aircraft. The minesweeper *Montrose* was damaged but was towed back to Harwich. *Wren* became the chief target for the aircraft and was sunk.

29 July 1940

Name	*Delight*	**Location**	English Channel, Portland harbour
Class	D class destroyer	**Cause**	Air attack
Built	2 June 1932		

Notes *Delight* was attacked by German aircraft off Portland on the 29th and set on fire. She managed to return to Portland but the fires proved too great and she sank there the next morning.

1 August 1940

Name	*Oswald*	**Location**	Mediterranean
Class	*Odin* class submarine	**Cause**	Ramming
Built	19 June 1928	**Casualties**	3
CO	Lt Cdr D.A. Fraser RN	**Survivors**	52

Notes Just after midnight *Oswald* was lying on the surface, going slowly ahead on one engine while charging the battery with the other. A lookout sighted the Italian destroyer *Ugolino Vivaldi* 1½ miles away on the starboard quarter and sounded the night alarm. Fraser came to the bridge but was night-blind since he had been in the wardroom deciphering signals without wearing red goggles. *Vivaldi* came in to ram but *Oswald* did not dive, take any avoiding action or attempt to engage the destroyer with torpedoes or the 4 in gun (it was subsequently admitted that the gun lock was not shipped). It was subsequently established that Fraser gave the order to abandon ship when *Vivaldi* was still 100 yards away and <u>before</u> his submarine was rammed. *Vivaldi* struck *Oswald*, not very violently, just aft of the conning tower on the starboard side. *Oswald* then fell astern of *Vivaldi*; as she did so *Vivaldi* dropped ten depth charges and then fired on *Oswald* with the forward 120 mm gun. *Capitano di Fregata* Giovanni Galati, *Vivaldi*'s commanding officer, increased speed to ram a second time but slowed quickly when he realised that the submarine had sunk and her crew were swimming in the water.

Oswald's ship's company were extremely discontented in captivity. There was a feeling that Fraser had not done all he should in fighting the *Vivaldi*. Matters came to a head at a PoW camp near Venice where the officers were seen to be enjoying better conditions; the ratings refused to obey the orders of their officers and wished to be separated from them. At the subsequent enquiry ratings testified that Fraser had summoned his ship's company together and told them, 'There seems to be some discontent and grousing going on. The officers have books, cigarettes and card; well, we paid for them. It is our money and we are entitled to them. If the Italians choose to give you cigarettes they can. You have got fuck all, you are entitled to fuck all and, as far as I am concerned, you will get fuck all. You say you have no pillows – sleep on your fucking boots, the same as the Italian soldiers.'

Lieutenant-Commander Fraser was court-martialled for the loss of *Oswald* on five charges. He was found guilty on three counts: negligent performance of duty in not taking evasive action by diving; negligent performance of duty in failing to engage the enemy, HMS *Oswald* being unable to dive; and negligent performance of duty in not issuing specific orders to the OOW. He was sentenced to forfeit all seniority as a lieutenant-commander, to be dismissed from HMS *Victory* and to be severely reprimanded.

Name	*Spearfish*	**Location**	Atlantic, 180 miles WSW of
Class	S class submarine		Stavanger
Built	21 April 1936	**Cause**	Submarine attack
CO	Lt Cdr J.H. Forbes RN	**Casualties**	29
		Survivors	1

Notes HMS *Spearfish* was caught on the surface by *U34* (*Kapitanleutnant* Wilhelm Rollmann) at the end of a very successful patrol during which the *U34* had also sunk the *Whirlwind* (see p. 123). In fairly rough seas Rollmann fired his remaining torpedo and was rewarded by the sound of an explosion. Rollmann then surfaced and went to the spot to find Able Seaman William Pester, who was on his first patrol and had joined *Spearfish* just before she sailed, swimming in a sea of diesel.

2/3 August 1940

Name	*Thames*	**CO**	Lt Cdr W.D. Dunkerley RN
Class	*River* class submarine	**Casualties**	61
Built	26 January 1932	**Survivors**	None

Notes HMS *Thames* left Dundee for a patrol on 22 June and nothing more was heard from her. On 26 July she attacked the German battle cruiser *Gneisenau* but at the moment of firing her range was fouled by the torpedo boat *Luchs,* which took the full force of the torpedo(es) intended for *Gneisenau*. *Luchs* blew up in a violent explosion and it has been suggested that *Thames* was a victim of this explosion or was struck by *Luchs'* sinking hull. A second theory, the more likely, is that *Thames* was the victim of a mine. Her patrol was subjected to numerous changes of area. The order sent at 1939 hrs on 23 July to move area took her across a German minefield that consisted of over 500 mines, while a second order issued at 1413 hrs on the 24th would have taken her back through the same field. At 1157 hrs on the 25th she was ordered to move again and this took her across another German minefield while her recall signal sent at 1400 hrs on 2 August would have taken her across a fourth. Since Dunkerley made no transmission while on patrol it is hard to assess *Thames'* loss. However, the explanation currently accepted by the Ministry of Defence is that *Thames* was mined while on her homeward passage on the night of 2 August in the vicinity of 56 45'N, 03 26'E.

10 August 1940

Name	*Transylvania*	**Location**	Atlantic, 40 miles N of Malin Head,
Class	AMC		55 50'N, 08 03'W
		Cause	Submarine attack

Notes The fourth AMC to be sunk on the Northern Patrol in the space of two months, *Transylvania* was torpedoed by *U56* (*Kapitanleutnant* Otto Harms).

23 August 1940

Name	*Hostile*	**CO**	Cdr A.P. Gibson RN
Class	*H* class destroyer	**Location**	Mediterranean, 18 miles SE of Cape
Built	24 January 1936		Bon, Tunisia, 36 53'N, 11 19'E
		Cause	Mine

Notes   *Hostile* was en route for Malta when she was mined in the area between Pantellaria and Cape Bon, previously thought to be safe. She eventually had to be scuttled by a torpedo fired by HMS *Hero* after her crew had been taken off.

24 August 1940

Name	*Penzance*	**Location**	Atlantic, W of Ireland, 56 16'N,
Class	Sloop		27 19'W
Built	10 April 1930	**Cause**	Submarine attack

Notes   *Penzance* was escorting convoy SC1 when she was torpedoed by *U37* (*Korvettenkapitan* Victor Oerhn). The last of the torpedoes blew the little sloop in half and it was impossible to lower boats or Carley floats.

27 August 1940

Name	*Dunvegan Castle*	**Location**	Atlantic, 120 miles SW of Ireland,
Class	AMC		55 05'N, 11 00'W
		Cause	Submarine attack

Notes   *Dunvegan Castle* was proceeding independently to Belfast after escorting an SL convoy when she was attacked by *U46* (*Kapitanleutnant* Engelbert Endrass) at 2310 hrs. She remained afloat long enough for her survivors to be taken off by the destroyer *Harvester* and the corvette *Primrose*. She sank at 0600 hrs on 28 August.

30 August 1940

Name	*Esk*	**Location**	North Sea off the Dutch coast,
Class	*E* class destroyer		53 30'N, 03 47'E
Built	19 March 1934	**Cause**	Mine

Notes   See the entry for HMS *Ivanhoe* below.

1 September 1940

Name	*Ivanhoe*	**Location**	North Sea off the Dutch coast,
Class	*I* class destroyer		53 25'N, 03 48'E
Built	11 February 1937	**Cause**	Scuttled following mine damage

Notes   The 20th Destroyer Flotilla (*Express, Esk, Icarus, Ivanhoe* and *Intrepid*) was the Royal Navy's only effective offensive minelaying force. On the night of 30 August the five destroyers left Immingham for a minelaying operation, CBX.5, off Vlieland on the Dutch coast. At 2200 hrs a large number of enemy ships were reported off Terschelling and the destroyers were ordered to jettison their mines and attack these vessels instead. At 2307 hrs *Express* was mined north of Terschelling: her bow was blown off as far back as the bridge. She was towed back to

Humber stern first but worse was to follow. At 2325 hrs *Esk* struck a mine and sank in less than 2 minutes. Then at 0051 hrs on 1 September *Ivanhoe* ran into a mine and was damaged. *Ivanhoe* tried to head westwards but was abandoned after an air attack. Her sinking hulk was found by HMS *Kelvin* and torpedoed at 1700 hrs.

6 September 1940

Name	*Godetia*	**Location**	Atlantic, 3 miles off Alatacarry Head, 55 18'N, 05 57'W
Class	*Flower* class corvette	**Cause**	Collision

Notes   *Godetia* was sunk in collision with the merchant vessel SS *Marsa*. *Marsa* had straggled from convoy OA.209 and crossed the path of convoy OA.207 which *Godetia* was escorting.

15 September 1940

Name	*Dundee*	**Location**	Atlantic, W of Ireland, 56 45'N, 14 14'W
Class	Sloop	**Cause**	Submarine attack

Notes   *Dundee* was torpedoed and sunk while escorting convoy SC.3 by *U48* (*Kapitanleutnant* Heinrich Bleichrodt).

10 October 1940

Name	*Triad*	**Location**	Mediterranean, SW of Calabria
Class	*T* class submarine	**Cause**	Gunfire and torpedo
Built	5 May 1939	**Survivors**	None
CO	Lt Cdr G.S. Salt RN		

Notes   The loss of HMS *Triad* took place in unique circumstances, and she remains the only submarine to have been sunk in a surface engagement with another submarine. *Triad* was on patrol in the Gulf of Taranto and encountered the Italian submarine *Enrico Toti* (*Capitano di Fregata* Bandino Bandini) on the surface shortly after midnight. There was a brief but intense gun duel in which *Triad* scored two hits on *Toti*'s casing but did little damage and fired a torpedo which passed astern of the Italian boat. Both submarines now passed so closely that those on *Toti*'s bridge could clearly hear *Triad*'s bridge party speaking English. A sailor on *Toti*'s casing even threw his boot at the British boat! *Toti* now used her superiority in close-range weapons to force *Triad*'s bridge party and gun crew below – a tactic which succeeded. *Triad* began to fire but as she did so *Toti* scored two hits on her pressure hull near the conning tower and also one hit with a torpedo. *Triad* then sank.

15 October 1940

Name	*Rainbow*	**Location**	Mediterranean
Class	*Rainbow* class submarine	**Cause**	Collision
Built	14 May 1930	**Casualties**	53
CO	Lt Cdr L.P. Moore RN	**Survivors**	None

Notes   HMS *Rainbow* was sunk in collision with the Italian merchant ship *Antonella Costa*.

The Italian submarine *Enrico Toti* which sank the British submarine *Triad* in a unique gun and torpedo action on the night of 10 October 1940. (Ufficio Storico Navale Militare, Rome)

The Italian merchant ship *Antonella Costa*, which was responsible for ramming and sinking HMS *Rainbow* in an accidental collision. (Dott. Achille Rastelli)

16 October 1940

Name	*Dundalk*	**Location**	North Sea, off Harwich, 52 03'N, 01 48'E
Class	Minesweeper	**Cause**	Mine

Notes   *Dundalk* was mined during routine sweeping operations off Harwich. She survived the explosion and was taken in tow by HMS *Sutton*. However, she foundered on the 17th in position 51 57'N, 01 27'E.

18 October 1940

Name	*H.49*	**Location**	North Sea, W of Texel
Class	*H* class submarine	**Cause**	Depth-charge
Built	15 July 1919	**Survivors**	1
CO	Lt R.E. Coltart DSC RN		

Notes   At 1510 hrs on the 18th Coltart brought *H.49* to the surface off the Dutch coast, west of the island of Texel. He hoped to use the thick fog as cover to get in an early battery charge. Alas, he surfaced almost under the bows – less than a mile – of the five trawlers of the German 5th A/S Flotilla commanded by *Kapitanleutnant* Wolfgang Kaden. For some reason *H.49*'s Asdic had failed to pick up the approach of these ships before the submarine surfaced. The trawlers sped to the spot and, after dropping a marker buoy, began a series of depth-charge attacks – in which a total of twenty-five depth-charges were dropped – which did enormous damage to the little submarine. The fore ends were flooded and had to be isolated, high pressure air was escaping from the main line, hull glands were leaking and water was pouring through the engine room hatch. Coltart made an attempt to surface but the submarine had taken on too much water and her HP air supplies were almost exhausted. Leading Stoker George Oliver was on duty in the engine room and remembered that the pressure in the boat was now so great that breathing out required a great effort. He remembered that he had no DSEA, since there were not enough to go around, and then lapsed into unconsciousness. It will never be explained how Oliver came to escape the submarine. All he could remember was being carried through the submarine's hull, which had been blown open either by the last depth-charge attack or by the excess pressure in the boat, and up to the surface where he was rescued. He subsequently joined Able Seaman Pester from *Spearfish* (see p. 127) and the pair were regarded with a certain amount of awe by their German captors.

In the mid-1980s the Dutch government successfully prosecuted amateur divers who had violated *H.49*'s status as a war grave.

Stoker George Oliver, the sole survivor from HM Submarine *H.49*. Oliver made a near miraculous escape from the submarine without breathing apparatus. (Royal Navy Submarine Museum).

19 October 1940

Name	*Venetia*	**Location**	Thames estuary, off the Knob Buoy,
Class	*V* class destroyer		51 33'N, 01 10'E
Built	29 October 1917	**Cause**	Mine

Notes   While proceeding down the swept channel in the Thames estuary, *Venetia* ran over a bottom-lying magnetic mine laid by German aircraft the previous evening.

22 October 1940

Name	*Margaree*	**Cause**	Collision
Class	*D* class destroyer	**Casualties**	140
Built	16 June 1932	**Survivors**	31
Location	Atlantic, 450 miles W of Ireland,		
	53 24'N, 22 50'E		

Notes   HMCS *Margaree* was the former HMS *Diana* which had been transferred to the RCN as a replacement for *Fraser* (see p. 122). *Margaree* was no more fortunate than her predecessor for she sank following a collision with SS *Port Fairey* in convoy OL.8.

30 October 1940

Name	*Sturdy*	**Location**	W coast of Scotland, island of Tiree,
Class	*S* class destroyer		56 29'N, 06 59'W
Built	June 1919	**Cause**	Grounded
		Casualties	3

Notes   HMS *Sturdy* grounded on Tiree in bad weather and was subsequently wrecked.

November 1940 *saw the loss of three armed merchant cruisers within two days in very different circumstances. Two were sunk following a humanitarian but reckless decision to rescue survivors from a sunken ship in an area where a U-boat was known to be operating. The third was sunk in a heroic single ship action against a pocket battleship.*

3 November 1940

Name	*Laurentic*	**Location**	Atlantic, NW of Ireland, 54 09'N,
Class	AMC		13 44'W
Built	1927	**Cause**	Submarine attack

Notes   See the entry for HMS *Patroclus* below.

Name	*Patroclus*	**Location**	Atlantic, NW of Ireland, 53 43'N,
Class	AMC		14 41'W
Built	1923	**Cause**	Submarine attack
CO	Capt R. Wynter DSO RN	**Survivors**	230

Notes   The sinking of two AMCs in just under two hours represented something of a *coup* for *Kapitanleutnant* Otto Kretschmer of *U99*. The whole incident is horribly reminiscent of the sinking of *Aboukir* and her consorts in 1914 (see pp. 8–9).

Kretschmer had just torpedoed the merchant ship *Casanare*, steaming independently, when he sighted a second ship, followed by a third, coming up astern. Careless use of the wireless enabled *U99*'s *Funkmaat* to identify the *Casanare* calling for help, and the other two ships, the armed merchant cruisers *Laurentic* and *Patroclus*. Kretschmer fired at *Laurentic*, hitting her amidships at 2107 hrs, and then at *Patroclus*, hitting her astern and just forward of the bridge. Both ships now lay stopped in the water surrounded by a cluster of lifeboats. Kretschmer was determined to sink both ships even though a destroyer could be seen in the distance. He finished off *Laurentic* with another torpedo in the stern; the after part of the ship broke away and *Laurentic*'s depth-charges exploded before she sank stern first. *Patroclus* took another four torpedoes: after the sixth torpedo the ship broke in half and sank very quickly.

5 November 1940

Name	*Jervis Bay*	**CO**	Capt E.S. Fogarty Fegen RN
Class	AMC	**Location**	E Atlantic, 52 41'N, 32 17'W
Built	1924	**Cause**	Gunfire

Notes   *Jervis Bay* was escorting convoy HX.84 when, just after 2000 hrs on 5 November, a report was received that the convoy was being shelled by a raider, the pocket battleship *Admiral Scheer*. While the convoy scattered under cover of smoke *Jervis Bay* advanced to engage the *Scheer*. It was a hopeless action: *Jervis Bay* was armed with seven 6 in guns against the *Scheer*'s six 11 in and eight 5.9 in. She was overwhelmed by gunfire and sank. Nevertheless her sacrifice had bought the convoy precious time – of the 37 ships in the convoy 31 survived. On 18 November it was announced that Captain Fegen had been posthumously awarded the Victoria Cross.

7 November 1940

Name	*Swordfish*	**Location**	English Channel, S of St Catherine's
Class	S class submarine		Point on the Isle of Wight
CO	Lt M.A. Langley RN	**Cause**	Mine
		Survivors	None

Notes   *Swordfish* had sailed from Gosport for a patrol off Brest on 7 November. Nothing further was heard from her even though she was ordered to report her position on 15 and 16 November. Lieutenant Langley had only recently been appointed to *Swordfish* from *H.49* (see p. 132), so he survived the sinking of his former boat by just three weeks.

It was always supposed that *Swordfish* was mined off Brest. However, this theory was suddenly dispelled with the discovery of the wreck in July 1983. *Swordfish* lies in 150 ft of water a few miles south of St Catherine's Point, the most southerly tip of the Isle of Wight. The wreck lies in two parts, indicating that she had been mined. The forward hydroplanes are set to 'dive' and the engine room telegraphs are at slow ahead. The after escape hatch is open, suggesting that some members of the crew escaped; however, even if they did reach the surface their chances of survival without prompt rescue were no better than if they had remained in the submarine. It is clear that *Swordfish* was mined a few hours after leaving Portsmouth, probably as she performed a trim dive prior to proceeding to her patrol area.

2 December 1940

Name	*Forfar*	**Location**	Atlantic, W of Ireland, 54 35'N,
Class	AMC		18 18'W
Built	1920	**Cause**	Submarine attack

Notes   *Forfar* was sailing independently to meet convoy SC.14 when she was torpedoed and sunk by *U99* (*Kapitanleutnant* Otto Kretschmer).

6(?) December 1940

Name	*Triton*	**Location**	Mediterranean, lower Adriatic
Class	*T* class submarine	**Casualties**	62
Built	5 October 1937	**Survivors**	None
CO	Lt G.C. Watkins RN		

Notes   *Triton* sailed for patrol on 28 November and nothing more was heard from her. She was possibly the victim of a depth-charge attack by the torpedo boats *Altair* and *Andromeda* following *Triton*'s sinking of the freighter *Olimpia* on 6 December but the evidence is inconclusive. She might also have been the victim of an attack by the torpedo boat *Clio* on 18 December; however, since *Triton* should have been clear of this area by 13 December in order to return to Malta on the 17th this is unlikely. The only other alternatives are that *Triton* was mined or was the victim of an accident.

7 December 1940

Name	*Regulus*	**Location**	Mediterranean, Straits of Otranto
Class	*Rainbow* class submarine	**Cause**	Mine
Built	11 June 1930	**Casualties**	53
CO	Lt Cdr F.B. Currie RN	**Survivors**	None

Notes   *Regulus* sailed from Alexandria on 18 November with orders to patrol south of 42°N in the entrance to the Adriatic. She was not heard from after leaving Alexandria and was formally listed as overdue on 7 December. It is presumed that she was the victim of either a mine or an accident.

14 December 1940

Name	*Branlebas*	**Cause**	Foundered
Class	French *La Melpomene* torpedo boat	**Casualties**	*c.* 100
Built	12 April 1937	**Survivors**	3
Location	English Channel, E of the Lizard		

Notes   *Branlebas* had been taken over by the Royal Navy in July 1940 and was still wearing the White Ensign four months later. In bad weather east of the Lizard her back broke and she foundered. The survivors were picked up by the destroyer *Mistral* – another former French ship in British hands.

15 December 1940

Name	*Cameron*	**Location**	English Channel, Portsmouth
Class	*Town* class destroyer		dockyard
Built	8 May 1919	**Cause**	Air attack
CO	Not in commission	**Casualties**	None

Notes   HMS *Cameron* was one of the fifty ex-American leased to Britain by the Americans vessels in September 1940. On the night of 15 December she was in dry dock at Portsmouth when the dockyard was bombed. A bomb fell and exploded in the dock causing the ship to topple over. She was considered beyond repair and broken up.

17 December 1940

Name	*Acheron*	**Location**	English Channel, S of the Isle of
Class	*A* class destroyer		Wight, 50 31'N, 01 31'E
Built	18 March 1930	**Cause**	Mine

Notes   Having just completed repairs to bomb damage sustained on 24 August when her stern had been blown off, *Acheron* was conducting high-speed trials south of the Isle of Wight when she was mined.

22 December 1940

Name	*Hyperion*	**Location**	Mediterranean, 24 miles E of Cape
Class	*H* class destroyer		Bon, 37 40'N, 11 31'E
Built	8 April 1936	**Cause**	Submarine attack

Notes   *Hyperion* was torpedoed at 0156 hrs by the Italian submarine *Serpente*. She was taken in tow by *Janus* but later had to be scuttled.

LOSSES 1941

10 January 1941

Name	*Gallant*	**Cause**	Mine
Class	G class destroyer	**Casualties**	60
Built	26 September 1935	**Survivors**	85
Location	Mediterranean, 120 miles W of Malta, 36 27'N, 12 11'E		

Notes *Gallant* was participating in operation *Excess*, the passage of a convoy from Gibraltar to the eastern Mediterranean. At 0834 hrs she struck a mine and her bows were blown off as far back as the bridge. She was towed back to Malta stern-first by HMS *Mohawk* and beached in Grand Harbour on the 11th. The journey was not without incident: on ten occasions *Mohawk* and her charge were attacked by Ju.87 dive-bombers. Early warning radar and well-directed AA fire from the cruiser *Bonaventure* served to drive off the attackers on each occasion. On 20 January, following a survey, *Gallant* was declared a total loss.

The wreck of HMS *Gallant* lying at Malta, showing the extent of the mine damage suffered on 10 January 1941. (Ufficio Storico Navale Militare, Rome)

11 January 1941

Name	*Southampton*	**Location**	Mediterranean, 180 miles E of
Class	*Southampton* class cruiser		Malta, 34 54'N, 18 24'E
Built	10 March 1936	**Cause**	Air attack and (possibly) submarine
CO	Capt B.C. Brooke RN	**Casualties**	80
		Survivors	727

Notes   *Southampton* was the second casualty of operation *Excess*. At 1522 hrs on the 11th *Southampton* and *Gloucester* were proceeding to take station ahead of the battle fleet when they were attacked by a force of twelve Ju.87 dive-bombers. The aircraft attacked out the sun and achieved complete surprise. *Southampton* was hit aft by one or more bombs which started a fire in the after engine room. Damage control parties could not contain the blaze and she had to be abandoned. Her survivors were taken off by the destroyer *Diamond* and later transferred to *Gloucester*. While the survivors were being transferred *Southampton* was attacked by the Italian submarine *Settimo* (CC Mario Spano) which fired three torpedoes and reported one explosion. *Southampton* was eventually despatched by three torpedoes fired by HMS *Orion*.

31 January 1941

Name	*Huntley*	**Cause**	Air attack
Class	*Hunt* class minesweeper	**Casualties**	18
Built	1917	**Survivors**	56
Location	Mediterranean, 30 miles W of Mersa		
	Matruh, 31 25'N, 26 48'E		

Notes   The capture of Tobruk on 18 January 1941 was a considerable achievement for the Eighth Army. However, the burden of supplying the Army as it forged westwards fell on the small ships of the Royal Navy's Inshore Squadron. *Huntley* was one of these vessels. The little minesweeper was overwhelmed by German aircraft and sunk by torpedoes, bombs and machine-gun fire.

11 February 1941

Name	*Snapper*	**Location**	Atlantic, SW of Ushant
Class	*S* class submarine	**Casualties**	39
Built	25 October 1934	**Survivors**	None
CO	Lt G.V. Prowse RN		

Notes   *Snapper* sailed for her thirteenth war patrol on 29 January 1941 in an area off Ushant. She was due to leave patrol on the night of 10 February to return to the UK. That same night the German minesweepers *M2*, *M13* and *M25* were attacked off Ushant while conducting an A/S sweep. The submarine, which was almost certainly *Snapper* since no other British submarine was in the area, broke surface after firing and was then hunted by the minesweepers which dropped over fifty depth-charges. Although no wreckage was recovered that might indicate a sinking, the strong HE contact faded and disappeared. While the possibility of loss by accident must always be considered for a submarine, the attack by the three German minesweepers seems the most likely explanation for *Snapper*'s loss.

22 February 1941

Name	*Terror*	**Location**	Mediterranean, off Tobruk, 32 40'N,
Class	Monitor		22 30'E
Built	18 May 1916	**Cause**	Air attack
CO	Cdr H.J. Haynes RN	**Casualties**	None
		Survivors	204

Notes   *Terror*'s 15 in guns had been invaluable to the Eighth Army in their advance on Tobruk and Benghazi. However, she was terribly exposed since air cover and AA defences were non-existent. At dawn on the 22nd she sustained damage from three near-misses at Benghazi and was then ordered to return to the relative safety of Tobruk. While leaving Benghazi, escorted by the corvette *Salvia* and the minesweeper *Fareham*, she set off two acoustic mines in her wake which severely shook the ship and caused flooding. Just after her lone Hurricane fighter escort had departed on the morning of the 23rd *Terror* was attacked by a force of five German aircraft. Two bombs fell along the starboard side and a third to port and her hull began to split between the bridge and the 15 in turret. An oil fuel fire broke out in the engine room which was only extinguished by the rising flood water. This in turn cut off steam to the engines, pumps and generators. An attempt by *Fareham* to tow the monitor failed as she was listing to starboard and settling by the bow. At 2000 hrs all officers and men except the AA gun crews were ordered off. *Terror* continued to settle and just before midnight she was abandoned by the remainder of her crew. She finally sank at 0420 hrs on the 24th, her end hastened by depth-charges dropped by *Salvia* and *Fareham*.

The monitor HMS *Terror* at Malta in 1935. Built in 1916, *Terror* served in both world wars before being sunk off the North African coast on 22 February 1941. (Wright & Logan)

24 February 1941

Name	*Dainty*	**Location**	Mediterranean, Tobruk harbour
Class	D class destroyer	**Cause**	Air attack
Built	3 May 1932	**Casualties**	33

Notes   *Dainty* was bombed and sunk by German aircraft while preparing to put to sea from Tobruk. Her loss emphasised the total lack of air cover for British ships on the North African coast which left German aircraft free to operate without hindrance.

25 February 1941

Name	*Exmoor*	**Location**	North Sea, off Lowestoft, 52 29'N,
Class	*Hunt* class destroyer		01 50'E
Built	25 January 1940	**Cause**	Torpedo

Notes   German *S-boote* became increasingly active in the North Sea in February 1941. The regular north–south convoy traffic was their target. On the night of 25 February a force of *S-boote* attacked convoy FN.417 and in the mêlée the destroyer *Exmoor* was torpedoed and sunk.

25(?) February 1941

Name	*Usk*	**CO**	Lt G.P. Darling RN
Class	*U* class submarine	**Location**	Mediterranean, off Cape Bon
Built	7 June 1940	**Survivors**	None

Notes   *Usk* is believed to have been mined off Cape Bon in the Mediterranean. Despite the absence of an alternative explanation, there is little or no evidence to support this view. The date of 25 February is given as it is that of the last recorded signal from the submarine.

21 March 1941

Name	*York*	**Location**	Crete, Suda Bay harbour
Class	*York* class cruiser	**Cause**	Explosive motor boat
Built	17 July 1928	**Casualties**	None

Notes   *York* was lying at anchor in Suda Bay when she was attacked by a force of six Italian MT explosive motor boats. The Italians had had the anchorage under observation for some time and *York* was seen as a prime target. She was struck by two MT boats driven by *STV* Angelo Cabrini and Mechanic 3rd Class Tullio Tedeschi. The two explosions blew open the side of the ship around the machinery spaces. Both engine room and boiler rooms were flooded and *York* settled in 4½ fathoms of water. She was subsequently damaged repeatedly by German air attacks until 22 May 1941 when she was beyond all salvage.

31 March 1941

Name	*Bonaventure*	**Location**	Mediterranean, 90 miles S of Crete,
Class	*Dido* class cruiser		33 20'N, 26 35'E
Built	19 April 1939	**Cause**	Torpedo
		Survivors	310

Notes   *Bonaventure* was escorting a convoy returning to Alexandria from the Aegean when she was unsuccessfully attacked by the Italian submarine *Dagabur* on the evening of 30 March. Six hours later she had moved into the patrol area of the Italian submarine *Ambra*, which attacked at 0244 hrs on the 31st. *Bonaventure* sank almost immediately, her survivors being taken off by the destroyer *Hereward*.

4 April 1941

Name	*Voltaire*	**Location**	Atlantic, 14 25'N, 40 40'W
Class	AMC	**Cause**	Gunfire
Built	1923	**Survivors**	None

Notes   On 5 April an intercepted German communiqué announced that the British 'auxiliary cruiser' *Voltaire* had been sunk in the Atlantic by a German raider. Although the German ship was not named, she is now known to have been the *Thor*. In reply to enquiries from the Admiralty, the CinCs of the South Atlantic and America and West Indies Stations replied that they had no knowledge of the *Voltaire*'s movements. The Canadian AMC *Prince Henry* reported steaming through oil and wreckage which may have come from the *Voltaire* on 7 and 9 April. When no further information was received and *Voltaire* failed to answer signals she was declared lost on 3 May.

4 April 1941

Name	*Cormorin*	**Cause**	Fire
Class	AMC	**Casualties**	20
Built	1924	**Survivors**	405
Location	North Atlantic, 54 34'N, 21 20'W		

Notes   *Cormorin* was en route to Freetown with stores and also providing an ocean escort for MV *Glenarty* when she caught fire. It proved impossible to control the blaze and she had to be abandoned. The survivors were taken off in worsening weather conditions by the destroyers *Broke* and *Lincoln* assisted by the *Glenarty*. The seamanship of the *Broke* was especially commended since for three hours, in a south-easterly gale, she remained on the leeward quarter of the *Cormorin* thus allowing 180 of the 405 survivors to jump clear. *Cormorin*'s blazing wreck was eventually finished off by a torpedo fired by *Broke*.

8 April 1941

Name	*Rajputana*	**Cause**	Torpedo
Class	Armed Merchant Cruiser	**Casualties**	40
Built	1925	**Survivors**	277
Location	North Atlantic, 64 50'N, 27 25'W		

Notes   *Rajputana* was on the dangerous Northern Patrol duty when she was attacked by *U108* (*Korvettenkapitan* Klaus Scholtz). The survivors were rescued by the destroyer *Legion* and taken to Iceland.

16 April 1941

Name	*Mohawk*	**Location**	Mediterranean, Kerkenah Bank
Class	*Tribal* class destroyer	**Cause**	Torpedo
Built	5 October 1937	**Survivors**	168

Notes   In the early hours of 16 April the British destroyers *Jervis*, *Janus*, *Nubian* and *Mohawk* intercepted a convoy of five Italian merchant vessels heading for North Africa escorted by the destroyers *Tarigo*, *Baleno* and *Lampo*. In the mêlée all eight Axis vessels were sunk but *Mohawk* was hit aft by a torpedo fired by the *Tarigo*. She lay stopped in the water but continued to engage the merchant ships using her two forward turrets. She was hit amidships, again by a torpedo fired by *Tarigo*, and capsized. Her hull was eventually sunk by gunfire from *Janus*.

27 April 1941

Name	*Wryneck*	**Location**	Mediterranean, S of Nauplia,
Class	V&W class destroyer		36 30'N, 23 34'E
Built	13 May 1918	**Cause**	Air attack
		Survivors	42

Notes   See the entry for HMS *Diamond* below.

Name	*Diamond*	**Location**	Mediterranean, S of Nauplia,
Class	D class destroyer		36 30'N, 23 34'E
Built	8 April 1932	**Cause**	Air attack
		Survivors	None

Notes   In the confusion surrounding the German attack on Greece, several British warships and transports were employed in evacuating British, Commonwealth and Greek forces. The Dutch transport *Slamat* was carrying over 700 troops when she was bombed and sunk on the 27th. *Diamond* and *Wryneck* came to her rescue and picked up 700 of *Slamat's* crew and passengers. In turn the two destroyers were attacked by nine Ju.87 aircraft and both were sunk. One officer and forty-one ratings from *Wryneck* were rescued along with eight soldiers from the *Slamat*. There were no survivors from *Diamond*.

May 1941 *is best remembered for the loss of the battle cruiser HMS* Hood *in action with the German battleship* Bismarck. *However, in the evacuation of the island of Crete following the German airborne invasion the Royal Navy lost 2 cruisers and 6 destroyers together with 2 battleships, 1 aircraft carrier and 5 cruisers; 4 destroyers were damaged. The Navy achieved its aim of preventing a seaborne invasion of Crete but the cost was immense.*

2 May 1941

Name	*Jersey*	**Location**	Malta, entrance to Grand Harbour,
Class	J class destroyer		Valetta, 35 54'N, 14 30'E
Built	26 September 1938	**Cause**	Mine

Notes   HMS *Jersey* together with *Gloucester*, *Kipling* and *Kashmir* were returning to Malta following operations against Axis convoy routes. *Jersey* was in the lead. As she entered the harbour she ran over the mine and sank, blocking the channel. Her three consorts remained under way outside the harbour until it became clear that *Jersey's* wreck could not be cleared, at which point they were ordered to Gibraltar.

4 May 1941

Name	*Fermoy*	**Location**	Mediterranean, island of Malta
Class	Hunt class minesweeper	**Cause**	Air attack
Built	1917		

Notes *Fermoy* was in dry dock for routine boiler cleaning and maintenance when she was bombed and damaged beyond repair during an Axis air raid on the island.

7 May 1941

Name	*Stoke*	**Location**	Mediterranean, Tobruk harbour
Class	*Hunt* class minesweeper	**Cause**	Air attack
Built	1917		

Notes *Stoke* was bombed and sunk by Axis aircraft during an attack on shipping at Tobruk.

12 May 1941

Name	*Undaunted*	**Location**	Mediterranean, off Zuara on the
Class	*U* class submarine		Libyan Coast
Built	20 August 1940	**Survivors**	None
CO	Lt J.L. Livesay RN		

Notes *Undaunted* sailed from Malta on 1 May for her first Mediterranean patrol in an area off Tripoli. On 12 May an Italian aircraft sighted a submarine off Zuara on the Libyan coast and consequently the Italian corvette *Pegaso* was detached from a nearby convoy. At 2028 hrs *Pegaso* rejoined the convoy and reported that she had carried out a number of depth-charge attacks and although no wreckage had been recovered, a large oil slick was observed forming on the surface. The only problem with this explanation is that, although the attack took place in *Undaunted*'s patrol area, *Undaunted* should not have been there – she should already have been on her way back to Malta. However, apart from being mined or lost by accident, there is no other explanation for her loss.

Name	*Ladybird*	**CO**	Cdr J.F. Blackburn DSO RN
Class	*Insect* class gunboat	**Location**	Mediterranean, Tobruk harbour
Built	12 April 1916	**Cause**	Air attack

Notes HMS *Ladybird* had been one of the most successful ships of the Inshore Squadron, protecting the right flank of the Eighth Army. With her shallow draft and powerful armament of two 6 in guns, she was a most effective vessel. Her end came in an air attack on 12 May in a massed attack by Ju.87s, most of whose pilots had little to thank *Ladybird* for – the night before she had pounded their airfield at Gazala for several hours. One bomb struck the gunboat's 2-pounder pom-pom, a second burst in the boiler room and blew out the sides of the ship. The little gunboat sank upright in shallow water, with her upperworks still above the water, so that soldiers from the 1st Battalion South Staffordshire Regiment were still able to use the 3 in gun on her deckhouse. Writing of her loss, Admiral Sir Andrew Cunningham commented, 'The loss of HMS *Ladybird* . . . is a matter for keen regret'.

13 May 1941

Name	*Salopian*	**Location**	Atlantic, 56 43'N, 38 57'W
Class	AMC	**Cause**	Torpedo
Built	1926	**Survivors**	278

Notes *Salopian* had been covering convoy SC.30 but had left the convoy at 1825 hrs on the 12th to return to Halifax independently. Just after 0630 hrs on the 13th she was struck by one torpedo (of four) fired by *U98* (*Korvettenkapitan* Robert Gysae). She remained afloat until 0945 hrs when a second torpedo from *U98* sank her. Most of her complement got away and were rescued by HMS *Impulsive*. *Salopian* was the fourteenth AMC to be sunk during the war: ten had been sunk by U-boats, three by raiders and one destroyed by fire.

20 May 1941

Name	*Widnes*	**Location**	Mediterranean, Suda Bay on the
Class	*Hunt* class minesweeper		island of Crete
Built	1917	**Cause**	Air attack

Notes *Widnes* was badly damaged in a German air attack and sank in shallow water. She was subsequently salved and commissioned into the *Kriegsmarine* as *UJ.2109*. Her end came on 17 October 1943 when she was sunk in Kalymnos harbour by gunfire of the British destroyers *Jervis* and *Penn*.

21 May 1941

Name	*Juno*	**Location**	Mediterranean, SE of Crete,
Class	*J* class destroyer		34 35'N, 26 34'E
Built	8 December 1938	**Cause**	Air attack
CO	Cdr St J.R.J. Tyrwhitt RN	**Survivors**	97

Notes *Juno* had been part of a force of two cruisers and four destroyers stationed to the north of the island throughout the 20th. On the morning of the 21st they were ordered to withdraw southwards through the Kaso Strait and from 0950 hrs they bombed incessantly. *Juno* succumbed at 1249 hrs – she sank in less than 2 minutes following an explosion in one of her magazines. The survivors were rescued by *Nubian*, *Kandahar* and *Kingston*.

22 May 1941

Name	*Greyhound*	**CO**	Cdr W.R. Marshall-A'Deane DSO
Class	*G* class destroyer		DSC RN
Built	15 August 1935	**Location**	Mediterranean, W of Crete
		Cause	Air attack

Notes *Greyhound*, operating to the north-west of Crete, had been detached from the main body of the fleet to sink a caique and was rejoining the screen at 1351 hrs when she was attacked and struck by two bombs. She sank stern first in less than 15 minutes. *Kingston* and *Kandahar* were detached to rescue survivors; they would be supported later by the cruisers *Fiji* and *Gloucester*. (This decision was to have tragic consequences – both cruisers would be sunk within hours.) While engaged in rescue work the ships, and their boats in the water, were repeatedly machine-gunned by German aircraft.

Commander Marshall-A'Deane survived the sinking of his ship and was rescued by *Kandahar*. Later that day, while *Kandahar* was rescuing survivors from *Fiji*, he dived over the side to rescue a seaman in distress. He was lost sight of in the darkness and never seen again.

Name	*Gloucester*	**Location**	Mediterranean, W of Crete,
Class	*Southampton* class cruiser		35 50'N, 23 00'E
Built	19 October 1937	**Cause**	Air attack
CO	Capt H.A. Rowley RN		

Notes   After rescuing *Greyhound*'s survivors *Gloucester* and *Fiji* pressed on at high speed. Both ships were very low on AA ammunition (a fact not known to the senior officer when he ordered them to stand by *Greyhound*). At 1550 hrs *Gloucester* was just astern of the fleet when she was the subject of very intense air attacks which left her dead in the water. She was badly on fire and her upper deck was a shambles. In view of the intensity of the attacks Captain William Powlett of the *Fiji* realised that he could not stay and support her, so after dropping all available boats and rafts, *Fiji* headed away to the south-east. *Gloucester* subsequently sank. As was becoming the pattern in the battle for Crete, her survivors were machine-gunned in the water. Captain Rowley's body, recognisable only from his uniform jacket and signals in his pockets, was washed up west of Mersa Matruh on the North African coast four weeks later.

Name	*Fiji*	Location	Mediterranean, S of Crete, 34 35'N,
Class	*Colony* class cruiser		23 10'E
Built	31 May 1939	Cause	Air attack
CO	Capt P.B. William-Powlett RN	Casualties	248
		Survivors	523

Notes   As *Fiji* headed away to the south-east she was repeatedly attacked by German aircraft – some twenty attacks were reported. William-Powlett carried out evasive manoeuvres at high speed to put the bombers off their aim and enforced a rigid economy of fire to preserve his ship's dwindling ammunition stocks. However, the end came just after 1845 hrs when a lone Me.109 dropped a bomb that fell along the port side amidships. The ship took a heavy list to port but could still steam at 17 knots. At 1915 hrs another aircraft dropped three bombs which all hit the ship above the 'A' boiler room. The list increased and she slowed to a stop. At 2015 hrs she finally rolled over, having expended every 4 in shell on board except six starshells. *Kingston* and *Kandahar* dropped boats and floats but withdrew to the south to avoid further attack. They returned after dark and rescued 523 officers and men. Among the survivors was Leading Stoker Walter Arnold, one of three survivors from HMS *Thetis* (see pp. 95–100).

23 May 1941

Name	*Kelly*	Location	Mediterranean, 13 miles S of Crete,
Class	*K* class destroyer		34 40'N, 24 10'E
Built	25 October 1938	Cause	Air attack
CO	Capt Lord Louis Mountbatten GCVO DSO RN	Survivors	128

Notes   See the entry for HMS *Kashmir* below.

Name	*Kashmir*	Location	Mediterranean, 13 miles S of Crete,
Class	*K* class destroyer		34 40'N, 24 10'E
Built	4 April 1939	Cause	Air attack
CO	Cdr H.A. King RN	Survivors	153

Notes   *Kelly* and *Kashmir* had been withdrawing to the south of Crete since dawn on the 23rd. At 0755 hrs when 13 miles south of Gavdo Island the two ships were attacked by a force of twenty-four Ju.87 dive-bombers. *Kashmir* was first to be hit and sank in under two minutes. *Kelly* was then struck amidships by a single bomb while turning under full helm at 30 knots. She rolled over to port with considerable way on and eventually sank after floating upside-down for half an hour. The survivors of both ships were machine-gunned in the water by German aircraft until HMS *Kipling*, which had observed the attack from the south, returned to rescue them. While heading south, with 281 survivors embarked, *Kipling* was attacked by over forty aircraft which dropped eighty-three bombs. Skilful ship handling ensured her escape but the evasive manoeuvring so exhausted her fuel bunkers that the net layer *Protector* had to be sent out from Alexandria to supply her with fuel.

24 May 1941

Name	*Hood*	**Location**	N Atlantic, Denmark Strait, 63 20'N, 31 50'W
Class	Battle cruiser		
Built	22 August 1918	**Cause**	Gunfire
CO	Capt Ralph Kerr RN, flagship of Vice Admiral L.A. Holland	**Casualties**	1,418
		Survivors	3

The last known photograph of HMS *Hood*, taken from HMS *Prince of Wales* on 23 May 1941. Twenty-four hours later Hood had sunk with the loss of all but three of her complement of over 1,400. (US Navy)

Notes   *Hood* was surely the most famous of all Royal Navy losses this century. For most people in Britain, and indeed the world, the battle cruiser *Hood* epitomised the strength of the Royal Navy during the interwar period. Her loss was a massive blow to British morale and prestige – out of all proportion to the value of the ship herself. *Hood*, the battleship *Prince of Wales* and six destroyers had left Scapa Flow on 22 May in response to reports that the German battleship *Bismarck*, with *Prinz Eugen*, was en route for the Atlantic. On the morning of the 24th the British, steering north-west, encountered the German ships steering south-west. Holland's ships were poorly positioned with the two German ships 'crossing his T'. Moreover the wind and heavy seas hampered *Hood*'s fire-control teams while Holland had forbidden the use of radar for fear that the transmissions would be picked up by the enemy. The Germans opened fire first. Just after 0555 hrs, as Holland ordered the British ships to begin a turn to port which would open their 'A-Arcs', *Bismarck*'s fifth salvo landed alongside *Hood*'s starboard quarter. *Hood* was suddenly rent apart by a massive explosion, the base of which seemed to be at the foot of the ship's mainmast. The forward part of the ship reared up to the vertical before sinking while the after part remained afloat for some minutes shrouded in smoke.

Only three men survived the sinking: Midshipman Robert Dundas and Able Seaman Ted Briggs, both of whom climbed out of the bridge, and Able Seaman Robert Tillburn, who literally walked off the upper deck into the water. The three men spent two hours in the water before being rescued by HMS *Electra*.

A number of theories have been advanced to account for *Hood*'s loss. The problem with nearly all of them is that they fail to account for the explosion observed at the base of the mainmast – there is no magazine in this area of the ship which could have produced such an explosion. The only likely explanation is that one or more shells from *Bismarck*'s fifth salvo travelled underwater and penetrated *Hood*'s side underneath the armoured belt before exploding. While such an explosion would be unlikely to detonate the large number of shells in this area it would start a massive fire in the 115 tons of cordite contained in the two after 15 in and 4 in magazines. The fire would produce a mass of cordite gas. For a while the ship's structure would contain this gas but eventually it would take the line of least resistance and blow forward through the bulkhead into the engine room and then up through the exhaust vents located at the base of the mainmast. The gas bursting through the bulkhead into the engine room would have caused a massive structural failure in the ship, causing her to break in half and sink.

Able Seaman Bob Tillburn, one of the three survivors from HMS *Hood*, on survivor's leave with his younger brother. (Author)

28 May 1941

Name	*Mashona*	**Location**	Atlantic, 100 miles W of Ireland,
Class	*Tribal* class destroyer		52 58'N, 11 36'W
Built	3 September 1937	**Cause**	Air attack
CO	Cdr W.H. Selby RN	**Casualties**	46

Notes   *Mashona* had been part of the 6th Destroyer Flotilla which had attacked *Bismarck* with such *elan* on the night before she was sunk. While returning to the UK after the action she was attacked by an He.111 which had been vectored on to the force by an Fw.200 reconnaissance aircraft. *Mashona* was hit by one bomb which penetrated the ship's side and exploded in no. 1 boiler room. While it was possible to shore up the after bulkhead separating the two boiler rooms, the forward bulkhead was riddled with splinter holes and the ship began to take on water. *Mashona* began to list over to starboard and, despite all surplus equipment being jettisoned, it proved impossible to restore the ship to an even keel. Eventually *Mashona* rolled over on to her beam ends. Commander Selby gave the order to abandon ship. He thought he was last to leave the ship but as he went over the side a junior rating, who had not heard the order to abandon ship, was seen behind him. Once both men were in the water, Commander Selby reminded the rating of a captain's privileges in no uncertain terms!

The survivors were picked up by HMS *Tartar* who then tried – and failed – to sink the wreck by torpedo. Eventually *Mashona*'s hull was sent to the bottom by gunfire from HMC *St Croix* and *Sherwood*.

29 May 1941

Name	*Imperial*	**Location**	Mediterranean, S of Crete, 35 23'N,
Class	*I* class destroyer		25 40'E
Built	11 December 1936	**Cause**	Scuttled after machinery failure
CO	Lt Cdr C.A. de W. Kitcat RN	**Casualties**	None

Notes *Imperial* and *Kimberley* were part of the British force of three cruisers and six destroyers which had just completed the evacuation of the last British and Commonwealth personnel from Heraklion. They were heading south at high speed when at 0345 hrs *Imperial*'s steering gear failed. The failure may be ascribed to shock damage suffered from a near miss on the evening of the 28th. Rear Admiral Rawlings decided that he could not afford to wait for *Imperial*'s engine room department to effect repairs since he needed to be as far away as possible from Crete by daybreak. He therefore ordered *Hotspur* to take off *Imperial*'s crew and passengers before sinking her.

Name	*Hereward*	**Location**	Mediterranean, 5 miles S of Crete,
Class	*H* class destroyer		35 20'N, 26 20'E
Built	10 March 1936	**Cause**	Air attack
CO	Lt Cdr W.J. Munn RN		

Notes The delay caused by the loss of *Imperial* meant that the British ships were running 90 minutes behind schedule. As they entered the Kaso Strait they were attacked by German aircraft. Fighter cover promised by the RAF failed to appear. *Hereward* was hit and had to drop out of the screen. Rear Admiral Rawlings took the difficult decision to leave her rather than try to save her – and thereby risk his entire force and the troops embarked. *Hereward* was last seen moving slowly towards Crete, shrouded in smoke. She was eventually sunk by air attacks close to land. Italian motor boats rescued the majority of the survivors.

1 June 1941

Name	*Calcutta*	**Location**	Mediterranean, 100 miles NW of
Class	*C* class cruiser		Alexandria, 3155'N, 28 05'E
Built	9 July 1918	**Cause**	Air attack
CO	Capt D.M. Lees DSO RN	**Survivors**	255

Notes The cruisers *Calcutta* and *Coventry* sailed from Alexandria on 1 June in order to give extra AA cover to the cruiser *Phoebe*, the minelayer *Ariadne* and three destroyers which had evacuated the last British and Commonwealth troops from Crete the previous evening. When only about 100 miles out they were attacked from out of the sun by two Ju.88s. *Coventry* avoided the first aircraft but two bombs from the second struck *Calcutta* which sank in a few minutes, just after 0920 hrs. In view of the fact that his position was now known to the Luftwaffe and that further attacks could be expected, Captain Carne of the *Coventry* abandoned the operation and returned to Alexandria.

10 June 1941

Name	*Pintail*	**Location**	North Sea, Humber estuary,
Class	Corvette		53 30'N, 00 32'E
Built	1939	**Cause**	Mine

Notes   *Pintail* was mined off the Humber while escorting convoy FN.477.

24 June 1941

Name	*Auckland*	**Location**	Mediterranean, 20 miles ENE of
Class	Sloop		Tobruk, 32 15'N, 24 30'E
Built	30 June 1938	**Cause**	Air attack
		Survivors	162

Notes   *Auckland* was escorting the petrol carrier *Pass of Balmaha* to Tobruk when she was overwhelmed by three formations of German aircraft – each consisting of sixteen Ju.87 aircraft. The survivors were rescued by HMAS *Parramatta* despite repeated air attacks. The petrol carrier was damaged in the attack and was abandoned but later successfully brought into Tobruk by HMAS *Waterhen*.

29 June 1941

Name	*Waterhen*	**Location**	Mediterranean, 100 miles E of
Class	*W* class destroyer		Tobruk
Built	26 March 1918	**Cause**	Air attack
		Casualties	None

Notes   At 2000 hrs on the 29th, while heading for Tobruk in company with the British destroyer *Defender*, *Waterhen* was attacked by German aircraft and sustained such damage that she was brought to a standstill. Her complement was taken off by *Defender* which then loitered in the area waiting for night to fall after which she would return and attempt to take the cripple in tow. At this stage the Italian submarine *Tembien* was sighted and engaged by *Defender*. The submarine dived quickly, thus allowing an erroneous claim from *Defender* to have sunk the submarine. It proved impossible to tow the *Waterhen* as flooding had spread from her engine room to her boiler room and at 0150 hrs on the 30th she rolled over and sank.

30 June 1941

Name	*Cricket*	**CO**	Lt Cdr E.B. Carnduff RN
Class	*Insect* class river gunboat	**Location**	Mediterranean, E of Mersa Matruh
Built	1916	**Cause**	Air attack

Notes   *Cricket* was escorting a convoy of two slow storeships from Mersa Matruh to Tobruk when the convoy was attacked by some sixty Ju.87s and Ju.88s with strong fighter cover provided by Me.110s and Italian G.50s. Fighter cover from 73, 250 and 274 Squadrons RAF and 1 Squadron SAAF drove off most of the attackers but *Cricket* had been badly shaken by a near miss. Tons of water from the explosion of the bomb had cascaded over the ship, buckling her hull, flooding her machinery spaces and depolarising the dynamo. She was taken in tow by the sloop *Flamingo*, herself badly damaged, and was returned to Alexandria. *Cricket* was subsequently surveyed and found unfit for further sea service. Accordingly she was employed as a floating AA platform. At some time in 1944 or 1945 – the precise date is unknown – her hull was scuttled off the south coast of Cyprus where she lay undisturbed until discovered by divers from the Royal Engineers in the 1980s.

11 July 1941

Name	*Defender*	**Location**	Mediterranean, 60 miles E of Tobruk
Class	D class destroyer	**Cause**	Air attack
Built	7 April 1932		

Notes *Defender* was en route for Tobruk in company with the destroyer *Vendetta* when she was attacked and damaged by German aircraft. *Vendetta* tried to take her in tow but *Defender*'s engine and boiler room were flooded and her back was broken. She settled lower in the water and eventually had to be sunk off Sidi Barrani.

19 July 1941

Name	*Umpire*	**Location**	North Sea, off the coast of Suffolk
Class	U class submarine	**Cause**	Collision
Built	30 December 1940	**Casualties**	22
CO	Lt M.R. Wingfield RN	**Survivors**	16

Notes *Umpire* was a brand-new *U* class submarine which had just been completed by the Royal Dockyard at Chatham and was being sent north to Dunoon to begin trials and work-up. Accordingly she joined the north-bound East Coast convoy EC4, though she was not declared as part of the escort. When the convoy was passing Aldeburgh a lone He.111 attacked the leading ships and *Umpire* performed her first dive at sea. When the attack was over *Umpire* returned to the surface but soon her port engine began to give trouble and she lagged behind the convoy.

Shortly after midnight, convoy EC4 was due to pass the southbound FS44. Both convoys were using the same swept channel through the minefields and it was the procedure for convoys to keep to the right side of the channel so that they would pass each other port side to port side. However, Wingfield was surprised to see that the convoys had passed starboard to starboard, and directly ahead of him he could see the blacked-out silhouettes of the leading merchant ships of the southbound convoy. The usual course of action would be to alter course to starboard but this would have meant *Umpire* crossing the path of the leading merchant ships of the convoy. Instead Wingfield altered course to port in the hope that the convoy would pass down his starboard side without incident. The merchant ships did not see the low-lying submarine, but a trawler, the *Peter Hendriks*, part of the convoy escort, did. Wingfield saw the trawler alter course toward him but could not go to starboard, the accepted procedure under these circumstances, because his way was blocked by the leading ships of the convoy. Instead, Wingfield went to port but the trawler followed him round and crashed into her starboard side mid-way between the bow and the conning tower.

The submarine lurched to port and for a few seconds the two vessels were locked together. Wingfield clutched at the trawler's side and shouted, 'You bloody bastard, you've sunk a British submarine' before he, the two lookouts and Lieutenant Tony Godden, the navigating officer, were swept off the bridge as *Umpire* sank beneath them. Of these four, only Wingfield was later picked up. By a stroke of luck the conning tower hatch slammed shut as *Umpire* sank and thus the control room was not flooded. *Umpire* settled with her bows on the bottom at a depth of 80 ft. There were two groups of survivors in the submarine; twenty were gathered in the engine room and were attempting to escape via the engine room hatch, while another four were crammed into the narrow conning tower. Of the latter group all four successfully escaped but only one, Sub Lieutenant Edward Young RNVR, was rescued. All those in the engine room escaped but only eighteen survived. The first man out from the engine room was CERA George Killen who donned a DSEA set, then made his way on to the casing, 'walked about a bit' (as he put it) to see that the hatch was not fouled, and then re-entered the engine room to supervise the escape of the rest. Killen was the last man out of the boat. For this feat of courage Killen was awarded the BEM, though many believe that he deserved a higher honour.

Wingfield went on to command the submarine *Taurus* with distinction and was one of only two British submarine commanders to sink a Japanese submarine. Sub Lieutenant Young become the first RNVR officer to be given command of a submarine, HMS *Storm*.

20 July 1941

Name	*Union*	**Location**	Mediterranean, SSW of Pantellaria
Class	*U* class submarine	**Cause**	Depth-charge
Built	1 October 1940	**Survivors**	None
CO	Lt R.M. Galloway RN		

Notes   Barely hours after *Umpire* had been rammed in the North Sea, *Union* was sunk by depth-charges from the Italian torpedo boat *Circe* after an attack on a convoy in position 36 26'N, 11 50'E. Galloway attacked the convoy at 1100 hrs but his torpedoes were spotted. *Circe* raced down the tracks, saw the submarine's periscope in the very clear and calm water and delivered a number of depth-charge attacks. A large bubble of air then came to the surface followed by a significant amount of oil. Since no other British or Allied submarine was in the area, *Circe*'s attack almost certainly accounted for *Union*.

23 July 1941

Name	*Fearless*	**Location**	Mediterranean, S of Sardinia,
Class	*F* class destroyer		37 40'N, 08 20'E
Built	12 May 1934	**Cause**	Air attack
CO	Cdr A.F. Pugsley RN	**Casualties**	27

Notes   *Fearless* was part of the escort for convoy GM.1 passing westwards through the Mediterranean from Gibraltar to Malta. Such was the importance of this convoy that it was escorted by Force H as well as a goodly portion of the Home Fleet. At 0942 hrs on the 23rd the convoy was subjected to a well-coordinated high- and low-level air attack by Italian aircraft. The cruiser *Manchester* was torpedoed and damaged but was able to return to Gibraltar. *Fearless* was hit aft by an air-dropped torpedo and completely disabled. There was nothing that could be done to save her so she was scuttled by HMS *Forester*.

30 July 1941

Name	*Cachalot*	**Location**	Mediterranean, off Benghazi,
Class	*Porpoise* class submarine minelayer		32 49'N, 20 11'E
Built	2 December 1937	**Cause**	Scuttled to avoid capture
CO	Lt Cdr R.B. Newton RN	**Casualties**	1

Notes   *Cachalot* had left Malta on 26 July to return to Alexandria with stores and passengers. After sunset on the 29th, after surfacing to take a fix, she was almost certainly sighted and reported by an Italian hospital ship.

After being forced to dive by a destroyer, *Cachalot* surfaced at 0250 hrs on the 30th and proceeded to hunt for an Italian tanker reported off Benghazi. Just after 0335 hrs a ship was sighted and identified as a tanker and *Cachalot* prepared to attack. Visibility was poor and *Cachalot* and the 'tanker' dodged in and out of visibility until the 'tanker', which was actually the Italian torpedo boat *Generale Achille Papa*, burst through the mist 800 yards away from the submarine and headed in to ram at full speed. Before Newton could dive the submarine safely, the *Papa* rammed *Cachalot* aft, failing to tear the pressure hull but holing the submarine's Z tank. Newton ordered the crew to abandon ship, the main vents were opened and *Cachalot* gently sank bows first in 200 ft of water.

In contrast to the machine-gunning of British survivors by German aircraft off Crete, the *Papa*'s commanding officer, *Capitano di Fregata* Gino Rosica, behaved with a chivalry worthy of an earlier age. He lowered boats to pick up *Cachalot*'s survivors and used his searchlights to find men in the water. He continued searching for the sole casualty (a Maltese steward) long after it became clear that the man had drowned and then formally sought Newton's permission to end the search. Lieutenant-Commander Newton was repatriated in September 1943 and then commanded the submarine *Selene* in the Pacific.

12 August 1941

Name	*Picotee*	**Location**	Atlantic, S of Ireland, 62 00'N, 16 00'W
Class	*Flower* class corvette		
		Cause	Submarine attack

Notes *Picotee* was torpedoed at 0310 hrs on the 12th by *U568* (*Kapitanleutnant* Joachim Preuss). At the time she was part of the escort for convoy ON.5.

18(?) August 1941

Name	*P.33*	**CO**	Lt R.D. Whiteway-Wilkinson RN
Class	*U* class submarine	**Location**	Mediterranean, off Tripoli
Built	28 January 1941	**Survivors**	None

Notes There is no clear evidence for the loss of *P.33*. She left Malta on 6 August for a patrol off Tripoli in company with *P.32* and *Unique*. On 18 August the sound of severe depth-charging was heard by *P.32* and *Unique* coming from *P.33*'s area. When the explosions ceased *P.32* tried to contact *P.33* by Asdic but received no reply. *P.33* may have been sunk in this attack, or she have been mined or lost by accident. The file remains open.

18 August 1941

Name	*P.32*	**Location**	Mediterranean, off Tripoli
Class	*U* class submarine	**Cause**	Mine
Built	15 December 1940	**Casualties**	28
CO	Lt D.A. Abdy RN	**Survivors**	2

Notes At 1530 hrs on the 18th, shortly after hearing the depth-charge barrage which may have marked the end of *P.33*, Abdy sighted a convoy of five merchant ships heading into Tripoli. Since he was badly positioned for an attack Abdy decided to run in under the minefield and attack from inside the swept channel. When he considered that he was in the swept channel, Abdy brought *P.32* to periscope depth to begin the attack; however, as he did so the submarine struck a mine and she sank to the bottom. A quick survey established that the whole of the submarine forward of the control room had been destroyed, killing the eight men who were there, and that any attempt at raising the boat was out of the question. Abdy then ordered the twenty-three survivors into the engine room to begin a compartment escape through the engine room hatch. Abdy's own account, written on his repatriation, continues: 'The Chief ERA passed the remark to me that there might be some difficulty in opening the engine room hatch. This, I put down at the time, would be because of the list on the submarine. Petty Officer Kirk has subsequently told me that he is of the opinion that the engine room hatch was clipped from the outside and further states that I gave orders after *P.32* had been bombed in June 1941 off Ferrol that the forward escape and engine room hatches were to be clipped shut from the outside before leaving for patrol. I do not recollect this order. I then ordered the first lieutenant, Lieutenant R.W. Morris RN, to read out the orders for working a DSEA set and personally made sure that every man knew what to do. Realising the congestion in the engine room, I then called for two volunteers to escape with me using the conning tower as an escape chamber. Petty Officer Kirk, the coxswain, and ERA Martin, the Chief ERA, both volunteered and, having told the first lieutenant to start flooding up as soon as we had left the engine room, manned the conning tower in the order ERA Martin at the top, PO Kirk in the middle and myself.' Abdy and Kirk managed to reach the surface but unfortunately Martin died during the ascent. The men were spotted by an aircraft which summoned an *Mas* launch from Tripoli. As in the case of *Cachalot*, the Italians showed themselves extremely punctilious in searching for survivors. When informed that more men could be expected to escape, the Italian commanding officer remained on the scene for some time, lowering a portable hydrophone to listen for any sounds from *P.32*, until it became clear that none of the twenty men remaining in the engine room could escape. If the engine room hatch was clipped shut from the outside then there was no way that those inside could get out. However, with a sad twist of irony, the men in the engine room may not have lived long enough to realise that the escape hatch was fastened from the outside. As the engine room was flooded up, with *P.32* lying in 210 ft of water, prior to the escape, the CO_2 level, already high since the boat had been dived for a long time, would have risen to seven times that of normal atmospheric pressure. The only escape from CO_2 poisoning would be to breathe the pure oxygen from their DSEA sets. However, at that pressure they would have quickly succumbed to oxygen poisoning, probably before finding out that their exit from the submarine was barred anyway.

Lieutenant Abdy and PO Kirk were the only two survivors from eight *U* class submarines sunk on patrol in the Mediterranean during the Second World War.

23 August 1941

Name	*Zinnia*	**Location**	Atlantic, W of Portugal, 40 43'N, 11 39'E
Class	*Flower* class corvette		
Built	28 November 1940	**Cause**	Submarine attack
CO	Lt Cdr C.B. Cuthbertson RN	**Casualties**	49

Notes *Zinnia* was part of the escort for convoy OG.71 when she was torpedoed at 0525 hrs by *U564* (*Korvettenkapitan* Reinhard Suhren). The considerable loss of life was due to the corvette exploding after being hit.

20 September 1941

Name	*Levis*	**Location**	Atlantic, S of Ireland, 60 07'N, 38 37'W
Class	*Flower* class corvette		
Built	4 September 1940	**Cause**	Submarine attack

Notes *Levis* was escorting convoy SC.44 when she was torpedoed at 0115 hrs by *U74* (*Korvettenkapitan* Eitel-Friedrich Kentrat). Kentrat saw the corvette flash a light signal with one word, 'Help', before it sank in less than 1 minute.

27 September 1941

Name	*Springbank*	**Location**	Atlantic, W of Ireland, 49 50'N,
Class	Auxiliary AA Ship		23 40'W
Built	1926	**Cause**	Submarine attack

Notes *Springbank* was escorting convoy HG.73 when she was attacked at 0210 hrs by *U201* (*Kapitanleutnant* Adalbert Schnee). She finally sank at 1915 hrs.

14 October 1941

Name	*Fleur de Lys*	**Cause**	Submarine attack
Class	*Flower* class corvette	**Survivors**	3
Location	Atlantic, approaches to Straits of Gibraltar, 36 00'N, 06 30'W		

Notes Towards mid-October 1941 there was evidence of a strong concentration of U-boats in the western approaches to the Straits of Gibraltar. Patrols were increased but at 0240 hrs on the 14th *U208* (*Kapitanleutnant* Hermann Opitz) torpedoed the corvette *Fleur de Lys*. The little corvette broke in half and sank very quickly. The three survivors were subsequently rescued by a Spanish steamer.

16 October 1941

Name	*Gladiolus*	**Location**	Atlantic, possibly 67N, 25W
Class	*Flower* class corvette	**Survivors**	None

Notes *Gladiolus* was one of the escorts for convoy SC.48, which was subjected to concentrated attacks by U-boats between 53 34'N, 29 57'W and 57N, 19W. *Gladiolus* disappeared after 1930 hrs on the 16th and nothing further was heard from her. At 2200 hrs the Canadian corvette *Wetaskiwin* received a signal purporting to come from *Gladiolus* requesting a signal for radar purposes on 325k/cs. *Wetaskiwin* doubted the authenticity of the signal, asked for identification but received no reply. At 0320 hrs on the 17th a massive explosion was heard from astern of the convoy: this may have been *Gladiolus* exploding following an attack by *U568* but the evidence is inconclusive.

18 October 1941

Name	*Broadwater*	**Location**	Atlantic, 57 01'N, 19 08'W
Class	*Town* class destroyer	**Cause**	Submarine attack
Built	1919		

Notes The second of two British warships sunk while escorting convoy SC.48, *Broadwater* was one of the fifty ex-US destroyers transferred to Britain in September 1940 in the 'Destroyers for Bases' deal with President Roosevelt. At 0400 hrs she was torpedoed by *U101* (*Kapitanleutnant* Ernst Mengersen) and she sank at 1340 hrs.

21 October 1941

Name	*Gnat*	**Location**	Mediterranean, N of Bardia, 32
Class	*Insect* class gunboat		08'N, 25 22'E
Built	1916	**Cause**	Submarine attack
CO	Lt Cdr S.R. Davenport RN		

Notes *Gnat* was en route for Mersa Matruh when she was torpedoed at 0445 hrs by *U79* (*Kapitanleutnant* Wolfgang Kaufmann). The torpedo struck on the port side forward and blew off the bow and a length of plating on the starboard side of the ship. The explosion flung the little gunboat on to her beam ends but she righted herself and lay dead in the water, down by the head and listing to starboard. Fires started by the explosion were put out and the engine room bulkhead shored up. Davenport tried to go astern to ease the strain on the engine room bulkhead but found that *Gnat*'s triple rudders made this impossible. Instead he risked going slowly ahead but this too proved impossible in the rising seas. By morning *Gnat* had lost all steerage way and was rolling heavily. Davenport had destroyed all charts and CBs and had ordered the Carley floats to be put in the water in case they had to abandon ship. However, help was on the way. *Gnat*'s signal reporting her damaged condition had been received and RAF fighter cover operated over the ship from dawn. The destroyers *Griffin* and *Jaguar* were detached from the 7th Cruiser Squadron and were speeding to her rescue. On arrival *Griffin* took *Gnat* in tow while *Jaguar* circled in case the U-boat was still in the area – in fact Kaufmann had cleared the scene immediately after the attack. On the 24th the damaged *Gnat* was finally brought into Alexandria.

 Gnat's hull was beached at Fanana near Port Suez; she was surveyed but found to be beyond repair. However, so useful were the *Insect* class gunboats that the idea of welding *Cricket*'s (see p. 149) bow to *Gnat*'s stern was given serious consideration. In the end the idea proved impracticable and *Gnat* was paid off on 7 December 1941.

23 October 1941

Name	*Cossack*	**Location**	Atlantic, W of Portugal, 35 36'N,
Class	*Tribal* class destroyer		10 04'W
Built	1937	**Cause**	Submarine attack
CO	Capt E. Berthon DSC RN		

Notes *Cossack*, one of the most famous destroyers in the Navy, was escorting convoy HG.75 home from Gibraltar when she was torpedoed by *U563* (*Kapitanleutnant* Klaus Bargsten). The torpedo struck on the port side forward and there was no immediate danger of the ship sinking. Despite the tremendous efforts made to save the ship, she sank three days later at 1043 hrs on the 27th.

25 October 1941

Name	*Latona*	**Location**	Mediterranean, N of Bardia,
Class	*Abdiel* class minelayer		32 15'N, 24 14'E
Built	20 August 1940	**Cause**	Air attack
		Casualties	37

Notes Operation Cultivate – the replacement of Australian troops in Tobruk with elements of the British 70th Division from Syria – involved one fast minelayer of the *Abdiel* class running between Alexandria and Tobruk, escorted by three destroyers, on a nightly basis. At 2105 hrs on the 25th *Latona* was some 30 miles from Tobruk on the outward run when she was attacked by German aircraft. One bomb exploded in *Latona*'s after engine room and she lay dead in the water. Fires started by the bomb spread to the upper deck where there was a considerable quantity of artillery and SA ammunition stowed for the Tobruk garrison. Both the cargo of ammunition and the ship's after 4.7 in magazine exploded: 4 officers, 20 ratings and 7 soldiers were killed, but the remainder were taken off by the destroyers *Hero* and *Encounter*.

27 October 1941

Name	*Tetrarch*	**Location**	Mediterranean, either in the Sicilian
Class	*T* class submarine		Channel or off Cavoli Island
Built	4 November 1939	**Cause**	Mine
CO	Lt Cdr G.H. Greenway RN	**Survivors**	None

Notes   *Tetrarch* sailed from Alexandria on 17 October 1941 for the UK via Malta and Gibraltar. After leaving Malta on 26 October she was ordered to conduct a short patrol off Cavoli Island before proceeding to Gibraltar on the 29th. On crossing longitude 7°E she was to report her position. No signal was made by the submarine, nor did she respond to further requests to report her position. As there are no Axis claims for her sinking, it is most likely that she was the victim of a mine. The last signal from *Tetrarch* was a series of informal messages to *P.34* on the 27th using SST while both submarines were in the Sicilian Channel. Courses, ranges and bearings were exchanged and *Tetrarch*'s position established as 37 28'N, 12 35'E. At that point she was passing through a heavily mined area and the possibility that she was mined there cannot be excluded. Equally she could have been mined off Cavoli where the Italians had laid down a number of minefields.

November 1941 *saw two of the Royal Navy's most significant losses. In the Mediterranean the aircraft carrier* Ark Royal, *whose sinking had been the subject of so many false claims by the Luftwaffe, fell victim to a single German torpedo, as did the battleship* Barham.

13 November 1941

Name	*Ark Royal*	**Location**	Mediterranean, E of Gibraltar
Class	Aircraft carrier	**Cause**	Submarine attack
Built	13 April 1937	**Casualties**	1
CO	Capt L.E. Maund RN		

Notes   *Ark Royal* was returning to Gibraltar following the successful completion of Operation *Perpetual*, an aircraft ferry trip to Malta, when at 1541 hrs she was struck by one torpedo fired by *U81* (*Kapitanleutnant* Friedrich Guggenberger). The torpedo exploded under the bridge on the starboard side and caused serious damage. All electric power failed and the ship assumed a list of 10° increasing to 12° within 3 minutes. However, it was found that although the starboard engine room was out of action, the port and centre engine rooms were undamaged. When the order was given to transfer all personnel to the destroyer *Legion* it was not made clear that damage control and engine room personnel should stand fast. As a result a number of these key officers and ratings transferred to *Legion* and it was impossible to retrieve them. This failure in damage control procedures was compounded by the ship's design. Flooding was able to spread into the centre and port boiler rooms through the smoke ducts which had no baffles fitted and which were placed too low down in the ship. There were no diesel dynamos so when the ship's own electrical power supply failed, there was no back-up. By 1815 hrs the destroyer *Laforey* was alongside to provide electric power but her efforts were hindered by the

HMS *Legion* comes alongside *Ark Royal*'s port quarter to take off survivors. (US Navy)

destroyer's officers not knowing the internal layout of the carrier and her pumps having different connections from those of *Ark Royal*. However. by 2059 hrs the ship was proceeding slowly toward Gibraltar in the tow of two tugs and by midnight steam had been raised in one boiler. At 0215 hrs on the 14th a fire broke out in the port boiler room and by 0430 hrs the list had increased to 35° and *Ark Royal* had to be abandoned. She sank at 0613 hrs, 29 miles east of Gibraltar.

19 November 1941

Name	*Sydney*	**Location**	Indian Ocean, off Western Australia,
Class	*Arethusa* class cruiser (modified)		26 00'S, 111'E
Built	22 September 1934	**Cause**	Surface action
CO	Capt J. Burnett RAN	**Casualties**	645
		Survivors	None

Notes Few warships have inspired such interest in their loss as the *Sydney*, an RAN cruiser which had just returned to Australian waters after a very successful commission in the Mediterranean. On 24 November the Australian Naval Board informed the Admiralty that *Sydney* had not arrived at Fremantle on the 20th when she was expected. Air and sea searches failed to find any trace of the cruiser and it was only after the merchant ship *Triocas* reported picking up twenty-five German sailors from a raft on the 24th and the arrival of another 290 German survivors on the coast of Western Australia that the story of *Sydney*'s loss became known.

The Germans were from the raider *Kormoran* (*Kapitan zur See* Detmers) which had sighted the *Sydney* on 19 November at about 1600 hrs. *Kormoran* was disguised as the Dutch vessel *Straat Malaka* but the disguise was evidently not convincing for *Sydney* closed to a position 1 mile abaft *Kormoran*'s starboard beam, both ships steaming a course of 250° at a speed of 15 knots. *Sydney* then asked the *Straat Malaka* to make the recognition signal currently in force, at which the merchant ship hoisted German colours and opened fire with guns and torpedoes. Her first salvo hit the *Sydney*'s bridge while her torpedo exploded under the cruiser's 'A' turret. *Sydney*'s guns opened fire and the action continued for about 25 minutes, after which both ships drifted apart, both blazing furiously. Detmers scuttled his ship just before midnight when the fires threatened to set off the *Kormoran*'s magazine and mine store.

Nothing more was heard of the *Sydney* and it is presumed that she sank after it became impossible to control the fires. There were rumours – fuelled when of one of *Sydney*'s Carley floats was washed up on the Australian coast covered in what appeared to be bullet holes – that the *Kormoran*'s crew had massacred the *Sydney*'s survivors. These stories were always stoutly denied by the Germans and no charges were ever brought against Detmers. The answer to *Sydney*'s loss may lie in the fact that she had just returned from an arduous commission in the Mediterranean and her crew may not have been too alert, in waters where the threat was considered to be low. *Kormoran* on the other hand was steaming in waters where every vessel could be presumed hostile – her crew would have been on their mettle.

24 November 1941

Name	*Dunedin*	**Location**	Atlantic, 900 miles W of Freetown,
Class	*D* class cruiser		03'N, 26'W
Built	19 November 1918	**Cause**	Submarine attack
CO	Capt R.S. Lovatt RN	**Casualties**	420
		Survivors	72

Notes HMS *Dunedin* was on routine patrol in the South Atlantic. On 25 November it was reported that she had failed to answer routine signals for over 24 hours. Concern over her whereabouts was increased by a German radio broadcast announcing the sinking of a *Dragon* class cruiser in the same area. The sloop HMS *Bridgewater* and the armed merchant cruiser HMS *Canton* were deployed to search for her but found nothing. On the 27th the US merchant ship *Nishmaha* picked up seventy-two exhausted survivors – all that was left of *Dunedin*'s crew. They reported that the ship had been struck by two torpedoes, fired by *U124* (*Kapitanleutnant* Johann Mohr) at 1326 hrs on the 24th, one of which wrecked the W/T office so that no distress signal could be sent.

No boats were launched before the ship sank and only six Carley floats supported the survivors in their 78 hour ordeal before they were rescued. As well as suffering from shortage of food and water the survivors were also repeatedly attacked by barracuda fish which caused several deaths. Five of the survivors subsequently died in hospital.

25 November 1941

Name	*Barham*	**Location**	Mediterranean, off the North African
Class	*Queen Elizabeth* class battleship		coast, 32 34'N, 26 24'E
Built	31 December 1914	**Cause**	Submarine attack
CO	Capt G.C. Cooke RN	**Casualties**	862
		Survivors	450

Notes HMS *Barham* had left Alexandria on 24 November in company with other units of the battle fleet to cover a cruiser and destroyer operation against an Italian convoy. At 1630 hrs on the 25th she was attacked by

U331 (*Kapitanleutnant* Franz-Dietrich Freiherr von Tiesenhausen). The U-boat penetrated the destroyer screen with ease and fired three torpedoes at *Barham*. *U331* briefly lost trim and broke surface on firing but escaped, passing so close down the side of HMS *Valiant* that the battleship's guns could not depress far enough to engage her.

The impact of the torpedoes was clearly felt by Admiral Cunningham in his flagship *Queen Elizabeth*. He rushed up to the bridge and saw, 'The poor ship rolled nearly over on to her beam ends, and we saw men massing on her upturned side. A minute or two later there came the dull rumble of a terrific explosion as one of her main magazines blew up. The ship became completely hidden in great clouds of yellowish-black smoke . . . When it cleared away the *Barham* had disappeared.' The destruction of the ship was primarily attributed to a failure on the part of the screening destroyers. *U331* passed between two of these destroyers at comparatively high speed but neither destroyer made contact. (One destroyer's Asdic operator did make contact but was told to disregard the echo.)

27 November 1941

Name	*Parramatta*	**Location**	Mediterranean, off Bardia, 32 20'N, 24 35'E
Class	Sloop		
Built	18 June 1939	**Cause**	Submarine attack
		Survivors	20

Notes The sloop *Parramatta* was escorting the SS *Hanne* to Tobruk with a desperately needed cargo of ammunition when she was attacked and sunk by *U559* (*Kapitanleutnant* Hans Heidtmann). The ship sank very quickly and only twenty ratings were rescued by HMS *Avon Vale*.

December 1941 *was undoubtedly the worst month of the war for the Royal Navy. A new theatre of war opened in the Far East with the entry of Japan into the conflict. The stunning blow delivered to the US Navy at Pearl Harbor was followed three days later by the seemingly effortless sinking of* Prince of Wales *and* Repulse *by Japanese land-based aircraft. In the Mediterranean, Force K's depredations of Axis shipping came to an abrupt end when the force ran into an Italian minefield. The year ended with the daring Italian* Maiale *attack on Alexandria in which the battleships* Queen Elizabeth *and* Valiant *were badly damaged.*

6 December 1941

Name	*Perseus*	**Location**	Mediterranean, off Cephalonia
Class	*P* class submarine	**Cause**	Mine
Built	22 May 1929	**Casualties**	52
CO	Lt Cdr G.H. Greenway RN	**Survivors**	1

Notes *Perseus* was returning to Alexandria from Malta and was to patrol off eastern Greece. At 2200 hrs on the 6th the submarine struck a mine and settled on her starboard side on the seabed. Only five junior rates survived the explosion, one of whom was Leading Stoker John Capes (**see** photograph overleaf) – ironically he was a passenger in the submarine returning from Malta. The five men set about rigging the escape trunk, but found it very difficult to do so since the submarine was lying on her starboard side and a number of holes in the pressure hull made it extremely difficult to pressurise the compartment for an escape. Eventually only Capes managed to escape from the submarine. What followed was nothing short of an epic. Capes swam nearly 5 miles to land and

Leading Stoker John Capes, the only survivor from HMS *Perseus*. (Author)

was lucky to be found by friendly villagers. For the next eighteen months Capes was sheltered by the Greeks before he was evacuated to Kioste and Alexandria, where his appearance was greeted with a good deal of scepticism!

7 December 1941

Name	*Windflower*
Class	*Flower* class corvette
Location	Atlantic, 46 19'N, 49 30'W
Cause	Collision

Notes   HMS *Windflower* collided with the merchant ship *Zypenberg* in thick fog; this was an inevitable consequence of warships and merchant ships manoeuvring in close company together.

8 December 1941

Name	*Peterel*
Class	River gunboat
Built	1927
CO	Lt Cdr H.D. Polkinghorn RNR
Location	China, port of Shanghai
Cause	Surface action

Notes   *Peterel* had been disarmed and moored at Shanghai since 1940 in order to provide secure W/T communications for the British Consulate in the city. On the morning of 8 December, following the Japanese attack on Pearl Harbor, *Peterel* was boarded by a delegation of Japanese naval officers from the cruiser *Idzumo* who demanded that the gunboat surrender immediately. Even though he was hopelessly outnumbered, Polkinghorn received the Japanese with the usual marks of respect, heard them out and then refused their demands. The Japanese officers were then seen over the side with all the traditional naval ceremonial due to their rank. When the Japanese ultimatum expired, the cruiser *Idzumo* opened fire and in a few salvoes sent the little gunboat to the bottom of the Whangpoo River. Lieutenant-Commander Polkinghorn's actions won the admiration of the Japanese, particularly because the latter delegation had boarded the US Navy gunboat *Wake* on an earlier occasion and found all the crew sound asleep in their hammocks. Polkinghorn and his ship's company received significantly better treatment in the Lunghua PoW camp as a result.

10 December 1941

Name	*Repulse*	**Location**	South China Sea, E of Malaya, 03 45'N, 104 24'E
Class	Battle cruiser		
Built	8 January 1916	**Cause**	Air attack
CO	Capt W.G. Tennant RN		

Notes   HMS *Repulse* sailed from Singapore on 8 December in company with HMS *Prince of Wales* and four destroyers in response to intelligence reports on Japanese landings on the east coast of Malaya. The reports were false but after the ships had been sighted by three Japanese aircraft at 1830 hrs on the 9th, Admiral Phillips decided to return to Singapore on the grounds that the operation was compromised. After investigating the port of Kuantan on the morning of the 10th, both ships received reports of enemy aircraft from one of their destroyers, HMS *Tenedos*, which had been sent on ahead and was herself being attacked. At 1020 hrs shadowing aircraft were spotted and shortly after 1100 hrs the first wave of enemy aircraft were sighted. The first attack was by high-level bombers and *Repulse* received one hit which started a small fire but was quickly brought under control. At 1156 hrs *Repulse* survived a combined high-level and torpedo-bomber attack but shortly after 1223 hrs was struck by no less than five torpedoes, one of which wrecked her steering gear. By 1227 hrs she was listing heavily. Captain Tennant ordered his crew to abandon ship and at 1233 hrs *Repulse* rolled over and sank.

Name	*Prince of Wales*	**Location**	South China Sea, E coast of Malaya,
Class	*King George V* class battleship		03 34'N, 104 26'E
Built	3 May 1939	**Cause**	Air attack
CO	Capt J.C. Leach MVO DSO RN		

Notes *Prince of Wales* survived *Repulse* but not by long. At 1144 hrs she was hit by at least one torpedo which did serious damage to her machinery and she was never again under complete control. Moreover this torpedo hit also damaged the dynamos, cutting the power supply to her electrically operated twin 5.25 in AA mountings. At 1223 hrs she sustained two more torpedo hits and another two at 1224 hrs. In a high-level attack she sustained at least one hit. By 1310 hrs she was settling rapidly in the water and at 1320 hrs turned turtle and sank.

Against the loss of these two capital ships the British could claim seven Japanese aircraft destroyed. More than anything this attack pointed to the vulnerability of the battleship, however modern, unless provided with air cover from an aircraft carrier (as opposed to land based air cover).

12 December 1941

Name	*Moth*	**Location**	Hong Kong harbour
Class	*Insect* class gunboat	**Cause**	Scuttled
Built	1916		

Notes *Moth* was in dry dock when the Japanese attacked Hong Kong. By the 11th Japanese artillery was shelling the dockyard. Since there were too few workmen remaining in the dockyard to undock the little gunboat, she was stripped of any useful equipment and then the graving dock was flooded. Within a few hours all that could be seen of *Moth* was her funnels and masts sticking out of an oily scum. *Moth* was raised by the Japanese and renamed *Suma*, but on 19 March 1945 she was destroyed when she ran over an American mine in the Yangtse River above Nanking.

14 December 1941

Name	*Galatea*	**Location**	Mediterranean, 30 miles W of
Class	*Arethusa* class cruiser		Alexandria, 31 12'N, 29 15'E
Built	9 August 1934	**Cause**	Submarine attack
CO	Capt E.W. Sim RN	**Casualties**	470
		Survivors	144

Notes *Galatea* was returning to Alexandria following an unsuccessful search for an Axis convoy when she was attacked by a U-boat which hit her with two torpedoes. The cruiser rolled over and sank very quickly, hence the heavy loss of life. The survivors were rescued by the destroyers *Griffin* and *Hotspur*.

19 December 1941

Name	*Neptune*	**Location**	Mediterranean, 20 miles N of	
Class	*Achilles* class cruiser		Tripoli, 33 15'N, 33 30'E	
Built	31 January 1933	**Cause**	Mine	
CO	Capt R. O'Conor RN	**Casualties**	763	
		Survivors	1	

Notes *Neptune* was the senior ship of a British force consisting of the cruisers *Neptune*, *Aurora* and *Penelope* together with the destroyers *Kandahar*, *Lance*, *Lively* and *Havock* which had sailed from Malta on the 18th to intercept an Italian convoy. At 0039 hrs on the 19th *Neptune* exploded a mine in one of her paravanes and immediately Captain O'Conor went full astern in order to clear the minefield. As he did so *Neptune* struck a mine which blew off her propellers and rudder and left the ship dead in the water. *Penelope* and *Aurora*, steaming astern of *Neptune*, immediately opened out to port and starboard; both struck mines but were able to reach Malta. At 0100 hrs *Neptune* hit a third mine. *Kandahar* went into the minefield in a brave attempt to rescue *Neptune*'s ship's company and in turn had her stern blown off by a mine. At 0400 hrs a fourth mine exploded under *Neptune*'s bridge. Five minutes later she rolled over and sank. Captain A.D. Nicholl of *Penelope*, the senior officer, was now faced with a cruel dilemma: it went against all his instincts and training to leave *Neptune*'s survivors in the water but hard reality dictated that he could not risk more ships by sending them into an enemy minefield. Since he was off an enemy coast and dawn was breaking, heralding the increased risk of air attack, he turned back for Malta.

Neptune's survivors abandoned the ship in a heavy sea and it proved impossible to clear away any more than two of the cruiser's Carley floats. By dawn on the 19th only Captain O'Conor and a few others remained alive. Over the next four days the survivors succumbed to exhaustion and hypothermia until only Leading Seaman J. Walters was left alive; he was rescued by an Italian torpedo boat on the 23rd.

Name	*Stanley*	**Location**	Atlantic, W of Portugal, 38 12'N,	
Class	*Town* class destroyer		17 23'W	
Built	1919	**Cause**	Submarine attack	
CO	Lt Cdr D.B. Shaw OBE RN	**Survivors**	25	

Notes The passage of convoy HG.76 to the UK from Gibraltar marked one of the finest episodes of the Battle of the Atlantic. The convoy got off to a good start with the sinking of two U-boats, *U131* and *U434*. *Stanley* had been involved in the sinking of both. At 0345 hrs on the 19th *Stanley*, in her position at the stern of the convoy, reported another U-boat. However, 30 minutes later she was torpedoed and blew up with a violent explosion. The submarine responsible was *U574* (*Oberleutnant zur See* Dietrich Gengelbach). Some 12 minutes later *U574* was rammed and sunk by HMS *Stork*.

Name	*H.31*	**Location**	Atlantic, NW coast of Spain, exact	
Class	*H* class submarine		position unknown	
Built	16 November 1918	**Survivors**	None	
CO	Lt F.B. Gibbs RN			

Notes The elderly *H.31* was despatched to sea hurriedly in December after reports that the battle cruisers *Scharnhorst* and *Gneisenau* were about to sail from Brest. Even by 1941 the veteran *H* class submarines had been relegated to training duties. Nevertheless *H.31* parted company with her escort off the Wolf Rock on the 19th and nothing more was heard from her. The rumours about the German ships proved false but when *H.31* was ordered to report her position on the night of 24 December, no reply was received. She is therefore presumed to have been mined some time from the 19th onwards. However, the possibility of loss by accident cannot be excluded, particularly in view of her age and mechanical condition.

20 December 1941

Name	*Kandahar*	**Location**	Mediterranean, 20 miles N of Tripoli, 33 15'N., 33 30'E
Class	K class destroyer		
Built	21 March 1939	**Cause**	Mine
CO	Cdr W.G.A. Robson RN	**Survivors**	174

Notes The circumstances under which *Kandahar* was mined have been described above (see *Neptune*). Throughout the 19th *Kandanar* drifted forlornly, sinking lower in the water all the time. However, she remained unmolested by enemy aircraft and was able to send signals to Malta. The destroyer *Jaguar* (Commander L.R.K. Tyrwhitt RN) was despatched to her assistance. Though aided by a radar-equipped Wellington bomber it was not until 0400 hrs on the 20th that *Jaguar* found the *Kandahar*. The sea was now so rough that it was impossible for Tyrwhitt either to take *Jaguar* alongside the *Kandahar* or to go bow to bow with her. Instead *Kandahar*'s survivors had to swim across, after which *Jaguar* sank her by torpedo.

The loss of *Neptune* and *Kandahar*, and damage to *Penelope* and *Aurora*, ended Force K's run of successes against Italian shipping.

21 December 1941

Name	*Cicala*	**CO**	Lt Cdr John Boldero DSC RN
Class	Insect class gunboat	**Location**	South China Sea, off Hong Kong
Built	1916	**Cause**	Air attack
		Casualties	1

Notes *Cicala* had endured over sixty-one dive-bombing attacks from Japanese aircraft since hostilities began on 7 December. Nevertheless the little gunboat acquitted herself well and continued to provide the army with fire support using her two 6 in guns. However, on 21 December she was overwhelmed in an air attack by four Japanese dive-bombers. She was struck by three bombs, two of which hit aft, causing serious flooding and fracturing the main steam line. Boldero decided to abandon ship and he and his men were taken off by *MTB.10*.

Although just one man had been killed in the sinking of the *Cicala*, only half of the remaining crew survived the war. One seaman died in the land battle but on 25 December *Cicala*'s survivors became prisoners of the Japanese when Hong Kong surrendered. Approximately half their number died in Japanese captivity, many when the transport vessel taking them to Japan was torpedoed and sunk by an Allied submarine.

Name	*Audacity*	**Location**	Atlantic, 500 miles W of Cape Finisterre, 44N, 20W
Class	Escort carrier		
Built	29 March 1939	**Cause**	Submarine attack
CO	Cdr D.W. Mackendrick RN		

Notes *Audacity* was the former German merchant ship *Hannover* which had been given a rudimentary conversion to allow her to operate aircraft. She had already demonstrated her value to convoy HG.76. In four days her aircraft had reported eight U-boats, shot down two Fw.200 aircraft and damaged another three. It was the usual procedure for *Audacity* to leave the convoy at nightfall and manoeuvre independently. Mackendrick wanted to remain on the starboard side of the convoy with one corvette as an escort. Commander Frederick Walker, the escort commander, had to refuse the corvette (since after *Stanley*'s loss he was stretched to cover the convoy properly) and suggested that *Audacity* operate on the port side of the convoy since all his intelligence indicated that U-boats were gathering on the convoy's starboard side. Mackendrick demurred since the convoy's zigzag to port would inconvenience his ship when having to maintain a steady course for launching or recovering aircraft. Since no clear chain of authority existed stating that the carrier was subordinate to the escort commander (or vice versa), Mackendrick simply took station unescorted on the convoy's starboard side where at 2035 hrs she was hit by two torpedoes fired by *U751* (*Kapitanleutnant* Gerhard Bigalk). Although most of her ship's company survived the sinking, many (including Mackendrick) were killed when aircraft secured to *Audacity*'s flight deck broke their tethers and crashed down into the sea.

24 December 1941

Name	*Salvia*	**Cause**	Submarine attack
Class	*Flower* class corvette	**Casualties**	900+
Location	Mediterranean, 100 miles W of Alexandria, 31 48'N, 28 00'E	**Survivors**	None

Notes On 23 December the merchant ship *Shuntien* was torpedoed and sunk by *U559* (*Kapitanleutnant* Hans Heidtmann). In addition to her crew the *Shuntien* was carrying 850 Axis PoWs, and the corvette *Salvia* was ordered to remain behind and collect survivors. Nothing further was heard from *Salvia*. HMS *Peony* found oil and wreckage in a position 90 miles east of where the *Shuntien* was sunk: it was concluded that *Salvia* had been torpedoed and then, grossly overloaded with survivors, capsized. That is indeed what happened. German records revealed that she had been torpedoed at 0158 hrs on the 24th by *U568* (*Kapitanleutnant* Joachim Preuss).

30 December 1941

Name	*Triumph*		
Class	*T* class submarine	**Location**	Aegean, off Hydra
Built	16 February 1938	**Cause**	Mine
CO	Lt J. Huddart RN	**Survivors**	None

Notes *Triumph* was on her first patrol under Huddart's command (her previous CO had been Commander W.J. 'Sam' Woods). She was regarded as a 'lucky' submarine – in December 1939 a drifting mine in the Skagerrak had blown off her bows but she had managed to return to port. She departed from Alexandria on 26 December and on the 30th Huddart reported that he had landed an SOE party near Bireans. His orders were then to patrol between 36° and 39°N and 25°E and then rescue a party of escaped PoWs on 9 January. However, *Triumph* failed to make the rendezvous and nothing more was heard from her. It is therefore presumed that she was mined at some time from the 30th onwards in the area off Hydra.

LOSSES 1942

9 January 1942

Name	*Vimiera*
Class	*V* class destroyer
Built	22 June 1917

Location	Thames estuary, off the East Spile Buoy, 51 28'N, 00 55'E
Cause	Mine

Notes   No further details are known.

17 January 1942

Name	*Gurkha*
Class	*L* class destroyer
Built	8 July 1940
CO	Cdr C.N. Lentaigne RN

Location	Mediterranean, N of Bardia, 31 50'N, 26 14'E
Cause	Submarine attack
Casualties	9

Notes   While proceeding off the Libyan coast at 17 knots *Gurkha* was hit aft at 0735 hrs by a torpedo fired by *U133*. The damage was extensive: a large hole was blown in the ship's side, the after superstructure collapsed and the ship started to flood. The fire main was fractured and thus it was impossible to fight the fire, fed by oil fuel from the after tanks, that enveloped the stern of the ship causing the ready use ammunition around 'X' and 'Y' mountings to explode. *Gurkha* lay dead in the water and with an increasing list to port. The Dutch destroyer *Isaac Sweers* then towed her clear of the burning oil fuel and took off her survivors. At 0913 hrs *Gurkha* rolled over and sank.

   This was the destroyer that had been paid for by the Gurkha Brigade of the British Army following the loss of the first *Gurkha* in April 1940 (see pp. 107–8). On this second sinking the gesture was not repeated!

17 January 1942

Name	*Matabele*
Class	*Tribal* class destroyer
Built	6 October 1937
CO	Cdr A.C. Stafford DSC RN

Location	Barents Sea, 69 21'N, 35 34'E
Cause	Submarine attack
Survivors	3

Notes   *Matabele* was part of the escort for convoy PQ.8 sailing to the Soviet port of Murmansk. At 1846 hrs *U454* (*Kapitanleutnant* Burkhard Hacklander) torpedoed the merchant ship *Harmatris*. Hacklander's second torpedo struck *Matabele* in the stern and the destroyer stopped. HMS *Somali* remained behind to screen the two damaged ships. Hacklander also remained in the area and at 2221 hrs he made a second attack on the destroyer, which blew up in a massive explosion. Hacklander, observing the blast through his periscope, considered it to have been over 2,000 ft tall. *Somali* rescued three survivors.

27 January 1942

Name	*Thanet*	**Location**	Off Endau, E coast of Malaya,
Class	Destroyer		02 40'N, 103 42'E
Built	5 November 1918	**Cause**	Gunfire
		Survivors	57

Notes   As the Japanese Army advanced down the Malayan Peninsula, the Japanese Navy occupied the port of Endau with a task force consisting of an aircraft carrier, a heavy cruiser, five light cruisers and five destroyers. Although the RAF tried to bomb the port their attacks were ineffectual and easily beaten off by the Japanese. On the night of 27 January 1942 the elderly destroyers *Vampire* and *Thanet* were despatched for a night attack on the port. As they approached the port they were engaged by the Japanese destroyers *Amagiri*, *Hatsuyuki* and *Shirayuki*. *Vampire* escaped under cover of smoke but *Thanet* was overwhelmed by the superior gunfire of the Japanese destroyers.

31 January 1942

Name	*Belmont*	**Location**	North Atlantic, off Halifax, Nova
Class	*Town* class destroyer		Scotia, 42 02'N, 57 18'W
Built	1919	**Cause**	Submarine

Notes   *Belmont* was escorting the Canadian troop convoy NA.2 to Britain when she was torpedoed by *U82* (*Kapitanleutnant* Siegfried Rollmann). Six days later *U82* was sunk by the corvettes *Rochester* and *Tamarisk*.

Name	*Culver*	**Location**	Atlantic, SW of Ireland, 48 43'N,
Class	Ex-USCG cutter		20 14'W
Built	1929	**Cause**	Submarine attack

Notes   *Culver* was escorting convoy SL.98 when she was attacked and sunk by *U105* (*Korvettenkapitan* Heinrich Schuch). Schuch had fired a four torpedo spread at the convoy and observed two hits and a big explosion. He first thought that he had hit an ammunition ship but in fact both torpedoes struck the *Culver* which blew up with massive force. *Culver* had been fitted with an operational automatic HF/DF set.

February 1942 *marked the rout of the Royal Navy from Singapore. On 11 February the Senior Naval Officer at Singapore described the waterfront as a 'mass of demoralised troops looking for any means of leaving the island'. Three river gunboats, nine minesweepers and over sixty other auxiliary vessels of all types were sunk by the Japanese during the evacuation. The fall of Singapore was swiftly followed by the collapse of subsequent efforts to assemble a credible fighting force from the surviving British, Dutch, American and Australian warships.*

5 February 1942

Name	*Arbutus*	**Location**	Atlantic, S of Iceland, 55 05'N,
Class	*Flower* class corvette		19 43'W
		Cause	Submarine attack

Notes   On the evening of 5 February the corvette *Arbutus* and the destroyer *Chelsea* were detached from the escort of convoy ON.63 in order to search for U-boats which had been detected by radar around the convoy.

Arbutus made one unsuccessful attack but while returning to the convoy was torpedoed and sunk by *U136* (*Kapitanleutnant* Heinrich Zimmerman).

9 February 1942

Name	*Herald*	**Location**	Singapore
Class	Survey ship	**Cause**	Scuttled

Notes   *Herald* had been damaged in an air raid and then abandoned in the dockyard at Singapore. She was repaired and recommissioned by the Japanese as the *Heiyo*. On 14 November 1944 she was mined and sunk in the Java Sea.

11 February 1942

Name	*Spikenard*	**Cause**	Submarine attack
Class	*Flower* class corvette (RCN)	**Survivors**	8
Location	Atlantic, S of Iceland, 56 10'N, 21 07'W		

Notes   *Spikenard* was the Senior Officer's ship for the escort of convoy SC.67. At 0033 hrs on 11 February she was torpedoed by *U136* (*Kapitanleutnant* Heinrich Zimmerman). There were a number of U-boat attacks on the convoy that night and in the confusion the rest of the escort did not realise that the Senior Officer's ship had been sunk until daylight on the 11th. It was then that HMS *Gentian* was sent back and rescued the eight survivors.

12 February 1942

Name	*Maori*	**Location**	Malta, Grand Harbour, Valetta
Class	*Tribal* class destroyer	**Cause**	Air attack
Built	2 September 1937	**Casualties**	1
CO	Cdr R.E. Courage DSO DSC RN		

Notes   On the night of 11 February *Maori* was secured at the Emergency Destroyer Buoy at the entrance to Dockyard Creek. In accordance with usual practice then in force at Malta, off duty personnel slept ashore at night. When the island was raided by German aircraft just after 0200 hrs *Maori* was struck by one bomb which exploded in her machinery spaces. The ship blew up, damaging HMS *Decoy*, and sank at her moorings. The next morning her bow and stern were visible above the water. On 5 July 1945 her remains were raised, towed out to sea and sunk in deep water.

13 February 1942

Name	*Tempest*	**Cause**	Scuttled following depth-charge attacks
Class	*T* class submarine		
Built	10 June 1941	**Casualties**	39
CO	Lt Cdr W.K. Cavaye RN	**Survivors**	24
Location	Mediterranean, Gulf of Taranto, 39 11'N, 17 47'E		

Notes *Tempest* was sunk as a result of an attack on the Italian tanker *Lucania* on 12 February by HMS *Una* (Lieutenant D.S. Martin RN). *Lucania* had been given a 'safe conduct' pass by the British because she was engaged on humanitarian work and thus the Italians were exceedingly angry that she had been sunk. Extra patrols were instituted to find the culprit but *Tempest* was the unlucky recipient of their attentions. At 0315 hrs on the 13th the torpedo boat *Circe* (Capitano di Corvetta Stefanino Palmas) got an Asdic contact with *Tempest* and then carried out seven hours of depth-charge attacks which reduced the inside of the submarine to a shambles. At 0942 hrs, with no. 3 battery producing great clouds of toxic chlorine gas, Cavaye gave the order to surface. Machine-gun fire from *Circe* prevented *Tempest*'s crew from bringing either the 4 in gun or their machine-guns into action so Cavaye gave the order to open main vents and set the scuttling charges before giving the order to abandon ship. The survivors were picked up by *Circe* but *Tempest* remained stubbornly afloat until 1605 hrs when she sank – just as *Circe*'s crew managed to secure a tow rope.

Name	*Scorpion*	**Location**	Sumatra, in the Banka Strait off
Class	River gunboat		Berhala Island
Built	1937	**Cause**	Gunfire
CO	Lt Cdr G.C. Ashworth RNVR	**Survivors**	20(?)

Notes *Scorpion* was sunk by gunfire from Japanese destroyers, although the exact details of her fate are unknown. She left Singapore for Batavia on 10 February and was later sunk by Japanese warships off Berhala Island in the Banka Strait.

14 February 1942

Name	*Dragonfly*	**Location**	E of Sumatra, off Posik Island
Class	*Dragonfly* class river gunboat	**Cause**	Air attack
Built	1938		

Notes *Dragonfly* also left Singapore on 10 February. Off Posik Island she was attacked by Japanese aircraft. Her commander decided to try to hide under the shelter of the land but it was too late. The little gunboat was hit aft and sank very quickly. The survivors, who were machine-gunned in the water, came ashore on Posik Island. The total number of casualties/survivors is difficult to ascertain in view of the number of passengers the ship was carrying and their subsequent fate while in Japanese captivity.

Name	*Grasshopper*	**CO**	Cdr J.S. Hoffman RN
Class	*Dragonfly* class river gunboat	**Location**	E of Sumatra, off Posik Island
Built	1938	**Cause**	Air attack

Notes *Grasshopper* was next to be attacked after *Dragonfly*. She was hit aft and a serious fire started which could not be fought because the bombs had wrecked the fire main. Hoffman beached his ship on Posik Island and evacuated crew, passengers and six captured Japanese aircrew. *Grasshopper* was then left to burn herself out. As with *Dragonfly* it is impossible to determine the number of casualties since *Grasshopper* was grossly overloaded with soldiers, nurses, civilian women (two of whom gave birth after the sinking and whose babies were delivered by the coxswain, Petty Officer G.L. White) and children, and PoWs. One survivor of note was the ship's dog, a Pointer bitch called Judy. She proved invaluable after the sinking in finding sources of fresh water and for the next three-and-a-half years shared the privations of Japanese captivity with her owners.

23 February 1942

Name	*P.38*	**CO**	Lt R.J. Hemingway RN
Class	*U* class submarine	**Location**	Mediterranean, N of Tripoli
Built	9 July 1941	**Cause**	Depth-charge

Notes   Ten days later *Circe* was escorting a convoy of four merchant ships to Tripoli when at 1014 hrs the asdic operator gained a submerged contact. This was Hemingway's *P.38*. While the senior officer altered course to lead the convoy away from contact *Circe* turned and increased speed to attack. *P.38* was blown to the surface by the first attack and then engaged by gunfire from the destroyer *Antoniotto Usodimare* before sinking again. Further depth-charge attacks were carried out by the *Usodimare* and the *Emmanuel Pessagno* until Palmas ordered the ships to cease firing so that his ECG operator could search for the submarine (*Circe* was the only ECG-fitted ship in the escort). Suddenly, just after 1040 hrs, *P.38* surfaced and as quickly as she had appeared dived again. *Pessagno* raced over the swirl and dropped a pattern of depth-charges. When calm had been restored *Circe*'s ECG operator regained contact but reported that the submarine was stationary on the bottom. On the surface was a spreading slick of diesel fuel. *Circe* steamed over the spot and recovered various items including a flag bag containing three Union Jacks and pieces of deck planking covered in linoleum.

27 February 1942

Name	*Electra*	**Location**	North of Java
Class	*E* class destroyer	**Cause**	Gunfire
Built	15 February 1934	**Casualties**	90
CO	Cdr C.W. May RN	**Survivors**	54

Notes   *Electra* was part of the combined American, British, Dutch and Australian force of five cruisers and nine destroyers that was attempting to frustrate the Japanese force of four heavy cruisers and twenty destroyers supporting the Japanese invasion of Northern Java. The allied ships were a heterogeneous bunch who had never worked together before; they faced an enemy who proved superior in every respect except that of courage. After an initial engagement between the cruisers the destroyer *Electra* led out HMS *Encounter* and *Jupiter* to launch a torpedo attack on the Japanese line. As *Electra* emerged from her smokescreen she engaged the Japanese destroyer *Asagumo*, to a halt with several well-directed broadsides. However, the Japanese destroyer mounted a heavier 5 in weapon and returned fire. *Electra* was repeatedly hit, caught fire and sank. Her survivors were subsequently rescued by the US submarine *S.38*.

Name	*Jupiter*	**Location**	off Surabaya, 06 45'S, 112 06'E
Class	*J* class destroyer	**Cause**	Mine
Built	27 October 1938	**Casualties**	95
CO	Lt Cdr N.V. Trew RN		

Notes   *Jupiter* inadvertently strayed into a Dutch minefield and ran into a mine at 2125 hrs. After the strained events of the day it is understandable that the ship's position – most likely established by dead reckoning – may have been slightly out. She sank four hours later.

March 1942 *saw the completion of the Japanese conquest of the East Indies, and the sinking of those ships that had survived the Java Sea engagement. In the Mediterranean the coming of spring brought with it an Axis air offensive against Malta of unparalleled ferocity which was to claim the loss of many ships and submarines before the summer was out.*

1 March 1942

Name	*Perth*	**Location**	Sunda Strait, 05 45'S, 106 13'E
Class	*Arethusa* class cruiser (modified)	**Cause**	Gunfire and torpedoes
Built	27 July 1934	**Survivors**	307
CO	Capt Waller		

Notes   HMAS *Perth* and USS *Houston* were making a night transit of the Sunda Strait heading for Tjilatjap. *Perth* made an enemy sighting report at 2330 hrs while rounding St Nicholas Point and thereafter nothing more was heard from her. It is now known that the two cruisers were engaged by the Japanese cruisers *Mogami* and *Mikuma*, escorted by a number of destroyers. Japanese excellence in night fighting paid off and both cruisers were torpedoed and then finished off with gunfire.

Name	*Exeter*	**Location**	Sunda Strait, off Bawean Island,
Class	*Exeter* class cruiser		05 00'S, 111 00'E
Built	18 July 1929	**Cause**	Gunfire and torpedo
		Survivors	300 +

The last moments of the cruiser HMS *Exeter* as she lies on her beam ends on 1 March 1942. Over 300 of her ship's company were rescued and became prisoners of the Japanese. (US Navy)

Notes After being damaged in the battle of the Java Sea on 27 February, *Exeter* had left Surabaya on the 28th in company with the destroyers HMS *Encounter* and USS *Pope*. At 0253 hrs on the 1st a signal from *Exeter* was received by HMS *Dragon* reporting three enemy cruisers steering west. Nothing more was heard from her. It is now known that she was attacked by the cruisers *Nachi* and *Haguro* but could offer little resistance, being able to steam at only 16 knots. She was reduced to a shambles by gunfire and then finished off just after 1100 hrs by a torpedo fired by the destroyer *Ikazuchi*. The survivors were rescued by the Japanese.

Name	*Encounter*	**Location**	Exact position unknown (but very
Class	*E* class destroyer		close to where *Exeter* was sunk)
Built	29 March 1934	**Cause**	Gunfire and torpedo

Notes *Encounter* did not long survive the *Exeter*. Armed with only four 4.7 in guns, she was overwhelmed at 1130 hrs by 8 in gunfire from the Japanese cruisers *Myoko* and *Ashigara*. Her consort USS *Pope* was sunk an hour later.

3 March 1942

Name	*Stronghold*	**Location**	220 miles S of Sunda Strait, 11 30'S,
Class	*S* class destroyer		109 03'E
Built	6 May 1919	**Cause**	Gunfire
CO	Lt Cdr G.R. Pretor-Pinney RN	**Casualties**	70

Notes *Stronghold* was escorting the Dutch MV *Zaandam*, the depot ship *Anking*, *MMS.51* and RFA *Francol* to Fremantle in company with HMAS *Yarra* when at 2315 hrs they were intercepted by a force of three Japanese cruisers and two destroyers. The action was very one-sided, and all the ships except the *Zaandam* were sunk by gunfire and torpedo. In addition to the seventy killed at the time of her sinking, a further five of her company died in Japanese captivity.

Name	*Yarra*	**Location**	220 miles S of Sunda Strait, 11 30'S,
Class	*Grimsby* class sloop		109 03'E
Built	28 March 1935	**Cause**	Gunfire and torpedo

Notes See the entry for HMS *Stronghold* above.

11 March 1942

Name	*Naiad*	**Location**	Mediterranean, N of Mersa Matruh,
Class	*Dido* class AA cruiser		32 01'N, 26 19'E
Built	3 February 1939	**Cause**	Submarine attack
CO	Capt Guy Grantham RN, flagship of	**Survivors**	82
	Rear Admiral Philip Vian		

Notes On 10 March the cruisers *Naiad* (flagship of Rear Admiral Philip Vian, flag officer commanding 15th Cruiser Squadron), *Dido* and *Euryalus*, together with nine destroyers, left Alexandria to attack an Italian convoy which had been reported by the RAF. At the same time the CinC decided to take this opportunity to bring out the cruiser *Cleopatra* and destroyer *Kingston* which had been languishing at Malta. The two forces joined up at 0800 hrs on the 11th but by then Admiral Vian had given up on finding the Italian convoy and had turned for home. Throughout the day the ships were subjected to a series of air attacks, but at 2005 hrs *Naiad* was struck by a torpedo fired by *U565* (*Kapitanleutnant* Johann Jebsen). *Naiad* was hit amidships and sank very quickly. 'Such a loss that little *Naiad*,' wrote Admiral Cunningham a few days later: 'A highly efficient weapon with a ship's company with a grand spirit.'

The men of the 15th Cruiser Squadron had an almost religious belief that whenever four *Dido* class cruisers sailed in company then there would be trouble. In this case it proved shockingly accurate.

15 March 1942

Name	*Vortigern*	**Location**	North Sea, off Cromer, 55 06'N,
Class	*V* class destroyer		01 22'E
Built	15 October 1917	**Cause**	Torpedo

Notes   *Vortigern* was escorting convoy FS.749 when the convoy was attacked by a force of German *S-boote*. In the mêlée that followed *Vortigern* was hit by two torpedoes, probably fired by *S-104*, and sank.

20 March 1942

Name	*Heythrop*	**Location**	Mediterranean, E of Tobruk,
Class	*Hunt* class destroyer		32 22'N, 25 28'E
Built	30 October 1940	**Cause**	Submarine attack
		Survivors	15

Notes   *Heythrop* was part of the 5th Destroyer Flotilla and was making an A/S sweep ahead of convoy MW.10 when at 1100 hrs she was torpedoed by *U652* (*Kapitanleutnant* Georg-Werner Fraatz). It seemed possible that the ship might be saved so she was taken in tow by HMS *Eridge* and headed toward Tobruk. Unfortunately she sank some 5 hours later, just after 1600 hrs.

24 March 1942

Name	*Southwold*	**Location**	Mediterranean, Malta, off Zonkor
Class	*Hunt* class destroyer		Point, 35 63'N, 14 35'E
Built	29 May 1941	**Cause**	Mine

Notes   *Southwold* was the second destroyer to be sunk during the passage of convoy MW.10. In the meantime, the convoy's escort had driven off an attack by the Italian battle fleet on 22 March in the Second Battle of Sirte. It was therefore all the more galling that, just as the convoy neared the safety of Malta, *Southwold* should be lost. She hit a mine at 1117 hrs and subsequently sank at 1759 hrs.

26 March 1942

Name	*Jaguar*	**Location**	Mediterranean, off Sidi Barrani,
Class	*J* class destroyer		31 53'N, 26 18'E
Built	22 November 1938	**Cause**	Submarine attack
		Survivors	53

Notes   *Jaguar* was escorting the oiler *Slavol* to Tobruk where she was to fuel the 5th Destroyer Flotilla. At 0445 hrs she was struck by two torpedoes fired by *U652* (*Kapitanleutnant* Georg-Werner Fraatz) and sank at once. The survivors were rescued by the South African A/S whaler *Klo*. Two hours later *U652* sank the *Slavol*.

Name	*Legion*	**CO**	Cdr R.F. Jessel RN
Class	*L* class destroyer	**Location**	Malta, Grand Harbour, Valetta
Built	26 December 1939	**Cause**	Air attack

Notes   *Legion* had been damaged in an air raid on 23 March while covering convoy MW.10. Now 'safely' in Malta she was hit again and sank alongside the jetty. Her crew were evacuated from Malta in HMS *Havock* (see p. 177); when that ship was wrecked, they were interned by the Vichy French.

Name	*P.39*	**Location**	Malta, alongside the submarine base
Class	*U* class submarine		at Manoel Island
Built	23 August 1941	**Cause**	Air attack
CO	Lt N. Marriott RN		

Notes   During an earlier raid on Malta, *P.39* had sustained serious shock damage to her hull, battery and machinery, and had been towed over to the dockyard to have her battery removed. During an air raid at 1800 hrs on the 26th, *P.39* was struck by a single bomb which effectively blew the submarine in two, the two 'halves' being held together only by the keel. She was saved because all watertight doors were closed but was clearly beyond repair so she was towed up the harbour to Kalkara and beached. Her hull was then extensively and ostentatiously camouflaged so that she received a lot of attention from the Axis air forces which might have been better directed elsewhere. It was very sad, though, for her crew to wait around and watch what they still regarded as 'their' boat being smashed to bits.

28 March 1942

Name	*Campbeltown*	**CO**	Lt Cdr S.H. Beattie RN
Class	*Town* class destroyer	**Location**	Western France, port of St Nazaire
Built	1919	**Cause**	Expended as blockship

Notes   In March 1942 it was decided that the great dock at St Nazaire – the only dock on the Atlantic seaboard capable of accommodating a battleship as large as the *Tirpitz* – had to be destroyed. The plan called for a blockship, *Campbeltown*, to be sunk in the lock entrance packed with delayed action explosives. The attacking force would then retire after doing as much damage to the docks and dock installations as possible. For this operation *Campbeltown*'s appearance was significantly altered so that she resembled a German *Wolf* class torpedo boat.

The operation went exactly to plan and at 0314 hrs on the 28th *Campbeltown* was driven into the lock gate and then scuttled. The landing force then withdrew after causing considerable mayhem ashore. Eleven hours later, at 1235 hrs, the explosives packed into *Campbeltown*'s forecastle exploded. A photograph taken shortly before the explosion shows the ship's forecastle packed with German officers surveying their 'prize'. The explosion shook the whole city and the dock was not repaired until well after the war. Lieutenant-Commander Beattie was awarded the Victoria Cross for the action and had the unusual distinction of having the citation read to him by the *Kommandant* of his PoW camp.

April 1942 *marked the escalation of the Axis air offensive against Malta with the loss of another two destroyers and two submarines alongside. At sea the Royal Navy lost two of its most successful commanding officers, Lieutenant-Commander M.D. Wanklyn VC DSO RN of HMS* Upholder *and Lieutenant-Commander E.P. Tomkinson DSO DSC RN of HMS* Urge. *In the Far East the Japanese continued their seemingly inexorable advance, entering the Indian Ocean and attacking British bases in Ceylon. Although they sank an aircraft carrier, two cruisers, two destroyers, a corvette and an armed merchant cruiser, this operation would mark the peak of the Japanese Navy's success. Two months later their main carrier force was devastated at the Battle of Midway.*

1 April 1942

Name	*P.36*	**Location**	Malta, alongside the submarine base
Class	*U* class submarine		at Manoel Island
Built	28 April 1941	**Cause**	Air attack
CO	Lt H.N. Edmonds RN	**Casualties**	None

Notes   Following the loss of *P.39* it became normal practice for submarines at Malta to lie dived on the bottom during the day. However, on 1 April *P.36* was caught alongside the jetty during an air raid. A bomb exploded in the water by the boat, smashing a hole in the pressure hull. Desperate measures were tried in order to keep her afloat, even to the extent of securing steel hawsers to her hull and then wrapping them around the massive columns supporting the arches of the submarine base building – a sixteenth-century quarantine hospital. At this point, when it looked as if *P.36*'s weight would cause the arches to collapse, Lieutenant Edmonds was heard to comment that it was bad enough to lose one's command without being sued for the destruction of an ancient monument as well! The hawsers were cut and *P.36* sank into the harbour.

In August 1958 *P.36* was raised, taken out to sea and scuttled.

Name	*Pandora*	**CO**	Lt R.L. Alexander RN
Class	*P* class submarine	**Location**	Malta, Grand Harbour, Valetta
Built	22 August 1929	**Cause**	Air attack

Notes   *Pandora* had arrived at Malta on 31 March carrying vital stores for the island, including fuel oil. As her cargo was urgently needed it was decided to risk keeping her on the surface during daylight so that it could be discharged. Between 1430 hrs and 1500 hrs the island received a very heavy air raid in which *Pandora* was struck by at least two bombs and sank in less than 4 minutes.

The wreck was subsequently raised and sent to join *P.39* at Kalkara Creek. In 1957 it was being broken up *in situ* when the skeletons of two of her crew were found in the compartment in which they had died fifteen years earlier. Their bodies were committed to the deep on 1 July 1957 from the submarine HMS *Tudor*. The burial service was read by Captain R.L. Alexander DSO RN.

5 April 1942

Name	*Hector*	**CO**	None appointed
Class	AMC	**Location**	Ceylon, port of Colombo
Built	1924	**Cause**	Air attack

Notes   *Hector* was not in commission at the time of her loss and was in the process of being re-converted for trade. Having only just undocked, she could not be sent to sea for safety when reports of the appearance of

Japanese carriers were received. Just before 0800 hrs, on Easter Sunday, 5 April, Colombo was attacked by a force of Japanese aircraft from the carriers *Akagi*, *Soryu* and *Hiryu*. *Hector* was struck by four bombs, caught fire and sank in shallow water with her upperworks awash. The fire was fuelled by the large amount of dockyard stores and combustible materials lying around on her upper deck and burned for fourteen days before being extinguished.

Name	*Tenedos*	**Location**	Ceylon, port of Colombo
Class	S class destroyer	**Cause**	Air attack
Built	21 October 1918	**Casualties**	33
CO	Lt Cdr R. Dyer RN		

Notes Like *Hector*, *Tenedos* could not be sent to sea owing to defects. She received two direct hits aft, a third near the foremast and a near miss astern, and quickly sank.

Name	*Cornwall*	**Location**	Indian Ocean, S of Ceylon, 01 54'N,
Class	*County* class cruiser		77 45'E
Built	11 March 1926	**Cause**	Air attack
CO	Capt P.C.W. Manwaring RN	**Casualties**	190

Notes *Cornwall* (in company with *Dorsetshire*) had cleared Colombo on 4 April and was steering 220° at 23 knots to join the main body of the fleet. At 0800 hrs on the 5th enemy reports began to come in and speed was increased to 27 knots. From 1100 hrs the ships were shadowed by aircraft, presumed hostile, and at 1340 hrs the first attack developed on *Cornwall* with bombs striking the hangar and falling alongside the port quarter. Bombs then fell continuously on and around the ship so that it was impossible to gain an accurate estimate of the sequence of events. A near miss on the port side abreast the bridge flooded large areas on the port side and dislocated electrical power supplies all over the ship. A bomb on the waterline abreast the hangar burst into the forward engine room, while all personnel in the after engine room were killed by a near miss on the starboard side. Both boiler rooms were also flooded and had to be evacuated. Further hits were received between the forward and centre funnels, between 'X' and 'Y' turrets, in the sick bay flat, the dynamo room and the forward messdecks. Most of the personnel on the bridge were killed by flying splinters. In less than five minutes the *Cornwall* was dead in the water, the port gunwhale was awash and the starboard outer propeller breaking surface. At 1355 hrs Captain Manwaring gave the order to abandon ship. Four minutes later *Cornwall* suddenly heeled over to about 70° and sank by the bows. The survivors had to spend some 30 hours in the water before being rescued by the cruiser *Enterprise* and the destroyers *Panther* and *Paladin*.

Name	*Dorsetshire*	**Location**	Indian Ocean, S of Ceylon, 01 54'N,
Class	*County* class cruiser		77 45'E
Built	29 January 1929	**Cause**	Air attack
CO	Capt A.W. Agar VC DSO RN	**Casualties**	234

Notes Just as *Cornwall* was receiving her first attack, three aircraft also attacked *Dorsetshire*. Although avoiding action was taken, she was hit by three bombs: one on the quarterdeck, one on the catapult and the third on the port side. Attacks then followed at intervals of a few seconds. Commenting after his ordeal Captain Agar said that it seemed to be the Japanese practice to have one bomb falling while the previous one was exploding. The Japanese were also aided by the fact that the ships were steering a southerly course – they could attack from down sun and from dead ahead – the cruisers' AA blind spot. Four minutes after the attack began *Dorsetshire* began to list to port. Looking aft from the bridge Captain Agar could see 'flames and smoke extending to the stern'. The ship had now been struck by a total of ten bombs and there were also several near misses that caused much shock damage. At 1346 hrs *Dorsetshire* rolled on to her beam ends and sank stern first. As with *Cornwall's* survivors, those from *Dorsetshire* had to endure 30 hours in the water before being rescued.

Name	*Lance*	**CO**	Lt Cdr R.W. Northcott RN
Class	*L* class destroyer	**Location**	Malta, Grand Harbour, Valetta
Built	28 November 1940	**Cause**	Air attack

Notes   *Lance* was in dry dock for repairs and thus was helpless when a German air raid developed on the 5th. She was damaged beyond repair, and a further attack on the 9th added to the damage.

Name	*Abingdon*	**Location**	Malta, Grand Harbour, Valetta
Class	*Hunt* class minesweeper	**Cause**	Air attack
Built	1917		

Notes   *Abingdon* suffered the same fate as *Lance*. Alongside the jetty for repairs she could not be moved when the air attack developed and was sunk.

Damage to the starboard side of HMS *Lance* while in dry dock at Malta, April 1942. (Dott. Achille Rastelli)

6 April 1942

Name	*Indus*	**Location**	Indian Ocean, off Fakir Point Light,
Class	Sloop		Akyab, 20 07'N, 92 54'E
Built	24 August 1934	**Cause**	Air attack
CO	Cdr J.E.N. Coope RIN		

Notes   *Indus* was sunk in an air attack by Japanese Army Air Force aircraft.

Name	*Havock*	**Location**	Mediterranean, off Kelibia, Tunisia,
Class	*H* class destroyer		36 48'N, 11 08'E
Built	7 July 1936	**Cause**	Grounding
CO	Lt Cdr R. Watkins RN	**Casualties**	1
		Survivors	100+ passengers.

Notes   *Havock* was making a night passage from Malta to Gibraltar with over 100 passengers on board. At 0415 hrs on the 6th she hit a sandbank off Kelibia while steaming at 30 knots. The turbines disintegrated, killing one and scalding five stokers. Watkins reported that he was destroying all equipment and CBs and requested that either Catalina aircraft or a submarine be sent to rescue the crew. However, no Catalinas were available and it was considered too risky to send a submarine. Accordingly Watkins, his ship's company and the passengers were interned by the Vichy French. They were kept at a camp at Laghouat, deep in the Sahara, where conditions were very bad.

9 April 1942

Name	*Hermes*	**Location**	Indian Ocean, off Batticaloa
Class	Aircraft carrier		(Ceylon), 07 35'N, 82 05'E
Built	11 September 1919	**Cause**	Air attack
CO	Capt R.F. Onslow MVO DSC RN	**Casualties**	307

Notes   The Japanese carriers returned to attack Trincomalee on 9 April. Owing to efficient dispersal measures the anchorage was empty and by the time they sank only a merchant ship and a floating dock. At 0858 hrs a Japanese signal reporting *Hermes* was intercepted by the British. Fighter cover for the carrier was requested (but never arrived owing to communications failures) and she was ordered to return to Trincomalee at full speed. At 1035 hrs the carrier reported that she was under air attack. According to her navigating officer the Japanese air attack was carried out 'perfectly, relentlessly and quite fearlessly'. Over the next 10 minutes *Hermes* was attacked from all directions and over forty hits were recorded. By 1050 hrs she lay dead in the water with the port side of the flight deck awash. At 1055 hrs, just after Captain Onslow had ordered abandon ship, she rolled over and sank. 'So quickly did she in fact go', wrote her navigating officer, 'that I merely stepped off the chart house level into the water.'

Name	*Vampire*	**Location**	Indian Ocean, off Batticaloa
Class	*V* class destroyer		(Ceylon), 07 35'N, 82 05'E
Built	21 May 1917	**Cause**	Air attack
CO	Cdr W.T. Moran RAN	**Casualties**	8

Notes   After sinking *Hermes* the Japanese aircraft turned their attention to her escorting destroyer. *Vampire* lasted less than 10 minutes under attack by more than fifteen aircraft. After a number of hits the ship broke in half: the forward part sank immediately but the after end exploded at 1105 hrs and sank. As the stern sank the depth-charges exploded in a massive underwater blast.

Some 600 survivors from *Hermes* and *Vampire* were rescued by the hospital ship *Vita*. Japanese aircraft had flown over the *Vita* several times throughout the day but had respected her Red Cross markings.

Name	*Hollyhock*	**Cause**	Air attack
Class	*Flower* class corvette	**Casualties**	53
CO	Lt Cdr T.E. Davies RNR	**Survivors**	16
Location	Indian Ocean, 30 miles SSE of		
	Batticaloa, 07 21'N, 81 57'E		

Notes   About an hour after the attacks on *Hermes* HMS *Hollyhock*, which was escorting the tanker *Athelstane* sighted nine aircraft approaching. Five of them peeled off and attacked the *Athelstane*, which sank almost immediately at 1205 hrs. The other four aircraft attacked the little corvette in pairs. In the first attack one bomb put no. 2 boiler out of action; in the second attack two bombs struck the stern which 'disintegrated' and she sank in less than 45 seconds. The survivors were rescued by *Athelstane*'s boat. As they headed for the shore seven FAA Fulmars flew overhead: the air cover requested for *Hermes* had finally arrived.

11 April 1942

Name	*Kingston*	**Location**	Malta, Grand Harbour, Valetta
Class	*K* class destroyer	**Cause**	Air attack
Built	9 January 1939		

Notes   The loss of *Kingston* showed just how hard the Axis air offensive was hitting Malta. *Kingston* had been damaged by gunfire during the Second Battle of Sirte on 22 March but had reached Malta for repairs. Since then she had been damaged in raids on 5 and 7 April. In dry dock on the 11th she could not evade her attackers and was damaged beyond repair.

14(?) April 1942

Name	*Upholder*	**CO**	Lt Cdr M.D. Wanklyn VC DSO RN
Class	*U* class submarine	**Survivors**	None
Built	8 July 1940		

Notes   *Upholder* sailed from Malta on 6 April for what was her twenty-first and last patrol in the Mediterranean. After this patrol she was to return to the UK for a refit and a well-earned rest for her crew. She met with *Unbeaten* on the night of the 10th to transfer an Army officer and thereafter nothing more was heard from her. The most widely accepted theory for *Upholder*'s loss is that she was a victim of a depth-charge attack by the Italian destroyer *Pegaso* on 14 April. However, the position of this attack, 34 47'N, 15 55'E is nearly 100 miles north of where *Upholder* was expected to be. Moreover *Pegaso* did not observe any wreckage or oil (the usual indication of a sinking) following her attack with just one pattern of depth-charges. Alternative explanations include mining in the Tripoli area on the night of 11 April where a submarine was sighted close to the minefield, or loss by accident. No clear evidence supports any one of these theories to the exclusion of the others. The file on *Upholder* remains open.

HMS *Kingston* lying on her beam ends in dry dock at Malta. The photograph was taken in April 1942. (Dott. Achille Rastelli)

In her brief career *Upholder* had sunk two Italian submarines, a destroyer and over 100,000 tons of Axis shipping. In a rare tribute to Wanklyn and his ship's company the Admiralty issued a communiqué which concluded: 'The ship and her company are gone but the inspiration and example remain.'

27 April 1942

Name	*Fitzroy*	**Location**	North Sea, NE of Great Yarmouth,
Class	*Hunt* class minesweeper		52 39'N, 02 46'E
Built	1917	**Cause**	Mine

Notes *Fitzroy* was mined 40 miles east-north-east of Great Yarmouth and sank in less than 10 minutes. It has been suggested that she struck a British mine. However, her loss was one of the inevitable hazards of operating in waters which were extensively mined by both sides.

29(?) April 1942

Name	*Urge*	**CO**	Lt Cdr E.P. Tomkinson DSO DSC
Class	*U* class submarine		RN
Built	19 August 1940	**Survivors**	None

Notes The most likely explanation for *Urge*'s loss is that she was the victim of an attack by Italian fighters, converted to the role, on 29 April off Ras el Hilal. The aircraft had sighted a submarine shelling the motor vessel *San Giusto* and attacked. Given that *Urge* had left Malta on 27 April, she could easily have been off Ras el Hilal on the 29th.

May 1942 *Although April 1942 had seen the Japanese Navy at the peak of its success, May saw the opening of a new theatre for the Royal Navy and one that was going to be a running sore for the rest of the war. The coming of spring and long daylight hours allowed the Germans to attack the convoys taking supplies of raw material to the Soviet ports of Murmansk and Archangel. May saw two cruisers and a destroyer lost in these inhospitable waters.*

1 May 1942

Name	*Punjabi*	**Location**	Atlantic, NE of Iceland, 66 00'N,
Class	*Tribal* class destroyer		08 00'W
Built	18 December 1937	**Cause**	Collision
CO	Cdr the Hon. J.M.G. Waldegrave DSC RN	**Survivors**	205

Notes   *Punjabi* was screening the capital ships of the Home Fleet which were providing distant cover for PQ convoys. The day had been calm but with frequent snow showers and patches of dense fog. The destroyer screen was stationed eight cables from the capital ships but when visibility worsened, the destroyers closed to four cables distance so as not to lose touch with the flagship. *Punjabi* was the second ship in the starboard column with *Martin* and *Marne* astern of her. It was just before 1600 hrs when the visibility suddenly worsened and the starboard leader closed in towards the battleships. *Punjabi* turned to follow the leader's fog buoy but lost it, and continued toward the fleet's line of advance at an angle of 80°. Suddenly the *King George V*, travelling at 25 knots, loomed out of the fog and crashed into *Punjabi*'s port side just aft of the engine room and sliced straight through her hull.

Punjabi's stern sank almost immediately and as it did so the ready-use depth-charges on the stern went off causing severe internal bruising to those of *Punjabi*'s crew who were already in the water. Both *King George V* and USS *Washington* sustained shock damage as a result of the explosions. The two destroyers astern of *Punjabi*, *Marne* and *Martin*, had to go hurriedly astern and were nearly run down by *Victorious* and *Wichita*.

Punjabi's forward section sank more slowly and 205 officers and men, including Commander Waldegrave, were rescued. Many men were picked unconscious out of the freezing cold water and could not be revived.

2 May 1942

Name	*Edinburgh*	**Location**	Barents Sea, 71 51'N, 35 10'E
Class	*Southampton* class cruiser (modified)	**Cause**	Scuttled following submarine and
Built	31 March 1938		destroyer attack
CO	Capt W. Faulkner RN (flagship of Rear Admiral Stuart Bonham-Carter DSO)	**Casualties**	58

Notes   HMS *Edinburgh*, flying the flag of Rear Admiral Stuart Bonham-Carter (who had commanded the blockship *Intrepid* at Zeebrugge, see p. 72), was escorting the homeward-bound convoy QP.11. Additionally *Edinburgh* was carrying 5 tons of Soviet gold – payment for Allied war material. Bonham-Carter decided to take *Edinburgh* out to a distance of 15 miles ahead of the convoy in order to be in a good position to head off any attacks by destroyers. It was while *Edinburgh* was in this exposed position that she was struck by two torpedoes fired by

U.456 (Kapitanleutnant Max-Martin Teichert). Petty Officer L.D. Newman was in 'B' turret when the first torpedo struck: 'I was leaning over the centre gun tray watching the card playing when suddenly the whole ship shook accompanied by a terrific explosion throwing me about two feet up into the air, and no sooner had I come down again when another similar explosion sent me up into the air. At the second explosion all the lights went out.'

The first torpedo had struck on the starboard side forward and had caused considerable flooding. The second virtually blew the stern off, although the port shafts remained intact. The force of the explosion blew the quarterdeck back over the guns of 'Y' turret. The explosion was seen from the convoy and the destroyers *Foresight* (Commander J.S. Salter) and *Forester* (Lieutenant-Commander C.P. Huddart) were sent to her assistance, followed shortly afterwards by two Russian destroyers. With the four destroyers providing a screen *Edinburgh* slowly began the 250 mile passage back to Murmansk.

The vigilance of the destroyers prevented Teichert from sinking the cruiser but he remained in contact and reported her movements. This information prompted the German Flag Officer Northern Waters to send the three destroyers based at Kirkenes to attack the convoy and its depleted escort; at 0100 hrs on 1 May *Z.24* (*Korvettenkapitan* Martin Salzwedel), *Z.25* (*Korvettenkapitan* Heinz Peters) and the *Hermann Schoemann* (*Korvettenkapitan* Heinrich Wittig) put to sea.

Meanwhile the *Edinburgh* had been making slow progress toward Murmansk. At 0600 hrs the two Soviet destroyers had to go ahead to Murmansk to fuel so HMS *Foresight*, which had been secured astern of the cruiser, acting as a drogue, cast off to resume her screening duties that, as *U.456* was still in the area, were of greater importance. Without the balancing weight of *Foresight* astern of her, *Edinburgh* now began to yaw from side to side. All that could be done to correct this was to go astern on one engine periodically but this reduced her speed to about 2 knots.

At 1800 hrs *Edinburgh*'s screen was reinforced by the Soviet tug *Rubin*, which alas lacked sufficient power to tow the *Edinburgh*, and later by the four minesweepers *Harrier*, *Gossamer*, *Niger* and *Hussar*. *Rubin* secured to *Edinburgh*'s port bow and, with *Gossamer* acting as a drogue aft, a speed of 3 knots was attained. The weather remained stable and there was every indication that the stricken cruiser would make the Kola Inlet. However, at 0627 hrs on the 2nd HMS *Hussar*, on *Edinburgh*'s starboard quarter, came under fire from the German destroyers which could just be seen through the fog. The destroyers tried to close the *Edinburgh* but once again were impeded by the aggressive tactics of the destroyers and the minesweepers. *Edinburgh* herself was not going to give up without a fight. On sighting the destroyers Captain Faulkner ordered the tug and *Gossamer* to cast off. Although the cruiser was slowly circling, totally out of control, the crew of 'B' turret brought its guns into action, firing by local control. *Edinburgh*'s second salvo hit the *Hermann Schoemann* doing considerable damage. Two of the 112 lb 6 in shells exploded in *Schoemann*'s engine room and she lost all steam and electric power. She took no further part in the action. Meanwhile *Foresight* and *Forester* were engaged in a running fight in and out of the smokescreens and snow flurries with *Z.24* and *Z.25*. Just after 0650 hrs *Forester* fired three torpedoes at the destroyers but was herself hit by three shells which killed her commanding officer, Lieutenant-Commander G.P. Huddart RN, wrecked no. 1 boiler room and 'B' and 'Y' mountings. Three minutes later *Z.24* fired four torpedoes at the *Forester*, all of which missed but sped on towards the *Edinburgh*. The cruiser could not take avoiding action and was struck on the port side almost exactly opposite where the first of *U.456*'s torpedoes had hit.

Captain Faulkner ordered an inspection of the damage and his engineer officer reported that the ship was completely open to the sea amidships on both sides and that at any moment her back might break. Bonham-Carter ordered the *Gossamer* alongside to take off the wounded and the Merchant Navy personnel embarked in *Edinburgh* for the passage. As the 440 officers and men were transferred to *Gossamer*, 'B' turret continued to fire and by doing so prevented *Z.24* and *Z.25* from going to the aid of the *Hermann Schoemann*. However, when the

The minesweeper HMS *Harrier* lies alongside the port side of HMS *Edinburgh* taking off her crew. Note the damage to the stern caused by *U.456*'s torpedo. (Novosti)

list reached 17°, the guns would no longer bear and the turret had to cease firing. Bonham-Carter gave Captain Faulkner the order to abandon ship: the 350 remaining officers and men were taken off by HMS *Harrier*. Bonham-Carter then ordered the wreck to be scuttled by *Foresight*.

In 1982 the wreck of HMS *Edinburgh* was located by a British salvage company and, following complex negotiations between the British and Soviet governments, most of the 5 tons of gold bullion was removed from the wreck.

5 May 1942

Name	*Auricula*	**Location**	Indian Ocean, Courier Bay, NE coast of Madagascar, 12 12'S, 49 19'E
Class	*Flower* class corvette		
CO	Lieutenant-Commander S.L. Maybury RN	**Cause**	Mine
		Casualties	None

Notes Though nominally an escort vessel *Auricula* had been fitted for minesweeping. While sweeping following the British landings on Madagascar she ran on a mine at 1138 hrs and broke her back. She was in no danger of sinking and remained where she was, anchored by her sweep gear. At 0740 hrs she broke in half and sank.

8 May 1942

Name	*Olympus*	**Location**	Mediterranean, off Malta
Class	O class submarine	**Cause**	Mine
Built	11 December 1928	**Casualties**	98
CO	Lt Cdr H.G. Dymott RN	**Survivors**	12

Notes *Olympus* left Malta at 0400 hrs on 8 May bound for Gibraltar. As well as her own ship's company she had thirty-six passengers – members of the crews of *P.36*, *P.39* and *Pandora*. In all ninety-eight persons were on board. Just after 0500 hrs, while proceeding on the surface, she was mined and sank in less than 9 minutes. Only twelve men managed to swim the 5 or 6 miles to shore.

11 May 1942

Name	*Lively*	**Location**	Mediterraean, 100m NE of Tobruk,
Class	L class destroyer		33 24'N, 25 38'E
Built	28 January 1941	**Cause**	Air attack
CO	Lt Cdr W.F. Hussey RN		

Notes At 2000 hrs on 10 May four destroyers of the 14th Flotilla – *Jervis* (Captain A.L. Poland RN, Captain D.14), *Lively*, *Jackal* and *Kipling* – sailed from Alexandria to intercept an Axis convoy en route from Taranto to Tripoli. It was hoped to intercept the convoy off Benghazi on the 12th providing the destroyers could escape detection. However, they were sighted by an Axis aircraft, although the ships' radar failed to spot the aircraft. At 1553 hrs on the 11th the monitoring service at Alexandria warned the force that air attacks could be expected. Reluctantly Poland gave the order to turn back. From 1600 hrs onwards fierce air attacks were made on the ships. Three or four bombs scored direct hits on or about *Lively*'s waterline abreast 'A' mounting. She listed to starboard as a second salvo of bombs fell alongside. A few seconds later she was on her beam ends. At 1645 hrs there was an explosion forward and *Lively* sank immediately. Her survivors were rescued by *Jervis* and *Jackal*.

Name	*Kipling*	**Location**	Mediterranean, 60 miles N of Mersa
Class	K class destroyer		Matruh, 32 28'N, 36 20'E
Built	19 January 1939	**Cause**	Air attack

Notes *Kipling* did not long survive the *Lively*. The sea was calm and visibility was excellent. The air attacks were pressed home with accuracy and determination. At 2007 hrs *Kipling* was repeatedly hit and sank. Her survivors and those from *Lively* were taken on board *Jackal*.

Name	*Jackal*	**Location**	Mediterranean, 32 23'N, 36 25'E
Class	J class destroyer	**Cause**	Scuttled following air attack
Built	25 October 1938		

Notes *Jackal* had been damaged in the same attack in which *Kipling* was sunk but *Jervis* had managed to take her in tow. However, the damage proved too great and at 0455 hrs on the 12th she was sunk by *Jervis*. The loss of three destroyers represented a major blow to the Mediterranean Fleet and highlighted the difficulties that British ships faced when operating without air cover against an enemy with fifteen airfields in the immediate operational area.

14 May 1942

Name	*Trinidad*	**Location**	Barents Sea, 100 miles N of
Class	*Colony* class cruiser		Murmansk, 73 37'N, 23 53'E
Built	21 March 1940	**Cause**	Air attack
CO	Capt L.S. Saunders RN	**Casualties**	81

Notes HMS *Trinidad*, which had been under repair at Kola since being hit by one of her own torpedoes on 29 March, was sufficiently seaworthy by the middle of May for the voyage back to Iceland from where she would proceed to the United States for permanent repairs. Flying the flag of Rear Admiral Bonham-Carter she sailed from Murmansk on the evening of 13 May – an inauspicious day as events were to show. She was escorted by the destroyers *Somali* (Captain J.W. Eaton, Captain of the 6th Destroyer Flotilla), *Matchless*, *Foresight* and *Forester*. Virtually the whole of the Home Fleet was mobilised to cover her passage. The four cruisers, *Nigeria*, *Kent*, *Norfolk* and *Liverpool*, under the command of Rear Admiral Burrough, were steaming to the west of Bear Island while the battle fleet consisting of *Duke of York* (flagship of the CinC), *Victorious*, *London*, USS *Washington*, USS *Tuscaloosa* and eleven destroyers provided further cover to the south-west.

The Luftwaffe found the ship the next morning at 0730 hrs. Weather conditions were poor initially, which gave the ship some degree of cover but during the afternoon the visibility began to clear. An air escort of Hurricanes and Pe.3 fighters of the Red Air Force, which was supposed to cover the cruiser for the first 200 miles of her passage, failed to appear although three Hurricane fighters did cover the ships for a period of 45 minutes. There were also a number of U-boat alarms while the icefield restricted movement to the north. By 1852 hrs on 14 May there were four aircraft shadowing the ships and from then on homing signals were virtually continuous.

The first air attacks materialised after 2200 hrs that evening when Ju.88s started a series of dive-bombing attacks on *Trinidad* and her escort. After about twenty-five of these attacks, which were unsuccessful although some ships had some very near misses, a force of ten torpedo-bombers was detected coming in fairly low. While attention focused on this attack a lone Ju.88 dived out of the cloud and released its stick of bombs on *Trinidad*'s starboard quarter from a height of 400 ft. One bomb struck the starboard side of the bridge and burst on the lower deck, starting a fire that rapidly spread between decks and over the bridge. The second bomb, which was either a hit or a very near miss, flooded the magazine for 'B' turret and adjacent compartments and blew in a temporary patch in the ship's side abreast the Marines' mess deck. Despite a 14° list to starboard *Trinidad* was still steaming at 20 knots and Captain Saunders was able to avoid the torpedoes from a second attack launched fifteen minutes later.

However, at 2315 hrs Captain Saunders had to stop the ship to reduce the draught which was fanning the flames. By midnight it was accepted that the fire was out of control. In view of the fact that *Trinidad* lay only 170 miles from the enemy-held coast, the presence of U-boats and the certainty of further air attack, it was decided to abandon the ship and scuttle her. The wounded were taken off by HMS *Forester* and the remainder by the other destroyers. Admiral Bonham-Carter, who had transferred his flag to *Somali*, found himself in the unenviable position of having to order his flagship to be scuttled for the second time in less than a fortnight (see p. 182). The *coup de grace* was administered by HMS *Matchless* and *Trinidad* finally sank at 0120 hrs on 15 May.

June 1942 *saw a massive attempt to supply the island of Malta by sailing two convoys to the island from Gibraltar (Operation Harpoon) and Alexandria (Operation Vigorous) simultaneously. Four merchant ships of the* Harpoon *convoy reached Malta but the Vigorous convoy turned back after being threatened by superior enemy forces.*

12 June 1942

Name	*Grove*	**Location**	Mediterranean, Gulf of Sollum,
Class	*Hunt* class destroyer		32 05'N, 25 30'E
Built	29 May 1941	**Cause**	Submarine attack
CO	Cdr W.J. Rylands RN	**Casualties**	110
		Survivors	80

Notes   HMS *Grove* was returning to Alexandria after escorting convoy AT.49 to Tobruk. The ship was running on one shaft only but because all available escorts were required for the Vigorous convoy to Malta, *Grove* was alone. At 0205 hrs on the 12th she grounded near Raz Azzaz and although refloated her speed was reduced to 8 knots. At 0655 hrs she was torpedoed by *U77* (*Kapitanleutnant* Heinrich Schonder) and sank quickly. The survivors were rescued by HMS *Tetcott*.

15 June 1942

Name	*Bedouin*	**Cause**	Air attack following damage by
Class	*Tribal* class destroyer		gunfire
Built	21 December 1937	**Casualties**	28
CO	Cdr B.G. Scurfield RN	**Survivors**	213
Location	Mediterranean, SW of Pantellaria,		
	36 12'N, 11 38'E		

Notes   *Bedouin* was part of the escort for the Harpoon convoy. At 0540 hrs on the 12 June two Italian cruisers and five destroyers were sighted closing the convoy at speed. *Bedouin* led out *Partridge*, *Ithuriel*, *Matchless*, *Marne* and the Polish *Kujawiak* to launch torpedo attacks on the Italian ships while the convoy turned towards the North African coast. The destroyers attacked from behind a smokescreen and closed to within 5,000 yards of the Italian cruisers before launching their torpedoes. However, the barrage of fire from the Italian ships was such that *Bedouin*'s superstructure was almost shot away. She had been struck by at least twelve 6 in shells and lay dead in the water. Efficient damage control managed to get the ship going again and soon *Partridge* took the crippled destroyer in tow. A confusing series of orders had both ships headed first for Gibraltar, then back to rejoin the convoy and then headed back to Gibraltar. At 1320 hrs the Italian cruisers reappeared and sped after *Partridge* while firing on the crippled *Bedouin* as they went by. At the same time a single Italian torpedo-bomber attacked from the starboard side. Although the aircraft was shot down the torpedo hit *Bedouin* in the engine room and almost blew the ship in two.

Bedouin's survivors were rescued by an Italian hospital ship (which was bombed by Italian aircraft during the operation) and became PoWs. In May 1945 Commander Scurfield was killed during a random RAF strafing attack on the column in which he was travelling.

Name	*Hasty*	Location	Mediterranean, SE of Crete,
Class	*H* class destroyer		34 10'N, 22 00'E
Built	5 May 1936	**Cause**	Torpedo
CO	Lt Cdr N.H. Austen RN		

Notes   *Hasty* was escorting the Vigorous convoy from the other end of the Mediterranean. At 0145 hrs the convoy reversed track owing to the risk of meeting the Italian battle fleet early the next morning. In the confusion of this night manoeuvre *Hasty* and a number of other warships fell behind. While speeding to catch up with the convoy they were attacked by a force of German *S-boote* based on Crete. *Newcastle* was hit by one torpedo well forward but could still steam at 24 knots. However, *Hasty* was hit by *S-55* at 0528 hrs and was so badly damaged that she had to be sunk.

Name	*Airedale*	Location	Mediterranean, S of Crete, 33 50'N,
Class	*Hunt* class destroyer		23 50'E
Built	12 August 1941	**Cause**	Scuttled after air attack
CO	Lt Cdr A.G. Forman RN		

Notes   *Airedale* was the second of three destroyers to be sunk escorting the Vigorous convoy. At about 1525 hrs on the 15th a force of between thirty and forty Ju.87s attacked the convoy. Twelve of the aircraft concentrated on the *Airedale* which was stationed on the convoy's starboard quarter. She was completely disabled and had to be sunk by gunfire by HMS *Hurworth* and finished off by a torpedo fired by HMS *Aldenham*.

16 June 1942

Name	*Hermione*	Location	Mediterranean, S of Crete, 33 30'N,
Class	*Dido* class cruiser		26 10'E
Built	18 May 1939	**Cause**	Submarine attack
CO	Capt G.N. Oliver DSO RN		

Notes   While the Vigorous convoy was retiring to Alexandria it was attacked by *U205* (*Kapitanleutnant* Franz-Georg Reschke). *U205* approached from the starboard quarter and Reschke aimed at a light cruiser doing about 13 knots. This was *Hermione* in her night position. One, or possibly two, torpedoes hit at 0127 hrs and she sank in less than 20 minutes.

Name	*Nestor*	Location	Mediterranean, S of Crete, 33 36'N,
Class	*N* class destroyer		24 27'E
Built	9 July 1940	**Cause**	Scuttled after air attack
CO	Cdr A.S. Rosenthal DSO RAN		

Notes   The third destroyer to be sunk during Operation Vigorous, *Nestor* had been disabled in an attack by Ju.87s at around 1800 hrs. She was badly holed from near misses and was taken in tow by *Javelin* escorted by three other destroyers but it was a difficult task since *Nestor* was down by the bow and yawed badly. At 0430 hrs on the 16th the tow parted for the second time. Simultaneously reports were received of a number of *S-boote* in the area. Commander Rosenthal took the view that trying to save his ship would merely invite the loss of *Javelin* and the other escorting destroyers. Accordingly *Nestor* was scuttled at 0700 hrs.

17 June 1942

Name	*Wild Swan*	**Location**	Atlantic, S of Bantry Bay, 49 52'N,
Class	*V&W* class destroyer		10 44'W
Built	17 May 1919	**Cause**	Collision after air attack

Notes *Wild Swan* had parted company with convoy HG.74 in the afternoon of the 17th to return to harbour. At 2005 hrs, while she was passing through a fleet of Spanish fishing vessels, she was attacked by twelve Ju.88s, which apparently mistook the fishing fleet for the convoy. *Wild Swan* was damaged in the air attack and then in the confusion collided with a Spanish fishing vessel – three of which were also sunk in this attack. *Wild Swan* subsequently sank at 2305 hrs and her survivors were picked up by *Vansittart*.

21 June 1942

Name	*P.514*	**Location**	E coast of Canada, 43 33'N, 53 40'W
Class	Ex-US *R* class submarine	**Cause**	Rammed
Built	24 December 1917	**Survivors**	None
CO	Lt Cdr R. Pain RN		

Notes *P.514* was an old American submarine (ex-*R-19*) which had been transferred to Britain and was used for the training of escort groups on Canada's east coast. *P.514* sailed on 20 June from Argentia, escorted by the corvette HMS *Primrose*, bound for St John's in Newfoundland, 65 miles to the north. On the same day the minesweeper *Georgian* sailed from St John's to rendezvous with the coastal convoy CL.43 which she was to escort to Sydney, a small township on Cape Breton Island. The rendezvous was made at 1430 hrs and passage began. *Georgian* had been informed that two U-boats were believed to be operating off Cape Race but a signal informing the minesweeper that *P.514* was at sea was not received.

In the early hours of 21 June *Georgian* picked up a faint but unmistakable echo of a diesel engine through the hydrophones. At the same time the echoes from another convoy, SC.88, passing 8 miles to the south of *Georgian* were also picked up. Thus, *Georgian*, convoy SC.88, and *P.514* and her escort were all in the same area at the same time. At 0307 hrs a darkened shape was seen crossing *Georgian*'s bows from starboard to port. No recognition procedures were carried out and *Georgian* rammed the submarine squarely amidships at full speed. When *Primrose* indicated the identity of the submarine, a search was begun for any survivors but none was found. In the inevitable investigation, it was found that *Georgian* had not received the signal warning of *P-514*'s presence and that under the circumstances, the minesweeper's commanding officer had acted correctly, although with tragic results.

24 June 1942

Name	*Gossamer*	**Location**	Arctic, Kola Inlet, 68 59'N, 33 03'E
Class	Minesweeper	**Cause**	Air attack
CO	Lt Cdr T.C. Crease RN	**Casualties**	23

Notes The port of Murmansk was gradually being reduced to a ruin by repeated German air attacks, during one of which *Gossamer* was sunk. Five Ju.88s were making attacks on shipping anchored in the Kola Inlet when one of their number broke off and approached *Gossamer* unseen with the sun behind him. His bomb struck her forward of the winch and blew the ship's bow off: she sank in less than 8 minutes.

30 June 1942

Name	*Medway*	**Location**	E Mediterranean, NE of Alexandria,
Class	Submarine depot ship		31 03'N, 30 35'E
Built	1928	**Cause**	Submarine attack
CO	Capt P. Ruck-Keene RN	**Casualties**	30
		Survivors	1,105

Notes   In the face of the seemingly unstoppable advance of the German and Italian armies in the Western Desert, the decision was taken to evacuate the base at Alexandria. Despite her 'non-combatant' status *Medway* was a vitally important unit of the fleet since she sustained the extremely combatant submarines of the 1st Flotilla (and did much other general maintenance work for the fleet besides). She left Alexandria on 29 June for Haifa, escorted by a cruiser and seven destroyers, but at 0925 hrs on the 30th she was attacked by *U372* (*Kapitanleutnant* Hans-Joachim Neumann). *U372* had penetrated the screen with ease and fired four torpedoes from a range of 1,500 yards. He then submerged to a depth of 375 ft to avoid counter-attacks and escaped. Three of the four torpedoes struck *Medway* in the engine room and dynamo room and she sank in 13 minutes. Ruck-Keene described the attack as 'perfect'. Neumann was unaware of the identity of his victim and merely claimed a 15,000 ton transport. The Germans did not learn of *Medway*'s loss for some months.

The survivors were rescued by *Zulu* and *Hero*. Among them was Third Officer Audrey Coningham WRNS, a cipher officer, who gave up her lifebelt to a rating whom she found struggling in the water. Coningham was subsequently Mentioned in Despatches – a rare occurrence for an WRNS officer. 'Mother Medway' was highly regarded by all who served in her as the best designed of all British submarine depot ships. It was often commented that she was so comfortable and well laid-out that her construction must have been a mistake! Her loss was a hard one for the 1st Submarine Flotilla, particularly as she was carrying nearly ninety torpedoes, which could not easily be replaced. Fortunately some forty-seven of these were later found floating and were recovered by HMS *Aldenham* and other small craft.

July 1942 *saw the passage of the infamous convoy PQ.17 to Russia, a convoy that was scattered by order of the Admiralty in the face of threat from German forces. Out of the 36 merchant ships, 24 were sunk by U-boats and/or aircraft but Royal Navy forces sustained no losses – a fact that did not go unnoticed by the Merchant Navy.*

5 July 1942

Name	*Niger*	**Location**	Atlantic, off Iceland, 66 35'N,
Class	*Halcyon* class minesweeper		23 14'W
CO	Cdr A.J. Cubison DSC RN	**Cause**	Mine

Notes   The PQ.17 convoy to Russia has been subject of any number of books and articles. However, the fate that befell the homeward-bound convoy QP.17 was equally disastrous and made all the worse because it occurred as a result of a navigational error. At 1900 hrs on 5 July the convoy was approaching the north-west corner of Iceland in five columns escorted by *Niger*, *Hussar*, *Roselys* and two trawlers. The weather was bad with visibility down to less than 1 mile, with rough seas and the wind coming from the north-east at Force 8. Bad weather had made it impossible to take star sights since 2 July and the convoy's position had been calculated by dead reckoning and therefore was considerably in doubt.

At 1910 hrs Cubison suggested to the Commodore that the convoy should be reduced to two columns in order to pass between Straumnes Point and the minefield to the north-west of Iceland. Soon afterwards

Commander Cubison gave his estimated position at 2000 hrs as being 66° 45'N, 22° 22'W, and suggested altering course to 222° to clear Straumnes Point. This was done. Two hours later *Niger*, which had gone ahead to make a landfall, leaving *Hussar* as a visual link with the convoy, sighted what she took to be the North Cape, one mile distant, and ordered course to be altered to 270°.

What *Niger* had actually sighted was an iceberg and the alteration of course to the north had the effect of taking the convoy directly into the minefield. At 2240 hrs *Niger* blew up and sank with heavy loss of life, including Commander Cubison. At that very moment a signal from *Niger* was being handed to the Commodore recommending a return to 222° and explaining the mistake. It was too late. Explosions were occurring all over the convoy as ships ran into mines. In the reduced visibility six ships struck mines: *Exterminator*, *Heffron*, *Hybert*, *Massmar* and *Rodina* all sank, and *John Randolph* was damaged. The escorts displayed conspicuous gallantry in entering, or remaining in, the minefield to rescue the survivors. The action of the French corvette *Roselys* (Lieutenant de Vaisseau A. Bergeret) was particularly noteworthy. Although Bergeret appreciated that the convoy had blundered into a minefield, he kept his ship in the highly dangerous waters for 6½ hours during which time he rescued 179 survivors.

August 1942   *This month, the Americans went on the offensive at Guadalcanal in the Pacific. In the naval battles that followed British and Commonwealth forces played only a small part, but their experience showed that they had a long way to go to equal the Japanese in night fighting tactics. It had not been possible to run a convoy to Malta in July 1942 owing to commitments elsewhere, but in August the Royal Navy made its most determined effort, Operation Pedestal, to fight through a convoy to Malta. The cost was high: a fleet carrier, two cruisers and a destroyer were sunk but Malta was saved. In Home Waters the raid on Dieppe proved a very expensive way of gaining amphibious experience in terms of casualties and equipment. The Royal Navy was lucky to escape with the loss of one destroyer.*

7 August 1942

Name	*Thorn*	**Location**	Mediterranean, E of Gevdo Island,
Class	*T* class submarine		Crete
Built	18 March 1941	**Cause**	Depth-charge
CO	Lt Cdr R.G. Norfolk RN	**Survivors**	None

Notes   At 1255 hrs on 7 August a Ju.88 covering the passage of the Italian merchant ship *Istria* escorted by the destroyer *Emmanuale Pessagno*, sighted a submarine and alerted the destroyer by machine-gunning the area of water where the periscope had been seen. *Pessagno* closed the position at speed, sighted a periscope, and after gaining ECG contact delivered seven depth-charge attacks. After the sixth attack oil and air bubbles began coming to the surface. There can be no doubt that the victim of *Pessagno*'s attack was *Thorn*.

9 August 1942

Name	*Canberra*	**Location**	Pacific, S of Savo Island, 09 15'S,
Class	*County* class cruiser		159 40'E
Built	31 May 1927	**Cause**	Gunfire and torpedoes
		Casualties	84

Notes   *Canberra* was the sole Commonwealth representative in a force of five cruisers which attempted to stop a force of five Japanese cruisers from attacking the anchorage at Guadalcanal. The Americans and Australians were no match for Japanese night fighting tactics and the Japanese ships slipped between two radar-equipped US destroyers and then attacked the cruiser line. *Canberra* was sunk by gunfire and torpedoes fired by the cruisers *Chokai, Aoba, Kako, Kinugasa* and *Furutaka*, and was eventually scuttled at 0800 hrs on the 9th by the USS *Ellet*. In what later became known as the Battle of Savo Island, the American cruisers *Quincy, Astoria* and *Vincennes* were sunk along with the *Canberra*.

11 August 1942

Name	*Eagle*	**Location**	Mediterranean, 65 miles S of
Class	Aircraft carrier		Majorca, 38 05'N, 03 02'E
Built	8 June 1918	**Cause**	Submarine attack
CO	Capt L.D. Mackintosh DSC RN	**Casualties**	163
		Survivors	927

Notes The last of five fleet carriers to be sunk in the Second World War, *Eagle* was escorting the *Pedestal* convoy to Malta. On the afternoon of the 11th the convoy began a complicated series of evolutions: the carrier *Furious* began to fly off Spitfire aircraft to Malta while at the same time destroyers began to leave the screen individually to take on fuel from the oiler. With such a number of ships all tearing through the water Asdic conditions were appalling and thus *U73* (*Kapitanleutnant* Helmut Rosenbaum) was able to penetrate the screen undetected. At 1315 hrs Rosenbaum fired her bow tubes at the carrier. All four torpedoes struck the *Eagle* on her port side within 10 seconds. She immediately assumed a heavy list to port and sank in 8 minutes. *U73* used the same poor Asdic conditions to facilitate her escape.

12 August 1942

Name	*Foresight*	**Location**	Mediterranean, 13 miles SW of
Class	F class destroyer		Galita Island, 37 40'N, 10 00'E
Built	29 June 1934	**Cause**	Scuttled following air attack
CO	Lt Cdr R.A. Fell RN	**Casualties**	4
		Survivors	140

Notes At 1835 hrs on 12 August the *Pedestal* convoy was attacked by over 100 aircraft, including Ju.87 and Ju.88 bombers with Italian S.79 torpedo-bombers. Although Fell took avoiding action *Foresight* was hit and disabled by a torpedo. She was taken in tow by *Tartar* (Commander St J. Tyrwhitt) and headed back to Gibraltar. Throughout the 13th they were persistently shadowed by aircraft and Tyrwhitt decided to sink the cripple lest his own ship be sunk too. Accordingly, after taking off *Foresight*'s crew, he sank her with a torpedo.

Name	*Cairo*	**Location**	Mediterranean, NE of Bizerta,
Class	C class cruiser		37 40'N, 10 06'E
Built	19 November 1918	**Cause**	Submarine attack
CO	Acting Capt C.C. Hardy DSO RN	**Casualties**	24
		Survivors	376

Notes Despite the loss of *Eagle* and *Foresight*, the *Pedestal* convoy was doing well, and the massed air attacks had been driven off. However, as the convoy formed up into two columns at the entrance to the Skerki Channel

The broken remains of HMS *Foresight* before she was scuttled on 13 August 1942. (Ufficio Storico Della Marina Militare)

between Sicily and North Africa, it was attacked by the Italian submarine *Axum* (*TV* Renato Ferrini). *Axum* fired four torpedoes at 1955 hrs and Ferrini heard detonations between a minute or so later. He claimed hits on a cruiser and a destroyer but his actual success was far greater. One torpedo hit the cruiser *Nigeria* which had to return to Gibraltar. A second hit the tanker *Ohio* while the other two blew off *Cairo*'s stern. It proved impossible to save her and she was scuttled the next day.

Axum's achievement, one cruiser sunk, another damaged and a tanker damaged with a single salvo, is unique in submarine history. The removal of *Nigeria* and *Cairo* meant that the convoy lost the only two ships fitted for fighter direction.

13 August 1942

Name	*Manchester*	**Location**	Mediterranean, 4 miles N of Kelibia,
Class	*Southampton* class cruiser		36 50'N, 11 10'E
Built	12 April 1937	**Cause**	Scuttled after torpedo damage
CO	Capt H. Drew DSC RN	**Casualties**	132
		Survivors	568

Notes   As the *Pedestal* convoy made its way through the Skerki Channel, *Manchester* was struck at 0120 hrs by a torpedo fired by one of the Italian torpedo boats *Ms16* and *Ms22* which had been lying in wait in French waters close to the wreck of the *Havock*. *Manchester* returned fire and claimed to have sunk one of the Italian craft. Some 120 non-essential members of the crew were taken off by the destroyer *Pathfinder* which then left to rejoin the convoy. Captain Drew tried to get his damaged ship moving but at 0430 hrs decided to scuttle her on the grounds that daylight would bring further air attacks which the ship was incapable of avoiding. *Manchester* sank at 0500 hrs and most of her ship's company reached the shore where they were interned by the French. Like *Havock*'s ship's company they endured great privation until liberated later in the year.

Manchester's loss was the subject of a typical Churchillian piece of intervention. He considered that the cruiser had been abandoned prematurely and wanted Captain Drew court-martialled. However, wiser councils prevailed on the Prime Minister.

19 August 1942

Name	*Berkeley*	**Location**	English Channel, 4 miles NW of
Class	*Hunt* class destroyer		Dieppe, 49 57'N, 01 04'E
Built	29 January 1940	**Cause**	Scuttled after air attack

Notes   During the raid on Dieppe the destroyer *Berkeley* was subjected to a number of air attacks. Repeated near misses resulted in serious structural damage and the ship had to be abandoned at 1318 hrs. Her hulk was eventually sunk by a torpedo fired by HMS *Albrighton*.

29 August 1942

Name	*Eridge*	**Location**	E Mediterranean, off Daba, 31 07'N,
Class	*Hunt* class destroyer		28 26'E
Built	20 August 1940	**Cause**	Torpedo
		Casualties	5

Notes   At 0415 hrs on 29 August the destroyers *Eridge*, *Croome* and *Hursley* carried out a bombardment of the Daba area on the coast of North Africa. At 0500 hrs *Eridge* was struck by a torpedo fired by *MTSM.228* (*STV* Piero Carminati). *MTSM* (*Motoscafo Turismo Silurante Modificato*) were fast two-man motor boats armed with one torpedo. *MTSM.228* was part of a land-based motorised column of such boats which roamed the North African coast searching for suitable Allied targets. British claims to have sunk *MTSM.228* were false since Carminati made good his escape. *Eridge* was less fortunate. Carminati's torpedo had struck her in the engine room. She was towed back to Alexandria by HMS *Aldenham* with a severe list to port. After survey she was condemned as a constructive total loss and was never repaired.

September 1942   *In the Mediterranean, a disastrous raid on Tobruk was carried out by the Army and Royal Marines with naval support. The operation was a failure but was justified by Admiral Harwood, the CinC, who was soon to be replaced, that it was 'better to have tried and failed than not to have tried at all'. It was an expensive failure for the cost was one AA cruiser and two fleet destroyers. In Home Waters convoy PQ.18 was fought through to Russia against terrific opposition with only two warship losses, both on the return QP.14 journey.*

11 September 1942

Name	*Charlottetown*	**Location**	W Atlantic, Gulf of St Lawrence,
Class	*Flower* class corvette		49 12'N, 66 48'W
Built	10 September 1941	**Cause**	Submarine attack
		Casualties	9

Notes   Convoy QS.33 was the subject of repeated U-boat attacks. Five merchant ships were lost as well as the *Charlottetown*, which was torpedoed at 1110 hrs on the 11th by *U517* (*Kapitanleutnant* Paul Hartwig). She sank in 3 minutes.

14 September 1942

Name	*Ottawa*	**Location**	W Atlantic, Gulf of St Laurence,
Class	C class destroyer		47 55'N, 43 27'W
Built	30 September 1931	**Cause**	Submarine attack
CO	Lt Cdr C.A. Rutherford RCN	**Casualties**	112
		Survivors	76

Notes *Ottawa* was torpedoed by *U91* while escorting convoy ON.127.

Name	*Sikh*	**Location**	Mediterranean, off Tobruk, 32 65'N,
Class	*Tribal* class destroyer		24 00'E
Built	14 December 1937	**Cause**	Shore battery fire
CO	Capt St J.A. Mickelthwaite DSO RN	**Casualties**	275

Notes *Sikh*, along with *Zulu* and the cruiser *Coventry*, were participating in the ill-planned raid on Tobruk. The operation did not go according to plan and at 0505 hrs *Sikh* was illuminated by a searchlight from the shore. It was bad luck that the searchlight belonged to a Luftwaffe 88mm *Flak* battery whose guns opened rapid fire on the destroyer. *Sikh* was hit repeatedly: one shell wrecked the gearing room and destroyed the force lubrication system for the main engines; another exploded on the forecastle, wrecking 'A' and causing ready mounting-use 4.7 in ammunition to explode; another shell did the same with demolition charges stacked around 'Y' mounting, and another shell destroyed the bridge. *Zulu* tried to tow her sister ship away but was hit hard herself and was ordered away by Captain Mickelthwaite. At 0708 hrs Mickelthwaite fired the scuttling charges and ordered his crew to abandon ship.

Name	*Coventry*	**Location**	Mediterranean, off Tobruk, 32 48'N,
Class	C class cruiser		28 17'E
Built	6 July 1917	**Cause**	Scuttled after air attack

Notes The damaged *Zulu* retired towards the *Coventry* for support but to no avail. At 1120 hrs a force of Ju.87 aircraft, which had not been spotted by radar, came out of the cloud and attacked. *Coventry* was so badly damaged that she had to be sunk by *Zulu* at 1445 hrs.

Name	*Zulu*	**Location**	Mediterranean, E of Tobruk,
Class	*Tribal* class destroyer		32 00'N, 28 56'E
Built	23 September 1937	**Cause**	Scuttled after air attack
CO	Cdr R.T. White DSO RN	**Casualties**	40

Notes After sinking *Coventry*, *Zulu* closed the *Hunt* class destroyers for mutual protection and headed east at 25 knots – the *Hunts*' maximum speed. At 1600 hrs six Ju.87s and twelve Ju.88s made a simultaneous attack on *Zulu* from all directions. One bomb exploded in the engine room and *Zulu* was brought to a halt. *Croome* came alongside and took off all the crew except for a towing party. The destroyer *Hursley* then took her in tow. It was a brave effort but by 1900 hrs it was clear that *Zulu* was sinking. *Hursley* cast off the tow but before *Croome* could come alongside to take off the towing party, *Zulu* rolled over and sank.

17(?) September 1942

Name	*Talisman*	**CO**	Lt Cdr M. Willmott RN
Class	*T* class submarine	**Location**	Mediterranean, S of Sicily
Built	29 January 1940	**Survivors**	None

Notes   *Talisman* sailed from Gibraltar on 10 September and at 0845 hrs on the 15th reported a U-boat north of Cape Bougaroni. Thereafter she failed to answer all signals. No Axis claims exist to account for her loss. The only likely explanations for her loss are that she was mined in the Sicilian Channel on or around 16/17 September, or that she was a victim of an accident.

20 September 1942

Name	*Leda*	**Location**	Barents Sea, W of Bear Island,
Class	Minesweeper		75 48'N, 06 00'E
CO	Cdr A.H. Wynne-Edwards RN	**Cause**	Torpedo

Notes   *Leda* was astern of convoy QP.14 when she was torpedoed by *U435* (*Kapitanleutnant* Siegfried Strelow) and sank quickly.

Name	*Somali*	**Location**	Barents Sea, W of Bear Island,
Class	*Tribal* class destroyer		75 40'N, 02 00'E, sank in 69 11'N,
Built	24 August 1938		15 32'W
CO	Lt Cdr C.D. Maud DSC RN	**Cause**	Submarine attack

Notes   At 1920 hrs on 20 September *Somali* was torpedoed by *U703* (*Kapitanleutnant* Heinz Bielfeld). The torpedo completely blew away the midships portion of the port side so that the ship was only held together by the upper deck and the starboard side as far down as the keel. The port turbine simply fell through the bottom of the ship. All non-essential personnel were transferred to other ships, leaving a towing party of eighty on board. The towing party were forbidden to go below and lived under a tarpaulin rigged on the forecastle. *Somali* was then taken in tow by *Ashanti*. The weather was excellent and throughout the 21st working parties came over from *Ashanti* and threw over all non-essential equipment. However, that evening *Somali*'s dynamo broke down and with that there was no power for the pumps. Hand-pumps could not keep the water under control so all available ships contributed lengths of cable so that power could be supplied from *Ashanti*. Within an hour power was restored and Somali's list had decreased from 17° to 12° and speed was increased to 6 knots. *Ashanti* now desperately needed fuel so when the oiling ship RFA *Blue Ranger* appeared on the 22nd she simply steamed ahead of *Ashanti* and floated a hose down to her. *Blue Ranger*, *Ashanti* and *Somali* were all now linked together.

By the evening of the 23rd the weather, which had been so fine, broke. Precautions were taken: *Blue Ranger* laid an oil slick ahead of *Somali* to calm the waves while the trawler *Lord Middleton* steamed astern of *Somali* ready to take off the towing party. But the storm proved so violent that the oil slick was quickly broken up and *Lord Middleton* could not get near enough to take off the survivors. Just after 0200 hrs on the 24th *Somali* simply folded in two. The stern half sank quickly while the bow section sank steadily and vertically. Survivors were rescued by the trawler *Lord Middleton* and *Ashanti*.

HMS *Somali* with a heavy list to port after being torpedoed by *U703* during the return passage of convoy QP.14 in September 1942. (Author)

A unique photograph showing, from left to right: the oiler RFA *Blue Ranger* refuelling HMS *Ashanti* which is towing HMS *Somali*, 22 September 1942. (Author)

25 September 1942

Name	*Voyager*	**Location**	Pacific, Timor Island, 09 11'S,
Class	*W* class destroyer		125 43'E
Built	8 May 1916	**Cause**	Grounding
		Casualties	None

Notes   *Voyager* grounded while landing reinforcements for the Australian garrison on Timor. While aground she was attacked by Japanese aircraft but in the end she was thoroughly wrecked by her own crew before she was abandoned since it was impossible to refloat her.

26 September 1942

Name	*Veteran*	**Location**	Atlantic, S of Iceland, 54 51'N,
Class	*W* class destroyer		23 04'W
Built	26 April 1919	**Cause**	Submarine attack
		Survivors	None

Notes   *Veteran*, along with HMS *Vanoc*, was escorting convoy RB.1; this was an unusual convoy of eight river steamers going from New York to Londonderry. The convoy was attacked by U-boats and the steamers *Boston* and *New York* were sunk on the 21st. *Veteran* had rescued eighty survivors from both ships and was rejoining the convoy at 16 knots when she was attacked at 1036 hrs on the 26th by *U404* (*Korvettenkapitan* Otto von Bulow). Nothing more was heard or found of her despite an intensive sea search.

2 October 1942

Name	*Curacoa*	**Location**	Atlantic, NW of Ireland, 55 50'N,
Class	*C* class cruiser		08 38'W
Built	5 May 1917	**Cause**	Collision
CO	Capt J.W. Boutwood DSO RN	**Casualties**	338
		Survivors	26

Notes   *Curacoa* was part of the escort for the liner *Queen Mary* on the final leg of her passage from the USA to the Clyde carrying US troops. Usually the *Queen Mary* sailed unescorted but in UK coastal waters and when within range of German aircraft, she was provided with cover. On 2 October *Curacoa* was stationed on the liner's starboard bow. In thick weather a look-out reported what he thought was a periscope and the cruiser turned to port to investigate. At the same time the *Queen Mary* (80,000 tons and travelling at 30 knots plus) turned to starboard. Captain Boutwood thought he had enough clearance to pass ahead of the liner but misjudged his and the liner's speed. *Queen Mary* ploughed in to the little cruiser on her port quarter, cutting her almost in half and carrying *Curacoa's* wreckage impaled on her bows for some distance. *Curacoa* then broke in half and sank.

A subsequent enquiry attributed most blame to the *Curacoa* although the *Queen Mary* did not escape censure.

10(?) October 1942

Name	*Unique*	**CO**	Lt R.E. Boddington RN
Class	*U* class submarine	**Location**	Atlantic, N of Spain
Built	6 June 1940	**Survivors**	None

Notes *Unique* was on passage to the Mediterranean and parted company with her escort on 9 October. Thereafter nothing further was heard from her. On 10 October *Ursula*, on patrol off northern Spain, reported the sound of explosions like depth-charging. However, no German claims exist to account for a submarine being attacked in these waters at that time. The only likely explanations for her loss are that she was the victim of a drifting mine on or around 10 October or that she was the victim of an accident.

November 1942 *saw the Royal Navy on the offensive with the landings in North Africa. The French, nursing their bitter memories of British action at Oran in July 1940, fought back hard.*

4 November 1942

Name	*X.3*	**Location**	Scotland, Loch Striven
Class	*X*-Craft	**Cause**	Accident
Built	1942	**Casualties**	None
CO	Sub Lt J.T. Lorimer RNVR	**Survivors**	3

Notes *X.3* was engaged in a routine training operation when the induction trunk valve failed, the craft took on a considerable amount of water and eventually bottomed in over 100 ft. Lorimer ordered the craft to be flooded-up to equalise the pressure and then all three men escaped. *X.3* was raised that evening and returned to Vickers for repair.

8 November 1942

Name	*Walney*	**Location**	Mediterranean, port of Oran
Class	Ex-US coastguard cutter	**Cause**	Gunfire
CO	Capt F.T. Peters RN		

Notes Before the main Anglo-American landings at Oran it was decided to launch a direct assault from the sea before dawn to prevent the French from destroying harbour installations or blocking the harbour entrance. Two ex-US coast guard cutters, *Walney* and *Hartland*, both in British service, were chosen for this operation – the rationale being that the French might be unfamiliar with their appearance and therefore less likely to open fire.

Walney came to the harbour entrance at 0245 hrs on the 8th and broadcast an announcement in French. The harbour batteries opened fire by way of reply. *Walney* then smashed through the boom at 15 knots but before she could secure alongside a jetty she was fired on by harbour batteries and ships in the harbour. She drifted out of control and was later abandoned, Captain Peters and the survivors being taken prisoner. Six hours later, at 0945 hrs, she exploded.

Captain Peters was swiftly released but was killed in an air crash during his return to the UK. He was posthumously awarded the Victoria Cross.

Name	*Hartland*	**Location**	Mediterranean, port of Oran
Class	Ex-US coastguard cutter	**Cause**	Gunfire
CO	Cdr G.P. Billot RNR		

Notes *Hartland* followed *Walney* through the boom and managed to reach her objective, the Quai de Dunkerque, despite being raked by point-blank fire from shore batteries and the destroyer *Typhon*. Like *Walney*,

Hartland's ship's company could not secure their ship to the jetty and she drifted out into the harbour where she was later abandoned.

Name	*Broke*	Location	Mediterranean, off Algiers, 36 50'N,
Class	*V&W* class destroyer		03 00'E; scuttled in 36 50'N, 00 40'E
Built	16 September 1920	Cause	Gunfire
CO	Capt H. St J. Fancourt RN		

Notes   The destroyer *Broke* was charged with a similar mission to that of *Walney* and *Hartland* but on this occasion at the port of Algiers. As *Broke* ran in towards the boom at 0405 hrs on 8 November Fancourt was blinded by the searchlights and made three unsuccessful attempts to pass the boom. Accordingly he hauled off until daylight gave better visibility. Soon after 0500 hrs he made a fourth attempt and at 0525 hrs smashed through the boom at 26 knots. Although fired by shore batteries *Broke* went alongside the Quai de Falaise as if 'she were being berthed at the Gladstone Dock in Liverpool'. The US Rangers got ashore and started their work but at 0930 hrs they were recalled because fire from light field guns was making *Broke*'s position alongside the Quai de Falaise untenable. At 0935 hrs *Broke* left the harbour badly on fire. She was screened and then taken in tow by *Zetland*, until she foundered in heavy weather at 1900 hrs on the 9th.

Name	*Gardenia*	Cause	Collision
Class	*Flower* class corvette	Casualties	None
Location	Mediterranean, off Oran, 35 49'N, 01 05'W		

Notes   *Gardenia* sank off Oran following a collision with the trawler *Fluellan* in fog.

10 November 1942

Name	*Martin*	Location	Mediterranean, 85 miles NE of
Class	*M* class destroyer		Algiers, 37 53'N, 03 57'E
Built	12 December 1940	Cause	Submarine attack
CO	Cdr C.P.R. Thompson DSO RN	Casualties	161
		Survivors	63

Notes   HMS *Martin* was attacked and sunk by *U431* (*Korvettenkapitan* Wilhelm Domnes). Domnes had identified his target as a *Leander* class cruiser and observed three of the four torpedoes he fired strike the target.

Name	*Ibis*	Location	Mediterranean, 10 miles N of
Class	*Black Swan* class sloop		Algiers, 37N, 03E
Built	28 November 1940	Cause	Air attack
		Survivors	102

Notes   At 1002 hrs on 10 October *Ibis* was attacked by a number of Italian aircraft. She defended herself well, shooting down three of her assailants, but one aircraft dropped a torpedo that struck the little sloop amidships. She capsized and sank almost immediately. The survivors had to wait till after dark before being rescued by the cruiser *Scylla*.

11 November 1942

Name	*Unbeaten*	**Location**	Atlantic, Bay of Biscay
Class	*U* class submarine	**Cause**	Air attack
Built	9 July 1940	**Survivors**	None
CO	Lt D.E. Watson RN		

Notes Under the command of Lieutenant-Commander E.A. Woodward HMS *Unbeaten* had been one of the most successful submarines in the famous 10th Submarine Flotilla operating from Malta. In the autumn of 1942 *Unbeaten* returned to the UK for a routine refit before sailing, now under the command of Lieutenant Donald Watson, for a patrol in the Bay of Biscay on 23 October 1942. She was ordered to intercept an outward-bound blockade runner and on 6 November reported the ship but did not attack. Nothing was ever heard from the submarine again.

When *Unbeaten* failed to make her rendezvous off the Bishop's Rock, an investigation into her probable fate was begun. In the course of the investigation it was found that an attack on a submarine in *Unbeaten*'s area had been made by Wellington F. Freddie of 172 Squadron. The aircraft had taken off at 1745 hrs on 10 November and the patrol report states:

At 0300 hrs in position 46° 55'N, 08° 43'W a message from base was received diverting 'F' to attack a submarine reported in position 46° 13'N, 07° 40'W at 2120 hrs and steering 040° true. Speed 15 knots. At 0129 hrs in position 48° 00'N, 07° 44'W aircraft set course for estimated position of the submarine. At 0216 hrs a S/E contact was obtained 8 miles, 20° to port. Aircraft then homed to within 3 miles when severe S/E interference was encountered. A course of 180° true was held and at ¼ mile range a submarine was sighted by L/E dead ahead.

The submarine was fully surfaced and on a course of 347° true, speed 12–15 knots. 'F' was flying at 200 ft and at 0222 hrs in position 46° 50'N, 06° 51'W made a steep dive down to starboard down to 75 ft in an endeavour to drop the depth-charges ahead of the submarine. . . . A column of water was observed to envelop the stern of the submarine and it was estimated that at least two explosions straddled the submarine which made a 90° turn to port and remained stationary at right angles to its original course. Aircraft then made three further runs on the target.*

This attack was within the bombing restriction area and in a position within 10 miles of *Unbeaten*'s estimated position. An investigation of the relevant German and Italian records show that it was not one of their boats which was the victim of the attack nor do the Axis claim to have sunk an Allied submarine in the area at the time. Despite this evidence and other circumstantial evidence, such as the fact that the S/E interference experienced by 'F' Freddie was probably caused by *Unbeaten*'s Type 291 air warning set, an RAF Board of Enquiry failed to come to any conclusions. Officially the file on the loss of HMS Unbeaten remains open, but it is almost certain that 'F' Freddie was responsible for her loss.

* Evans A.S., *Beneath the Waves*, London, William Kimber, 1986, pp. 327–8.

Name	*Hecla*	**Location**	Atlantic, 180 miles W of Gibraltar,
Class	Repair ship		35 43'N, 09 57'W
Built	1940	**Cause**	Submarine attack

Notes   *Hecla* was proceeding to Gibraltar where she was to augment the dockyard facilities in dealing with the number of ships damaged in the North African operations. At 2315 hrs she was torpedoed and sunk by *U515* (*Kapitanleutnant* Werner Henke). Henke thought that his target was a *Southampton* class cruiser. It was very much Henke's night for 2 hours later he blew the stern off *Hecla*'s erstwhile escort, the destroyer HMS *Marne*. Unlike *Hecla*, *Marne* reached the safety of Gibraltar.

12 November 1942

Name	*Tynwald*	**Location**	Mediterranean, off Bougie, 36 42'N,
Class	Auxiliary AA ship		05 10'E
Built	1936	**Cause**	Submarine attack

Notes   *Tynwald* had already been damaged in an air attack but at 0600 hrs on the 12th she sank following an underwater explosion. At first it was thought that she had been mined but in fact her attacker was the Italian submarine *Argo* (*TV* Pasquale Gigli).

15 November 1942

Name	*Algerine*	**Location**	Mediterranean, off bougie, 36 47'N,
Class	*Algerine* class minesweeper		05 11'E
Built	22 December 1942	**Cause**	Submarine attack

Notes   *Algerine* was torpedoed off Bougie by the Italian submarine *Ascianghi* (*TV* Rino Erler).

Name	*Avenger*	**Location**	Atlantic, W of Gibraltar, 36 15'N,
Class	*Archer* class escort carrier		07 45'W
Built	27 November 1940	**Cause**	Submarine attack
CO	Cdr A.P. Colthurst RN	**Survivors**	12

Notes   The sinking of the *Avenger* was perhaps the most serious loss suffered by the Royal Navy in the North African campaign. This little ship had already proved her worth several times over in the PQ.18/QP.14 convoy battles to and from Russia. She was returning to the UK covering convoy MKF.1 when at 0414 hrs she was torpedoed by *U155* (*Kapitanleutnant* Adolf Piening). The torpedo caused a sympathetic detonation of the contents of the carrier's bomb room and she sank very quickly. The twelve survivors were rescued by HMS *Glaidale* after spending some time in the water.

Name	*Sanguenay*	**Cause**	Collision
Location	Atlantic, E of Newfoundland		

Notes   *Sanguenay* was damaged in a collision with the merchant ship *Azara*. The collision caused the accidental release of *Saguenay*'s depth-charges which exploded, blowing the ship's stern off. She was towed to St John and then Halifax but was never repaired.

25 November 1942

Name	*Utmost*	**Location**	Mediterranean, off Marittimo
Class	*U* class submarine	**Cause**	Depth-charge
Built	20 April 1940	**Survivors**	None
CO	Lt J.W. Coombe RN		

Notes   At 1210 hrs on the 25th the Italian destroyer *Groppo*, which was escorting a convoy to Bizerta, was alerted to the presence of a submarine by an aircraft. *Groppo* left the screen and after obtaining ECG contact delivered two depth-charge attacks which were considered to have sunk the submarine. The submarine was almost certainly *Utmost* whose route took her across the convoy's path.

December 1942   *Throughout December 1942 the North African operations continued to exact a steady toll of British warships. However, the same month saw the heroic defence of Russian convoy JW.51B by five destroyers against a pocket battleship, a heavy cruiser and a number of destroyers. The Battle of the Barents Sea, despite the loss of a minesweeper and a destroyer, did much to exorcise the ghosts of the Russian convoy battles of 1942.*

1 December 1942

Name	*Armidale*	**Cause**	Air attack
Class	Minesweeper	**Survivors**	30
Location	Pacific, off Timor, 10S, 128E		

Notes   While on a routine mission to Timor with relief personnel *Armidale* was attacked and sunk by Japanese aircraft. One boat with twenty personnel on board was recovered by HMAS *Kilgourie* while a further ten survivors were rescued by RAAF flying boat.

2 December 1942

Name	*Quentin*	**Location**	Mediterranean, off Galita Island,
Class	*Q* class destroyer		37 40'N, 08 55'E
Built	5 November 1941	**Cause**	Air attack

Notes   *Quentin* was part of Force Q, a strike force based on Bone and tasked with stopping Axis convoys heading for Tunis. While returning from a very successful night operation against a convoy in which four transports were sunk, together with three escorts, the force was attacked by a number of Ju.88 aircraft and *Quentin* was sunk.

3 December 1942

Name	*Penylan*	**Location**	English Channel, 5 miles S of Start
Class	*Hunt* class destroyer		Point, 50 08'N, 08 39'W
Built	17 March 1942	**Cause**	Torpedo
		Survivors	117

Notes   *Penylan* was escorting convoy PW.257 when at 0630 hrs the convoy was attacked by German *S-boote*. *Penylan* and one merchant ship, the *Gatinais*, were sunk in this attack.

HMS *Traveller* returns to Beirut after a successful patrol along the North African coast. Shortly after this photograph was taken she sunk in Taranto Bay during a reconnaissance for a special operation. (Royal Navy Submarine Museum)

4(?) December 1942

Name	*Traveller*	**CO**	Lt Cdr D. St Clair Ford
Class	*T* class submarine	**Location**	Mediterranean, Gulf of Taranto
Built	27 August 1941	**Survivors**	None

Notes   As part of the preparations for Operation Principal – an attack by British 'chariot' human torpedoes on Italian ports – *Traveller* was despatched to the Gulf of Taranto to make a reconnaissance of the harbour approaches. The area was known to be well defended and heavily mined. The most likely cause of her loss is striking a mine some time around 4 December.

9 December 1942

Name	*Marigold*	**Cause**	Air attack
Class	*Flower* class corvette	**Casualties**	40
Location	Mediterranean, off Algiers, 36 50'N, 03 00'E	**Survivors**	6 officers and 37 ratings

Notes   *Marigold* was sunk by an aircraft torpedo while escorting convoy MKS.3.

Name	Porcupine	**Location**	Mediterranean, 70 miles NE of
Class	P class destroyer		Oran, 36 40'N, 00 04'E
Built	10 June 1941	**Cause**	Submarine attack

Notes   On the night of 9 December Porcupine was escorting the submarine depot ship Maidstone from Algiers to Gibraltar. At 2330 hrs on the 9th she was torpedoed by U602 (Kapitanleutnant Philipp Schuler). Her engine room and other compartments were flooded but she managed to make the port of Arzeu in the tow of the destroyer Vanoc and then the corvette Exe. She arrived at Arzeu drawing 25 ft aft and listing 28° to port. After survey it was decided to separate the damaged stern from the rest of the ship and then send both parts, referred to rather unkindly as 'Porc' and 'Pine', back to the UK for repair. Although this was carried out Porcupine was never repaired and restored to service.

11 December 1942

Name	Blean	**Location**	Mediterranean, 60 miles W of Oran,
Class	Hunt class destroyer		35 55'N, 01 50'E
Built	15 January 1942	**Cause**	Submarine attack
		Survivors	94

Notes   HMS Blean was attacked and sunk by U443 (Oberleutnant zur See Konstantin von Puttkamer) while escorting convoy MKF.4. The survivors were rescued by HMS Wishart.

12 December 1942

Name	P.222	**Location**	Mediterranean, off the island of
Class	S class submarine		Capri
Built	20 September 1941	**Cause**	Depth-charge
CO	Lt A.J. Mackenzie RN	**Survivors**	None

Notes   P.222 (the only S class boat not to be named) was on her fifth Mediterranean patrol when she was sunk by the Italian destroyer Fortunale which was escorting a convoy bound for Tunis. At 1734 hrs Fortunale sighted a submarine coming to the surface 3,500 yards away. While the destroyer Ardito shepherded the convoy away, Fortunale turned in to attack. After three depth-charge attacks, bubbles were observed coming to the surface, after which a fourth and final attack was delivered.

17 December 1942

Name	Firedrake	**Location**	Atlantic, 600 miles S of Iceland,
Class	F class destroyer		50 50'N, 25 15'W
Built	28 June 1934	**Cause**	Submarine attack
		Survivors	26

Notes   HMS Firedrake was one of the escorts of convoy ON.153. At 2010 hrs on the 17th, when just outside the range of aircraft based in Iceland, she was torpedoed and sunk by U211 (Kapitanleutnant Karl Hause). She broke in half immediately. The bow portion sank quickly, leaving no survivors. About thirty-five of the crew clung to the stern portion and attracted the attention of HMS Sunflower by firing starshells. However, the stern sank as Sunflower approached and she was able to rescue only twenty-six men in the very heavy seas.

18 December 1942

Name	*Partridge*	**Location**	Mediterranean, 50 miles W of Oran, 35 50'N, 01 35'E
Class	P class destroyer		
Built	5 August 1941	**Cause**	Submarine attack
		Survivors	173

Notes   While screening Force H *Partridge* was attacked and sunk by *U565* (*Kapitanleutnant* Wilhelm Franken). The survivors were rescued by HMS *Penn*.

19 December 1942

Name	*Snapdragon*	**Cause**	Air attack
Class	*Flower* class corvette	**Survivors**	59
Location	Mediterranean, off Benghazi, 32 18'N, 19 54'E		

Notes   *Snapdragon* was escorting a convoy from Benghazi when she was attacked by German aircraft. One bomb struck the ship amidships and she sank in three minutes. The survivors were rescued by HMS *Erica*.

25 December 1942

Name	*P.48*	**Location**	Mediterranean, off Zembra Island
Class	U class submarine	**Cause**	Depth-charge
Built	15 April 1942	**Survivors**	None
CO	Lt M.E. Faber		

Notes   *P.48* left Malta on 21 December for her third Mediterranean patrol in the approaches to Tunis. At 1120 hrs on the 25th the destroyers *Ardito* and *Ardente* were escorting a northbound convoy from Tunis when the latter got an ECG contact. Two depth-charge attacks were made after which the ECG operator indicated that the submarine was stationary on the bottom. A third depth-charge attack was then delivered after which a considerable number of bubbles came to the surface. Again the ECG indicated that the submarine was stopped so a fourth and final pattern of depth-charges was dropped.

30 December 1942

Name	*Fidelity* (ex-*Rhin*)	**Cause**	Submarine attack
Class	Special service vessel	**Survivors**	None
Location	Atlantic, 43 25'N, 27 07'W		

Notes   *Fidelity* was a unique vessel. She looked like a tramp steamer but was designed for special operations and was fitted with a concealed aircraft catapult and two landing craft. She had been 'inherited' from the French in 1940 and was now on her way out to the Far East with convoy ON.154 where it was felt she could be of more use. At dusk on 28 December the Senior Officer of the escort endeavoured to fly off *Fidelity*'s aircraft to cover an alteration of course but the plane crashed on take-off. *Fidelity*'s single engine then broke down and she was ordered to make for Gibraltar if repairs permitted – if not a tug was being sent for her. At 1130 hrs on the 30th she sent a routine signal reporting her position as 42N, 28W – nothing more was heard from her. That evening at 1638 hrs she was torpedoed and sunk by *U435* (*Kapitanleutnant* Siegfried Strelow).

31 December 1942

Name	*Bramble*	**Location**	Barents Sea, exact position unknown
Class	Minesweeper	**Cause**	Gunfire
CO	Cdr H.T. Rust DSO RN	**Survivors**	None

Notes   *Bramble* was proceeding independently from the main body of convoy JW.51B to look for stragglers. At 1039 hrs she made a signal reporting one enemy cruiser in sight, and thereafter nothing more was heard from her. It is now known that she was overwhelmed by 11 in gunfire from the pocket battleship *Lutzow* and sank.

Name	*Achates*	**Location**	Barents Sea, 73 18'N, 30 06'E
Class	*A* class destroyer	**Cause**	Gunfire
Built	4 October 1929	**Survivors**	81
CO	Lt Cdr A.H.T. Johns RN		

Notes   The story of the loss of the *Achates* is one of the great naval epics of the Second World War. The little destroyer was at the stern of convoy JW.51B and thus when the cruiser *Admiral Hipper* appeared at 1115 hrs *Achates* was clearly visible. The German gunnery was very accurate and *Achates* was hit hard. Lieutenant-Commander Johns was killed, together with forty of his crew. Command devolved on Lieutenant Peyton-Jones, the first lieutenant, who found that damage to the ship's machinery prevented her from conforming to the Senior Officer's order to station herself at the head of the convoy to screen the damaged *Onslow*. Unable to communicate his position to the Senior Officer, Peyton-Jones disregarded his orders and remained at the stern of the convoy, continuing to make the smokescreen that was shielding the merchant ships. Subsequently Admiral Tovey totally endorsed Peyton-Jones's conduct: 'I consider the action of Lt Cdr A.H.T. Johns RN and subsequently Lt L.E. Peyton-Jones RN to have been gallant in the extreme. They had only one idea, to give what protection they could to the convoy, and this they continued to do up to the moment of sinking. The behaviour of all officers and ratings was magnificent.'

By 1300 hrs it was clear that she could not survive much longer. *Achates*' list had increased to 60° and an hour later she lost all power. Throughout the action Peyton-Jones had refrained from signalling for help since he knew his fellow escorts were hard pressed, but once his ship lost power then he felt he had no choice but to ask for assistance. The *Northern Gem* came alongside just as *Achates* capsized at 1330 hrs. Eighty-one of her crew were picked up by the trawler and Skipper Lieutenant Aisthorpe RNR was commended for the 'courageous and seamanlike handling of the *Northern Gem*'.

LOSSES 1943

2 January 1943

Name	*Alarm*	**Location**	Mediterranean, port of Bone
Class	Minesweeper	**Cause**	Air attack

Notes   *Alarm* was damaged during a German air raid on the night of 3 January. A survey established that she was beyond repair so she was beached and abandoned. Her 4 in gun passed to the Army who used it to fire starshell for coastal defence purposes.

2(?) January 1943

Name	*P.311*	**CO**	Cdr R.D. Cayley DSO RN
Class	*T* class submarine	**Location**	Off Northern Sardinia
Built	5 March 1942	**Survivors**	None

Notes   *P.311*, the only *T* class submarine not to be named, was tasked with taking 'chariots' to attack Italian shipping at La Maddalena. She successfully reported her passage through the Sicilian Channel at 0130 hrs on 31 December but thereafter nothing was heard from her. No Axis claim exists to account for her loss so it is presumed that she was lost in one of the many minefields around La Maddalena.

29 January 1943

Name	*Pozarica*	**Location**	Mediterranean, NW of Bougie
Class	Auxiliary AA ship	**Cause**	Air attack
Built	1937		

Notes   *Pozarica* was damaged in an attack by Italian torpedo aircraft but managed to make the port of Bougie in tow of the minesweeper *Cadmus*. However, during salvage operations at Bougie on 13 February she capsized and was written off.

30 January 1943

Name	*Samphire*	**Cause**	Submarine attack
Class	*Flower* class corvette	**Survivors**	4
Location	Mediterranean, 30 miles NE of Bougie, 37 47'N, 05 32'E		

Notes   *Samphire* was torpedoed by either the Italian submarine *Platoon* or the German *U596*. Both submarines claim to have sunk this vessel. Whatever the identity of her attacker she sank very quickly leaving only four survivors to be rescued by HMS *Zetland*.

February 1943 *began with the loss of one of the Royal Navy's versatile Abdiel class minelayers. The steady run of losses in North African waters continued and the month also saw the loss of the first of three experienced submarines and their crews.*

1 February 1943

Name	*Welshman*	**Location**	Submarine attack
Class	*Abide* class minelayer	**Cause**	Mediterranean, 45 miles E of
Built	4 September 1940		Tobruk, 32 12'N, 24 52'E
CO	Capt D. Friedburger RN	**Casualties**	152

Notes   HMS *Welshman* was en route for Alexandria from Malta when at 1832 hrs on 1 February she was torpedoed by *U617* (*Fregattenkapitan* Albrecht Brandi). *U617* fired three torpedoes fitted with non-contact fuses: all exploded aft, wrecking *Welshman*'s shafts. However, the ship still had power and damage control measures were put in hand to shore up bulkheads and reduce the flooding. The destroyer *Tetcott* reported that she was coming to *Welshman*'s assistance and would be on the scene at 0030 hrs. Despite the damage control efforts water began to appear on the mine deck. At 2035 hrs the ship lurched to starboard and then rolled over on to her beam ends before sinking by the stern within three minutes. As she sank a depth-charge that had not been set to safe exploded in the water, killing a number of survivors. *Tetcott* and *Belvoir* were on the scene by 0020 hrs on the 2nd and rescued the survivors.

   Considerable concern was expressed as to why the ship should have sunk so quickly. The Board of Enquiry found that once the flooding had spread to the mine deck, which ran almost the full length of the ship, she became dangerously top heavy. The ship's officers 'believed their ship to be in no danger until she capsized and this was brought about by a lack of appreciation that, in the absence of any sub-division between the mining and upper decks over a large portion of the ship's length, the mining deck was the upper deck for the purposes of stability'. Although it was considered that grave errors of judgement had been made, Friedburger and his officers were exonerated.

6 February 1943

Name	*Louisberg*	**Cause**	Air attack
Class	*Flower* class corvette	**Casualties**	1
Location	Mediterranean, 60 miles N of Oran,	**Survivors**	50
	36 15'N, 00 15'E		

Notes   HMCS *Louisberg* was sunk by aircraft while escorting convoy KMS.8. She was the eleventh Canadian warship to be sunk in the war, but the first to be sunk by aircraft and the first to be sunk in the Mediterranean. The survivors were rescued by HMS *Lookout*.

9 February 1943

Name	*Erica*	**Cause**	Mine
Class	*Flower* class corvette	**Casualties**	None
CO	Lt A.C.C. Seligman RNR	**Survivors**	73
Location	Mediterranean, between Benghazi		
	and Derna, 32 48'N, 21 10'E		

Notes   HMS *Erica* was mined in a field laid by the British submarine *Rorqual* in July 1941 but whose existence had not been plotted. The complete ship's company was rescued by HMS *Southern Maid*.

22 February 1943

Name	*Weyburn*	**Location**	Mediterranean, 4 miles W of Cape
Class	*Flower* class corvette		Spartel, 35 48'N, 06 02'W
CO	Lt Cdr T.M. Golby RCNR	**Cause**	Mine

Notes   *Weyburn* was escorting convoy KMS.8 when she struck a mine. As she sank, her depth-charges, which had not been set to safe, exploded, damaging HMS *Wivern* which was rescuing survivors.

24 February 1943

Name	*Vandal*	**Location**	W coast of Scotland, Inchmarnock
Class	*U* class submarine		Water
Built	23 November 1942	**Cause**	Accident
CO	Lt J.S. Bridger RN	**Survivors**	None

Notes   *Vandal* was a brand-new submarine and in February 1943 was just completing her work-up on the Clyde. The conclusion to this activity was a three-day independent exercise to test crew and boat under war conditions. *Vandal* was due to return to Holy Loch at 1900 hrs on the 24th and was seen leaving the anchorage at Lochranza on the Isle of Arran at 0830 hrs on that day. She was never seen or heard from again. As part of the exercise *Vandal* had to perform a deep dive in Inchmarnock Water on the 24th and it was presumed that she was lost during this exercise. In 1996 her wreck was discovered by divers and now holds the preserved status of a war grave.

27 February 1943

Name	*Tigris*	**Location**	Mediterranean, 6 miles SE of Capri
Class	*T* class submarine	**Cause**	Depth-charge
Built	31 October 1939	**Survivors**	None
CO	Lt Cdr G.R. Colvin DSO RN		

Notes   At 1050 hrs on the 27th the German A/S vessel *UJ2210*, which was escorting a convoy, made ECG contact with a submerged submarine south-east of Capri and at 1114 hrs launched the first of four attacks totalling sixty depth-charges. After the fourth attack large air bubbles and wreckage came to the surface. Undoubtedly the submarine concerned was *Tigris*, for her patrol area was south of Naples.

11 March 1943

Name	*Harvester*	**CO**	Cdr A. Tait RN
Class	Ex-Brazilian *Jarua*	**Location**	Atlantic, 51 23'N, 28 40'W
Built	29 September 1939	**Cause**	Submarine attack

Notes   *Harvester* was part of the escort for convoy HX.228. On 11 March she detected *U444* on radar, ran down the bearing, blew the submarine to the surface with depth-charges and then rammed her. She ran completely over the U-boat until the latter was wedged solidly in the destroyer's 'A' brackets. The two ships remained locked together for some time until *U444* broke free, only to be rammed by the French corvette *Aconit*. However, *Harvester* had sustained considerable damage in the attack and while making her way slowly back to the convoy she was torpedoed by *U432* (*Kapitanleutnant* Hermann Eckhardt). The few survivors were rescued by the *Aconit* which then sank *U432*.

12 March 1943

Name	*Lightning*	**Location**	Mediterranean, off Bizerta, 37 53'N,
Class	*L* class destroyer		69 50'E
Built	22 April 1940	**Cause**	Torpedo
CO	Cdr H.G. Walters RN	**Casualties**	46
		Survivors	170

Notes   *Lightning* was attacked and sunk by German *S-boote* of the *7th Flotille* while returning from a sweep with Force Q. The torpedo struck right forward and Walters ordered the ship to stop in order to reduce damage to the bows. As the way fell off the ship she was struck by a second torpedo which struck forward of the engine room. *Lightning* broke in half and sank, the bow and stern sections remaining vertical in the water for a while. The survivors were picked up by HMS *Loyal*.

14 March 1943

Name	*Thunderbolt* (ex *Thetis*)	**Location**	Mediterranean, off Cap San Vito,
Class	*T* class submarine		Sicily
Built	1 June 1939	**Cause**	Depth-charge
CO	Lt Cdr C. Crouch DSO DSC RN	**Casualties**	62
		Survivors	None

Notes   In her new name and with an outstanding commanding officer, *Thunderbolt* had to rest laid the ghost of the unlucky *Thetis* . On 12 March *Thunderbolt* attacked and damaged the merchant ship *Esterel* and then survived a depth-charge attack by the escort *Libra*. On the 13th the destroyer *Cicogna* (*TV* Augusto Migliorini) sailed from Trapani to work over the area where *Libra* had reported attacking a submarine and at 0516 hrs on the 14th she obtained a firm ECG contact in near perfect conditions. Migliorini proved extraordinarily patient and it was not until 0845 hrs, by which time he had twice sighted *Thunderbolt*'s periscope, that the first pattern was dropped. *Cigogna* was just turning to begin her second run when a massive explosion blew the submarine's stern out of the water. The stern hung there at 90° for a while, in an uncanny reminder of the dreadful photographs of June 1939, before sinking in a boil of water and oil. Migliorini dropped another two depth-charges and saw more oil and wreckage come to the surface.

   Thunderbolt lay undisturbed until 9 November 1995 when her wreck was discovered. She lies upright on a sloping bottom. Her conning tower and periscope standards are wreathed in fishing nets and wires. The forward hydroplanes are set at 'hard to dive'. There is a large hole on her port side just forward of the conning tower. Verification of the identity of the wreck was provided when a bronze tally on the submarine's 4 in gun was filmed. The tally read simply: '*Thetis* No. 1027' (1,027 was *Thetis*' Cammell Laird yard number).

14(?) March 1943

Name	*Turbulent*	**CO**	Cdr J.W. 'Tubby' Linton DSO RN
Class	*T* class submarine	**Casualties**	62
Built	12 May 1941	**Survivors**	None

Notes Linton was one of the most experienced submarine commanding officers in the Mediterranean. On 24 February 1943 *Turbulent* sailed from Algiers for her last patrol before returning to the UK. Gus Britton, a signalman in HMS *Tribune*, remembered: '"Tubby" Linton saluted, bade farewell to Captain Fawkes at the head of *Maidstone*'s gangway and then descended to his boat. He was saluted by his first lieutenant as he went on board and he then emerged on the bridge wearing a white sweater. *Turbulent* let go her breasts and springs, water swirled at her stern as she slowly moved ahead and whistles sounded as she exchanged salutes with other ships in the harbour.' On 20 March *Turbulent* was given her return route to Algiers but failed to acknowledge this signal. There are any number of possible explanations for *Turbulent*'s loss but the two most likely are a depth-charge attack by a Ju.88 aircraft and the destroyer *Ardito* on 6 March in the Bay of Naples, or being mined somewhere along the north and east coast of Sardinia between 12 and 14 March. *Turbulent*'s route back to Algiers lay along the east coast of Sardinia, an area that was intensively mined. The Italian authorities have conducted exhaustive investigations into her fate but can find no clear evidence to support any one theory. Until a wreck is found the file on HMS *Turbulent* remains open.

Commander Linton was posthumously awarded the Victoria Cross. The award was unusual in that it was made for his persistent waging of war against the enemy rather than for one specific act of courage.

HMS *Turbulent* (outboard boat) at Algiers in February 1943 before her last patrol. (US Navy)

Commander J.W. 'Tubby' Linton (right), commanding officer of HMS *Turbulent*, lost with his ship in March 1943. Linton was posthumously awarded the Victoria Cross. (Commander Arthur Pitt)

19 March 1943

Name	*Derwent*	**CO**	Lt P.R.C. Higham RN
Class	*Hunt* class destroyer	**Location**	Mediterranean, port of Tripoli
Built	22 August 1941	**Cause**	Air attack

Notes *Derwent* was at anchor in Tripoli when the port was attacked by Italian aircraft dropping *Motobomba* circling torpedoes. *Derwent* was hit and was beached with her machinery spaces flooded. Although she was salvaged and returned to England, she was never repaired.

27 March 1943

Name	*Dasher*	**Location**	Firth of Clyde, Cumbrae Light
Class	*Archer* class escort carrier		5 miles, 55 37'N, 05 00'W
Built	12 April 1941	**Cause**	Petrol explosion
CO	Capt L.A. Boswell RN	**Casualties**	379
		Survivors	149

Notes   *Dasher* was peacefully at anchor in the Clyde when she was destroyed by a vast explosion. A subsequent enquiry, noting that *Dasher* had just been removed from the JW.53 convoy to Russia on account of her poor material condition, ascribed this to petrol vapour igniting. The wreck was located on 12 January 1944 and has been dived on fairly frequently since then. At the last official survey, in April 1984, *Dasher* was found lying upright at a depth of 170 metres, surrounded by a large debris field.

11 April 1943

Name	*Beverley*	**Location**	Atlantic, SW of Iceland, 62 19'N,
Class	*Town* class destroyer		40 28'W
Built	1919	**Cause**	Submarine attack

Notes   HMS *Beverley* was escorting convoy ONS.176 and had already been damaged in a collision with the merchant ship *Cairnvalona* on the 9th. She was retained with the escort even though her Asdic and degaussing equipment were not in use. At 0400 hrs on the 11th she was torpedoed and sunk by *U188* (*Kapitanleutnant Siegfried Lüdden*) and sank with heavy loss of life.

16 April 1943

Name	*Pakenham*	**Location**	Mediterranean, 12 miles off Cape
Class	P class destroyer		Granitola, Sicily, 37 26'N, 12 30'E
Built	28 January 1941	**Cause**	Scuttled

Notes   At 0248 hrs on 16 April *Pakenham* and *Paladin*, which were engaged in a sweep in the Sicilian Narrows, encountered the Italian torpedo boats *Cigno* and Cassiopea. *Pakenham* sank the *Cigno* with gunfire and a torpedo but not before the latter had put one lucky 3.9 in shell into *Pakenham*'s engine room, bringing the ship to a standstill. *Paladin* took her in tow but at 0800 hrs on the 11th scuttled her. The decision to sink *Pakenham* was made on the grounds that the two destroyers had already received one air attack and more could be expected, they were only making five knots, and it would be some hours before they were under the umbrella of Malta-based fighters. This decision was supported by CinC Mediterranean, who was surprised that two under-gunned Italian torpedo boats should have put up such a good showing.

18(?) April 1943

Name	*Regent*	**Location**	Adriatic, off Bari
Class	R class submarine	**Cause**	Mine
Built	11 June 1930	**Casualties**	53
CO	Lt W. Knox RN	**Survivors**	None

Notes   *Regent* is believed to have been mined off Bari some time between 18 and 25 April. On 1 May the first of four bodies wearing British uniform came ashore between Brindisi and Otranto; the others came ashore on 15 and 16 May. Post mortem examination established that the men had been dead for just over three weeks. The current flowing along the Apulia coast flows towards the Mediterranean at a speed of no more than half a knot. This would mean that the men had died off Bari at some time between 18 and 25 April.

18 April 1943

Name	*P.615*	**Location**	Atlantic, off Liberian coast, 06 49'N,
Class	*P.611* class, submarine ex-Turkish		13 09'W
Built	1 November 1940	**Cause**	Submarine attack
CO	Lt C.W. St C. Lambert RN	**Survivors**	None

Notes *P.615* was employed on ASW training duties in West Africa. On 17 April she left Freetown for a routine passage to Takarodi with *MMS107* as an escort. Just after 0905 hrs on the 18th she was attacked by *U123* (*Oberleutnant zur See* Horst von Schroeter) and blew up. *MMS107* later reported that *P.615* had been struck on the starboard side under the conning tower.

21 April 1943

Name	*Splendid*	**Location**	Mediterranean, off Capri
Class	*S* class submarine	**Cause**	Depth-charge
Built	19 January 1942	**Casualties**	18
CO	Lt I.L. McGeoch DSO RN	**Survivors**	27

Notes At 0838 hrs on 21 April a look-out in the German-manned (but British-built) destroyer *Hermes* (ex-Greek *Vasilefs Georgios 1*) sighted a periscope 3,000 yards off the destroyer's port bow. Almost immediately *Hermes* established Asdic contact and between 0843 hrs and 0924 hrs she delivered three attacks using forty-three depth-charges. The submarine was the British *Splendid*. *Hermes'* third attack did such damage that water

A photograph taken from the German destroyer *Hermes* on 21 April 1943 showing HMS *Splendid* on the surface shortly before she was abandoned. (US Navy)

began to flood into the submarine and she sank below 500 ft (operational diving depth was 250 ft). McGeoch decided that he had no choice but to surface and abandon the submarine. When *Splendid* surfaced she was still under way and turning since her helm was jammed. *Hermes* evidently thought that the turn was the prelude for a torpedo attack so opened fire on the submarine with her main armament. A number of hits were scored, which hastened her sinking even though McGeoch had opened the main vents. Less than a year after being taken prisoner McGeoch escaped, despite having lost his right eye during *Splendid*'s sinking, and eventually reached England in May 1944.

24 April 1943

Name	*Sahib*	**Location**	Mediterranean, off Cape Milazzo,	
Class	S class submarine		Sicily	
Built	19 January 1942	**Cause**	Depth-charge	
CO	Lt J.H. Brommage RN	**Casualties**	None	
		Survivors	46	

Notes   At 0450 hrs on 24 April *Sahib* attacked and sank the freighter *Galiola* in a convoy escorted by the torpedo boats *Gabbiano*, *Euterpe* and *Climene*. As she fired she broke surface and she was spotted at 0506 hrs by a Ju.88 which dropped a bomb to attract the escorts' attention. At 0530 hrs *Gabbiano* launched her first depth-charge attack, after which Ju.88s made two bombing runs over the area. At 0540 hrs *Euterpe* delivered an attack with thirty depth-charges which blew the compressor outlet valve clean off *Sahib*'s side, leaving a 1.5 in diameter hole in her pressure hull. This leak could not be plugged and as the submarine started to sink Brommage gave the order to surface and abandon ship. As *Sahib* came to the surface, she was fired on by the corvettes, but they checked fire when they realised that the submarine was being abandoned.

No fewer than twenty-three of *Sahib*'s crew made escapes from PoW camps, twelve of them reaching the Allied lines.

20 May 1943

Name	*Fantome*	**Location**	Mediterranean, off Cape Bon
Class	Minesweeper	**Cause**	Mine
Built	22 September 1942	**Casualties**	1

Notes   *Fantome* was mined during clearance operations off Cape Bon. Her stern was blown off but she was towed back to Bizerta. A survey found her to beyond repair so she was paid off as a constructive total loss.

Name	*Untamed*	**Location**	W coast of Scotland, off Sanda Island
Class	U class submarine	**Cause**	Accident
Built	8 December 1942	**Casualties**	36
CO	Lt G.M. Noll RN	**Survivors**	None

Notes   *Untamed* was lost as a result of a series of errors, beginning with the improper operation of the boat's Otway log (a device used for measuring the vessel's speed). This caused massive flooding in the submarine, causing her to settle on the bottom in 160 ft of water. Just over 3 hours later, at 1815 hrs, when it proved impossible to raise the submarine, the decision was taken to escape. The delay in making this decision was a second factor. By this time the air in the boat was extremely foul and all on board would have been feeling the effects of CO_2 poisoning. Thirty-four of her crew (two had remained in the tube space to try to reassemble the log and had died there) moved aft to the engine room. The third factor was that the rapid flood valve, which admitted water to the compartment prior to an escape, was wrongly assembled. Flooding up the engine room to equalise the pressure started using other means but it was a slow business, compounded by the fact that because the underwater drain cock gun was open, water was leaving the compartment almost as fast as it was being admitted so there was hardly any hope of pressure being equalised. Sometime around 2200 hrs, CO_2 poisoning killed the thirty-four crewmen.

Untamed was raised and recommissioned as *Vitality*. She was broken up in March 1946.

11 June 1943

Name	*Wallaroo*	**Location**	Western Australia
Class	Minesweeper	**Cause**	Collision

Notes   HMAS *Wallaroo* sank off Fremantle following a collision with the merchant ship *Gilbert Costin*.

August 1943 *saw the introduction of a new German weapon, the radio-controlled glider bomb.*

7(?) August 1943

Name	*Parthian*	**CO**	Lt C.A. Pardoe RN
Class	*P* class submarine	**Location**	Adriatic
Built	22 June 1929	**Survivors**	None

Notes   On 26 July *Parthian* left Malta and thereafter nothing was heard from her. She failed to arrive at Beirut on 11 August and is presumed to have been mined, although the possibility of accident cannot be eliminated.

14 August 1943

Name	*Saracen*	**CO**	Lt M.G.R. Lumby RN
Class	*S* class submarine	**Location**	Mediterranean, off Bastia
Built	16 February 1942	**Cause**	Depth-charge

Notes   *Saracen* had been sighted by coastwatchers off Bastia on 12 August and on 13th the torpedo boats *Euterpe* and *Minerva* were despatched to search for her. At 0014 hrs on the 14th *Minerva* had an excellent *ECG* contact and at 0046 hrs dropped thirty-two depth-charges. This attack flooded *Saracen*'s after ends which were evacuated – the watchkeeper left so quickly that he could give Lumby no description of the damage other than flooding! *Saracen* began to sink by the stern, which Lumby attempted to correct by ballast adjustments. These had the effect of making the submarine porpoise up and down alarmingly. At 0053 hrs her conning tower broached between *Euterpe* and *Minerva* but sank quickly. Lumby decided that the position was hopeless and gave the order to surface. The crew mustered in the control room with DSEA sets and prepared to abandon ship. *Saracen* came to the surface at 0059 hrs and sank after being abandoned.

27 August 1943

Name	*Egret*	**Location**	Atlantic, 30m W of Vigo, 42 10'N,
Class	Sloop		09 22'W
Built	31 May 1938	**Cause**	Guided missile
		Casualties	194

Notes   HMS *Egret* was on anti-submarine duties in the Bay of Biscay when she was attacked by thirteen Dornier aircraft, one of which released an Hs.293A glider bomb. The missile was observed to fly across the wind, being directed by one of the aircraft, before plunging down on the little sloop, which disappeared in a massive explosion. When the smoke cleared all that remained of *Egret* was her bow floating upside down on the surface. HMS *Egret* therefore enjoys the dubious distinction of being the first warship to be sunk by a guided missile.

September 1943 *saw a revival of activity in the Mediterranean and in the Atlantic. On 3 September 1943, the day of the first Allied landings in Italy, the Italian government, now without Mussolini, concluded an armistice with the British and Americans. Once again the Royal Navy would be committed to supporting the Army ashore in the face of German opposition. In the Atlantic the Germans renewed the U-boat offensive and introduced another new weapon – the acoustic homing torpedo. In the battles around convoys ONS.18 and ON.202 four escorts were lost to this new weapon, but counter-measures were swiftly developed. In the Arctic, Operation Source was the operational debut of the British X-Craft midget submarines. Though all six craft involved in the operation were lost, the battleship* Tirpitz *was very badly damaged.*

9 September 1943

Name	*Welman 10*	**Location**	Firth of Clyde, alongside the depot
Class	Midget submarine		ship HMS *Forth*
Built	1943	**Cause**	Accident
CO	Lt B. Pedersen (Norwegian Army)	**Casualties**	None
		Survivors	1

Notes   *Welman 10*, one of the first of a new kind of one-man submarine designed and operated by SOE, sank virtually alongside the depot ship HMS *Forth*. Pedersen behaved with commendable courage: he flooded up the craft and then pushed open the hatch and swam to the surface.

10 September 1943

Name	*Abdiel*	**Location**	Mediterranean, port of Taranto
Class	*Abdiel* class minelayer	**Cause**	Mine
Built	23 April 1940	**Casualties**	48, plus 120 soldiers

Notes   As part of preparations for the announcement that the Italian government had concluded an armistice, the British moved swiftly to occupy the important port of Taranto. A holding force was put together consisting of the battleship *Howe*, the US cruiser *Boise*, HMS *Abdiel* and a number of destroyers, the whole being known as Force Z. They then embarked 435 soldiers from the British 1st Airborne Division whose task was to hold the town until more substantial reinforcements arrived from the Western Desert. Force Z arrived at Taranto on the afternoon of the 9th and received a friendly welcome. *Abdiel* remained anchored in the Mare Grande, intending to disembark her troops later on the 10th, but at 0015 hrs that morning a violent explosion took place under the ship, breaking her back and causing her to sink in 2 minutes. Casualties would have been heavier but for the fact that the watches had only just been changed and the watch that had just been relieved had not yet turned in. In addition to the loss of life, *Abdiel* lost the large amount of stores she was carrying, together with eight jeeps, seven 6 pdr AT guns, motorcycles and pedal cycles.

It was later established that she had been sunk by one of twenty-two German GS-type magnetic mines laid the previous evening by *MFP478* and two *S-boote*, *S-54* and *S-61*. The mines were fused with 24-hr delay mechanisms and PDMs of between two to four actuations. Thus the mines would have become live just after midnight on the 10th. *Abdiel*, which had switched off her degaussing gear after anchoring, must have swung across the mine the requisite number of times to detonate it.

16 September 1943

Name	*X.9*	**Cause**	Foundered, presumably as a result of
Class	*X*-Craft		a broken tow rope
Built	1943	**Casualties**	3
CO	Sub Lt E.A. Keaton RNVR	**Survivors**	None
Location	Norwegian Sea		

Notes   In the tow of HM Submarine *Syrtis* (Lieutenant M.H. Jupp DSC RN) *X.9* had dived at 0120 hrs on the 16th after a routine period on the surface to ventilate the boat. At 0855 hrs *X.9* was ordered to come to the surface again but when *Syrtis* surfaced it was found that the tow rope had parted. Jupp reversed his course but could find nothing. The only explanation for *X.9*'s loss is that her manila tow rope had parted and that the little submarine, weighed down by 600 ft of waterlogged rope, plunged to the depths and destruction.

17 September 1943

Name	*X.8*	**Location**	Norwegian Sea
Class	*X*-Craft	**Cause**	Scuttled
Built	1943	**Casualties**	None
CO	Lt J. Smart RNVR	**Survivors**	3

Notes   On the morning of the 17th *X.8* began to experience difficulties in maintaining her trim. Air could be heard escaping from the starboard side cargo. It was decided that the starboard side cargo would have to be jettisoned. The charge was set to 'safe' and released in 180 fathoms of water. However, the fuse malfunctioned fand the charge exploded when *X.8* and *Seanymph* were only 1,000 yards away. Then the port charge began to show signs of leaking so it was decided that this one should be jettisoned as well. The fuse was set to allow *X.8* 2 hours to get clear but it exploded prematurely, the explosion doing a considerable amount of damage. It was clear that she could no longer proceed with the operation (no armament and in a terrible condition), so she was scuttled.

20 September 1943

Name	*Lagan*	**Location**	Atlantic, SW of Iceland, 57 09'N,
Class	Frigate		27 28'W
		Cause	Submarine attack

Notes   HMS *Lagan* was one of the escorts for convoy ON.202, the convoy selected by Admiral Donitz to renew the Battle of the Atlantic following the defeat of the U-boats in May. This time the U-boats had a new weapon: the T5 or *Zaunkonig* acoustic torpedo (*GNAT* in British parlance). *Lagan* was the first victim of this new weapon. She was torpedoed at 0305 hrs and her stern was blown off by *U270* (*Kapitanleutnant* Paul Friedrich Otto). She was towed to the UK by the tug *Destiny* but not repaired.

Name	St Croix	Location	Atlantic, SW of Iceland, 57 30'N,
Class	*Town* class destroyer		31 10'W
CO	Lt Cdr A.H. Dobson DSC RCN	Cause	Submarine attack
		Survivors	80

Notes Fourteen hours after *Lagan* was torpedoed the destroyer *St Croix* was torpedoed at 1758 hrs by *U305* (*Kapitanleutnant* Rudolf Bahr). She lay dead in the water until a second attack by the same submarine sank her. The survivors were rescued by HMS *Itchen*.

Name	Polyanthus	Cause	Submarine attack
Class	*Flower* class corvette	Casualties	84
Location	Atlantic, SW of Iceland, 57 00'N, 31 10'W		

Notes *Polyanthus* was the third escort of ON.202 to be torpedoed. At 2236 hrs she was sunk by *U952* (*Kapitanleutnant* Oscar Curio) using a T5. The little corvette sank almost immediately.

22 September 1943

Name	Itchen	Cause	Submarine attack
Class	*River* class frigate	Casualties	147
Location	Atlantic, south of Greenland, 53 25'N, 39 42'W	Survivors	3

Notes *Itchen* was the first British frigate to be sunk during the Second World War and the fourth escort to be sunk in the battles around convoy OB.202. At 2355 hrs she was torpedoed by *U666* (*Kapitanleutnant* Herbert Engel). The forward magazine blew up and the ship sank almost immediately. She was carrying eighty survivors from the *St Croix* as well as her own ship's company, but only three survived; two from *Itchen*, the other from *St Croix*.

Name	X.6	Location	Norway, Kaafjord
Class	*X*-Craft	Cause	Scuttled
Built	1943	Casualties	None
CO	Lt Donald Cameron RNR	Survivors	4

Notes *X.6* successfully penetrated *Tirpitz*'s anchorage and, despite being detected at the last minute, laid both her charges under the battleship's 'B' turret. Cameron then ordered the inside of the boat to be wrecked, surfaced and abandoned the craft. A launch tried to take the submarine in tow but she foundered. Her hull would have been destroyed when the charges exploded just after 0810 hrs.

Name	X.7	Location	Norway, Kaafjord
Class	*X*-Craft	Cause	Scuttled
Built	1943	Casualties	2
CO	Lt G. Place RN	Survivors	2

Notes   *X.7* also laid her charges under *Tirpitz* but was spotted at 0740 hrs. Place dived deep but at 0810 hrs *X.7* became caught in the net; she was subsequently blown free by the explosion of the charges. The submarine was considerably damaged so Place decided to surface alongside a battle practice target. No sooner had Place left the submarine than water flooded in through the hatch and she sank. The remaining three crew escaped using DSEA: Sub Lieutenant Aitken survived and was taken prisoner; Sub Lieutenant Whittam was drowned but his body was retrieved and later buried at Tromso; no trace was ever found of ERA Whitley's body.

22(?) September 1943

Name	*X.5*	**CO**	Lt H. Henty-Creer RN
Class	*X*-Craft	**Casualties**	4
Built	1943	**Survivors**	None

Notes   *X.5* disappeared. She had been successfully released by her towing submarine, *Thrasher* and had been sighted on 20 September by *X.7*, but thereafter nothing was heard of her. The Germans claim to have sunk a third *X*-Craft at 0843 hrs and a periscope was sighted by Sub Lieutenant Lorimer of *X.6* from his vantage point on board *Tirpitz*. However, a number of postwar hydrographic surveys of Kaafjord have failed to find any trace of her. It seems reasonable that she was lost by accident, possibly as a result of plunging to below her crush depth on hitting a pocket of fresh water. The file on *X.5* remains open.

27 September 1943

Name	*Intrepid*	**Location**	Mediterranean, port of Leros
Class	*I* class destroyer	**Cause**	Capsized after air attack
Built	17 December 1936	**Casualties**	15

Notes   At 0700 hrs on 26 September the destroyer HMS *Intrepid* and the Greek destroyer *Vasillisa Olga* arrived at Leros following an anti-shipping sweep. At 0915 hrs there was a German air raid on the island and the *Vasillisa Olga* was sunk and *Intrepid* damaged amidships. Repairs were made but at 1715 hrs there was a further air raid and she was damaged aft. She was then abandoned by her crew as she was considered to be beyond repair; she capsized at 0200 hrs on the 27th.

3 October 1943

Name	*X.10*	**Location**	North Sea
Class	*X*-Craft	**Cause**	Scuttled
Built	1943	**Casualties**	None
CO	Lt K.R. Hudspeth RANVR	**Survivors**	4

Notes   *X.10* had been ordered to attack the battle cruiser *Scharnhorst* lying in Altafjord. However, the British were not aware that the vessel was not at her moorings that day: *Kapitan zur See* Julius Hintze had taken his new command to sea for target practice. During her run up the fjord *X.10* was plagued with a series of break-downs and machinery failures, and Hudspeth was well behind schedule in reaching the target. He heard the explosions of *X.6* and *X.7*'s charges and realised that the defences would now be very much on the alert. Accordingly he made the difficult decision to withdraw on the evening of 22 September. Hudspeth then made his way along the coast, without compass and with *X.10*'s periscope jammed in the 'up' position, in increasingly bad weather until he met with *Stubborn* at sea at 0055 hrs on the 28th. However, *X.10*'s troubles were not yet over for the weather worsened and, reluctantly, at 2047 hrs on 3 October on direct orders from Flag Officer Submarines, she was scuttled.

Name	*Usurper*	Location	Mediterranean, exact position
Class	U class submarine		unknown
Built	24 September 1942	Survivors	None
CO	Lt D.R. Mott RN		

Notes *Usurper* left Algiers for patrol on 24 September. Thereafter nothing was heard from her. She may have been sunk in minefield QB.192 in the Gulf of Genoa or she may have been the victim of an attack by *UJ.2208* on 3 October.

9 October 1943

Name	*Carlisle*	Location	Mediterranean, Scarpanto Straits,
Class	C class cruiser		35 48'N, 27 38'E
Built	9 July 1918	Cause	Air attack
		Casualties	20

Notes While returning from an anti-shipping sweep west of Kos, *Carlisle* was subjected to a series of dive-bomber attacks by Ju.87 aircraft from 1205 hrs onwards. Severely damaged, she was saved only by the appearance of USAAF P.38 Lightning aircraft which chased off the Stukas and then gave cover. *Carlisle* was taken in tow by *Rockwood* and reached Alexandria. However, it was considered that she was beyond economic repair and she was declared a constructive total loss .

Name	*Panther*	Location	Mediterranean, Scarpanto Straits,
Class	P class destroyer		35 48'N, 27 38'E
Built	28 May 1941	Cause	Air attack

Notes *Panther* was escorting the *Carlisle* but was not so fortunate. Under what the commanding officer of HMS *Petard* described as 'unlimited' Stuka attacks, *Panther* was sunk.

10 October 1943

Name	*Trooper*	CO	Lt J.S. Wraith RN
Class	T class submarine	Casualties	60
Built	5 March 1942	Survivors	None

Notes *Trooper* left Beirut for a patrol west of the Dodecanese on 26 September. Nothing further was heard from her. She may have been mined but the possibility of accident cannot be ruled out.

11 October 1943

Name	*Hythe*	Location	Mediterranean, off Bougie, 37 04'N,
Class	Minesweeper		05 00'E
Built	4 September 1941	Cause	Submarine attack

Notes HMS *Hythe* was torpedoed and sunk by *U371* (*Kapitanleutnant* Waldemar Mehl).

21 October 1943

Name	*Chedabucto*	**Location**	Atlantic, Gulf of St Lawrence,
Class	Minesweeper		48 14'N, 69 16'W
Built	14 April 1941	**Cause**	Collision

Notes   HMCS *Chedabucto* was damaged in collision with the SS *Lord Kelvin*. She survived the collision but was beached. After a survey she was declared a constructive total loss.

22 October 1943

Name	*Hurworth*	**Location**	Mediterranean, E of Kalymnos,
Class	*Hunt* class destroyer		36 59'N, 27 06'E
Built	10 April 1941	**Cause**	Mine
CO	Cdr R.H. Wright DSC RN	**Survivors**	80

Notes   HMS *Hurworth* was mined at 2200 hrs while engaged in a diversionary operation with the Greek destroyer *Adrias* (also mined but which survived) to cover the landing of stores on Leros by HMS *Jervis* and HMS *Pathfinder*. The survivors came ashore in Turkey; they found the Turkish authorities most helpful and were soon repatriated. The Turks stated that that very morning they had seen caiques under German colours lay the minefield in which *Hurworth* was sunk.

23 October 1943

Name	*Charybdis*	**Location**	English Channel, N of Ile de Batz,
Class	*Dido* class cruiser		48 59'N, 03 39'W
Built	17 September 1940	**Cause**	Torpedo
CO	Capt G.A. Voelcker RN	**Survivors**	107

Notes   German destroyers based at Brest and Cherbourg were competently handled and were proving more than a match for the British *Hunt* class destroyers engaged in regular sweeps up and down the Brittany coast. Accordingly the cruiser *Charybdis* and the destroyer *Grenville* were detached from the Home Fleet to strengthen the Channel forces. On 22 October *Charybdis* left Devonport in company with the fleet destroyers *Grenville* and *Rocket* and the *Hunt* class destroyers *Limbourne*, *Talybont*, *Stevenstone* and *Wensleydale*. The ships were known as Force 28 and were to sweep down the Brittany coast to search for a suspected German convoy. The operation had the codeword *Tunnel*.

On her first operation *Charybdis* was torpedoed at 0135 hrs on the 23rd by the torpedo boats *T.23* and *T.27*. She was struck by two torpedoes and sank very quickly. The first torpedo hit her port side, flooding no. 2 dynamo room and 'B' boiler room. By the time Commander Oddie, the Executive Officer, got down on to the upper deck from the bridge to take charge of damage control, the ship was already listing 20° to port. As Commander Oddie made his way aft *Charybdis* was hit again aft on the port side. This hit caused serious damage: all electric light failed, the after engine room flooded and the list increased to 50°. All communication with the bridge had failed so Oddie ordered the ship to be abandoned. Shortly afterwards *Charybdis* sank by the stern until her bows were vertical above the water: she remained like this for nearly half an hour before she disappeared at 0230 hrs.

In his well-written memoirs, *Destroyer Captain*, Commander Roger Hill DSO RN, Commanding Officer of *Grenville*, gives a very interesting account of the operation. Hill states that he argued that the German coastal radar stations tracked the route taken by the British ships on these sweeps down the Brittany coast, and that the route should therefore be changed. Although Hill received the support of Captain Voelcker, he could not persuade the CinC Plymouth, Admiral Sir Charles Little. Accordingly the operation went ahead as planned with the results that Hill predicted. Force 28 was detected by the radar station at Perros at 0027 hrs on the 23rd and by Paimpol radar at 0040 hrs. A German convoy was at sea but the 4th TB Flotilla screening the convoy was detached and took up position between the convoy and the British ships. Until the Germans fired their torpedoes at 0143 hrs they were kept continually informed of Force 28's movements. Though commended for his part in the affair in taking command of the force in very confused circumstances, Hill was subsequently very outspoken about the conduct of the operation in particular and staff officers in general. Not surprisingly his post-war career in the Royal Navy did not prosper.

Name	*Limbourne*	Location	English Channel, N of Ile de Batz,
Class	*Hunt* class destroyer		48 59'N, 03 39'W
Built	12 May 1942	Cause	Torpedo
CO	Cdr W.J. Phipps OBE RN	Survivors	103

Notes *Limbourne* was torpedoed at 0152 hrs. The torpedo blew away the bows but the boiler room bulkhead held, the ship had power and there was no immediate danger of her sinking. However, power was subsequently lost as sea water contaminated oil fuel lines. The commanding officer and first lieutenant were suffering from concussion, so command devolved on Sub Lieutenant D.H. Cunliffe-Owen RN. Eventually steam was recovered and communications throughout the ship restored, but it proved impossible to get the ship going on any course other than a circle. Concerned that she might drift ashore (the enemy-held coast was no more than 5 miles away), Cunliffe-Owen gave orders for the motor boat to be swung out and the rafts prepared. As this was being done, *Grenville* and the rest of Force 28 appeared. While *Grenville* and *Rocket* carried out a sweep to the west, *Talybont*, *Stevenstone* and *Wensleydale* rescued *Charybdis'* survivors and prepared to take *Limbourne* in tow. However, it proved impossible to tow the ship owing to the drogue effect of her shattered bows, so she was scuttled by torpedoes from *Talybont* and *Rocket* at 0640 hrs.

Name	*Cromarty*	Cause	Mine
Class	Minesweeper	Survivors	62
Location	Mediterranean, W approaches to Bonifacio Straits		

Notes HMS *Cromarty* was mined and sunk at 1124 hrs while minesweeping at the western entrance to the Bonifacio Straits. This area had been heavily mined by both Germans and Italians and was one of the most hazardous places for minesweeping in the Mediterranean.

24 October 1943

Name	*Eclipse*	Location	Mediterranean, E of Kalymnos,
Class	*E* class destroyer		37 01'N, 27 11'E
Built	12 April 1934	Cause	Mine
		Casualties	+ 140

Notes HMS *Eclipse* was carrying 200 soldiers to reinforce the garrison on Leros when she was mined. In addition to the losses in her own ship's company, 140 of the soldiers were also killed.

November 1943 *At the eastern end of the Mediterranean the British occupation of the Dodecanese Islands gave the Luftwaffe its last opportunity to demonstrate the effectiveness of air attack on warships without air cover.*

11 November 1943

Name	*Rockwood*	**Location**	Mediterranean, 5 miles E of Kos,
Class	*Hunt* class destroyer		36 50'N, 27 30'E
Built	13 June 1942	**Cause**	Air attack

Notes On 10 November *Rockwood*, *Petard* and the Polish *Krakowiak* carried out a bombardment of Levitha Harbour to forestall the anticipated German invasion of Leros. It was while returning from this operation that *Rockwood* was attacked by German aircraft and disabled by an Hs.293A glider bomb. She was towed by *Petard* to the Bay of Losta in the Gulf of Doris. On the 15th HMS *Blencathra* arrived with a metal patch to place over the hole in her side. At 1730 hrs on the 16th *Rockwood* proceeded to Alexandria in the tow of *Blencathra*; they arrived on the 19th but *Rockwood* was not repaired.

13 November 1943

Name	*Dulverton*	**Location**	Mediterranean, 5 miles E of Kos,
Class	*Hunt* class destroyer		36 50'N, 27 30'E
Built	1 April 1941	**Cause**	Air attack
		Survivors	109

Notes The Germans invaded Leros on 13 November. That day the cruiser *Phoebe* and the destroyers *Dulverton*, *Belvoir* and *Echo* were sent into the Aegean north of Rhodes to look for landing forces. At 0130 hrs on the 13th *Dulverton* was hit by an Hs.293A glider bomb and sank 2 hours later. The survivors were rescued by *Echo* and *Belvoir*.

15 November 1943

Name	*Quail*	**Location**	Mediterranean, port of Bari
Class	*Q* class destroyer	**Cause**	Mine
Built	1 June 1942		

Notes The port of Bari on the east coast of Italy was the object of repeated minelaying sorties by the Luftwaffe. HMS *Quail* was the victim of one of these mines while entering harbour on the 15th. Her stern was badly damaged and her after 4.7 in gun mounting was blown over the side. She was beached and remained at Bari until June 1944 when arrangements were made to tow her to Taranto for repairs. On 18 June 1944 she capsized while under tow in the Gulf of Taranto, at 40 05'N, 17 52'E. Some accounts say that *Quail* struck another mine but there is no evidence for this.

18 November 1943

Name	*Chanticleer*	**Location**	Atlantic, 250 miles ENE of the
Class	*Black Swan* class sloop		Azores, 39 47'N, 20 12'W
Built	24 September 1942	**Cause**	Submarine attack
		Casualties	28

Notes HMS *Chanticleer* was escorting the combined convoys MKS.30 and SL.139 when she was torpedoed and damaged by *U515* (*Kapitanleutnant* Werner Henke) using a T5 acoustic torpedo. Her stern was blown off but she was towed to the Azores and paid off. She was subsequently recommissioned as the *Lusitania* and served as a base ship at Horta until 1945.

19(?) November 1943

Name	*Simoom*	**Location**	Mediterranean, exact position
Class	S class submarine		unknown
Built	12 October 1942	**Cause**	Mine
CO	Lt G.D. Milner RN	**Casualties**	48
		Survivors	None

Notes *Simoom* left Port Said on 2 November for a patrol in the Aegean. Thereafter nothing was heard from her although she was ordered to leave patrol on the 15th. She may have been the victim of a mine, *U595* claimed to have attacked and sunk a submarine at 2345 hrs on the 19th. However, the position of this attack is well away from *Simoom*'s route back to Port Said. Loss by accident is another possibility. *Simoom* was the last British submarine to be sunk in the Mediterranean during the Second World War.

22 November 1943

Name	*Hebe*	**Cause**	Mine
Class	Minesweeper	**Casualties**	38
Location	Adriatic, off the port of Bari, 41	**Survivors**	72
	08'N, 16 52'E		

Notes German minelaying off Bari was extremely effective. Following the loss of the *Quail* (see p. 223) sweeping operations were organised. It was while engaged in this work that *Hebe* was mined in an area which had <u>twice</u> been swept over the previous day! Thirty-eight of the survivors were wounded, most suffering fractures from being thrown up in the air by the explosion.

Name	*Welman 46*	**Location**	Norway, port of Bergen
Class	Midget submarine	**Cause**	Captured
Built	1943	**Casualties**	None
CO	Lt B. Pedersen (Norwegian Army)	**Survivors**	1

Notes *Welman 46* was one of four midget submarines engaged in operation *Barbara*, an attack on the Laksevag floating dock at Bergen. They had been taken by MTB to Norway where they lay up for a while before deciding to launch the attack on the night of 21/22. While waiting the crews had been less than discreet and had been spotted by a number of civilians. It is possible that the operation was compromised from the start. As they ran in towards Bergen, Pedersen found the defences very much alert. He encountered a net in Westbyfjord and on coming to the surface was spotted by the patrol boat *NB59*. Pedersen tried to scuttle the craft but he was blinded by searchlights and was captured along with *Welman 46*. The Germans made great use of the midget submarine and many of its features reappeared in German midget submarines such as the *Biber*. This operation was the only operational use of the *Welman* submarine. *Welman 45*, *47* and *48* were abandoned by their operators (who were all later recovered to the UK by MTB) in the same operation.

Pedersen was lucky not to be handed over to the *SD* (*Sicherheitdienst* – the security agency responsible for dealing with spies and saboteurs under the notorious *Nacht und Nebel* order). Instead of being shot as a saboteur, he was placed in a naval PoW camp. After a lucky escape from the firing squad he might be forgiven for keeping a low profile but he attempted three escapes. His fourth attempt was frustrated by the arrival of the British Army in May 1945.

December 1943   *Even with the array of counter-measures deployed against them, German U-boats were still capable of inflicting considerable damage. In attacks against convoy KMS.34 over two days U-boats sank two* Hunt *class destroyers and damaged a new frigate beyond repair.*

11 December 1943

Name	*Cuckmere*	**Location**	Mediterranean, off Algiers, 36 56'N,
Class	Frigate		03 01'E
		Cause	Submarine attack

Notes   HMS *Cuckmere* was torpedoed by *U223* (*Kapitanleutnant* Karl-Jurg Wachter). She was towed into Algiers but the damage was such that she was not repaired.

12 December 1943

Name	*Tynedale*	**Location**	Mediterranean, off Bougie, 37 10'N,
Class	*Hunt* class destroyer		06 05'E
Built	5 June 1940	**Cause**	Submarine attack

Notes   The next day, at 0710 hrs *U593* (*Kapitanleutnant* Gerd Kelbling) attacked and sank HMS *Tynedale* with a homing torpedo.

Name	*Holcombe*	**Location**	Mediterranean, off Bougie, 37 20'N,
Class	*Hunt* class destroyer		05 50'E
Built	14 April 1942	**Cause**	Submarine attack

Notes   In the confusion following the sinking of the *Tynedale*, *U593* made a second attack at 1456 hrs (while the other escorts were hunting for her) and sank the *Holcombe*, again using a T5 acoustic homing torpedo.

18 December 1943

Name	*Felixstowe*	**Cause**	Mine
Class	Minesweeper	**Casualties**	None
Location	Mediterranean, 3 miles E of Cape Ferro Sardinia, 41 10'N, 08 40'E		

Notes   HMS *Felixstowe* was mined during routine sweeping operations off the coast of Sardinia.

23 December 1943

Name	*Worcester*	**Location**	North Sea, off Smiths Knoll Buoy
Class	*V&W* class destroyer	**Cause**	Mine
Built	20 April 1919	**Casualties**	None

Notes   HMS *Worcester* had done great work earlier in the war and in particular had made a valiant attempt (sustaining much damage in the process) to torpedo the German battle cruisers *Scharnhorst* and *Gneisenau* during the famous 'Channel Dash'. By December 1944 she was reduced to escort work on the east coast and was mined off Smiths Knoll. Though her stern was blown off, she was taken in tow by the tug *Champion* and reached Yarmouth. Later she was taken to Harwich. There the decision was taken not to repair this great fighting destroyer. Three days later the *Scharnhorst*, the ship *Worcester* had tried so hard to sink, was sunk at the battle of the North Cape.

24 December 1943

Name	*Hurricane*	**Location**	Atlantic, 45 10'N, 22 05'W
Class	Ex-Brazilian *Japarua*	**Cause**	Submarine attack
Built	29 September 1939		

Notes   At 0758 hrs on 24 December HMS *Hurricane* and HMS *Glenarm* from the escort group B.1 were detached to reinforce the US Navy TG.21.14 which was engaged in anti-blockade runner operations. At 2000 hrs she was torpedoed by *U415* (*Kapitanleutnant* Kurt Neide) and reported that she had no power but was in no danger of sinking. She was screened by the *Glenarm* until the arrival of the destroyer *Watchman*. Her condition remained unchanged but at 1305 hrs on the 25th she was sunk by *Watchman* on the direct orders of CinC Western Approaches on the grounds that drifting in her crippled state she would act as a magnet for further U-boat attacks.

31 December 1943

Name	*Clacton*	**Cause**	Mine
Class	Minesweeper	**Survivors**	43
Location	Mediterranean, E coast of Corsica		

Notes   HMS *Clacton* was on passage from La Maddalena to Bastia in company with *LST.411* when she struck a mine at 0832 hrs and sank immediately. The survivors were rescued by HMS *Polruan*.

LOSSES 1944

January 1944 *saw the Allied landings at Anzio on the west coast of Italy. Once again the Royal Navy was committed to the support of the army in face of opposition from a determined German air force now equipped with new weapons such as the Hs.293A glider bomb.*

7 January 1944

Name	*X.22*	**Location**	Scotland, Pentland Firth
Class	*X*-Craft	**Cause**	Collision
Built	1943	**Casualties**	3
CO	Lt B.M. MacFarlane RAN	**Survivors**	None

Notes *X.22* was in the tow of HM Submarine *Syrtis* on passage to Scapa Flow where she was to spend some time testing the harbour defences. The Royal Navy was concerned that one of the three *X*-Craft lost in Operation Source (see pp. 216–17) might have fallen into German hands intact – they did not want the Germans staging a repeat performance in Scapa Flow. While crossing the Pentland Firth – the strip of water between the north of Scotland and the Orkneys – *Syrtis* was swamped by a large wave which washed her OOW, Lieutenant C. Blyth RNR, off the bridge. *Syrtis* turned to look for Blyth and in so doing ran down on *X.22* and inadvertently sank her.

Name	*Tweed*	**Location**	Atlantic, W of Cape Ortegal,
Class	*River* class frigate		44 18'N, 21 19'W
Built	24 November 1942	**Cause**	Submarine attack
CO	Lt Cdr R.S. Miller DSC RD RNR	**Survivors**	52

Notes *Tweed* was attacked by *U305* (*Kapitanleutnant* Rudolf Bahr) using a T5 homing torpedo. She sank in less than 2 minutes, with the fifty-two survivors being rescued by HMS *Nene*.

23 January 1944

Name	*Janus*	**Location**	Mediterranean, off Anzio, 41 26'N,
Class	*J* class destroyer		12 38'E
Built	10 November 1938	**Cause**	Air attack
CO	Lt Cdr W.B. Morrison RN	**Casualties**	162

Notes *Janus* was torpedoed at 1815 hrs in an attack launched at dusk by aircraft armed with both conventional torpedoes and glider bombs. The torpedo set off her magazine and she blew up with heavy loss of life.

29 January 1944

Name	*Spartan*	**Location**	Mediterranean, Anzio Bay, 41 26'N,
Class	*Bellona* class cruiser		12 41'E
Built	27 August 1942	**Cause**	Air attack
CO	Capt P.V. McLaughlin RN	**Casualties**	64
		Survivors	523

Notes   In another dusk raid by the Luftwaffe the cruiser *Spartan* was hit at 1820 hrs by an Hs.293A glider bomb. The explosion started fierce fires which could not be controlled, largely because of the failure of the ship's electrical supplies and the inability of the crew to restore them. The ship sank about 1 hour later.

One post-war consequence of the loss of *Spartan* (and, to a certain, extent of that of *Ark Royal*, see p. 156) was that the Royal Navy considered that the generation and supply of electricity in a warship should no longer be a secondary responsibility of the torpedo department, as it had been up to then. Instead a specialist electrical branch was created.

30 January 1944

Name	*Hardy*	**Location**	Arctic, S of Bear Island, 73 37'N,
Class	*U* class destroyer		18 06'E
Built	18 March 1943	**Cause**	Submarine attack
CO	Capt W.G. Robson DSO DSC RN	**Casualties**	40

Notes   *Hardy* was escorting convoy JW.56B when she was attacked at 0405 hrs by *U278* (*Kapitanleutnant* Joachim Franze) with a homing torpedo. Three minutes later her magazine exploded and she had to be scuttled by a torpedo fired by HMS *Venus*.

18 February 1944

Name	*Penelope*	**Location**	Mediterranean, W of Naples,
Class	*Arethusa* class cruiser		40 55'N, 13 25'E
Built	15 October 1935	**Cause**	Submarine
CO	Capt G.D. Belben DSC AM RN	**Casualties**	415
		Survivors	85

Notes   HMS *Penelope*, affectionately known as 'Pepperpot' after the number of holes in her sides sustained during repeated air raids in 1942, was steaming at 26 knots when she was attacked by *U410* (*Oberleutnant zur See* Horst-Arno Fenski). The first torpedo hit at 0730 hrs and was followed, 16 minutes later, by another, after which she sank very quickly.

20 February 1944

Name	*Woodpecker*	**Location**	Atlantic, S of Iceland, 48 49'N,
Class	*Black Swan* class sloop		22 11'W
Built	29 June 1942	**Cause**	Submarine attack
CO	Cdr H.L. Pryse RD RNR	**Casualties**	None

Notes   HMS *Woodpecker*, part of Captain Walker's renowned 2nd Escort Group, was attacked by *U764* (*Oberleutnant zur See* Hanskurt von Bremen) with a T5 homing torpedo. The explosion blew *Woodpecker's* stern off but she remained afloat and it was considered that she was worth salvaging. She was taken in tow but sank in a gale on 27 February in position 49 39'N, 06 08'W.

Name	*Warwick*	**Location**	English Channel, 20 miles SW of
Class	*V&W* class destroyer		Trevose Head, 50 27'N, 05 23'W
Built	28 December 1917	**Cause**	Submarine attack
CO	Cdr D.A. Rayner DSC RN	**Casualties**	67
		Survivors	93

Notes   HMS *Warwick* was attacked by *U413* (*Kapitanleutnant* Gustav Poel). The explosion of *U413's* torpedo was followed very quickly by an internal explosion, whereupon *Warwick* rapidly sank.

25 February 1944

Name	*Inglefield*	**Location**	Mediterranean, off Anzio, 41 26'N,
Class	*I* class destroyer leader		12 36'E
Built	15 October 1936	**Cause**	Air attack
CO	Cdr C.F. Churchill DSC RN	**Casualties**	35
		Survivors	157

Notes   The third British victim of a Luftwaffe dusk raid on the Anzio beachhead, *Inglefield* was hit by an Hs.293A glider bomb and sank quickly.

Name	*Mahratta*	**Location**	Arctic, 280 miles W of the North
Class	*M* class destroyer		Cape, 71 17'N, 13 30'E
Built	28 July 1942	**Cause**	Submarine attack
CO	Lt Cdr E.A.F. Drought RN	**Casualties**	220
		Survivors	16

Notes   HMS *Mahratta* was escorting convoy JW.57 to Murmansk when she was attacked and sunk by *U990* (*Kapitanleutnant* Hubert Nordheimer) using a T5 homing torpedo. *Mahratta*, a destroyer seconded to the operation from the Home Fleet, was at the stern of the convoy. The destroyer *Impulsive* was sent back and picked up sixteen survivors.

The loss of the *Mahratta* need not have occurred had the Home Fleet destroyers been as well trained in anti-submarine warfare as their colleagues in Western Approaches Command. The latter specialised in U-boat hunting and were wise to their tactics and latest weapons. However, in the Atlantic the surface threat was non-existent and the air threat negligible, so the Western Approaches forces could concentrate on U-boat hunting. They also had the benefit of an operational research division ashore in Liverpool where U-boat and escort tactics could be analysed. This information was not generally available to the Home Fleet destroyers working on the Arctic convoys, who had to give equal consideration to the threat from aircraft and submarines. Lieutenant-Commander Reginald Whinney, in command of HMS *Wanderer*, one of the ships of the B.1 group, wrote of his concern that only two destroyers were covering the stern of the convoy when it had become clear that U-boats were making successful attacks undetected down-wind and down-sea. However, he did not signal his concern to the Senior Officer. Whinney recalled: 'The destroyer *Mahratta*, one of the two ships astern of the convoy called up the Admiral on R/T. Up on the bridge I heard the educated and entirely calm voice – it could have been Drought the commanding officer, who had been at prep school and again at Dartmouth with me: "Have been hit by a torpedo aft and am stopped." This was obviously a Gnat which had homed on the destroyer's propeller noises. This report was followed by a pause before the next. "Have been struck by a second torpedo." Then there was another pause, probably Drought was trying to get all watertight doors shut and summing up the desperate situation. "Life saving equipment is being cleared away." Still the same calm, unemotional tones. Then, probably due to a fault in the R/T set, an unhappy warble developed in the voice. "We are abandoning ship. We are sinking. We cannot last much longer." And that was it. It appeared that the Admiral sent two destroyers to rescue survivors. There were very few rescued. I believe at least some of the life-saving gear was frozen up. So far as we in *Wanderer* could make out no ship was sent out after the U-boat. Personally, for sheer incompetence and rasping anguish, the *Mahratta* incident compared with . . . the staggering horror of the sinking of the mighty *Hood*.'

1 March 1944

Name	*Gould*	**Location**	Atlantic, NNE of the Azores,
Class	*Captain* class frigate		45 46'N, 23 10'W
Built	1943	**Cause**	Submarine attack
CO	Lt D.W. Unged RN	**Casualties**	123
		Survivors	14

Notes   HMS *Gould* was one of a number of escorts chasing a submarine contact to the north-north-east of the Azores. Contact had been made initially by HMS *Garlies* at 0507 hrs on 29 February but the U-boat proved determined and cunning, constantly manoeuvring and changing depth throughout the 29th and most of 1 March, though with one or other of the frigates in contact most of the time. At 1920 hrs on the 1st HMS *Gould* had just completed an attacking run and had lost contact with the U-boat which was off her port quarter. The next ship astern, HMS *Affleck*, had just acquired the contact when a sudden improvement in the echo was observed. The U-boat (*U358*, commanded by *Kapitanleutnant* Rolf Manke) had come shallow and promptly torpedoed HMS *Gould*. *U358* was eventually sunk by HMS *Affleck*.

9 March 1944

Name	*Asphodel*	**Location**	Atlantic, WNW of Cape Finisterre,
Class	*Flower* class corvette		45 24'N, 18 09'W
Built	1941	**Cause**	Submarine attack
CO	Lt A.M. Halliday RNZN	**Casualties**	92
		Survivors	5

Notes   HMS *Asphodel* was torpedoed and sunk by *U575* (*Oberleutnant zur See* Rudolf Boehme).

16 March 1944

Name	*Stonehenge*	**Location**	Indian Ocean, N end of the Malacca
Class	*S* class submarine		Strait
Built	23 March 1943	**Casualties**	48
CO	Lt D.S. Verschoyle-Campbell RN	**Survivors**	None

Notes   *Stonehenge* sailed from Ceylon on 25 February for patrol in an area around the island of Great Nicobar and the north coast of Sumatra. The patrol was a hurried one, ordered in response to reports of Japanese fleet movements out of Singapore. Nothing further was heard from her and it is presumed that she was lost either in a minefield or as the result of an accident.

28(?) March 1944

Name	*Syrtis*	**Location**	Norwegian Sea, exact position
Class	S class submarine		unknown
Built	4 February 1943	**Casualties**	48
CO	Lt M.H. Jupp RN	**Survivors**	None

Notes   HM Submarines *Taku*, *Satyr* and *Syrtis* were preparing for an operation in which they would force an entrance to the Skagerrak. On 16 March all three submarines were hurriedly ordered to sail from Lerwick for patrol off Norway. Intelligence had been received that the German battleship *Tirpitz* was ready to move following repairs to damage sustained in the *X*-craft attack of the previous year. Lieutenant-Commander Arthur Pitt of HMS *Taku* watched *Syrtis* sail: '"And goodbye to you too", called back Michael Jupp as the grey shape of the *Syrtis* drew clear astern. There she stopped for an instant until, with a rattle and a shudder, her diesels started. They quickly settled down to a steady drumming as she passed about twenty yards away, heading for the open sea. Michael's voice and the grey shape of *Syrtis* heading for the open sea was to be the last sight and sound of them to their friends.' It is known that she sank a small ship by gunfire on 22 March. On the 28th she was ordered to return to Lerwick but the signal was not acknowledged. There is no clear explanation for her loss. The Germans claimed to have sunk a submarine by shore battery fire off Bodo around this time but there is no evidence to back this up. Alternative explanations include loss by mining or as the result of an accident.

30 March 1944

Name	*Laforey*	**Location**	Mediterranean, NE of Palermo,
Class	L class destroyer		38 54'N, 14 18'E
Built	15 February 1941	**Cause**	Submarine attack
CO	Capt H.T. Armstrong DSO DSC RN	**Casualties**	177
		Survivors	69

Notes   The destroyers *Laforey*, *Ulster* and *Tumult* were carrying out a routine anti-submarine sweep when *Ulster* gained a firm Asdic contact at 0450 hrs on 29 March. The destroyers launched a series of depth-charge attacks until 1222 hrs when *Ulster* was detached to Palermo having expended all her depth-charges. Her place was taken by *Wilton*. At 1530 hrs the destroyers *Hambledon* and *Blencathra* joined in and the attacks continued. During the night the destroyers simply maintained contact, intending to resume attacks at daybreak. Maintaining contact was not easy since throughout the night the U-boat (*U223*, commanded by *Oberleutnant zur See* Peter Gerlach) manoeuvred fast and evasively in an effort to throw off her pursuers or break through the screen. At 0050 hrs on the 30th the sound of tanks being blown was heard, the U-boat surfaced and all ships opened fire. Almost simultaneously *Laforey* was hit by a torpedo and sank very quickly. In the confusion the U-boat tried to escape on the surface at 15 knots — a futile exercise when pitted against two fleet destroyers and three escort destroyers. She finally sank by the stern at 0110 hrs having been on the receiving end of twenty-seven depth-charge/Hedgehog attacks followed by gunfire.

   HMS *Laforey* was the last British vessel to be sunk by a submarine in the Mediterranean during the Second World War.

29 April 1944

Name	*Athabaskan*	**Location**	Atlantic, 12 miles N of the Ile de
Class	*Tribal* class destroyer		Vierge, 40 48'N, 04 32'W
Built	18 November 1941	**Cause**	Torpedo
CO	Lt Cdr J.H. Stubbs RCN		

Notes Despite the sinking of *Charybdis* and *Limbourne* in 1943, operation *Tunnel* was continued on a regular basis by a mixed cruiser/destroyer force based at Devonport. They had a number of successes: on 25/26 April 1944 *Haida*, *Athabaskan* and *Huron* sank the German torpedo boat *T.29* north of the Ile de Batz. Two days later *Haida* (Commander H.C. de Wolf RCN) and *Athabaskan* sailed from Devonport for the same area to prevent two German *Elbing* class torpedo boats, *T.27* and *T.28*, based at St Malo, from interfering with a minelaying operation.

The two German ships did put to sea and were sighted by the two Canadian *Tribals* at 0414 hrs on the 29th. The two German ships were taken by surprise by the Canadian ships' starshell and at once turned away to starboard, making smoke and firing torpedoes. The Canadians turned to follow at 0417 hrs and at that moment *Athabaskan* was hit by a torpedo aft which set her on fire and brought her to a standstill. The Canadians also seem to have been taken by surprise for afterwards it was discovered that at the time of the engagement *Athabaskan*'s torpedo tubes were not turned outboard. Ten minutes later, at 0427 hrs, the ship exploded. This may have been caused by a second torpedo or the explosion of her after magazine where the fire had been raging. Meanwhile *Haida* had chased the two German ships and had driven *T.27* aground before returning to find over a hundred of *Athabaskan*'s crew in the water. All of *Haida*'s floats were dropped into the water together with her motor boat, and as many men were brought on board as possible. By 0515 hrs Commander de Wolf felt that he could not remain under an enemy-held coast for much longer and withdrew to the north leaving all floats and boats behind. *Haida* arrived at Devonport at 0840 hrs.

Haida's motor boat, loaded with *Athabaskan*'s survivors, had an epic journey of her own. The coxswain, Able Seaman W. McClure, headed north at full speed, chased by three German minesweepers who gave up the chase after half an hour. Undeterred, McClure continued on the 100 mile journey back to Devonport and was fortunate to be spotted by two Spitfires in mid-Channel. At 2145 hrs that evening *Haida*'s motor boat was met by a motor launch which took off the crew and the survivors.

The subsequent enquiry into *Athabaskan*'s loss found that 'the exchange of a *Tribal* class destroyer for an *Elbing* cannot be regarded as a satisfactory transaction while the unpreparedness of the British [sic] torpedo armament is inexplicable'.

4 May 1944

Name	*Elgin*	**Location**	English Channel, 9 miles E of
Class	*Aberdare* class minesweeper		Portland, 50 28'N, 02 11'W
Built	1917	**Cause**	Mine
		Casualties	None

Notes HMS *Elgin* was disabled when an acoustic mine exploded 150 ft from her stern. She did not sink but was towed to Portsmouth. There she was surveyed but the damage was considered so great that she was not repaired.

7 May 1944

Name	*Valleyfield*	**Location**	Atlantic, 40 miles E of Cape Race,
Class	Frigate		46 03'N, 52 24'W
Built	17 July 1943	**Cause**	Submarine attack
CO	Lt Cdr D.T. English RCN	**Casualties**	121
		Survivors	38

Notes   HMS *Valleyfield* was attacked and sunk by *U548* (*Kapitanleutnant* Eberhard Zimmerman) using a T5 homing torpedo. The survivors were rescued by HMCS *Giffard*.

June 1944   *D-Day, 6 June, saw the launch of the long-awaited Anglo-American landings on the coast of Normandy. British losses were comparatively light given the scale of the enterprise.*

6 June 1944

Name	*Wrestler*	**Location**	English Channel, NW of Le Havre,
Class	*V&W* class destroyer		49 36'N, 0 27'W
Built	25 February 1918	**Cause**	Mine
CO	Lt Cdr R.W. Lacon DSC RN		

Notes   HMS *Wrestler* was mined at 0545 hrs on 6 June while shepherding landing craft through the mine barrage in mid-Channel. Lieutenant-Commander Lacon had done extremely valuable work in keeping the groups of assault craft closed up and on their way despite the bad weather. In doing so he accepted the risk of straying into unswept waters. The old destroyer survived the explosion and was towed to Portsmouth but after survey she was never repaired.

8 June 1944

Name	*Lawford*	**Location**	English Channel, Seine Bay, Juno
Class	*Captain* class frigate		Beach area
Built	1943	**Cause**	Air attack
CO	Lt Cdr M.C. Morris RN	**Casualties**	24

Notes   HMS *Lawford* was the HQ ship for the assault forces off Juno beach. On 8 June, while off Courcelles, she was attacked and sunk by German aircraft.

9 June 1944

Name	*Centurion*	**Location**	English Channel, off Arromanches
Class	*King George V* class battleship	**Cause**	Scuttled as blockship
Built	18 November 1911	**Casualties**	None
CO	Not in commission		

Notes   The first part of the construction of the Mulberry harbours off the Normandy beaches was the construction of a 4 mile breakwater made up of fifty-three old warships and merchant ships about 1,500 yards offshore. *Centurion* was one of the ships involved.

Name	Durban	CO	Not in commission
Class	D class cruiser	Location	English Channel, off Arromanches
Built	29 May 1919	Cause	Scuttled as blockship
		Casualties	None

Notes   See the entry for HMS *Centurion* above.

Name	Alynbank	CO	Not in commission
Class	Auxiliary AA ship	Location	English Channel, off Arromanches
Built	1925	Cause	Scuttled as blockship
		Casualties	None

Notes   See the entry for HMS *Centurion* above.

12 June 1944

Name	Halsted	Built	1943
Class	Captain class frigate	Location	English Channel, Seine Bay
		Cause	Torpedo

Notes   At 0315 hrs on 12 June *Halsted* was attacked by *S-boote* of *9 Schnellboote Flotille* and her bows were blown off. She returned to Portsmouth – astern and under her own power – but was not repaired.

12(?) June 1944

Name	Sickle	CO	Lt J.R. Drummond RN
Class	S class submarine	Location	Mediterranean, Aegean
Built	27 August 1942	Survivors	1

Notes   HMS *Sickle* had left Malta on 31 May for a patrol in the Aegean. On 4 June Drummond carried out a gun attack on shipping at Mitylene and at 1255 hrs on 12 June he reported the sighting of a convoy in the Steno Channel. Nothing more was heard from the submarine. There is no clear explanation for *Sickle*'s loss. No definite claim for sinking her was made by Axis forces. Her last signal was made at 1255 hrs on the 12th. It is presumed that she was either mined or lost as the result of an accident. *Sickle* was the last British submarine to sink in the Mediterranean during the Second World War.

Her sole survivor was Able Seaman Richard Blake, a member of the submarine's 3 in gun crew. During the bombardment of Mitylene on 4 June the submarine had been engaged by the German patrol vessels *GA76* and *GA91*. A 3.7 in shell from one of these vessels had burst near *Sickle*'s gun, killing one man and wounding two more, and blowing Blake over the side. Since fire from the two German ships was becoming very accurate, Drummond had to dive the boat leaving Blake in the water. He was later picked up by the Germans and became a PoW.

13 June 1944

Name	Boadicea	Location	English Channel, 12 miles SW of
Class	B class destroyer		Portland Bill, 50 26'N, 02 34'W
Built	23 September 1930	Cause	Air attack
CO	Lt Cdr F.W. Hawkins RN	Casualties	175
		Survivors	12

Notes   HMS *Boadicea* was escorting a westbound Channel convoy when she was attacked by Ju.88 aircraft. The destroyer was hit by two torpedoes: her magazine then exploded and she sank very quickly.

15 June 1944

Name	*Blackwood*	**Location**	English Channel, 50 04'N, 02 15'W
Class	Frigate	**Cause**	Submarine attack
Built	1943	**Casualties**	58
CO	Lt Cdr L.T. Sly RD RNR		

Notes   HMS *Blackwood* was torpedoed by *U674* (*Oberleutnant zur See* Hanskurt von Bremen) using a T5 homing torpedo. The explosion blew off *Blackwood*'s bows but she remained afloat. She was taken in tow but foundered at 0410 hrs on the 16th, 23 miles south-east of Portland. Subsequently *Blackwood*'s wreck was assessed as being a bottomed U-boat by a Canadian escort group engaged in anti-submarine operations. The subsequent depth-charge attack set off the frigate's own remaining depth-charges in a terrific explosion.

Name	*Mourne*	**Location**	English Channel, 49 20'N, 05 30'W
Class	Frigate	**Cause**	Submarine attack
Built	24 September 1942	**Casualties**	110
CO	Lt Cdr R.S. Holland RD RNR		

Notes   *Mourne* was attacked by *U767* (*Oberleutnant zur See der Reserve* Walter Dankleff) using a T5 homing torpedo. Unusually, the torpedo hit *Mourne* forward (T5s usually struck aft where the engine noise was greater) and blew off her bows. The frigate sank in less than 1 minute.

21 June 1944

Name	*Fury*	**Location**	English Channel, Normandy, Sword
Class	F class destroyer		Beach area
Built	10 September 1934	**Cause**	Mine

Notes   At 1045 hrs on 21 June HMS *Fury* became another mine casualty off the Normandy beaches. She was taken in tow and it was intended to return her to Portsmouth. However, she broke free from her tow in bad weather and was driven ashore at 2300 hrs where she became a constructive total loss.

23 June 1944

Name	*Scylla*	**CO**	Flagship Rear Adm P.L.V. Vian
Class	*Dido* class cruiser	**Location**	English Channel, Normandy, off
Built	24 July 1940		Sword Beach, 49 25'N, 00 24'W
		Cause	Mine

Notes   HMS *Scylla* ran over a German acoustic mine and sustained massive shock damage to her midships section and total loss of power. She was towed to Portsmouth but was never repaired. Her shattered hull lingered in the dockyard until 1950 when she was finally sold for breaking up.

24 June 1944

Name	*Swift*	**Location**	English Channel, Seine Bay, Sword
Class	S class destroyer		Beach area
Built	15 June 1943	**Cause**	Mine
CO	Lt Cdr J.R. Gower RN		

Notes HMS *Swift* was mined, possibly by an acoustic mine, off Ouisterham. The explosion broke the destroyer's back and she later broke in half and sank.

25 June 1944

Name	*Goodson*	**Location**	English Channel, SE of Start Point
Class	*Captain* class frigate	**Cause**	Submarine attack
Built	1943		

Notes HMS *Goodson* was torpedoed by *U984* (*Oberleutnant zur See* Hans Sieder) with a T5 homing torpedo. Her stern was blown off but she subsequently reached Portland in the tow of HMS *Bligh*. However, after survey she was not repaired.

27 June 1944

Name	*Pink*	**Location**	English Channel, ENE of Barfleur,
Class	*Flower* class corvette		29 48'N, 00 49'W
		Cause	Submarine attack

Notes HMS *Pink* was attacked by *U988* (*Oberleutnant zur See* Erich Dobberstein). The damage was restricted to the loss of her propeller and shaft but after survey at Portsmouth it was decided that she was not worth repairing.

July 1944   *The continuing need to support the Allied armies as they fought their way off the Normandy beaches saw the Royal Navy exposed to a new threat: German 'human torpedoes'. Though these weapons were crude and probably more lethal to their operators than they were to the British, they nevertheless absorbed a considerable amount of resources. An increasing feature of British naval operations is the number of ships not repaired following action damage, indicative of Britain's growing materiel superiority.*

6 July 1944

Name	*Magic*	**Location**	English Channel, Normandy, Sword
Class	*Algerine* class minesweeper		Beach area
CO	Lt Cdr T.P. Davies RNR	**Cause**	Human torpedo
		Casualties	25

Notes *Magic* was the first victim of a *Neger/Marder* sortie on the night of 5 July. She was hit at 0353 hrs on the 6th and sank quickly. Most of her survivors were taken aboard her flotilla-mate *Cato*.

Name	*Cato*	**Location**	English Channel, Normandy, Sword
Class	*Algerine* class minesweeper		Beach area
CO	Lt R.W. Harris RN	**Cause**	Human torpedo
		Casualties	26

Notes   *Cato* was the next victim of that night's operations, being sunk at 0511 hrs.

8 July 1944

Name	*Pylades*	**Location**	English Channel, Normandy, Sword
Class	*Algerine* class minesweeper		Beach area
CO	Lt M. Harris RN	**Cause**	Human torpedo

Notes   HMS *Pylades* was sunk in the Northern Defence Line by either a *Neger* or *Marder* one-man human torpedo. Her stern was blown off and she sank very quickly. Chief ERA Allan Smales in HMS *Pylades* described the sinking: 'At about 0650 hrs we were hit in the stern by what we later learned was a *Neger*. Fortunately I was ERA on watch in the forward engine room at the time of the explosion and I was able to get out. I remember having a laugh as I got out of the ship to see a seaman sailing merrily past on one of the Oropesa floats clad only in his vest.' Able Seaman Fred Holmes in HMS *Cockatrice* recalled: 'I was standing on the afterdeck of *Cockatrice* when we heard the explosion and saw the stern of *Pylades* blown clean off and then the forward part of the ship just tipped and sank almost immediately.'

20 July 1944

Name	*Isis*	**CO**	Lt H.D. Durwell RN
Class	*I* class destroyer	**Location**	English Channel, Seine Bay
Built	12 November 1936	**Survivors**	20

Notes   HMS *Isis* was sunk some time after 1800 hrs on the 20th. Little is known about the circumstances of her loss other than that she suffered a violent explosion. Her loss was not discovered until 0209 hrs on the 21st when HMS *Hound* picked up twenty men from the water. They were the only survivors of her ship's company. There are three possible explanations for the destroyer's loss: firstly, that she was lost as a result of hitting or running over a mine; secondly, that she was sunk by a *Neger* or *Marder* human torpedo; or thirdly, that she was the victim of a *Dackel* slow running, circling and air launched German torpedo.

21 July 1944

| **Name** | *Chamois* | **Location** | English Channel, Seine Bay |
| **Class** | Minesweeper | **Cause** | Mine |

Notes   HMS *Chamois* was mined in the Seine Bay. She was towed back to Portsmouth but not repaired.

24 July 1944

Name	*Goathland*	**Location**	English Channel, Seine Bay
Class	*Hunt* class destroyer	**Cause**	Mine
Built	3 February 1942		

Notes HMS *Goathland* had been modifed to act as an HQ ship for troops ashore and while acting in this role that she was mined north-north-east of Courcelles. She was towed back to Portsmouth but not repaired.

3 August 1944

Name	*Quorn*	**Location**	English Channel, Seine Bay
Class	*Hunt* class destroyer	**Cause**	Human torpedo
Built	27 March 1940	**Casualties**	130
CO	Lt J. Hall RN		

Notes At 0251 hrs on 3 August HMS *Quorn* was torpedoed by either a *Neger* or *Marder* one-man human torpedo. It struck on the starboard side amidships and the ship assumed a 40° list to starboard and less than a minute after the attack she rolled over on to her beam ends. Although she temporarily righted herself, *Quorn* was broken in two amidships. Both ends sank rapidly, leaving 30 ft of the stern and 15 ft of the bow above the water.

6 August 1944

Name	*Regina*	**Location**	English Channel, off Trevose Head,
Class	Corvette		Cornwall, 50 42'N, 05 03'W
Built	14 October 1941	**Cause**	Submarine attack

Notes HMCS *Regina* was escorting convoy EBC.66 when she was attacked by *U667* (*Oberleutnant zur See* Karl-Heinz Lange). The ship rolled over and sank almost immediately.

21 August 1944

Name	*Kite*	**Location**	Arctic, 220 miles SW of Bear Island,
Class	*Black Swan* class sloop		73 01'N, 03 57'E
Built	13 October 1942	**Cause**	Submarine attack
CO	Lt A.N. Campbell RN	**Casualties**	183
		Survivors	9

Notes HMS *Kite* was escorting convoy JW.59 to Russia when she was attacked by *U344* (*Kapitanleutnant* Ulrich Pietsch) using a spread of FAT homing torpedoes. *Kite* sank almost immediately with heavy loss of life.

Name	*Orchis*	**Location**	English Channel, Seine Bay
Class	*Flower* class corvette	**Cause**	Mine
Built	15 October 1940		

Notes HMS *Orchis* was mined off Courcelles in Normandy. The explosion blew off the bows as far back as the gun. *Orchis* was subsequently beached as a constructive total loss.

Name	*Alberni*	**Location**	English Channel, Isle of Wight, SE of
Class	Corvette		St Catherine's Point, 50 18'N, 00
Built	22 August 1940		51'W
CO	Lt I. Bell RCN	**Cause**	Submarine attack
		Casualties	59

Notes   HMCS *Alberni* was torpedoed by *U480* (*Oberleutnant zur See* Hans-Joachim Forster). *Alberni* was hit amidships and sank in less than 30 seconds.

22 August 1944

Name	*Nabob*	**Location**	Arctic, 120 miles WNW of the
Class	*Ruler* class escort carrier		North Cape, 71 42'N, 19 11'E
Built	9 March 1943	**Cause**	Submarine attack
CO	Acting Capt H.N. Lay RCN		

Notes   HMCS *Nabob* was the first aircraft carrier to join the greatly expanded Royal Canadian Navy. *Nabob* had just participated in a Home Fleet air attack on the *Tirpitz* and was then detached to fuel some of convoy JW.59. While doing so she was attacked at 0020 hrs by *U354* (*Kapitanleutnant* Hans-Jurgen Sthamer) which was outward bound to the Atlantic. The torpedo struck aft and did serious damage. Nevertheless *Nabob* remained afloat and managed the 1,000 mile return trip to Rosyth under her own power. However, she was not repaired and was subsequently broken up.

HMCS *Nabob* down by the stern but still under way after being torpedoed by *U354* on 22 August 1944. With the sea lapping around her quarterdeck the damaged carrier made the return trip to Rosyth under her own power. (Public Archives of Canada)

Name	*Bickerton*	**Location**	Arctic, 120 miles WNW of the
Class	*Captain* class frigate		North Cape, 71 42'N, 19 11'E
Built	1943	**Cause**	Submarine attack
CO	Cdr G.D. MacIntyre DSO RN	**Casualties**	38

Notes   HMS *Bickerton* was torpedoed at 0022 hrs on 33 August by *U354* (*Kapitanleutnant* Hans-Jurgen Sthamer) in the same attack and lost her stern. The ship was salvageable but the force commander ordered that she be scuttled and this was done 3 hours later. He did not wish to be burdened with two crippled ships and, since *Nabob* was the more valuable unit, *Bickerton* had to be abandoned and was later sunk by the destroyer *Vigilant*.

Name	*Loyalty*	**Location**	English Channel, S of the Nab Tower,
Class	Minesweeper		50 09'N, 00 41'W
CO	Lt Cdr J.E. Maltby DSC RD RNR	**Cause**	Submarine attack

Notes   HMS *Loyalty* was torpedoed by *U480* (*Oberleutnant zur See* Hans-Joachim Forster) within 10 miles of where the U-boat had sunk HMCS *Alberni*. *Loyalty* sank in less than 7 minutes.

27 August 1944

Name	*Hussar*	**Location**	English Channel, off Cap d'Antifer
Class	*Halcyon* class minesweeper	**Cause**	Air attack (own side)
CO	Lt R. Nash MBE RN	**Casualties**	55

Notes   See the entry for HMS *Britomart* below.

Name	*Britomart*	**Location**	English Channel, off Cap d'Antifer
Class	*Halcyon* class minesweeper	**Cause**	Air attack (own side)
CO	Lt Cdr J.A. Galvin DSC RN	**Casualties**	22

Notes   The sinking of *Hussar* and *Britomart* was the worst 'friendly fire' incident involving ships of the Royal Navy during the Second World War. On a clear, sunny afternoon ships of the 1st Minesweeping Flotilla (1st MSF) were attacked by rocket-firing RAF Typhoon fighter-bombers. HMS *Hussar* and *Britomart* were sunk, HMS *Salamander* so badly damaged that she was beyond repair, and two other ships damaged. In total, 78 officers and ratings were killed and 149 wounded, many seriously.

The ships of the flotilla had been deployed off the Normandy beaches since the beginning of the invasion. On 5 and 6 June the ships had swept channels through to Sword Beach for Assault Convoy S1 and thereafter had been employed in routine clearance of the swept channel between Portsmouth and Arromanches. However, on 22 August they were ordered to clear a field of German magnetic mines laid 5 miles off the French coast between Fecamp and Cap d'Antifer. The clearance of this minefield would enable the battleship HMS *Warspite* and the monitors *ERebus* and *Roberts* to move close to the shore and bombard German positions around Le Havre in preparation for the assault on the city by the Canadians. After four days of work clearing this field, the flotilla, now reduced to *Jason* (SO), *Britomart*, *Hussar* and *Salamander*, enjoyed a rest day at Arromanches.

On the evening of the 25th, Commander Trevor Crick DSC RN, commanding officer of HMS *Jason* and senior officer of the flotilla (the commanding officer of the flotilla was away) received orders that the flotilla was to return to its previous work of clearing the Portsmouth/Arromanches channel on the morning of the 27th. Crick argued that the work of clearing the coastal field was not yet complete and secured a 24 hour extension from the staff after which his ships would return to the Portsmouth–Arromanches channel. The flotilla staff circulated the amended orders to other service commands. It was essential for all shipping movements off the French coast to be disclosed, not just to other naval commands but also to the relevant army and air force commands, in order to prevent misunderstandings.

The signal amending the flotilla's orders was received in *Jason* early on the morning of Sunday 27 August, shortly before the ships weighed anchor for the day's operations. It was a fine day with almost perfect conditions for minesweeping. *Britomart*, *Jason* and *Salamander* were abreast of each other with *Salamander* nearest the shore. Astern of *Britomart* came *Hussar* whose sweep gear was defective. Inshore of *Salamander* was the trawler *Colsay* which was laying DAN buoys to mark the swept channels, while the trawler *Lord Ashfield*, another DAN layer, steamed astern. Shortly before noon, an RAF aircraft made a low pass over the ships, the pilot acknowledging the waves from members of the ships' companies idling on deck.

The flotilla had just begun the third leg of its sweep at about 1330 hrs when a group of aircraft came diving down out of the sun and attacked. The aircraft were clearly recognised as Typhoons, and Crick reported at once that his ships were being attacked by friendly aircraft and repeated the signal two minutes later at 1334 hrs. The Typhoon attack literally ripped *Britomart* apart. The bridge and funnel were destroyed, Lieutenant Commander Galvin was killed, and the upper deck turned into a mass of twisted metal so that it was impossible for anyone at the after end of the ship to go forward and vice versa. The Engineer Officer, Warrant Officer J.R.D. Gregson, gallantly severed the Double L sweep that the ship was towing, which was still pumping out 5,000 amps into the water, by cutting it with an axe. Lieutenant-Commander H. Johnson, an officer embarked in *Britomart* to gain minesweeping experience while awaiting an appointment to his own command, now found himself as senior surviving officer; he decided that he had no choice but to order the crew to abandon ship. It was clear that *Britomart* was beyond salvage and, moreover, she was drifting helplessly in the middle of a minefield.

Astern of *Britomart* was HMS *Hussar*. Her bridge was raked with rocket and cannon fire. Her navigating officer was killed instantly and Lieutenant-Commander Nash was severely wounded in both legs and his right elbow was shot away. All communication with the engine room was lost, but a rating courageously used the emergency stop lever situated in the cross-passage forward of the wardroom to alert the engine room staff to stop the engines. Leading Stoker Hal Booth was off watch and had been sunbathing on the upper deck at the time of the attack: 'I had dozed off but woke up suddenly at a strange noise and saw the minesweeper ahead of us [*Britomart*] surrounded by a mass of little waterspouts with a plane diving on her. We jumped up and ran – there were men running on all sides. As we dashed down the ladder to the mess deck the action bells sounded and I ran to my action station in the engine room but before I could get there the whole engine room area was aflame after being hit by rockets and in the passage outside a lot of washing hung up to dry was burning fiercely. Inside all was utter chaos with men lying dead and others terribly injured, one man with both legs smashed.'

Coder Stan Timothy had also been among those taking it easy on the upper deck: 'Just afterwards *Hussar* gave a tremendous shudder and started to heel over to port. The degaussing and electrical systems were damaged and I think we now hit a magnetic mine. We – the wireless staff – managed to get up to the upper deck which was now at an angle of 45 degrees, and as some of the upper superstructure was breaking away, I made for the starboard rail. Climbing up the sloping deck I noticed that a hatch cover was moving and was able to help those inside by loosening a spring wire which was fouling it. A head appeared and a voice said, "About time too!" I slid down the starboard side and swam away with others of the crew.' *Hussar* sank by the stern with her bows above water.

By 1342 hrs the attack was over. It had taken less than 12 minutes for the little minesweeper to sink. From *Jason*'s bridge, Commander Crick surveyed the remains of his flotilla. *Britomart* was burning and listing heavily to port. *Hussar* had sunk leaving only the tip of her bows above the water. *Salamander* was drifting helplessly with a severe fire engulfing her stern. Crick's own ship had been raked by cannon fire as had the trawlers *Colsay* and *Lord Ashley*. Crick could do no more than wireless an immediate request for tugs and begin to pick up the survivors. The *Colsay* was rescuing men from the *Britomart*, so Crick took *Jason* over to where *Hussar*'s survivors were swimming in the water. As rescue work commenced both ships came under fire from German shore batteries who had been passive witnesses of the events. Crick had no choice but to retire out of gun range and order *Colsay* to do the same and then send back small boats to pick up those still in the water. The shelling was accurate and took a heavy toll of the survivors.

Lieutenant-Commander Johnson from *Britomart* was picked up by a whaler: 'We were transferred to an RAF launch on which there were some pretty terrifying cases, but all displaying amazing courage. There was a Petty Officer from *Hussar* with not only his right arm and shoulder missing but a good part of his rib cage too. He was half lying, half sitting, chain smoking, with this dreadful mess exposed to a glaring sun. I dropped a wet handkerchief over it but he said, "It doesn't matter, I can't feel it anyway".'

At 1500 hrs the rescue work was complete. *Britomart* had turned right over and so *Pytchley* was ordered to sink her with gunfire along with *Hussar*. The rescue ships then returned to Arromanches, *Jason* stopping en route to bury her dead. At Arromanches the wounded were transferred to hospital ships and the other survivors to Army camps ashore before being sent back to Portsmouth. There they were thoroughly debriefed and sent on the usual fourteen days survivors' leave with a strict injunction not to say anything of their ordeal: it was an order most were only too happy to obey. Other attempts at damage limitation were more inventive. On board HMS *Gozo*, the commanding officer cleared lower deck and thanked the ship's company for their rescue work: 'I remember that he said, "Yes, the Typhoons and Spitfires were British, but these had been captured and flown by the Germans". Somehow that statement made us feel better and we all agreed that it was the bastard Germans and it just increased our hate for them.'

Admiral Sir Bertram Ramsay lost no time in ordering an enquiry. This found that the primary cause of the disaster was the failure of the staff on board HMS *Ambitious*, the minesweepers' headquarters ship, to inform the Flag Officer British Assault Area (FOBAA), Rear Admiral J.W. Rivett-Carnac, of the change made on the evening of 26 August to the following day's minesweeping programme. As a result FOBAA's staff were unaware that the 1st MSF would be in the area. A staff officer had simply forgotten to write '(R)FOBAA' [Repeated to FOBAA] on the signal amending 1st MSF's operational orders.

On the morning of 27 August, the ships of the 1st MSF were detected by a shore radar station and were identified as hostile since the orders for that day indicated no 'friendly' ships operating in that area. An RAF reconnaissance was ordered to confirm the identity of the ships and reported a force of minesweepers and trawlers which 'appeared to be friendly'. The RAF consulted FOBAA's staff who confirmed that no friendly ships were in the area. However, in view of the doubt raised by the pilot's identification of the ships as possibly friendly, FOBAA's staff attempted to contact HMS *Ambitious* to confirm that no minesweepers were in the area. A breakdown in telephone communications resulted in this enquiry not being received and FOBAA's staff did not press the matter or try alternative means of communication.

Accordingly a flight of eight Typhoons of 263 and 266 (Rhodesia) Squadrons RAF took off from landing strip B3 in France under the command of Wing Commander J. Baldwin DSO DFC AFC. Baldwin lacked nothing when it came to aggression but was unhappy at his orders to attack shipping provisionally identified as 'friendly'. Twice in the air he questioned his orders but when confronted with a definite order to proceed, he had no choice. The Enquiry found that 'staff work fell short of the highest standards in several respects' and made certain recommendations for disciplinary action. Three officers were court-martialled at Rouen for their role in the affair. FOBAA's Staff Officer Operations, Lieutenant-Commander Franks DSO OBE RN, and Captain Minesweepers Seine Bay, Captain the Lord Teynham DSC RN, were both acquitted, the latter having been away on the day in question. The Deputy to Captain Minesweepers Seine Bay, Commander D. Venables DSC RN, was also court-martialled, found guilty of negligence and severely reprimanded.

1 September 1944

Name	*Hurst Castle*	**Cause**	Submarine attack
Class	*Castle* class corvette	**Casualties**	None
CO	Lt H. Chesterman DSC RN	**Survivors**	105
Location	Atlantic, W of Ireland, 55 27'N, 08 12'W		

Notes   HMS *Hurst Castle* was torpedoed by *U482* (*Kapitanleutnant* Hartmut Graf von Matuschka) north of Troy Island off the coast of Donegal at 0825 hrs. The explosion wrecked *Hurst Castle's* stern and the frigate sank in 6 minutes. The 105 survivors were rescued by HMS *Ambuscade*.

27 September 1944

Name	*Rockingham*	**Location**	North Sea, SE of Aberdeen, 56 47'N, 01 30'W
Class	*Town* class destroyer		
Built	7 May 1919	**Cause**	Mine
CO	Lt Cdr J.C. Cooper RNVR	**Casualties**	None

Notes   HMS *Rockingham* had lost her front line role and was serving as an aircraft target ship when she was mined at 0446 hrs. She was taken in tow but subsequently sank at 2026 hrs in position 56 29'N, 00 57'W.

4 October 1944

Name	*Chebogue*	**Location**	Atlantic, WSW of Cape Clear, 49 20'N, 24 20'W
Class	Corvette (RCN)		
Built	16 August 1943	**Cause**	Submarine attack
		Casualties	7

Notes   HMCS *Chebogue* was torpedoed at 2204 hrs by *U1227* (*Oberleutnant zur See* Friedrich Altmeier). The explosion blew her stern off but she was taken in tow by HMCS *Chambly* which took her nearly 900 miles to Port Talbot in South Wales where she was paid off and not repaired.

8 October 1944

Name	*Mulgrave*	**Location**	English Channel, Seine Bay
Class	Minesweeper	**Cause**	Mine
Built	2 May 1942		

Notes   HMS *Mulgrave* was mined off Normandy. Initially her wreck was beached but she was later refloated and towed to Portsmouth. However, she was never repaired.

12 October 1944

Name	*Loyal*	**Location**	Tyrrhenian Sea
Class	*L* class destroyer	**Cause**	Mine
Built	8 October 1941		

Notes   HMS *Loyal* ran over an acoustic mine and suffered immense shock damage. Every item of machinery and armament on board was affected by the blast. She was paid off, never repaired and broken up in 1948.

14 October 1944

Name	*Magog*	**Location**	W Atlantic, mouth of the
Class	River class frigate (RCN)		St Lawrence River
Built	22 September 1943	**Cause**	Submarine attack
		Casualties	2

Notes   In a revival of the U-boat war on the US/Canadian east coast the frigate *Magog* was torpedoed by *U1223* (*Oberleutnant zur See* Albert Kneipe). Her stern was blown off but she was towed back to port. However, she was never repaired.

18 October 1944

Name	*Geelong*	**Location**	New Guinea, 06 04'S, 147 50'E
Class	Minesweeper (RAN)	**Cause**	Collision
CO	Lt M. Matthews RANR	**Casualties**	None
		Survivors	70

Notes   *Geelong* sank after colliding with the merchant ship SS *York*.

25 October 1944

Name	*Skeena*	**Location**	Iceland, port of Reykjavik
Class	*B* class destroyer	**Cause**	Grounded
Built	10 October 1930	**Casualties**	15
		Survivors	123

Notes   HMCS *Skeena* was anchored at Reykjavik when at 0200 hrs on the 25th she dragged her anchors in a gale and was driven ashore on Videy Island. The continuing bad weather meant that salvage could not be attempted and in December she was written off as a total loss.

1 November 1944

Name	*Whittaker*	**Location**	Atlantic, off Lough Swilly, 53 30'N,
Class	*Captain* class frigate		07 39'W
Built	1943	**Cause**	Submarine attack
		Casualties	92

Notes HMS *Whittaker* was torpedoed and sunk by *U483* (*Kapitanleutnant* Hans-Joachim von Morstein). The torpedo's explosion was quickly followed by another when the propellant for the twenty-four Hedgehog projectiles on their launcher forward of the bridge exploded. This explosion blew off the bows and wrecked the bridge structure. *Whittaker* was towed into Belfast and laid up. She was not repaired.

10 November 1944

Name	*Hydra*	**Location**	English Channel, off Ostend
Class	*Algerine* class minesweeper	**Cause**	Mine
Built	1942		

Notes HMS *Hydra* was mined off Ostend and was abandoned because it was thought likely that she would sink. However she remained afloat, so she was reboarded and towed back to Sheerness. She was never repaired and was subsequently broken up.

22 November 1944

Name	*Stratagem*	**Location**	Malacca Strait
Class	*S* class submarine	**Cause**	Depth-charge
Built	21 June 1943	**Casualties**	41
CO	Lt C.R. Pelly RN	**Survivors**	8

Notes On 18 November *Stratagem* had attacked a Japanese convoy and sunk the tanker *Nichinan Maru*. Although she cleared the area, on 22 November, while 3 miles south-west of Malacca, she was sighted by an aircraft and was then attacked by a destroyer. Undoubtedly the aircraft had spotted the submarine in the clear blue water and called reinforcements. Alternatively, the aircraft may have been one of the few Japanese aircraft fitted with Magnetic Anomaly Detectors. Just after 1210 hrs the destroyer delivered two depth-charge attacks which wrecked the submarine's lighting and damaged the pressure hull – water was heard pouring into the boat. Pelly ordered the main ballast blown but to no effect.

Lieutenant C.R. Douglas, the torpedo officer, and thirteen ratings managed to survive in the fore ends but all other compartments were flooded. Since it was impossible to isolate the fore ends owing to the flood of water coming through the door, Leading Seaman Gibbs began to remove the clips from the escape hatch with Lieutenant Douglas's help to carry out an *ad hoc* escape. As the last clip came off the hatch was blown open, by the extreme pressure in the compartment and Gibbs was blown out of the boat. The hatch then clanged shut, striking Douglas on the head; no sooner had it done so than the pressure blew it open again and Douglas shot out of the boat. Ten of the fourteen men in the compartment managed to escape from *Stratagem*, although only eight survived the ascent to the surface. The men were picked up by the destroyer and began a nine-month ordeal in Japanese captivity. Only Lieutenant Douglas, Leading Seaman Gibbs and Able Seaman Robinson survived – the other five died in Japanese captivity.

24 November 1944

Name	*Shawinigan*	**Cause**	Submarine attack
Class	Corvette (RCN)	**Casualties**	51
Location	E coast of Canada, 47 34'N, 59 11'W	**Survivors**	None

Notes   HMCS *Shawinigan* was attacked in the Cabot Strait off Cape Breton by *U1228* (*Oberleutnant zur See* Friedrich-Wilhelm Marienfeld) at 0115 hrs with a homing torpedo. The little corvette blew up and sank with the loss of all hands.

30 November 1944

Name	*Duff*	**Location**	Mine
Class	*Captain* class frigate	**Cause**	English Channel, N of Ostend
Built	1942	**Casualties**	3

Notes   *Duff* was mined north of Ostend. She managed to return under her own power to Harwich but was laid up and never repaired.

6 December 1944

Name	*Bullen*	**Location**	N of Scotland, 58 42'N, 04 12'W
Class	*Captain* class frigate	**Cause**	Submarine attack
Built	1943	**Casualties**	71
CO	Lt Cdr A.H. Parish RN	**Survivors**	97

Notes   HMS *Bullen* was torpedoed at 0950 hrs by *U775* (*Oberleutnant zur See* Erich Taschenmacher) 7 miles north-east of Cape Wrath. The torpedo hit amidships and the frigate broke in half. The bow portion sank almost immediately, but the stern portion remained afloat for two more hours. The survivors were rescued by HMS *Hesperus*.

14 December 1944

Name	*Aldenham*	**Location**	Adriatic, SE of Pola, 44 30'N,
Class	*Hunt* class destroyer		14 50'E
Built	27 August 1941	**Cause**	Mine
CO	Cdr J.G. Farrant RN	**Survivors**	63

Notes   HMS *Aldenham* was mined at 1530 hrs while 45 miles south-east of the port of Pola (now Pula). The survivors were rescued by HMS *Atherstone*.

24 December 1944

Name	*Clayoquot*	**Location**	E coast of Canada, 44 30'N, 63 20'W
Class	Minesweeper	**Cause**	Submarine attack
Built	1943	**Survivors**	64

Notes   HMCS *Clayoquot* was torpedoed by *U806* (*Kapitanleutnant* Klaus Hornbostel) using a T5. A second T5 fired by *U806* detonated in the CAT gear of the corvette *Transcona*, but she survived the attack.

25 December 1944

Name	*Dakins*	**Location**	English Channel, 51 25'N, 02 44'E
Class	*Captain* class frigate	**Cause**	Mine
Built	1943		

Notes   HMS *Dakins* ran over a ground mine at 2110 hrs while 14 miles north-west of Ostend. The ship took on a lot of water in her forward compartment but good damage control enabled her to return to the UK under her own power – although stern first. However, she was not considered worth repairing.

26 December 1944

Name	*Capel*	**Location**	English Channel, 49 48'N, 01 43'W
Class	*Captain* class frigate	**Cause**	Submarine attack
Built	1943	**Casualties**	77
CO	Lt B.G. Heslop DSC RN		

Notes   HMS *Capel* was torpedoed by *U486* (*Oberleutnant der Reserve* Gerhard Meyer) off Cap de la Hague at 1237 hrs. The explosion blew the bridge structure aft until it rested on the funnel. *Capel* sank very slowly and finally capsized at 1602 hrs.

Name	*Affleck*	**Location**	English Channel, 49 48'N, 01 41'W
Class	*Captain* class frigate	**Cause**	Submarine attack
Built	1943		

Notes   While searching for HMS *Capel*'s assailant HMS *Affleck* was also torpedoed by *U486* (*Oberleutnant der Reserve* Gerhard Meyer) using a T5 homing torpedo. The explosion blew off 60 ft of *Affleck*'s stern but she reached Cherbourg under her own power. She was later towed to Portsmouth but never repaired.

LOSSES JANUARY–JULY 1945

January 1945   *As the war in Europe drew to a close a feature of British losses is the number of ships damaged by mine or torpedo that a year ago would have been repaired but were now being laid up unrepaired.*

6 January 1945

Name	*Walpole*	**Location**	North Sea, off Flushing, 52 33'N, 03 06'E
Class	*V&W* class destroyer		
Built	12 February 1918	**Cause**	Mine
		Casualties	2

Notes   HMS *Walpole* struck a mine while escorting a cross-Channel convoy. The explosion caused flooding of her machinery spaces and she was towed back to Sheerness. She was written off as a constructive total loss.

9(?) January 1945

Name	*Porpoise*	**CO**	Lt Cdr H.B. Turner DSC RN
Class	*Porpoise* class submarine	**Survivors**	None
Built	30 August 1942		

Notes   *Porpoise* had sailed from Trincomalee on 2 January to lay two minefields west of the southern end of Penang Island. The mines were to be laid on or around 9 January. However, the submarine failed to report the completion of the operation and on 19 January was declared lost. Postwar clearance operations failed to find the fields she should have laid, so it assumed that she was sunk sometime between 2 and 9 January. There are several possible explanations for her loss. A Japanese air attack by a MAD-fitted aircraft is said to have led to anti-submarine craft coming out from Penang to find and sink her but no evidence can be found in existing Japanese documents to support this. Alternative theories are that she was mined or sunk by accident. *Porpoise* was the fifth of her class of six minelaying submarines to be sunk in the war (*Narwhal*, *Seal*, *Grampus* and *Cachalot* were the others).

12 January 1945

Name	*Regulus*	**Location**	Mediterranean, off Sista Island, near Corfu
Class	Minesweeper		
		Cause	Mine

Notes   *Regulus* was engaged in the seemingly never-ending task of clearing the Mediterranean of mines – both Allied and Axis – when she struck a mine south of Corfu at 1350 hrs. At first the damage seemed slight – her propellers were off – and she was taken in tow. However, damage control could not stop the ship taking on water and she capsized at 1438 hrs.

15 January 1945

Name	*Thane*	**Location**	W coast of Scotland, Firth of Clyde,
Class	*Ruler* class escort carrier		55 10'N, 05 30'W
Built	15 July 1943	**Cause**	Submarine attack
		Casualties	10

Notes   HMS *Thane* was lying peacefully at anchor when she was torpedoed by *U482* (*Kapitanleutnant* Hartmut Graf von Matuschka). *U482* had been operating in the area for some time with seeming immunity from anti-submarine measures. However, while withdrawing from the area the next day she was sunk by *EG.22*. *Thane* was surveyed and considered not worth repairing. She was laid up in the Gareloch and never repaired.

26 January 1945

Name	*Manners*	**Location**	Irish Sea, 21 miles W of Anglesey
Class	Frigate	**Cause**	Submarine attack
Built	1943	**Casualties**	36

Notes   At 0945 hrs HMS *Manners* was attacked by *U1172* with a T5 homing torpedo. Her stern was blown off but she was towed to Barrow. Like *Thane* and *Walpole* she was laid up unrepaired.

February 1945   *One area where the U-boats could still operate with considerable success was the Arctic, where the water was deep and Asdic conditions poor. The geography of the area also gave them a natural 'choke point' as convoys entered and left Kola Inlet which led to the port of Murmansk. February saw three RN escorts sunk or damaged beyond repair in this theatre.*

11 February 1945

Name	*Pathfinder*	**Location**	Coast of Burma, Pakseik
Class	*P* class destroyer		Taungmauw, S of Akyab
Built	10 April 1941	**Cause**	Air attack

Notes   HMS *Pathfinder* was supporting army operations in the area when she was attacked by JAAF aircraft. At the time Pathfinder was in shallow water and as a result, although she was not hit by any bombs, several near misses inflicted considerable shock damage (almost as if she had been mined). *Pathfinder* was immobilised and towed to Chittagong. There she was surveyed and not repaired.

12 February 1945

Name	*Delhi*	**Location**	Adriatic, port of Spalato (now Split)
Class	*D* class cruiser	**Cause**	Explosive motor boat
Built	23 August 1918		

Notes   HMS *Delhi* was lying at anchor at Spalato when she was attacked by German *Linssen* EMBs, similar to the Italian craft that had damaged HMS *York* (see p. 140) in 1941. The EMBs were carried to the entrance of the harbour by former Italian *MS*-type torpedo boats now under German control. At the time of the attack *Delhi* was moored with her starboard side to the Molo S. Doimo. Inboard of her was the Yugoslav merchant ship *Balcik* and secured to her starboard side was *LCF.8*. To reach the cruiser the EMBs had to break through the harbour entrance, then make a sweeping turn to starboard so that they were aiming at *Delhi*'s port quarter.

The EMBs attacked just after 0530 hrs on 12 February. At least four EMBs were used in the attack: one turned back; a second was hit by gunfire, ran out of control and exploded against the breakwater; a third entered the harbour but was destroyed by *LCF.8*'s or *Delhi*'s gunfire just as she was beginning to make the big turn to starboard; and the fourth did the damage. The boat struck the cruiser right aft, damaging the rudder and rudder head, as well as inflicting much other damage.

Delhi was not repaired and was left *in situ* until 1948 when she was sold for breaking up. She remains one of only two British warships to have been 'sunk' by this weapon.

13 February 1945

Name	*Denbigh Castle*	**Location**	Arctic, entrance to the Kola Inlet,
Class	*Castle* class frigate		69 20'N, 33 33'E
Built	1943	**Cause**	Submarine attack
CO	Lr G. Butcher DSC RNR		

Notes   HMS *Denbigh Castle* was escorting the last merchant ship of convoy JW.64 into the Kola Inlet when just after midnight, in appalling weather, she was torpedoed by *U992* (*Oberleutnant zur See* Hans Falke). She was taken in tow by HMS *Bluebell* but the torpedo had struck right forward and as she was under tow the bow submerged. Just after 0700 hrs she was beached but later capsized and slid off into deeper water.

17 February 1945

Name	*Lark*	**CO**	Cdr H. Lambton RN
Class	Sloop	**Location**	Arctic, Kola Inlet, 69 30'N, 34 33'E
Built	28 August 1943	**Cause**	Submarine attack

Notes   HMS *Lark* was minesweeping ahead of convoy RA.64, which had just cleared the Kola Inlet, when she was attacked by *U968* (*Oberleutnant* Otto Westphalen) with a T5. Her stern was blown off but she was towed back to the Kola Inlet. There she was surveyed but found to be so badly damaged that it was not worth organising local repairs and then towing her back to the UK. She was stripped of anything useful and then in a 'goodwill gesture' was transferred to the USSR, the date of transfer being 13 June 1945. Her ultimate fate is uncertain: some sources say that she was never repaired, others that she was recommissioned into the Soviet Navy.

Name	*Bluebell*	**Location**	Arctic, 8 miles NE of the Kola Inlet,
Class	*Flower* class corvette		69 36'N, 25 29'E
CO	Lt G.H. Walker DSC RN	**Cause**	Submarine attack
		Survivors	1(2?)

Notes   HMS *Bluebell* was the second of RA.64's escorts to be torpedoed. At 1523 hrs she was attacked by *U711* (*Kapitanleutnant* Hans-Gunther Lange) with a T5 which hit the little corvette aft. Immediately there was a second massive explosion as *Bluebell*'s depth-charges exploded. When the smoke cleared *Bluebell* had disappeared. From torpedo strike to sinking had taken less than 30 seconds.

20 February 1945

Name	Vervain	**Location**	Irish Sea, 20 miles S of Waterford, 51 47'N, 07 06'W
Class	Flower class corvette	**Cause**	Submarine attack

Notes HMS *Vervain*'s bows were blown off by a torpedo fired by *U1208* (*Korvettenkapitan* Georg Hagene) at 1155 hrs. Twenty-one minutes after the attack *Vervain* sank.

22 February 1945

Name	Trentonian	**Cause**	Submarine attack
Class	Flower class corvette	**Casualties**	6
Location	English Channel, E of Falmouth, 50 06'N, 04 50'W		

Notes HMCS *Trentonian* was attacked by *U1004* (*Oberleutnant zur See* Rudolf Hinz) at 1230 hrs. She was damaged aft but the flooding spread forward and the ship sank 10 minutes later.

6 March 1945

Name	XE.11	**Location**	Loch Striven
Class	XE-Craft	**Cause**	Collision
Built	1944	**Casualties**	3
CO	Lt A. Staples SANF (V)	**Survivors**	2

Notes The *XE*-Craft were a variant of the *X*-Craft design intended for operations in the Far East. On 6 March *XE.11* was proceeding dived while calibrating instruments. She drifted out of the declared exercise area and towards a BDV that was laying nets. Unaware of the presence of the vessel, *XE.11* collided with it. The impact made two holes in her pressure hull and she sank to the bottom of the loch. All five men tried to escape using DSEA sets. Sub Lieutenant Jim Morrison RNVR and ERA Swatton survived but Staples and two ratings were killed.

It was the custom to give *XE*-Craft 'unofficial' names, usually beginning with an *X*. Staples had challenged this tradition by naming his *Lucifer*. In doing so, he had offended against an even older tradition that no ship should ever be named after the Devil.

17 March 1945

Name	Guysborough	**Cause**	Submarine attack
Class	Minesweeper	**Casualties**	54
Location	Atlantic, Bay of Biscay, 46 43'N, 09 20'W		

Notes HMCS *Guysborough* was attacked and sunk by *U878* (*Kapitanleutnant* Hans Rodig) at 1835 hrs. She sank just after 2000 hrs.

20 March 1945

Name	*Lapwing*	**Location**	Arctic, 6 miles off Kola Inlet,
Class	Sloop		69 26'N, 33 44'E
Built	16 July 1943	**Cause**	Submarine attack
CO	Acting Cdr E.C. Hutton RN		

Notes   HMS *Lapwing* was escorting convoy JW.65 on its approach to the Kola Inlet when she was attacked by *U968* (*Oberleutnant* Otto Westphalen) with a T5. The sloop broke in half and she sank 20 minutes later.

26 March 1945

Name	*Puffin*	**Cause**	Midget submarine
Class	Corvette	**Casualties**	None
Location	North Sea, off the Schelde		

Notes   The loss of HMS *Puffin* is quite unique. On the night of 25 March *Puffin* was patrolling off the Dutch coast with *MTBs.764* and *758*. The sea was flat calm and visibility was about 1.5 miles. At 0326 hrs a radar contact was reported which was at first assessed as a DAN buoy. However, a short time later the DAN buoy started to move! It was illuminated with a searchlight and was seen to be a midget submarine. It was now only a cable from *Puffin's* starboard bow and under the depression of *Puffin's* 4 in gun. Accordingly the corvette turned to ram the submarine aft of the conning tower. Just after the corvette hit the submarine there was massive explosion as the U-boat's two G7e torpedoes detonated. *Puffin* was lifted bodily into the air and then fell steeply into a trough with water and burning petrol (indicating that the craft was a *Biber*) cascading down on to the bridge until it was nearly 3 ft deep. With the water and fuel oil came wreckage including gauges, a chair, fragments of a chart and the remains of the submarine's operator. *Puffin* returned to port under her own power but was paid off and not repaired.

29 March 1945

Name	*Teme*	**Location**	English Channel, 6 miles N of Lands
Class	Frigate		End, 50 07'N, 05 45'W
Built	11 November 1943	**Cause**	Submarine attack
		Casualties	4

Notes   HMCS *Teme* was torpedoed by *U246* (*Kapitanleutnant* Ernst Raabe) with a T5. *Teme* lost her stern. She was towed to Falmouth, but laid up and not repaired.

April 1945   *In the Pacific the US Navy was engaged in a massive struggle off Okinawa. In the waters around the UK, however, events were rather more quiet.*

16 April 1945

Name	*Esquimalt*	**Cause**	Submarine attack
Class	Minesweeper	**Casualties**	44
Location	W Atlantic, off Halifax Nova Scotia,		
	44 28'N, 63 10'W		

Notes   HMCS *Esquimalt* was attacked and sunk by *U190* (*Oberleutnant* Hans-Edwin Reith).

Name	Ekins	Location	English Channel, 24 miles NW of
Class	Frigate		Ostend
Built	1943	Cause	Mine

Notes   HMS *Ekins* struck a mine at 2125 hrs. The explosion flooded her boiler room and she lay dead in the water. She then drifted on to a second mine at 2140 hrs which caused further flooding. However, her ship's company got her going again and she returned to the Medway under her own power. After survey she was paid off and not repaired.

27 April 1945

Name	Redmill	Location	Irish Sea, 25 miles NW of Blacksod
Class	Frigate		Bay, 54 23'N, 10 36'W
Built	1943	Cause	Submarine attack
		Casualties	22

Notes   HMS *Redmill* was attacked by *U1105* (*Oberleutnant zur See* Hans Joachim Schwarz). She lost her stern and propellers but was towed to Londonderry. The ship was then paid off and not repaired.

29 April 1945

Name	Goodall	Location	Arctic, entrance to the Kola Inlet, 69
Class	Frigate		25'N, 33 38'E
Built	1943	Cause	Submarine attack
CO	Lt Cdr J.V. Fulton RNVR		

Notes   HMS *Goodall* was the last British warship to be sunk by submarine attack. The frigate was engaged in an anti-U-boat sweep to clear the waters off the Kola Inlet of submarines before the departure of convoy RA.66. After the torpedo hit, *Goodall*'s magazine exploded and blew away the forward part of the ship. She was beyond salvage so was abandoned and scuttled.

May 1945   *Germany's surrender came into effect at 2301 hrs on 8 May 1945. The war in Europe was over. Even so the menace posed by extensive minefields continued to inflict a number of losses.*

9 May 1945

Name	Prompt	Location	English Channel, 12 miles NW of
Class	Minesweeper		Ostend
		Cause	Mine

Notes   HMS *Prompt* was mined at 1705 hrs – 18 hours after peace had been declared! She was towed to Southend but not repaired.

July 1945 *saw the last British naval losses in the Second World War. Against the high drama of events taking place in the seas around Japan, the sinking of two minesweepers off the west coast of Thailand went almost unnoticed.*

24 July 1945

Name	*Squirrel*	**Cause**	Mine
Class	Minesweeper	**Casualties**	7
Location	Gulf of Thailand, off Phuket Island		

Notes   *Squirrel* was engaged in preparatory clearing operations for Operation Zipper, the forthcoming landings in Malaya, when she was mined. Efforts to save the ship failed and she was scuttled by gunfire.

26 July 1945

Name	*Vestal*	**Cause**	Air attack
Class	Minesweeper	**Casualties**	20
Location	Gulf of Thailand, off Phuket Island, 07 05'N, 97 50'E		

Notes   HMS *Vestal* is the only RN warship to be *sunk* following severe damage by a JAAF Japanese *Kamikaze* aircraft. After the attack she was scuttled by the destroyer *Racehorse*.

LOSSES
OCTOBER 1945–TO DATE

October 1945 *The war was barely over when a British destroyer was sunk by a mine in a classic 'freedom of the seas' operation that went badly wrong.*

22 October 1945

Name	*Saumarez*	**Location**	Mediterranean, Corfu Straits
Class	S class destroyer	**Cause**	Mine
Built	20 November 1942	**Casualties**	31

Notes The Albanian government had claimed the waters between the mainland and the island of Corfu and, to emphasise the point, had mined them with Yugoslav assistance. A force of British destroyers had been ordered to pass through the Straits in order to test their right of free passage. In what is now known as the Corfu Channel incident *Saumarez* and *Volage* both struck mines during the transit. Both destroyers returned to Malta but the damage to *Saumarez* was such that she was never repaired. Britain was subsequently awarded damages in the International Court – which have never been paid.

12 January 1950

Name	*Truculent*	**Cause**	Rammed
Class	T class submarine	**Casualties**	46 ship's company, 18 dockyard
Built	12 September 1942		workers
CO	Lt O.P. Bowers RN	**Survivors**	15
Location	Thames estuary		

Notes On the night of 12 January HMS *Truculent* was proceeding up the River Thames to Sheerness following post-refit trials at sea. The OOW observed the lights of what he thought was a stationary vessel on the north side of the channel. In fact it was the Swedish tanker *Divina* proceeding downstream and wearing an additional red light at the masthead to indicate that she was carrying a dangerous cargo. Bowers ordered a turn to port to clear the 'stationary' vessel but this manoeuvre took *Truculent* directly across *Divina*'s bows: the tanker ploughed into the submarine, striking her on the starboard side just forward of the conning tower.

Bowers and four other men on the bridge were thrown clear by the collision but it was nearly an hour before they were picked up by the Dutch vessel, *Almdyk*. Inside the submarine ten men drowned immediately following the collision. The remaining sixty-four went aft to the engine room under the command of First Lieutenant, F.J. Hindes RN. Hindes was familiar with the findings of the recent Ruck-Keene Committee report on submarine escape (most of these findings had been accepted but then dropped on the grounds of economy) and knew that there were too many men in the compartment for a successful escape to take place. The CO_2 level would rise to above danger level before the last men had got out. The story of the loss of the *Untamed* (see p. 214) undoubtedly influenced Hindes in his decision to get out of the submarine quickly. Accordingly Hindes took some men with him

The remains of HM Submarine *Truculent* are raised from the Thames following her loss in January 1950. (Author)

into the after ends while the remainder stayed in the engine room under the command of CERA Sam Hine. The noise of propellers was clearly audible in the submarine. Hindes and Hine took this as a sign that rescue craft were on the surface and both men then supervised flawless escapes from their part of the submarine.

The real tragedy of *Truculent* was that when they reached the surface they found that they were entirely alone. The engine noises they had heard were those of normal river traffic. Of the sixty-four men who successfully escaped from the submarine all but ten were carried out to sea and certain death by the ebb tide. Among those who did not survive were Lieutenant Hindes and CERA Hine, both of whom were posthumously awarded the Albert Medal. Four years earlier the Ruck-Keene Committee had recommended that submariners be provided with immersion suits for precisely this eventuality. Fifty-four men died through drowning or exposure because of lack of suitable clothing that had been recommended four years earlier. Such was the price of 'austerity'.

16(?) April 1951

Name	*Affray*	**Casualties**	75, including 4 RM Commandos and
Class	*A* class submarine		20 officers under training and their
Built	12 April 1945		instructors
CO	Lt J. Blackburn RN	**Survivors**	None
Location	English Channel, NW of Alderney,		
	49 49'W, 02 34'W		

Lessons learned from the loss of *Truculent*. A sailor wears a specially designed immersion suit intended to protect submariners from hypothermia while on the surface following an escape. Such a suit would have saved the lives of a good many of those who escaped from *Truculent*. (Author)

Notes   HMS *Affray* sailed for Portsmouth on 16 April to participate in exercise Training Spring – a free-ranging exercise in which *Affray* was to simulate the conditions of a war patrol as much as possible. The only binding restriction was that, for safety reasons, she was to report her position between 0900 hrs and 1000 hrs daily. As an additional precaution she was to report her position to 19 Group RAF by 0900 hrs every day. By 1000 hrs on 17 April *Affray* had failed to make either report so the submarine rescue organisation was activated. Nothing was found and on the evening of the 19th the Admiralty admitted that there could be no hope of saving life from *Affray*. The operation now became one of location and salvage rather than rescue.

After a prodigious hunt *Affray* was found lying upright in 278 ft of water on 14 June. Divers and underwater photography using a TV camera found no evidence of collision damage and confirmed that all hatches were closed. However, they did find that the snort induction mast had broken off and was lying down by *Affray*'s side. This seemed to indicate the cause of her loss. Although the snort mast was found to have broken off there was no sign of any impact or collision damage which might have caused this to happen. Although poor welding was later found on the snort mast, this in itself would not have caused the mast to break. If the snort mast had broken then the induction valve, designed to close if ever the head of the mast dipped below the surface, should have closed automatically. If the induction valve had failed then the submarine would have flooded very quickly and sunk stern first. Yet *Affray*'s stern was undamaged. An alternative explanation was that her loss was due to a battery explosion which split the external battery ventilation trunking, allowing water to flood into the battery.

It was therefore imperative to establish whether this valve was open or not. This was to be done using radioactive isotope photography. The task proved harder than expected and great chunks of *Affray*'s casing had to be ripped away using a grab before the valve could be exposed. Then on 23 October a diver accidentally dropped one of the radioactive isotopes, which rolled under the hull. Diving operations were first suspended while safety advice was sought and then cancelled altogether on safety grounds. The file on HMS *Affray* remains open.

Among the seventy-five men killed in *Affray* was Sub Lieutenant John Linton, the son of Commander J.W. 'Tubby' Linton of HMS *Turbulent* (see p. 209) and sub Lieutenant Anthony Frew who had survived the sinking of *Truculent* (see p. 255).

16 June 1955

Name	*Sidon*	**Cause**	Accident
Class	*S* class submarine	**Casualties**	13
Built	4 September 1944	**Survivors**	No figures are available as to how
CO	Lt H.T. Verry RN		many men were on board at the time
Location	English Channel, Portland harbour		of the accident.

Notes HMS *Sidon* was alongside the depot ship *Maidstone* in Portland harbour when at 0825 hrs she was shaken by a considerable explosion. The hydrogen peroxide propellant in one of her torpedoes had leaked inside the confined space of the torpedo tube. The result was a build-up of heat and pressure which resulted in an explosion. A sheet of flame shot out of *Sidon*'s conning tower, followed by a shower of debris. Both the bow and rear doors of the tube were blown off and the sea poured into the submarine. The submarine flooded and sank alongside *Maidstone* at 0845 hrs. Great gallantry was shown by members of her crew in rescuing men overcome by smoke from the interior of the submarine. In particular Surgeon Sub Lieutenant C.E. Rhodes RNVR, a national serviceman and non-submariner, ran from HMS *Maidstone* and made four trips into *Sidon*'s smoke-filled interior. On each occasion he returned with an unconscious man. He went back a fifth time but on this occasion he did not return — he was last seen lying unconscious at the foot of the conning tower ladder. Rhodes was posthumously awarded the Albert Medal for his heroic endeavours.

1 July 1971

Name	*Artemis*	**Cause**	Accident
Class	*A* class submarine	**Casualties**	None
Built	26 August 1946	**Survivors**	9 men together with 3 SCC cadets
CO	Lt Cdr R. Godfrey RN		who were on board at the time of the
Location	English Channel, Portsmouth harbour,		accident
	alongside the jetty at HMS *Dolphin*		

Notes On 1 July 1971 *Artemis* returned to HMS *Dolphin*, the submarine base in Portsmouth harbour, following a maintenance period in the floating dock. That evening the submarine prepared to 'first fill' the after fuel tanks

HMS *Sidon* after being raised from the bottom of Portland harbour, June 1955. (US National Archives)

with water prior to fuelling the next day. Unfortunately, because of a series of misunderstandings and failures of communications, the submarine was much heavier in the water than her officers realised. At the same time, a series of separate and unrelated events had resulted in six out the seven hatches on the casing being left open.

As the submarine took on water her stern dipped until water began to pour down the after escape hatch – the hatch nearest the stern. The lid for this hatch was down but had not been clipped 'shut', thus leaving a small gap through which water poured for some 20 minutes. The stern dipped further, covering the after escape hatch until water began to pour down the open after torpedo loading hatch, the next hatch forward along the casing, and *Artemis* began to sink (**see** photograph overleaf). Six of the nine men on board at the time, together with three Sea Cadets visiting the boat, got out just before she sank. Petty Officer David Guest, MEM Donald Beckett and LMEM Robert Croxen were trapped in the fore ends. They flooded up the compartment to make an escape but because of the shallow depth of water in which *Artemis* was lying, it was over 10 hours before they reached the surface.

The subsequent enquiry pulled no punches. *Artemis* had been lost because, 'too many people had forgotten the basic principle of submarine safety–ship stability'. The loss of *Artemis* had uncanny echoes of the loss of *H.29* in 1926 (see p. 90). Six days after the sinking *Artemis* was raised from the bottom and subsequently sold for scrap. For many years her rusting remains could be seen from the M27 motorway lying at Pounds' Portsmouth scrap yard.

The scene on the jetty at HMS *Dolphin* after *Artemis* sank on 1 July 1971. The top of her conning tower can be seen resting on the port saddle tanks of HMS *Ocelot*. On *Ocelot*'s starboard bow is the tug *Setter* which is keeping *Ocelot* in position so that *Artemis* does not roll over completely. (Author)

20 September 1976

Name	*Fittleton*	**Cause**	Collision
Class	*Ton* class minesweeper	**Casualties**	12
Built	3 February 1954	**Survivors**	17
Location	North Sea		

Notes   HMS *Fittleton*, a minesweeper seconded to the Royal Navy Reserve, capsized and sank following a collision with the frigate HMS *Mermaid* during exercise Teamwork '76.

May 1982   On 1 April 1982 the Argentine government sought to resolve the long-running dispute with Britain over the possession of the Falkland Islands by military action. After years of dithering about the future of the islands, the British response was surprisingly robust. A naval task force was despatched to the South

Atlantic with the clear aim of recovering the islands and returning their inhabitants to British rule. Once again the Royal Navy was committed to supporting the army's land operations in a theatre of operations where the enemy's air force was superior in every field except skill and courage.

4 May 1982

Name	*Sheffield*	**Location**	South Atlantic, S of E Falkland
Class	Type 42 destroyer	**Cause**	Air attack – missile
Built	10 June 1971	**Casualties**	20
CO	Capt J. Salt RN	**Survivors**	266

Notes   *Sheffield* was one of three Type 42 destroyers deployed to the east of Port Stanley in a radar picket line. The ships had been detected by an Argentine Navy Neptune reconnaissance aircraft and two Super Etendard aircraft, flown by *Capitan di Corbeta* A. Bedacarratz and *Teniente di Navio* A. Mayora and armed with Exocet missiles, had taken off from Rio Gallegos with orders to find and attack them.

The Etendards flew at very low level and only 'popped up' to allow their Agave radar to acquire the targets and then fire the missiles when about 12 miles from the ships. They made no attempt to verify their targets – the two pilots simply fired at the first contacts they encountered. At that range the missiles had a flight time of one minute. On board *Sheffield* there was barely enough time to issue a warning and no time to fire chaff. The missile hit the ship on her starboard side just aft of the bridge. The 370 lb warhead itself did not explode but the kinetic energy released by the impact and deceleration ignited the missile's unused fuel and started a massive fire. Fire fighting was hampered by the fire main having been broken (for economy reasons the Type 42s were built with only one fire main). The ship's company fought heroically to save *Sheffield*. PO D.R. Briggs was posthumously awarded the DSM for repeatedly returning to the smoke-filled forward damage control store to collect urgently required equipment. Eventually he was overcome by the flames. POMA G. Meager (later awarded the QGM) went into the compartment and recovered Briggs' body but could not resuscitate him. The computer room teams remained at their posts and were all overcome by smoke. Eventually the fires proved impossible to control and when they threatened to spread to the Sea Dart magazine, Captain Salt ordered the ship to be abandoned: 225 of his crew were taken off by HMS *Arrow*, 6 went to HMS *Yarmouth*, and 35 were evacuated by helicopter.

Sheffield remained afloat although the fires continued to burn: at night she was observed to be glowing red. For a while *Sheffield* acted as a bait to tempt any Argentine submarine into revealing herself by attacking the derelict but no such attack was forthcoming. Eventually she was taken in tow by *Yarmouth* and headed for South Georgia. However, on 10 May the weather worsened and *Yarmouth*'s towing party were removed for safety reasons. *Sheffield*'s list to starboard increased as water poured in through the hole in her side made by the missile and at 0702 hrs she capsized.

Captain Salt was the son of Lieutenant Commander Salt, killed in *Triton* in 1940 (see p. 135).

21 May 1982

Name	*Ardent*	**Cause**	Air attack
Class	Type 21 frigate	**Casualties**	22
CO	Cdr Alan West RN	**Survivors**	179
Location	Falkland Islands, San Carlos Water		

Notes *Ardent* was proceeding up Falkland Sound on her way back to San Carlos after carrying out a bombardment of the airstrip at Goose Green. While in the exposed waters of the Sound at 1344 hrs she was caught by four A-4Q aircraft of the Argentine Navy. The aircraft attacked from astern, rendering *Ardent*'s bow-mounted 4.5 in gun useless. Of the nine 500 lb bombs dropped three hit the ship, two exploding in the hangar and one ending up in the Auxiliary Machinery Room (where it did not explode). Fires were started but *Ardent* continued to head for San Carlos and the protection of the ships anchored there. Just after 1400 hrs she was attacked by another three A-4Qs and all three aircraft scored hits with their 500 lb bombs. The after end of the little frigate was now a shambles and, after receiving advice from his heads of department that the frigate could not be saved, West ordered that she be abandoned. The survivors crossed from *Ardent*'s bow to *Yarmouth*'s flight deck, with Commander West being the last to leave the ship at 1455 hrs.

23 May 1982

Name	*Antelope*	**Location**	Falkland Islands, San Carlos
Class	Type 21 frigate		Water
Built	16 March 1972	**Cause**	Air attack
CO	Cdr Nicholas Tobin RN		

Notes *Antelope* was lightly damaged in an attack by four A-4s: two bombs hit the ship but remained unexploded in the POs mess and the air conditioning unit. The ship could still steam and fight. However, the bombs had to be made safe and to that end *Antelope* was boarded by army bomb disposal experts. The bomb in the air conditioning unit was tackled first. While the ship's company waited on the forecastle the disposal men sought to disable the bomb with a controlled explosion. Instead the bomb exploded, killing one of the disposal team and starting fires which spread across the width of the ship and between three decks. She was abandoned at 1820 hrs. Within 10 minutes of the last man leaving the ship the ready-use Seacat SAM magazine exploded, followed shortly afterwards by the main Seacat and torpedo magazines. The image of *Antelope* silhouetted against the explosions on board was captured by press photographer Martin Cleaver and remains one of the most indelible images of the war. *Antelope* burned throughout the night and, following another explosion probably caused by the second 1,000 lb bomb, she broke her back and sank.

25 May 1982

Name	*Coventry*	**Location**	South Atlantic, N of Pebble Island
Class	Type 42 destroyer	**Cause**	Air attack
Built	21 June 1974	**Casualties**	19
CO	Capt J. Hart-Dyke RN	**Survivors**	253

Notes Argentina's National Day was 25 May and an all-out effort was expected by the Argentines. *Coventry* was operating in the highly exposed 'missile trap' north of Pebble Island, together with the frigate *Broadsword*. *Coventry*'s Sea Dart SAM could take care of the air threat at high and medium level while *Broadsword*'s Seawolf SAM was more than capable of dealing with the low level and missile threat. *Coventry* had been highly successful in the AA war and intercepted Argentine radio messages indicates that they 'wanted to get that Type 42'.

A strike of four A-4Bs of the V Air Brigade was detected by *Coventry* but their easterly heading seemed to indicate that they were heading for San Carlos. However, the aircraft suddenly changed course and began to head inland over West Falkland. The Combat air patrol from 800 NAS went after the four A-4s but was called off as the Argentine aircraft entered *Coventry*'s Sea Dart missile 'envelope'. At this critical moment *Coventry*'s Sea Dart failed – possibly because the missile loading doors on the launcher were jammed shut with sea salt – and *Broadsword*'s Seawolf radar could not acquire the targets. The two ships were left with nothing more than small arms with which to defend themselves. Of the four 1,000 lb bombs from the first pair of A-4s, three missed while the fourth hit the water and bounced up through *Broadsword*'s flight deck, wrecking the Lynx helicopter, but failed to explode. No sooner had the first pair of A-4s attacked than the second pair bored in. This time *Broadsword*'s Seawolf system was tracking the aircraft perfectly but at the critical moment *Broadsword*'s range was fouled by *Coventry* and the system was 'blinded'. Three of the four 1,000 lb bombs dropped hit the destroyer and opened up her port side. She began to heel over at once and within 15 minutes was lying on her beam ends before sinking.

Royal Navy divers subsequently visited the wreck to recover/destroy classified equipment. Among the items recovered was a steel cross which has since been placed in Coventry Cathedral.

8 June 1982

Name	*Sir Galahad*	**Location**	East Falkland, Bluff Cove
Class	Logistic landing ship	**Cause**	Air attack
Built	19 April 1966	**Casualties**	50
Master	Capt P.J. Roberts RFA		

Notes RFA *Sir Galahad* was sent to Bluff Cove with 16 Field Ambulance RAMC, a Rapier SAM troop, a large amount of stores and ammunition, and a rifle company and support company of 1st Battalion, the Welsh Guards. She arrived at Bluff Cove on 8 June to find that the other LSL which had preceded her, RFA *Sir Tristram*, had not yet finished unloading. Bluff Cove was an exposed anchorage: SAM defences were not yet in place and it was overlooked by a number of Argentine OPs. It was therefore imperative to get both ships unloaded and away before the Argentines could mount an air attack. Yet throughout the day there was a lack of a sense of urgency and arguments among the various army units as to who should be disembarked first. By early afternoon barely any progress had been made in unloading troops or stores from *Sir Galahad*.

Just after 1315 hrs five A-4B aircraft came in from the west. They had flown round the coast of East Falkland and had either seen the ships or been vectored in on the anchorage by an Argentine OP. There was barely time to take any precautions before *Galahad* was hit by three 500 lb bombs. The explosions started massive fires which were fuelled by ammunition stored in her tank deck. Firefighting efforts were to no avail and at 1415 hrs Captain Roberts ordered his ship to be abandoned.

Casualties were high: 50 dead and 57 wounded, many of them horribly burned. The majority of the casualties – 39 dead and 28 wounded – were Guardsmen. That there were not more casualties was due to the superb flying skills of the Sea King pilots who plucked men from the burning ship or from the sea, despite explosions of ammunition, or used the down from their rotors to blow liferafts away from *Galahad*'s hull. The sinking was recorded by TV cameramen and the pictures of the shocked and burned survivors coming ashore are among the most searing of the Falklands War.

In June 1982 *Galahad*'s burned-out hulk was sunk in deep water as a war grave by the submarine *Onyx*.

Name	*F.4 (ex L.3507)*	**Location**	S Atlantic, coast of East Falkland
Class	Landing craft (LCU type)	**Cause**	Air attack
Built	1963	**Casualties**	4
CO	Colour Sgt Brian Johnstone RM	**Survivors**	None

Notes   Landing Craft *F.4* was making a daylight trip from Bluff Cove to Darwin to collect the HQ and communications vehicles of 5 Infantry Brigade. It was a risky operation sending out the little LCU, armed with only one 7.62 mm GPMG, unescorted in daylight. However, the operation was considered worth the risk since 5 Brigade desperately needed their vehicles to run the land battle efficiently. It was sheer bad luck that *F.4* was caught by four A-4B Skyhawk aircraft of V Air Brigade on the return journey; they sank her with bombs and cannon fire.

SELECT BIBLIOGRAPHY

PRIMARY SOURCES

Public Record Office, London
Relevant Reports of Proceedings of HM Ships and Submarines together with appropriate RAF Squadron Operational Record Books.
Admiralty, Anti-Submarine Warfare Division, *Monthly Anti Submarine Reports*, September 1939–December 1945.
Admiralty, *Monthly Intelligence Reports 1939–1945* and *Weekly Intelligence Reports 1939–1945*.
Admiralty, Naval Staff, Operations Division, *Daily Summary of Naval Events*.

Naval Historical Center, Washington DC
US Navy, *Anti Submarine Bulletin, 'Yellow Peril'*, June 1943–May 1945.

Admiralty Monographs
Admiralty: Naval Staff History of the Second World War: Battle Summaries nos 15 and 16; *Naval Operations off Ceylon 29 March to 10 April 1942* and *Naval Operations at the Capture of Diego Suarez (Operation Ironclad) May 1942*; London, 1943.
Admiralty: Naval Staff History of the Second World War: Battle Summary no. 41; *The Evacuation of Dunkirk, Operation Dynamo, 26 May to 4 June 1940*; London, 1949.
Admiralty: Naval Staff History of the Second World War: Battle Summary no. 22; *Arctic Convoys 1941–45*; London, 1954.
Admiralty: Naval Staff History of the Second World War: Battle Summary no. 29; *The Attack on the Tirpitz by Midget Submarines, 23 September 1943, Operation Source*; London, 1948.
Admiralty: Naval Staff History of the Second World War: Battle Summary no. 49; *The Campaign in North West Europe, June 1944–May 1945*; London, 1952.
Admiralty: Naval Staff History of the Second World War: *Submarines Volume 1 – Operations in Home, Northern and Atlantic Waters*; London, 1953.
Admiralty: Naval Staff History of the Second World War: *Submarines Volume 2 – Operations in the Mediterranean*; London, 1955.
Admiralty: Naval Staff History of the Second World War: *Submarines Volume 3 – Operations in Far Eastern Waters*; London, 1956.
Admiralty: Naval Staff History of the Second World War, *British Mining Operations, 1939–1945, volume 1*; London, 1973.

Secondary Sources

Aichelburg, W. *Die Unterseeboote Osterreich-Ungarns*: (Graz, Akademische Druck u Verlagsanstalt, 1981), 2 vols.
Bacon, Admiral Sir Reginald. *The Dover Patrol* (London, Hutchinson, 1919), 2 vols.

Bagnasco, E. & Rastelli, A. *Sommergibile in Guerra* (Parma, Albertelli Editore, 1989).

Bagnasco, E. & Spertini, M. *I. Mezzi d'Assalto Della Xᵃ Flottiglia MAS* (Parma, Albertelli Editore, 1991).

Barnett, C. *Engage the Enemy More Closely* (London, Hodder & Stoughton, 1992).

Beesely, P. *Very Special Intelligence* (London, Hamish Hamilton, 1977).

Bekker, C. *K-Men – The Story of the German Frogmen and Midget Submarines* (London, Wm Kimber, 1955).

Borghese, J.V. *The Sea Devils* (London, Andrew Melrose, 1952).

Brown, D. *Warship Losses of World War Two* (London, Arms and Armour Press, 1990).

Burn, A. *The Fighting Captain* (London, Leo Cooper, 1993).

Campbell, G. *My Mystery Ships* (London, Hodder & Stoughton, 1928).

Campbell, J. *Naval Weapons of World War Two* (London, Conway Maritime Press, 1985).

Chatterton, E.K. *Beating the U-boats* (London, 1943).

Compton-Hall, Commander P.R. *The Underwater War* (Blandford Books, 1982).

———. *Monsters and Midgets* (Newton Abbot, Blandford Books, 1985).

———. *Submarine vs Submarine* (London, David & Charles, 1988).

Connell, G.G. *Arctic Destroyers – the 17th Flotilla* (William Kimber, 1982).

Corbett, Sir Julian S. & Newbolt Sir Henry. *History of the Great War, Naval Operations* (London, Longman, 1920–31), 5 vols.

Coulter, Surgeon Captain J.L.S. *The Royal Naval Medical Service; Vol. 2: Operations* (London, HMSO, 1956).

Cruikshank, C. *SOE in the Far East* (Oxford, Oxford University Press, 1983).

Donitz, K. *Memoirs – Ten Years and Twenty Days* (London, Greenhill Books, 1990).

Edwards, K. *We Dive at Dawn* (London, Rich & Cowan, 1939).

English, J. *The Hunts* (World Ship Society, 1987).

Evans, A.S. *Beneath the Waves* (London, William Kimber, 1986).

Fayle, C.E. *Official History of the Great War, Seaborne Trade* (London, Murray, 1920–24), 3 vols.

Gayer, A. *Die deutschen U-boote in ihrer Kriegfuhrung 1914–1918* (Berlin, Mittler, 1930).

Gibson, R.H. & Prendergast, M. *The German Submarine War 1914–1918* (London, Constable, 1931).

Grant, R.M. *U-boats Destroyed* (London, Putnam, 1964).

———. *U-boat Intelligence 1914–1918* (London, Putnam, 1969).

———. *Known Sunk: German Warship Losses 1914–1918* (USNI *Proceedings*, vol. 64 (1938) pp. 66–77).

Gray, E. *Few Survived: A History of Submarine Disasters* (London, Leo Cooper, 1986).

Gretton, Vice Admiral Sir Peter. *Convoy Escort Commander* (London, Cassel, 1964).

———. *Crisis Convoy* (London, Peter Davies, 1974).

Groener, E. *German Warships, vol. 2* (London, Conway Maritime Press, 1991).

Hague, A. & Ruegg, B. *Convoys to Russia, 1941–45* (World Ship Society, 1992).

Halpern, P. *A Naval History of World War I* (London, UCL Press, 1994).

Hill, Roger. *Destroyer Captain* (London, William Kimber, 1975).

Holloway, A. *From Dartmouth to War – A Midshipman's Journal* (Buckland Press, 1993).

Jones, G. *Submarine vs U-boat* (London, William Kimber, 1986).

Kemp, Paul. *Die Royal Navy auf der Donau* (Graz, Herbert Weishaupt Verlag, 1987).

———. *The T Class Submarine* (London, Arms & Armour Press, 1990).

———. *Midget Submarines* (London, Arms & Armour Press, 1990).

———. *Convoy! Drama in Arctic Waters* (London, Arms & Armour Press, 1994).

———. *Friend or Foe* (London, Leo Cooper, 1995).

———. *Underwater Warriors* (London, Arms & Armour Press, 1996).

———. *U-boats Destroyed* (London, Arms & Armour Press, 1997).

Kemp, P. & Wilson, M. *Mediterranean Submarines* (Crecy Books, 1997).

Keyes, Admiral Sir Roger. *Naval Memoirs Vol. 2, From Scapa Flow to the Dover Straits* (New York, 1935).

Le Bailly, Vice Admiral Sir Louis. *The Man Around the Engine* (Kenneth Mason, 1990).

MacIntyre, D. *U-boat Killer* (London, Weidenfeld & Nicholson, 1958).

Milner, M. *North Atlantic Run, The Royal Canadian Navy and the Battle for the Convoys* (Annapolis, Naval Insititute Press, 1985).

———. *The U-boat Hunters* (Annapolis, Naval Institute Press, 1994).

Ministry of Defence. *The U-boat War in the Atlantic, 1939–45* (London, HMSO, 1989).

O'Neill, Richard. *Suicide Squads* (London, Salamander Books, 1978).

Padfield, P. *Donitz, The Last Fuhrer* (London, Gollancz, 1984).

———. *War Beneath the Sea* (London, John Murray, 1995).

Rastelli, A. *Le Navi del Re* (Sugar Co Se Edizione, 1988).

Rohwer, J. *The Critical Convoy Battles of March 1943* (London, Ian Allen 1977).

———. *Axis Submarine Successes* (Cambridge, PSL Ltd, 1983).

Rohwer, J. & Hummelchen, G. *Chronology of the War at Sea 1939–1945* (London, Greenhill Books, 1992).

Sainsbury, A. & Shrubb, R. *The Royal Navy Day by Day* (Centaur Press, 1979).

Shelford, W.O. *Subsunk: The Story of Submarine Escape* (London, Harrap & Co., 1960).

Simpson, Rear Admiral G.W.G. *Periscope View* (London, Macmillan 1972).

Sokol, H.H. *Osterreich Ungarns Seekrieg 1914–1918* (Graz, Akademische Druck u Verlagsanstalt, 1967), 2 vols.

Spindler, Admiral Arno. *Der Krieg zur See 1914–1918, Der Handelskrieg mit U-booten* (Berlin, Mittler, 1932–1966), 5 vols.

Sternhall, C.M. & Thorndike, A.M. *Antisubmarine Warfare in World War Two*, Operational Evaluation Group Report no. 51 (Washington, 1946).

Strutton, B. & Pearson, M. *The Secret Invaders* (London, Hodder & Stoughton, 1958).

Tarrant, V.E. *The U-boat Offensive 1914–1945* (London, Arms & Armour Press, 1989).

———. *The Last Year of the Kriegsmarine* (London, Arms & Armour Press, 1994).

Terraine, J. *Business in Great Waters, The U-boat Wars 1916–1945* (London, Leo Cooper, 1989).

Thetford, O. *British Naval Aircraft since 1912* (London, Puttnam, 1977).

Thompson, J. *The Imperial War Museum Book of the War at Sea* (London, Sidgwick & Jackson, 1996).

Ufficio Storico Della Marina Militare. *La Marina Italiana Nella Seconda Guerra Mondiale*, Vol. II; *Navi Miliare Perduti* (Rome, 1975), 5th edn.

———. *La Marina Italiana Nella Seconda Guerra Mondiale*, Vol. XIV; *I Mezzi D'Assalto* (Rome, 1992), 4th edn.

Vian, Admiral of the Fleet Sir Philip. *Action this Day* (London, Frederick Muller, 1960).

Waldron, T.J. & Gleeson, J. *The Frogmen – The Story of Wartime Underwater* (Evans Brothers, 1970).

Warren, C.E.T. & Benson, J. *Above Us the Waves* (London, Harrap & Co., 1953).

Whinney, R. *The U-boat Peril* (London, Blandford, 1987).

Whitley, M.J. *German Coastal Forces in World War Two* (London, Arms & Armour Press, 1992).

Williams, J. *They Led the Way – The Fleet Minesweepers at Normandy, June 1944* (J. Williams, 1994).

Wingate J. *The Fighting Tenth* (London, Leo Cooper, 1991).

Winton, J. *The Forgotten Fleet* (London, Michael Joseph, 1969).

Woodman, Richard. *Arctic Convoys 1941–45* (London, John Murray, 1994).

Woodward, Admiral Sir John. *One Hundred Days – The Memoirs of the Falklands Battle Group Commander* (London, Harper Collins, 1992).

Young, Edward. *One of Our Submarines* (London, Hart Davis, 1954).

ALPHABETICAL LIST OF SHIPS

A.1 1
A.3 5
A.4 2
A.7 6
A.8 2
AE.1 8
AE.2 18
Abdiel 216
Abingdon 176
Aboukir 8
Acasta 120
Achates 205
Acheron 136
Affleck 247
Affray 256
Afridi 111
Airedale 186
Alarm 206
Alberni 238
Alcantara 30
Aldenham 246
Algerine 200
Alynbank 234
Alyssum 50
Amphion 7
Anchusa 76
Andania 121
Antelope 262
Arabis 29
Arbutus (1917) 60
Arbutus (1942) 166
Ardent (1916) 38
Ardent (1940) 120
Ardent (1982) 261
Arethusa 29

Argyll 24
Ariadne 55
Ariel (1907) 3
Ariel (1918) 78
Ark Royal 156
Armidale 201
Arno 67
Artemis 258
Asphodel 230
Aster 53
Athabaskan 232
Attack 61
Auckland 149
Audacious 10
Audacity 163
Auricula 181
Avenger (1917) 53
Avenger (1942) 200

B.2 6
B.10 41
Barham 158
Basilisk 118
Bayano 16
Bedford 5
Bedouin 185
Begonia 57
Belmont 166
Ben-my-Chree 46
Bergamot 55
Berkeley 192
Beverley 212
Bickerton 240
Bittern (1918) 69
Bittern (1940) 111

Black Prince 38
Blackwater 4
Blackwood 235
Blanche 103
Blean 203
Bluebell 250
Boadicea 234
Bonaventure 140
Boxer 66
Bramble 205
Branlebas 135
Brazen 125
Brilliant 73
Britannia 83
Britomart 240--2
Broadwater 154
Broke 198
Bullen 246
Bulwark 13

C.3 70
C.11 5
C.12 80
C.14 6
C.16 50
C.26 69
C.27 69
C.29 23
C.31 14
C.32 58
C.33 21
C.34 54
C.35 69
CMB.1 53
CMB.2 76

CMB.8 57
CMB.10 74
CMB.11 59
CMB.18A 70
CMB.33A 70
CMB.39B 74
CMB.40 78
CMB.42 78
CMB.47 78
CMB.50 76
CMB.71A 81
Cachalot 151
Cairo 190
Calcutta 148
Calgarian 66
Calypso 120
Cameron 136
Campania 83
Campbeltown 173
Canberra 189
Candytuft 60
Capel 247
Carinthia 119
Carlisle 220
Cassandra 84
Cato 237
Centurion 233
Chamois 237
Champagne 57
Chanticleer 223
Charlottetown 192
Charybdis 221
Chebogue 243
Chedabucto 221
Cheerful 53
Cicala 163
Clacton 226
Clan MacNaughton 15
Clayoquot 246
Codrington 126
Comet 78
Comfort 116
Coquette 31

Cormorin 141
Cornwall 175
Cornwallis 46
Cossack 155
Courageous 102
Coventry 193
Coventry 262
Cowslip 73
Cressy 9
Cricket 149
Cromarty 222
Cuckmere 225
Culver 166
Curacoa 196
Curlew 116

D.2 13
D.3 66
D.5 13
D.6 75
Dainty 140
Dakins 246
Daring 106
Dasher 211
Decoy 1
Defence 36
Defender 150
Delhi 249
Delight 127
Denbigh Castle 250
Derwent (1917) 52
Derwent (1943) 211
Diamond 142
Dorsetshire 175
Dragonfly 168
Drake 57
Duchess 104
Duff 246
Duke of Albany 43
Dulverton 223
Dundalk 132
Dundee 130
Dunedin 158

Dunnon 111
Dunvegan Castle 129
Durban 234

E.1 68
E.3 10
E.4 42
E.5 30
E.6 27
E.7 23
E.8 69
E.9 68
E.10 15
E.13 21, 22
E.14 64
E.15 16
E.16 43
E.17 28
E.18 34
E.19 68
E.20 25, 26
E.22 32
E.24 31
E.26 39
E.30 45
E.34 76
E.36 46
E.37 45
E.41 42
E.47 55
E.49 49
E.50 65
Eagle 190
Eclipse 222
Eden 39
Edinburgh 180
Effingham 115
Egret 215
Ekins 253
Electra 169
Elgin 232
Encounter 171
Erica 207

Eridge 192

Erne 15

Escort 125

Esk 129

Esquimalt 252

Exeter 170

Exmoor 140

Exmouth 106

F.4 (ex-L.3507) 264

Fairy 75

Falcon 68

Falmouth 42

Fandango 85

Fantome 214

Fauvette 31

Fearless 151

Felixstowe 225

Fermoy 142

Fidelity (ex-Rhin) 204

Fiji 145

Firedrake 203

Fittleton 260

Fitzroy 179

Fleur de Lys 154

Flirt 43

Foresight 190

Forfar 135

Formidable 14

Fortune 38

Foxglove 125

Foyle 49

Foylebank 123

Fraser 122

Fury 235

G.7 82

G.8 62

G.9 56

G.11 84

Gaillardia 67

Gala 4

Galatea 161

Gallant 137

Gardenia 198

Geelong 244

Genista 43

Gentian 85

Gladiator 4

Gladiolus 154

Glatton 79

Glorious 119

Gloucester 144

Glowworm 107

Gnat 155

Goathland 237

Godetia 130

Goldfinch 15

Goliath 18

Good Hope 11

Goodall 253

Goodson 236

Gossamer 187

Gould 230

Grafton 116

Grampus 121

Grasshopper 168

Grenade 117

Grenville 106

Greyhound 144

Grove 185

Gurkha (1917) 48

Gurkha (1940) 107

Gurkha (1942) 165

Guysborough 251

Gypsy 103

H.3 40

H.5 66

H.6 28

H.10 63

H.29 90

H.31 162

H.41 86

H.42 88

H.47 91

H.49 132

Halsted 234

Hampshire 39

Hardy (1940) 108

Hardy (1944) 228

Hartland 197

Harvester 208

Hasty 186

Havant 118

Havock 177

Hawke 9

Hazard 64

Hebe 224

Hecla 199

Hector 174

Herald 167

Hereward 148

Hermes (1914) 11

Hermes (1942) 177

Hermione 186

Heythorp 172

Hilary 52

Hogue 9

Holcombe 225

Hollyhock 178

Hood 146

Hoste 45

Hostile 129

Hunter 109

Huntley 138

Hurricane 226

Hurst Castle 243

Hurworth 221

Hussar 240

Hydra 245

Hyperion 136

Hythe 220

Ibis 198

Imogen 125

Imperial 148

Indefatigable 34

India 21

Indus 177
Inglefield 229
Intrepid (1918) 72
Intrepid (1943) 219
Invincible 36
Iphigenia 72
Irresistible 16
Isis 237
Itchen (1917) 54
Itchen (1943) 218
Ivanhoe 129

J.6 81
Jackal 182
Jaguar 172
Janus 227
Jason 50
Jersey 142
Jervis Bay 134
Juniper 119
Juno 144
Jupiter 169

K.1 59
K.4 64
K.5 86
K.13 47
K.15 87
K.17 65
Kale 67
Kandahar 163
Kashmir 145
Keith 117
Kelly 145
Khartoum 122
King Edward VII 28
Kingston 178
Kipling 182
Kite 238

L.9 89
L.10 80
L.24 89

L.55 85
Ladybird 143
Laforey (1917) 50
Laforey (1944) 231
Lagan 217
Lance 176
Lapwing 252
Lark 250
Lassoo 41
Latona 155
Laurentic (1917) 47
Laurentic (1940) 133
Lavender 52
Lawford 233
Leda 194
Lee 5
Legion 173
Levis 153
Lightning (1915) 21
Lightning (1943) 209
Limbourne 222
Lively 182
Louis 25
Louisberg 207
Loyal 244
Loyalty 240
Lynx 21

M.1 89
M.2 93
M.15 59
M.21 81
M.25 86
M.27 86
M.28 63
ML.196 88
Magic 236
Magog 244
Mahratta 229
Majestic 20
Manchester 191
Manners 249
Maori (1915) 18

Maori (1942) 167
Margaree 133
Marigold 202
Marmion 58
Marmora 76
Martin 198
Mary Rose 58
Mashona 147
Matabele 165
Medusa 32
Medway 188
Mignonette 49
Mohawk 141
Moldavia 75
Monmouth 12
Montague 3
Mosquito 118
Moth 161
Mourne 235
Mulgrave 243
Myrmidon 50
Myrtle 85

Nabob 239
Naiad 171
Narborough 62
Narwhal 126
Nasturtium 32
Natal 27
Negro 45
Neptune 162
Nessus 79
Nestor (1916) 35
Nestor (1942) 186
Niger (1914) 13
Niger (1942) 188
Nomad 35
North Star 72
Nottingham 42
Nubian 44

Ocean 16
Oceanic 8

Odin 121
Olympus 182
Opal 62
Orama 58
Orchis 238
Orpheus 122
Oswald 127
Otranto 80
Ottawa 193
Otway 54
Oxley 101

P.32 152
P.33 152
P.36 174
P.38 169
P.39 173
P.48 204
P.222 203
P.311 206
P.514 187
P.615 213
Pakenham 212
Pandora 174
Panther 220
Paragon 49
Parramatta 159
Parthian 215
Partridge (1917) 60
Partridge (1942) 204
Pathan 122
Pathfinder (1914) 7
Pathfinder (1945) 249
Patia 75
Patroclus 133
Pegasus 8
Penelope 228
Penylan 201
Penzance 129
Perseus 159
Perth 170
Peterel 160
Petersfield 92

Pheasant 48
Phoenix (1906) 3
Phoenix (1918) 74
Phoenix (1940) 125
Picotee 152
Pincher 76
Pink 236
Pintail 149
Polyanthus 218
Porcupine 203
Porpoise 248
Poseidon 91
Pozarica 206
Primula 30
Prince of Wales 161
Princess Irene 20
Prompt 253
Puffin 252
Punjabi 180
Pylades 237

Quail 223
Queen Mary 35
Quentin 201
Quorn 238

Racoon 62
Raglan 63
Rainbow 130
Rajputana 141
Raleigh 88
Ramsey, The 21
Rawalpindi 103
Recruit (1915) 18
Recruit (1917) 55
Redmill 253
Regent 212
Regina 238
Regulus (1940) 135
Regulus (1945) 248
Repulse 160
Rhododendron 74
Rockingham 243

Rockwood 223
Royal Oak 102
Russell 32

Sahib 214
Salmon 124
Salopian 143
Salvia (1917) 53
Salvia (1941) 164
Samphire 206
Sanguenay 200
Saracen 215
Saumarez 255
Scorpion 168
Scotstoun 121
Scott 79
Scylla 235
Seagull 80
Seahorse 105
Seal 111--15
Setter 52
Shark (1916) 36
Shark (1940) 123
Shawinigan 245
Sheffield 261
Sickle 234
Sidon 258
Sikh 193
Simoon (1917) 47
Simoom (1943) 224
Sir Galahad 263
Sirius 73
Skeena 244
Skipjack 118
Snapdragon 204
Snapper 138
Somali 194
Southampton 138
Southwold 172
Sparrowhawk 37
Spartan 228
Spearfish 128
Speedy 7

Sphinx 106
Spikenard 167
Splendid 213
Springbank 154
Squirrel 254
St Croix 218
Stanley 162
Starfish 105
Staunch 59
Sterlet 110
Stoke 143
Stonehenge 230
Stratagem 245
Strongbow 57
Stronghold 171
Sturdy 133
Success 13
Surprise 61
Swift 236
Sword Dance 85
Swordfish 134
Sydney 157
Syrtis 231

TB.046 27
TB.064 16
TB.9 41
TB.11 31
TB.13 29
TB.24 47
TB.56 3
TB.84 2
TB.90 74
TB.96 25
TB.117 52
Talisman 194
Tara 25
Tarpon 109
Teme 252
Tempest 167
Tenedos 175
Terror 139
Tetrarch 156

Thames 128
Thane 249
Thanet 166
Thetis (1918) 71
Thetis (1939) 95--100
Thistle 109
Thorn 189
Thunderbolt (ex-Thetis) 209
Tiger 4
Tigris 208
Tipperary 37
Tornado 61
Torrent 60
Transylvania 128
Traveller 202
Trentonian 251
Triad 130
Trinidad 184
Triton 135
Triumph (1915) 19
Triumph (1941) 164
Trooper 220
Truculent 255
Tulip 51
Turbulent (1916) 38
Turbulent (1943) 209
Tweed 227
Tynedale 225
Tynwald 200

Ulleswater 78
Ulysses 82
Umpire 150
Unbeaten 199
Undaunted 143
Undine 105
Union 151
Unique 196
Unity 110
Untamed 214
Upholder 178
Urge 179
Usk 140

Usurper 220
Utmost 201

Valentine 115
Valerian 91
Valleyfield 233
Vampire 177
Vandal 208
Vanguard 54
Vehement 77
Velox 24
Venetia 133
Vervain 251
Vestal 254
Veteran 196
Viknor 14
Vimiera 165
Vindictive 74
Vittoria 86
Voltaire 141
Vortigern 172
Voyager 196

Wakeful 116
Wallaroo 215
Walney 197
Walpole 248
Warrior 39
Warwick 229
Waterhen 149
Waverley 117
Welman 10 216
Welman 46 224
Welshman 207
Wessex 115
Weyburn 208
Whirlwind 123
Whitley 115
Whittaker 244
Widnes 144
Wild Swan 187
Windflower 160
Wolverine 60

Woodpecker 228
Worcester 226
Wren 127
Wrestler 233
Wryneck 142

X.3 197
X.5 219
X.6 218
X.7 218
X.8 217

X.9 217
X.10 219
X.22 227
XE.11 251

Yarra 171
York 140

Zinnia 153
Zulu (1916) 44
Zulu (1942) 193